Development in Human Learning

DEVELOPMENT IN LEARNING

———

DEVELOPMENT IN LEARNING

BEHAVIOUR: LEARNING: EDUCATION

II

Development in Human Learning

———

EDITED BY

E. A. LUNZER

AND

J. F. MORRIS

STAPLES PRESS

First published 1968 by Staples Press
3 Upper James Street Golden Square London W1
Copyright © Staples Press 1968
Printed in Great Britain by
Cox & Wyman Limited
London, Reading and Fakenham

SBN: 286.62611.X

CONTENTS

Contents

CHAPTER 2. SOCIAL LEARNING AND
   IDENTIFICATION *by H. R. Schaffer*

CHAPTER 3. EXPERIMENTAL APPROACHES TO
   CONCEPT DEVELOPMENT IN YOUNG
   CHILDREN *by Marion Blank*

CHAPTER 4. SKILL *by G. F. Reed*

CHAPTER 5. LANGUAGE AND MENTAL
DEVELOPMENT *by M. M. Lewis*

Contents

Contents xi

PREFACE

Development in Learning is a comprehensive introduction to the psychology of education, designed to serve as a basic text for students preparing for advanced diplomas and degrees in education or in psychology. *Development in Human Learning* is in both senses the central core of the trilogy. Theoretical problems of learning were analysed in *The Regulation of Behaviour*, while problems arising out of individual difference in learning are dealt with in the last volume of the series, *Contexts of Education*, where the reader will also find discussions of social psychological and sociological considerations, as they affect pupils in the context of a changing educational pattern. The present volume is therefore wholly devoted to the treatment of child development from birth to adolescence.

Throughout the pages that follow, considerable emphasis is placed on achieving a deeper understanding of the ways in which the child progressively builds up his own image of the world – and at the same time elaborates new instruments to be used in this construction. It is our belief that such an understanding forms a necessary foundation upon which to base the efforts of educators in devising new curricula and new modes of instruction. One of us has argued that this may properly be regarded as the central function of educational psychology (Chapter 14).

While many aspects of the developing social consciousness of the child and its implications are discussed in Volume III, we have thought it quite proper to include in the present volume two chapters which deal specifically with development in human learning in this area, which is so crucial to the orientation of the child in his world.

In the main, the order of chapters is developmental, so that aspects of development which are most prominent in the early years appear first, and so on. More specialized topics are nested in as appropriate; for instance the development of language and the teaching of reading are considered after early conceptual development, and before that of more rigorous logical thought. Other orders would doubtless have been possible, but each student will almost certainly select his own order when he studies the several topics presented here. Often, the same topics have been treated from slightly different points of view in different chapters, and the index and table of contents should prove useful in this respect. But the areas of overlap are relatively small, and we believe that, such as they are, they are useful. For they contribute to a more rounded picture in a developing and often controversial field. Nevertheless, we feel that there is an overall unity about the present work, a unity which springs not only from a common attitude of respect for the findings of careful research, but also from a similarity in approach to what are the essential problems in the field.

Such a work as this is essentially a team effort, and in concluding this short preface, we have only to express our most grateful appreciation for the wholehearted support and collaboration of the contributors who have lent their expertise, their scholarship and their wisdom to its compilation, and have shown the utmost forbearance towards the editors in the face of what must have seemed quite unpredictable oscillation between long periods of delay alternating with sudden and insistent bouts of nagging. We would also like to thank Mr P. Herriot for undertaking the considerable task of indexing.

E.A.L.
J.F.M.

CONTRIBUTORS

M. BLANK, B.A., M.S. in Ed., Ph.D., Assistant Professor, Department of Psychiatry, Albert Einstein College of Medicine, Yeshiva University, New York.

P. HERRIOT, B.A., B.Ed., Lecturer in Education (Psychology of Language), University of Manchester.

H. KAY, M.A., Ph.D., Professor of Psychology, University of Sheffield.

M. M. LEWIS, M.A., Ph.D., Emeritus Professor of Education, University of Nottingham.

K. LOVELL, B.Sc., M.A., Ph.D., Reader at the Institute of Education, University of Leeds.

E. A. LUNZER, M.A., Ph.D., Senior Lecturer in Child Psychology, Department of Education, University of Manchester.

J. F. MORRIS, B.Sc.(Econ.), Ph.D., Senior Lecturer in Psychology, Manchester Business School (within the University of Manchester).

E. A. PEEL, M.A., Ph.D., D.Lit., Professor of Education, University of Birmingham.

G. F. REED, M.A., M.Litt., Ph.D., Senior Lecturer in Psychology, University of Aberdeen.

G. R. ROBERTS, M.A., Lecturer in Education, University of Manchester.

H. R. SCHAFFER, B.A., Ph.D., Senior Lecturer in Psychology, University of Strathclyde.

R. R. SKEMP, M.A., Ph.D., Senior Lecturer in Psychology, University of Manchester.

M. D. VERNON, M.A., Sc.D., Emeritus Professor of Psychology, University of Reading.

ACKNOWLEDGEMENTS

WE WOULD like to express our grateful appreciation to the following authors and publishers for permission to reproduce illustrations appearing in this book:

In Chapter 1: To J. Piaget and B. Inhelder, and to Messrs. Routledge and Kegan Paul Ltd. for figure 1 (from *The Child's Conception of Space*, 1956); to J. Piaget and the editors of *Archives de Psychologie* for figure 2b (from 'La résistance des bonnes formes à l'illusion de Müller-Lyer', Vol. **34** (1954), p. 159); to H. Würsten and the same editors for figure 3 (from 'L'évolution des comparaisons de longueurs de l'enfant à l'adulte', Vol. **32** (1947), p. 138); to E. J. Gibson and the editors of the *Journal of Comparative and Physiological Psychology* for figure 4 (from 'A developmental study of the discrimination of letter-like forms', Vol. **55** (1962), p. 898); to P. A. Osterrieth and the editors of *Archives de Psychologie* for figure 5 (from 'Le teste de copie d'une figure complexe', Vol. **30** (1945), p. 212); to L. Ghent and the American Psychological Association for figure 6 (from 'Perception of overlapping and embedded figures by children of different ages', *American Journal of Psychology*, Vol. **69** (1956), p. 580); to E. S. Gollin and to the editors of *Perceptual and Motor Skills* for figure 7 (from 'Developmental studies of visual recognition of incomplete objects', Vol. **II** (1960), p. 290); and to the British Psychological Society for figure 8 (from 'Learning from graphical material' by M. D. Vernon, *British Journal of Psychology*, Vol. **36** (1946), p. 148).

In Chapter 7: To M. L. J. Abercrombie and Messrs. Hutchinson and Co. for figure 2 (from *The Anatomy of Judgement*, 1960).

In Chapter 9: To the authors and to Messrs. Routledge and Kegan Paul Ltd. for figure 3 (from *The Child's Conception of Geometry* by J. Piaget, B. Inhelder and A. Szeminska, 1960); and to Harper Brothers Inc. for figure 4 (based on figures in *Productive Thinking* by M. Wertheimer, 1945).

In Chapter 12: To Her Majesty's Stationery Office for figure 2 (from *Teaching Machines and their Use in Industry* by H. Kay, J. Annett and M. E. Syme, 1963); and to the authors and publishers, City Publicity Services, London, for figure 4 (from *Programmed Learning in Perspective* by C. A. Thomas, I. K. Davies, D. Openshaw and J. B. Bird, 1963).

E.A.L.
J.F.M.

Development in Human Learning

1

Perception and Perceptual Learning

M. D. VERNON

I. INTRODUCTION

THROUGH his perception of his environment and the objects within it, the child develops and maintains his contact with the real world around him. He learns to adapt his behaviour in such a way as to preserve his life in constantly varying surroundings, and to satisfy his needs by reacting to and using these objects. Thus his perceptions must be reasonably correct, and in some circumstances extremely rapid. But his perceptual capacity is acquired; the infant does not appear to perceive the world as we do. He reacts spontaneously to certain external and internal sensory stimuli, but without knowledge of their nature or origin. Only gradually does he develop the ability to understand what objects are like and what he can do with them. This he does by means of his actions; he continually checks the 'veridicality' or truthfulness of his perceptions in the light of the effectiveness of his response to them. Hence even in later life, though perception may not immediately lead to action, action is always implicit; otherwise, sooner or later, a failure in adaptation would result, producing mistakes, frustrations, even danger.

In experiments on the perception of children, a certain artificiality may be apparent in that it is usually impossible to observe the spontaneous reactions of the children to what they perceive. The experimenter may require certain reactions to be made – selection of an object from its surroundings, choice between two objects, or, in older children, the verbal responses of naming, etc. Otherwise it would be impossible to determine what the child had perceived. But these responses are not necessarily the ones the child would make spontaneously. Thus the difficulties experienced by children in carrying out experimental tasks, and the errors they make, appear in some cases to be due to difficulties in response performance rather than in perception. For this reason, the observations of spontaneous behaviour in infants made by Piaget may be more valid than are experimental data, because

1

the sequences he noted, 'perception – response – modification of perception – further response', are natural ones which demonstrate how perception and action become integrated together and co-ordinated in 'schemata' of behaviour. Unfortunately such observations are difficult to make in a controlled and systematic manner; and we cannot be certain to what extent the behaviour of any particular infant is influenced by his peculiar environmental circumstances and by his motivation. For instance, in discussing the development of 'perceptual activity' at 3 years and upwards (see pp. 11 and 12), Piaget may not take into account the possibility that the child might show well-developed systematic exploratory activities with objects in which he is naturally interested.

Doubtless a repetition of Piaget's observations is needed. But in making this, the recording of isolated actions, however accurate, is not adequate. We need data on co-ordinated sequences of behaviour, and the relation of different sequences to each other and to the whole experience and maturation of the child. As yet, no such data are available. Therefore, inevitably, tracing the development of perception in young children must depend largely on Piaget's observations. But in the following discussion some attempt has been made to relate the observations and experiments of other psychologists to the thesis which Piaget has put forward.

II. REFLEX RESPONSES

The earliest forms of behaviour which indicate awareness of the environment are the innate reflex responses: simple automatic reactions to light, sound, touch, taste, smell and sensations from the internal organs. The primary function of these reactions is to preserve the life of the new-born infant. The first reflex is the gasp for breath to fill the lungs. A complex set of reflexes involved in sucking, swallowing and digesting food also develops at an early age. The new-born infant is responsive to touch. A light touch on the face or lips produces turning of the head and often sucking. Light touch on the hand arouses reflex grasping of the object which touches it. But stronger or painful touch to the limbs induces withdrawal or defensive movements, or even wriggling the whole body and crying. There is also a gradually developing set of 'startle' responses to jarring or sudden change of position.

Although reflex reactions to touch, taste and internal sensation play the most important part in sensori-motor behaviour during the first weeks of life, visual and auditory reflexes are also demonstrated. Blinking and contraction of the pupil in response to bright light appear during the first week. There is also reflex turning of the head and neck towards a stationary bright object, and pursuit movements of the eyes following a moving bright object. At an early age, sudden and loud noises produce blinking, general bodily changes in breathing, etc., and the 'startle' responses.

We may say that the infant possesses the physiological sensory and nervous mechanisms which enable him to respond and adjust to his environment. But the events which arouse reflexes are simple and crude, and there is no discrimination of their detailed characteristics. Moreover, it is clear that these stimuli give rise to behaviour which is of direct importance to the maintenance of life and the satisfaction of immediate needs. The stimuli have no significance for the infant apart from this, and he does not understand their nature nor realize their source. There is no differentiation between those which arise within his body, those which stimulate the body surface and those which originate at a distance. All that happens is that a particular sense organ is stimulated, and an appropriate pattern of activity is automatically engendered.

III. ATTENTION AND DISCRIMINATION

1. *The direction of attention*

It is possible to observe other innate behaviour in infants which appears to be a probable forerunner of later perceptual development. Although looking at and following the movements of a bright object may begin as reflex responses, they quickly lead to something like an attentive examination of this, which is accompanied by a general decrease in other activity (Gesell *et al.*, 1949). The infant spends a significant amount of time in gazing round him, as if to explore the visual environment. Furthermore, his attention is caught from time to time by objects at which he stares intently; often these are new and unfamiliar ones. Experimental observations have shown that he may direct his gaze at particular objects presented to him. A recent experiment by Hershanson (1964) showed that even within the first four days of life the infant's gaze might be consistently directed at certain types of stimulus. Stimuli of moderate brightness were fixated longer than were brighter or dimmer stimuli; and a simple half-white half-black surface was looked at for a longer time than a less simple chequer board. But as age increased, more complex patterns were increasingly fixated. Fantz (1958) found that at 1–2 months infants looked at striped rather than at plain surfaces, even with the stripes only 1/8th in. wide at a distance of 10 in. This indicated a high degree of visual acuity (Fantz *et al.*, 1962). Thomas (1965) presented pairs of stimuli to infants of 2–26 weeks, which included a striped and a chequered pattern, a picture of a face and a picture of a girl. The younger infants, aged 2–14 weeks, looked longer at the more complex chequered pattern than at the less complex stripes; but the pictures were too complex for them and they ignored them. The older infants fixated the picture of the face for longer than all others. Spears (1964) found that at 4 months a bullseye pattern was regarded longer than other patterns; and red and blue surfaces than grey ones. However, when colour and pattern were combined, pattern had the predominant influence on the direction of gaze.

Another sign of attention to particular aspects of the environment is given by the response of smiling. This has sometimes been classed as an instinctive social response to the human face. Ambrose (1961) has shown that this response reaches its maximum frequency at about 3 months in infants brought up at home, and at about 4 months in institutionally reared children. If the human face itself smiles, this reinforces the infant's response, which otherwise tends to die out. However, here is evidence to show that at an earlier age other stimuli may arouse smiling; for instance, two bright balls (Kaila, 1932) and a pair of black dots (Ahrens, 1954). And Salzen (1963) obtained a smiling response from one child of 8–11 weeks to a flashing light or a rotating card with black and white sectors on it. This suggests that initially smiling may be associated with the infant's delight and pleasure in anything which interests and excites him. But the smiling response becomes more specifically associated with the human face, and later with the smiling and the familiar human face. Also, the amount of smiling and of time spent on gazing are greater in infants who have been handled regularly than in those who have lain for most of the time passively in their cots (White and Castle, 1964).

It has sometimes been maintained that infants are comparatively inattentive to sounds other than loud noises which arouse 'startle'. However, Wertheimer (1961) reported that a new-born infant, at the sound of a click, ceased crying, opened his eyes and directed them towards the source of the sound. Piaget (1955) noted that at 2 months an infant turned his head in the direction of a human voice, and a little later looked attentively at the person who spoke. Again, a smiling response to a human voice was observed at 2–4 months (Hetzer and Tudor-Hart, 1927).

It has been noted that in the early months of life, touch and internal sensation play a larger part in the infant's experiences than does sensation from distant objects. Indeed, it has been argued by Birch (1963) that there is a hierarchical organization of sensory systems that determines which part of the environment appears 'figural' – that is to say, stands out as an object of attention, the remainder of the surroundings providing a background. In the young infant, the tactile and internal sensory systems predominate, and are only later replaced by the visual. Thus it is not surprising to find that much early exploratory activity is tactile. The infant fingers and grasps his own body and any object within his reach, and if possible puts them in his mouth.

However, it has been noted that visual pursuit of a moving object may occur at birth, or soon after, and that specific direction of visual attention develops within the first few weeks. Although exploration in the early months is largely tactile, from the age of about 4 months this becomes increasingly integrated with active visual exploration. White *et al* (1964) found that at about 5 months, when a highly coloured toy was presented to the infant, he looked at it intently, and also repeatedly looked to and fro between his hand and it; he might hit at it, but could not grasp it because his fist remained closed. Some grasping began at about 4 months; but not until $4\frac{1}{2}$–5 months did he lift his hand out of his visual field, open it as it approached the object, and then grasp the object deliberately. Handling and inspection then became prolonged, and it appeared that the infant was increasingly associating together complex visual and tactile sensory patterns to constitute what Piaget has called a 'schema', in which the co-ordinated sensory patterns become attached to a particular object. This is the first stage in the identification of objects. But the actual age at which it appears probably varies somewhat in different infants; Piaget noted it somewhat earlier than did White *et al.*

2. *Discrimination*

Now it is clear that in all these acts of attention, discrimination is involved. The infant must be able to differentiate one part of the environment from the remainder. At first, discrimination is very crude. A bright object is discriminated from its darker background; a moving object from its stationary surroundings; certain sounds from a background of noise; that which is touched at any one moment from that which is not being touched. Chase (1937) showed that at 15 days infants are able to discriminate moving coloured papers from a differently coloured background, by following them with their eyes. We have seen also that infants distinguish patterned from unpatterned surfaces. At 6 months there is some discrimination between differently shaped pieces of wood – circular, square, oval, triangular (Ling, 1941). Infants look longer at some colours than at others even when these are stationary (Stirniman, 1944); but discrimination is not accurate until the second year of life (Welch, 1939). However, both Ling and Welch tried to teach infants to remember the differences between objects or colours by responding consistently to the object or colour which was accompanied by a reward; and this is a much more difficult task than merely perceiving a difference.

Another type of task is the matching of an object of a particular shape or colour to a similar one among a group of objects of different shapes or colours; and this again is difficult for the young child. Thus Cook (1931) found that at 2 years children could match the primary colours, red, blue, green and yellow, with about 45 per cent accuracy; but accuracy was not complete until 6 years. And Meyer (1940) showed that children who were required to place objects inside one another, in a nest, and to pull objects through holes which fitted them, adopted a purely trial-and-error procedure up to the age of $2\frac{1}{2}$ years. At 3 years, they began to appreciate the necessity of matching the shapes of the objects and the holes, but they did not grasp the shape relationships accurately until over 4 years. This type of task is even harder if the number of shapes is increased. Thus in an experiment by Skeels (1932), children of 2–4 years were presented with a series of formboards and asked to fit shapes into the corresponding holes on the boards. At 2 years, they could place four discs or four squares into their appropriate holes. But the task increased in difficulty if the shapes on any formboard varied, and if the number of shapes was increased.

Now it has been found with adult observers that perceptual discrimination increases in difficulty both with the number of stimuli presented and also with the number of possible alternative responses (Garner, 1962). The same effect appears to operate with children even with the very simple stimuli presented by Skeels. The task became even harder as there were more pieces to deal with; and also when there were several differently shaped holes in the board, only one of which matched a particular piece. Thus we may infer that only as age increases can the more complex tasks involving differentiation be adequately performed.

3. *Summary of Sections II and III*

The mechanisms which govern the direction of attention, beginning with the simple reflexes described in Section II, combine with the processes of differentiation to produce discriminatory behaviour. But the evolution of this behaviour is gradual. It begins with selective attention to particular stimuli, in which at first the different sensory modes are unco-ordinated. But integration develops in exploratory behaviour towards the middle of the first year. Discrimination of particular visual characteristics of objects, in addition to perception of objects as wholes, also appears early; but accurate discrimination, leading to discrimination learning, develops slowly and is not fully operative until a later period, which will be discussed in Section V.

IV. IDENTIFICATION AND CATEGORIZATION

1. *Identification of objects*

It seems possible that tasks such as those of Welch and Skeels really depend on the capacity to identify particular shapes, rather than merely to discriminate them. Now Francès (1962) has stressed the difference between simple discrimination and identification. The former is the more elementary type of behaviour; the observer has merely to perceive if two or more stimuli presented to him are the same or different. In identification, he has to select and co-ordinate together those aspects of an object which enable him to recognize it from past experience; to know what it is, what it does and what he can do with it. This may require not only the co-ordination of different types of behaviour schemata associated with these various activities; but also the breakdown of earlier types of schemata into their constituent sequences, and the re-integration of these into new schemata.

It seems probable, from the observations of Piaget (1955), that familiar objects are the earliest things to be identified; and that the first step towards identification is made when the infant of 3–5 months begins to co-ordinate together visual and tactile sensory data, in grasping and handling an object which he also examines visually. Certain combinations of such sensory data, corresponding to particular objects, recur frequently in his experience, and he becomes familiar with the appearance of these objects, seen from all angles, as he turns them round in his hands. He gets to know what they feel like to his touch; and that they are solid, and cannot be squeezed up like water. Moreover, he experiments to discover what can be done with them, by striking, rubbing, banging and shaking them; and these actions are often repeated as he attempts to identify the objects. But Piaget considers that the crucial stage in identification is reached when the infant realizes that the objects have a continuing existence, even when they are out of sight; thus he continues to look for them when they are hidden from view.

Identification of objects, however, does not imply merely that the infant learns what they look and feel like, thus being able to recognize them again in terms of appearance. He also learns to attribute 'meaning' to them; and this meaning is constituted for him by what they do and what he can do with them. Thus his explorations are designed to discover the behaviour and functions of objects, and not merely to study their appearance. It seems clear from Piaget's observations that during the second half of the first year the infant spends much time investigating cause and effect, and especially what actions of his or of adults around him produce particular events. Thus he finds that wriggling about makes his cot move, and pulling a chain shakes a rattle suspended from the framework over the cot. In this way, he discovers gradually that there must be some physical contact or connexion between a person or an object which causes movement, and the object which is caused to move. We shall discuss later the significance of these causal events. But as the child grows older, he acquires an increasing knowledge of what he can do to objects, and what functions they possess, and thus improves his capacity to identify them.

However, the infant and the young child are not always consistent in their choice of the identifying characteristic of an object. They do not always differentiate the object from its surroundings, and it may therefore appear to belong to a particular setting, rather than existing independently. Again, objects and people in whom he is interested possess a number of recognizable characteristics and functions, all of which may appear from time to time, but not all of which may be perceived on any one occasion. Thus he has to learn which combination of these is essential to the identity of a particular object, and which may be ignored. He may mistakenly select a characteristic which is irrelevant; or he may choose one characteristic on one occasion, another on another. Thus Vurpillot and Brault (1959) found that children of 5–6 years, asked to select from a set of photographs the one which most resembled a familiar object presented previously, tended to choose in accordance with some dominant detail, such as the flower on a cup. We shall return later to the problem of selecting significant and rejecting irrelevant features.

2. *Cues to categorization*

The process of identification improves considerably during the second year of life as the child broadens his schemata and acquires the ability to classify objects and name the class as well as individual objects. Now we have already noted that discrimination is more difficult the greater the number of things to be discriminated. So also identification is harder the greater the number of possible alternative identifications; and this number naturally increases as the child becomes more mobile and encounters more and more new things. One means of overcoming this difficulty is to classify or group together objects of a particular type. Thus when a new object appears, it can be allocated to its appropriate class, and the child will then have some idea what kind of thing it is, what type of identity it possesses. He will also come to realize that there are certain things of which there is only a single example – his mother, his pet dog – and others which belong to a class of similar objects, such as 'ball', 'train', etc. He is of course greatly assisted in grouping by adults who tell him which objects fall into a class with a single name. But his ability to classify matures only gradually. Thus Inhelder and Piaget (1964) found that children of 3–5 years, when asked to group objects together, were often influenced by irrelevant perceptual characteristics. They might associate together those which formed a pattern, or those which 'belonged' together – for instance, a triangle which represented the roof of a house, a square being the house. Bruner (1964) showed that children of 6 years tended to use mainly perceptual characteristics in grouping, colour, size, etc. Grouping by function of object then developed, but often these functions were arbitrary and egocentric ('*I* can do this with them'). This was maximal at 9 years; and grouping by appropriate functions was not complete until 12 years.

Naming seems to be of paramount importance throughout development from about one year and upwards. Even very simple perceptual procedures are assisted by naming, which is used to label and to identify objects and fix them in memory. Thus Liublinskaya (1957) showed that children of 1–2 years learnt to find a sweet under a red cup more quickly when the name 'red' was spoken at the same time; and to recognize a butterfly from the stripes on its wings when the word 'stripes' was spoken. Again, Luria (1961) found that children of 12–30 months learnt to choose between a red and a green box more quickly when the experimenter named the two colours. With children of 3–5 years, identification of an animal picture from among four others was learnt more easily when the animals were named than when they were not (Weir and Stevenson, 1959). Remembering of faces by 3-year-old children was also facilitated when the children were taught to associate names with them (Cantor, 1955). The discrimination of meaningless shapes may be affected by naming even in older children. Thus one group of children aged 7–9 years was taught to associate a common label (a nonsense syllable) with two rather similar irregular silhouettes, while another group learnt different labels for the two (Katz, 1964). Subsequently, the first group perceived the silhouettes more often as being identical, and took longer to learn to discriminate between them even than those who had been given no labels at all; whereas those who had learnt different labels were more accurate throughout.

The identification of 'meaningless' shapes probably develops later than the identification of objects, not only because the former are less interesting to the child than are the latter, but also because identification depends on shape alone, and is not associated with the perception of other characteristics such as colour, activity, function, etc. But here the use of naming is equally important, as was apparent in the 2-year-old child described by Gellerman (1933), who learnt to identify the shape of a triangle by tracing it with her finger and calling it 'A'. Subsequently she could recognize it even when it was turned upside down, reversed from white to black, or outlined in dots. Babska (1965) again required groups of children aged 1½–5 years to choose from among three others a box with a particular picture of an object or geometrical shape on its lid, the child having previously been shown that this box contained a toy. Babska found that correct selection of the appropriate lid developed rapidly at about the age of 3 years, and was considerably assisted by naming the picture or shape. It should be noted that this response depends not merely on discrimination between two or more objects but on remembering through identification of particular objects.

In Gellerman's experiment, the child did not identify the triangle merely by glancing at it and naming it, but also by exploring it both visually and by touch. So again we saw that in the early stages of identification of familiar objects, both tactile and visual exploration were essential. Luria (1961) showed that even at 5 years children found it easier to classify shapes as triangles when they handled them before making their decisions. Now Piaget and Inhelder (1956) have maintained that the difficulty experienced by young children in identifying certain shapes is due to 'passivity'. They are said to be incapable of the 'perceptual activity' necessary to explore all the characteristics of objects and shapes and as a result of this exploration to pick out those characteristics which are essential to determine their identity. In identifying shapes by touch, children hold them passively or merely examine one or two of the more obvious characteristics. They must learn to explore more extensively and more systematically before they are capable of accurate tactile identification of certain kinds of shape. So also in visual perception they must acquire the capacity for exploration by the eyes before they can perceive and identify the more complex types of visual figure.

It seems surprising perhaps that children at this age should show passivity and failure to explore in tasks such as these, when one remembers how actively the infant explores objects, both visually and by touch, in his attempts to identify them and comprehend their nature. However, the child of 7–9 months in exploring objects tries to assimilate his percepts to existing schemata. He adopts a random unsystematic trial-and-error procedure, and thus identification is to some extent a matter of chance. It is not until later that he is capable of making a deliberate and analytical exploration, differentiating characteristics of the object, comparing them with those of other objects, noting differences and similarities, and finally establishing new and appropriate schemata. It is possible also that the children in the tactile experiments of Piaget and Inhelder had little interest in trying to identify meaningless shapes, and hence their behaviour appeared passive.

But there are other factors to be considered in the task of identification by touch alone. Piaget and Inhelder required their children to match shapes which they had only touched against drawings of these which they perceived visually. The younger children, aged about 2 years, were unable to do this because they merely held the shapes passively. Then, at 3 years, they were able to match some shapes because certain 'topological' characteristics were easy to distinguish by means of a cursory tactile exploration. For instance, the children could distinguish open from closed shapes, a ring from a circle, a surface with holes from one without holes, intertwined from separated rings (see Figure 1). But not until about $4\frac{1}{2}$ years could they differentiate between geometrical shapes – square, triangle, etc. – because to do this it was essential to obtain more detailed and accurate tactile impressions.

Fisher (1965), however, found no evidence of passive handling by the age of 3 years. He argued that an essential stage in the identification of shape was the use of language; and that young children found it easier to describe and name 'topological' than geometrical characteristics. In

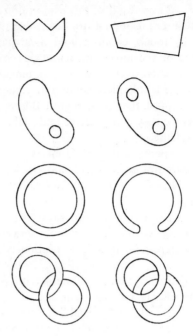

Figure 1

agreement with this argument, it should be noted that some of the children observed by Piaget and Inhelder named the geometrical shapes in terms of familiar objects; for instance, one child of $3\frac{1}{2}$ years called the triangle 'un planté' (a dibber). Fisher also supported his argument by an experiment in which he taught children of 2–5 years to associate nonsense syllables as names with three visually presented 'topological' shapes (similar to those in Figure 1), and three geometrical shapes such as a square, circle, triangle. Subsequently the children had to handle these shapes and match them against photographs. A control group of children viewed the shapes first without naming them. This control group did identify more 'topological' than geometrical shapes; but the children who had learnt names identified more geometrical than 'topological' shapes. We must conclude, therefore, that the children in the experiments of Piaget and Inhelder may have carried out sufficient tactile exploration of both 'topological' and geometrical shapes to determine their principal characteristics, but that those of the latter were more readily associated with names than were those of the former.

3. *Summary*

It would appear that identification of objects is a process of great importance in the development of perception, in which the infant first co-ordinates together a variety of sensory cues, which association he refers to one and the same object existing outside himself; and he then learns that this existence is permanent, even in the absence of the relevant sensory stimulation and that the object will reappear in the same form. Moreover, he acquires the expectation of certain characteristic behavioural relations between himself and the object, for instance, causal relations.

Almost immediately also he begins to classify objects, showing that he recognizes that they possess certain characteristic likenesses and differences of appearance and behaviour, which enable him to assign them to categories of objects with known properties, functions, etc. But learning to select and recognize the significant cues of classification takes place only gradually. It is assisted by tactile exploration and through the use of verbal symbols.

V. THE PERCEPTION OF SHAPE CHARACTERISTICS AS SUCH

1. *Perception of parts within the whole*

We must now consider the argument that children find the accurate visual perception of complex shapes difficult, and especially perception of the inter-relationships of their parts, because they lack the capacity to explore these systematically, to attend to the relevant characteristics and ignore the irrelevant. Now the adult, especially when he is set the task of viewing complex figures and making judgements as to their construction and the relations and sizes of their parts, directs his gaze from one significant part to another until he has obtained a general and balanced view of the whole. The child under the age of about 7 years may wander aimlessly about the field, his gaze sometimes straying away from it altogether; or, as we noted with the infant, he may be attracted by some interesting or striking part of the field, and his eyes remain fixed upon it while he ignores the remainder of the figure. This behaviour Piaget (1961) has called 'centering'; and he considers that in order to make accurate judgements the child must acquire the ability to decentre, to view all the significant aspects of the field and to compare them together. Piaget and Vinh Bang (1961) have in fact recorded the eye movements of younger and older children and have demonstrated

B

these differences in viewing. Further, Piaget (1961) considers that the perceptual centering of children under 7 years gives rise to the over-valuation of the centred parts of the field, and even to overestimation of their size. Thus centering the arrow-heads of the Müller-Lyer figure (see Figure 2a) leads to a greater overestimation of the length of the upper by comparison with the lower horizontal line in children than in adults; and in children the illusion is not decreased by prolonged inspection, as it is in adults. Again, with lines divided into two unequal parts, children tend to centre on the larger rather than the smaller part,

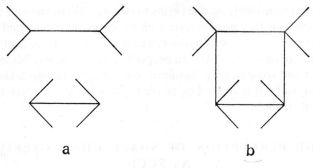

a   b

Figure 2

and therefore to overestimate its length. The same phenomenon appears if a line is divided into two equal parts, but one is cross-hatched (Vur-pillot, 1963). However, with some figures (for instance, Figure 3), the youngest children show the smallest illusion – that is to say, they do not overestimate the length of the vertical in relation to that of the hori-zontal line – because they make separate centerings of the two lines, and do not compare or contrast them (Würsten, 1947). But in other cases, where adults largely overcome the illusion by taking into account the whole figure, the younger children, who do not do this, retain the full amount of the illusion. This was shown by Piaget *et al.* (1954) with Figure 2b; for adults, the top and bottom lines of the square were estim-ated to be almost equal to each other, because they saw them as parts of the square. But again it must be pointed out that children may have little interest in perceiving accurately figures such as these; and also, in line with Fisher's argument, they do not possess the verbal facility of adults to describe the figures in words.

The inability to perceive the interrelations between the parts of com-plex figures is an important characteristic of children's perception up to the age of 7–8 years. Now it was stated by the Gestalt psychologists that the perceptions of children are global; they perceive undifferentiated wholes and ignore their parts. It has indeed been shown that the Rorschach ink-blots may be perceived at 2–5 years in terms of the whole blot or its larger details, and some organization of the parts within the whole does not occur until 3–4 years (Ames *et al.*, 1953). Maccoby and Bee (1965) have pointed out that children who at the age of 3–5 years cannot copy a circle or a triangle recognizably can nevertheless differentiate between them, presumably because copying necessitates more

Figure 3

accurate perception of a greater number of attributes. Again, general shape characteristics of simple outline shapes (angles, triangles, etc.) may be reproduced before the details can be copied correctly (Graham *et al.*, 1960). Lovell (1960) found that difficulty in copying increased with the number of parts of the figure to be introduced.

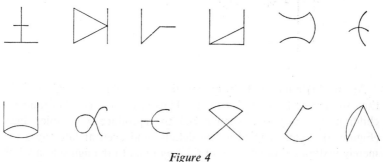

Figure 4

Gibson *et al.* (1962), however, showed that certain details of form are perceived at an earlier age than are others. Children of 4–8 years were required to identify each of the shapes shown in Figure 4 from a number of alternatives showing slight 'transformations'. It was found that 'topological' transformations – breaks in lines and closure of breaks –

were readily noticed even at 4 years. Reversals, rotations, and changes from curved to straight lines and vice versa, were overlooked by the youngest children, but these errors were eliminated by 8 years. Changes in slant or tilt of 45° were still largely ignored at 8 years. Thus it appears that there is considerable differentiation between the details of shape in children of these ages, some being perceived accurately at an earlier age than others. But Wohlwill and Wiener (1964) found that outline shapes containing some interior detail were discriminated accurately from inversions of the same shapes at 4–4½ years, though not at 3 years; and from left-right reversals only slightly less accurately.

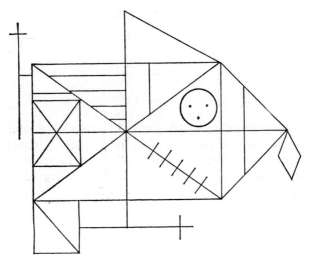

Figure 5

Again, children do not always perceive the outline of the whole rather than the parts of a complex figure. Thus Osterrieth (1945) found that children of 4–5 years, when asked to reproduce a complex figure (Figure 5), simply copied a few details; and even at later ages they merely juxtaposed them without relating them to the figure as a whole. It was not until 11–12 years that the children could reproduce the essential structure. Thus the more complex the shape, the harder it is for children to analyse it, because they are unable to direct attention systematically towards the significant features and compare and relate them together correctly. Difficulty in perceiving significant features has also been demonstrated with figures the outlines of which were obscure or incomplete (Piaget and Stettler-Von Albertini, 1954); and when simple figures, presented previously in isolation, were 'embedded' in more complex ones (see Figure 6). The second task was impossible for children of 4 years; and though performance improved with age, it was not perfect even at 8 years (Ghent, 1956).

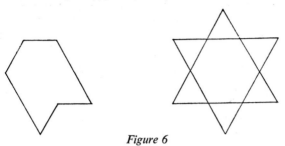

Figure 6

2. *The effect of perception on concept formation*

Inability to select the essential features from a complex field not only produces inaccuracy or inadequacy of perception, but also influences the formation of abstract concepts. In Piaget's very numerous studies of the development of concepts of number, quantity, weight, etc., it appeared again and again that the younger children tended to make judgements on the basis of their immediate perceptions, and failed to analyse and abstract those aspects of the situation relevant to particular concepts. Now it is well known that young children find it more difficult to enumerate a heterogeneous than a homogeneous group of objects, presumably because the perceptual differences within the former impede the abstraction of a group characteristic, its number, to which these differences are irrelevant. Again, Wohlwill (1960) required children of 4–7 years to match a card with three squares on it against other cards on which were 2, 3 or 4 differently formed or differently coloured shapes. Even after preliminary practice in matching according to number, the younger children often selected matching cards with the same shapes or colours, rather than with the same number of shapes. Equalization was even harder when the shapes on the cards were differently arranged. Piaget (1952) and other experimenters following him found that the number of objects in a row was said by 5-year-old children to be greater when the objects were placed far apart than when they were near together. The scattered objects covered a larger area and therefore looked more numerous. Although the children learnt to discount this appearance to some extent by practice, they could not overcome and reject it entirely through verbal logical reasoning (Wohlwill and Lowe, 1962). When water was poured from a wide vessel into a narrow one, it could be perceived to rise higher; and when a ball of plasticine was rolled out into a thin cylinder, it appeared longer. In both cases the amount was judged from its appearance to be greater.

These errors seem attributable to overdetermination through centration on one particular pre-potent perceptual aspect of the situation – shape, size, etc. Thus Bruner (1964) presented the problem of pouring water from a wide to a narrow vessel with the vessels screened in such a way that the children could not see the actual level of the water. He found that children of 5 years, and even some of 4 years, then gave the correct answer, that the volume of water remained the same. But when the vessels were unscreened, the 4-year-olds, but not the 5-year-olds, changed their response to the incorrect one. Some of the latter continued to respond correctly when vessels of different sizes were used.

The greater the number of perceptual characteristics which must be taken into account and compensated for, the more difficult the problem. When children were asked which of a pair of vessels of different sizes was the fuller, the younger ones judged simply by the total volume of water – greater in larger vessels. At the next stage, up to 7 years, they took into account the total volume of filled space and of empty space. But not until after this age were they able to judge the ratio of volume of water to size of container.

The effect on judgements of obvious perceptual characteristics is especially comprehensible in the case of the effect on weight estimation of size or volume, since these aspects are readily visible, whereas weight is not. Even adults, when they merely handle objects, tend to estimate the larger as being heavier than the smaller; this is known as the size-weight illusion. But young children persist in this misconception even when they are allowed to see the different-sized objects weighed on a balance (Smedslund, 1961). Halpern (1965) found that some children aged 5–7 years who could rank objects accurately in order of weight when the objects were of the same size, were unable to do so with objects of different sizes, particularly when the order of perceived size conflicted with the order of weight. Thus we can understand that not only must the child learn to correct his immediate perceptions by more careful and extensive viewing and analysis of the visual field. He must also learn in certain circumstances to reject what is immediately obvious, and rely upon logical reasoning. Again, it should be noted that although as they grow older children do learn to use these concepts more accurately, they can never learn to avoid completely the effects on perception of field factors. Some illusions persist in adults even after prolonged perceptual activity.

3. *Summary*

It is clear that the ability to discriminate between and identify objects does not depend on or necessarily result in the capacity to perceive accurately details of shape and their relation to each other. This capacity develops gradually, varying considerably with different types of shape; and it seems closely bound up with the ability to direct attention systematically to all parts of the field. Yet immediate and imprecise perception often has a compulsive effect on the younger child, preventing him from utilizing processes of reasoning to establish a fuller understanding of the nature of objects and their physical qualities.

VI. 'CONSTANCY' IN PERCEPTION

1. *The nature of 'constancy'*

In perceiving shapes and objects children as they increase in age learn to avoid some of the effects of centering and the undue influence of surroundings. They learn to select the significant aspects of what is presented to them; but in general their percepts correspond fairly closely with the sensory impressions falling on the retina. However, there are circumstances in which perception diverges increasingly from the immediate sensory impressions, in order that greater 'veridicality' may be achieved, and information supplied as to the 'real' nature and identity of objects which may not correspond exactly with the immediate sensory impressions. Clearly, the observer is more concerned to know what these objects really are than with the variations in their appearance produced by varying external circumstances. These 'veridical' perceptions are achieved in some cases only gradually, but are reasonably well developed by the age of 10 years. The child then disregards to a considerable extent the changes in shape and size of the images of objects projected on the retina, and perceives these objects, whatever their environmental position, largely in terms of their shape when they are situated at right angles to the line of sight, and of their size when they are fairly close to him. And he perceives the brightness and colour of objects as similar to their familiar brightness and colour when they are seen in normal daylight, and comparatively unmodified by variations in the brightness and colour of the surrounding illumination.

These phenomena were termed by the Gestalt psychologists the 'constancies', to indicate that the appearance of objects tends to remain constant in spite of variations in the sensory impressions obtained from them which are caused by variations in their environmental settings. Piaget (1961) hypothesized that we acquire the ability to compensate for these variations. For instance, we compensate for decrease in size of the retinal image with increasing distance of the object by taking this distance into account. Indeed, adults often overcompensate, overestimating the size of distant objects by comparison with nearer ones.

It has been pointed out that during the first year of life infants learned to identify objects by turning them round in their hands, and observing that their identity remained unchanged although the images projected on the retina varied in shape with variation in orientation. So also it seems that children learn that identity remains unchanged although retinal image size decreases with increase in distance; though this identification persists over only comparatively short distances. Thus Cruikshank (1941) found that infants of 6 months could discriminate between a rattle close to them, and another rattle three times the size presented at three times the distance (and therefore projecting the same sized retinal image).

2. *Problems in the measurement of size-constancy*

It has generally been supposed until recently that size-constancy is not as great in young children as in adults, and that the former do perceive more distant objects as smaller than nearer ones, since they have not the ability to compensate for increase in distance. Thus Zeigler and Leibowitz (1957) claimed that size-constancy was less on the average for children than for adults in matching the sizes of near and far objects of indefinite shape, such as wooden stakes. Piaget (1961) obtained a similar under-constancy for children up to about 8 years.

It should be noted that, especially in the earlier experiments on size-constancy, no careful distinction was made between judgements of the real or actual size of the object, and the size it appeared to be, which could approximate to a size corresponding to that of the angle it subtended at the retina – called the 'projected size'. Numerous recent experiments have indicated that, according to the instructions and the arrangement of the experimental materials, adult subjects may make either or both of these judgements; but that unless the instructions are highly specific, it is not always clear which type of judgement is being made. Then 'real' and 'projected' size judgements may be averaged together to produce a mean value lying between the two. This seems to have occurred in the experiments of Zeigler and Leibowitz. For Smith and Smith (1966) found that some children, even as young as 5 years, made fairly accurate judgements of real size, whereas others made judgements of projected size. This dichotomy appeared also in older children and adults, though it seems to have been more frequent in younger children. Smith and Smith, on analysing the results of Zeigler and Leibowitz, found the same dichotomy.

Though, according to Smith and Smith, children could spontaneously make either real or projected size judgements, it might seem somewhat difficult to convey to them instructions sufficiently specific to ensure that either real or projected size judgements were made invariably. However, Piaget and Lambercier (1951) claim to have obtained projected size judgements from children, and to have found that the 7–8-year-olds could make these judgements more accurately than could older children and adults. Hence, they suggested, younger children are relatively more aware of projected size, and tend to compensate less in order to make real size judgements. However, the results of Smith and Smith would seem to question this.

Normally, it is found that adults can neither perceive nor make accurate judgements of real size if their view of the surroundings is restricted, and they cannot perceive the relationship of objects to the spatial dimensions of the field of view, and hence compensate for distance. However, they may possess sufficient intelligence to utilize partial cues to spatial location, and make inferences as to real size; whereas, according to Lambercier (1946), children are less able to make such inferences.

In identifying and judging the size of objects situated at a great distance, inference is inevitable. Animals, vehicles and buildings appear minute when they are observed at great distances, for instance, when looking down from a mountainside; and no amount of compensation can make them appear otherwise. Children under the age of about 7 years may be incapable of making these inferences; they may not recognize the objects at all, or they may think that, for instance, houses in a distant village are 'toys' (Piaget, 1951).

That much study has been devoted to the phenomenon of size-constancy is due not only to its theoretical interest, but also to its practical importance in other types of perception, notably in the perception of distance. As we have noted, we tend to perceive a decrease of size in the retinal image, not as a decrease of real size of the object, but as an increase of its distance. Thus distance is a cue to real size; and one of the important cues to the perception and estimation of distance is decreased retinal size. We must therefore consider, in Section VII, the development in children of the ability to perceive distance as a function of this and other cues.

3. *The other constancies*

As regards the other constancies, it appears that these increase with increasing age. Up to the age of about 10 years, judgements of the shapes of objects tilted at an angle to the line of sight become nearer to the shapes when seen at right angles to the line of sight (Brunswik, 1956); but the former are never estimated to equal the latter. Much the same is true of brightness or colour of objects seen in dim or coloured light.

4. *Summary*

As the child learns to relate his perceptions of objects to his perception of their surroundings in the total field of view, so he learns to compensate for certain changes in the appearances of these objects which are produced by temporary variations in the surroundings. Thus he will perceive objects as relatively constant in shape, size, brightness and colour, whatever their situation, and will learn to make accurate judgements of the real shape, size, etc., of objects. However, the possibility of perceptual compensation is limited by the nature of the situation; and inferential judgements must sometimes be made, which may be difficult for the young child.

VII. PERCEPTION OF SPACE AND MOVEMENT

1. *Perception of distance*

It appears that, although infants perceive distance at an early age, their perceptions increase greatly in accuracy and sensitivity as they learn to co-ordinate together a variety of sensory data, all of which give cues to distance, but which are more reliable in combination than in isolation. We have noted that infants gain some idea as to the distance of objects by finding that certain things are within and others outside their reach. But also they possess the ability to estimate distance of continuous surfaces. Walk and Gibson (1961) showed that if an infant of 8 months was placed on a horizontal sheet of glass with a chequered surface immediately beneath one half of it, and another chequered surface 4 ft. below the other half, he would crawl across the former when his mother beckoned to him from the further side, but not across the latter. Now the immediate inference would be that since infants of this age can co-ordinate the direction of the two eyes fairly accurately – that is to say, they can fixate both eyes upon the same point – they were utilizing binocular disparity. For it is known that adults can compare distances with extreme accuracy by virtue of the fact that binocular images of the point of fixation fall on the same points of the retinas, whereas binocular images of points at distances different from the fixation point do not. Thus they fuse these unlike or disparate images, obtaining the impression of recession in space such as is perceived in the stereoscope. However, Walk and Dodge (1962) found that an infant of 10½ months with only one eye (who had probably never possessed any sight in the other eye) also refused to cross the surface over the 'visual cliff'. Thus it was concluded from this, and from similar behaviour in young animals which do not possess binocular vision (Walk and Gibson), that perception of distance did not depend on binocular disparity. It seemed also from the animal experiments that retinal size differences between the two chequered patterns were not utilized. Perception of distance was in fact thought to depend on motion parallax – relative movement of the retinal images of objects at different distances when the head is moved. Corroborative evidence for the utilization of this factor was found by Bower (1965). He showed that infants of 40–60 days could discriminate monocularly by motion parallax through head movement, between the distances of solid cubes, even when these projected the same sized retinal images. But the infants could not discriminate the distances of flat projections of shapes on screens, because motion parallax was not operative, though all other cues to distance were the same.

Gibson (1950) considered that in judging distances adults utilize sensory 'gradients' – gradual and regular changes in the perceived perspective and surface texture of objects over receding distances. It is possible to demonstrate these effects in experimental conditions by requiring observers to judge the distances of points on surfaces on which surface texture gradually increases in density; or on grids of lines approaching each other, as in perspective (Wohlwill, 1962). Children of 7 years showed by the manner in which they located points that they perceived these depth effects in much the same way as did adults; and both judged more accurately with the grid than with the graded texture surface. Perspective is of course formed by the steadily decreasing apparent size of objects with increasing distance. Therefore at this age children can make use of size cues to distance. But it seems that they do not necessarily comprehend at all clearly the nature of perspective relationships. Thus Piaget and Inhelder (1956) found that if children were required to draw lines receding in perspective, at the age of 6–7 years they drew them curving to meet at a point. Correct perspective reproduction was not achieved until 8 years or more.

During the first year of life, the infant scarcely realizes the existence of objects in distant space; or else he perceives the latter as a flat picture screen far outside his reach. But as he begins to move about, he extends the boundaries of his near space until it becomes continuous with gradually receding distant space. However, his judgements of far distances remain uncertain until 5–6 years, and these distances are probably underestimated. Indeed, it seems likely that accurate judgements of far distances develop only when the child possesses the capacity to reason about the changing aspects of far distant objects – the lack of clarity of their outlines, their change of colour to blue-grey, and so on.

2. *Spatial judgements*

Piaget and Inhelder (1956) consider that the concept of continuous Euclidean space does not fully incorporate all percepts and judgements of spatial relations until the age of 9–10 years. Thus before that age the child cannot understand the manner in which the characteristically different appearances of, for instance, mountains, or models of mountains, seen from different points of view, are related together. We see, therefore that just as with other types of perception, the fully developed perception of space is modified from the immediate primary perceptions by the co-ordination together of sensory and ideational data within a universal logical schema.

It must not be forgotten that our spatial schemata include two-dimensional space – the visual perception of the horizontal and vertical dimensions and their integration with the gravitational senses which enable us to adjust the body in space. Again, the immediate perceptions and their integration together develop early in life and are reasonably adequate by the time the child can balance his body effectively. But Piaget and Inhelder (1956) have shown that ideas about the horizontal and vertical co-ordinates do not develop until later. Thus when children under 7–8 years were asked to draw people and trees on a sloping hillside, they placed them at right angles to the slope rather than vertically.

Again, the surface of water in a tilted jar was drawn at right angles to the side of the jar, rather than horizontally.

3. *Perception and judgement of movement*

There may be some doubt as to when and how the child first perceives space and distance, but there is no doubt that he perceives movement at a very early age. We have seen that infants soon after birth perceive moving objects against a stationary background. It seems possible that they perceive movement as such, rather than specific objects in movement. Indeed, this perception of movement as such persists into adult life and occurs when, for instance, an object which cannot be clearly seen when stationary suddenly moves at the edge of the field of vision. It is not perhaps surprising that this is one of the earliest visual perceptions to develop, since there is evidence that the sensory and nervous mechanisms of vision are particularly sensitive to rapid change and movement.

We have seen also that awareness of the nature and identity of objects develops in conjunction with the movements imparted to them by infants, when the latter reach for and grasp objects, turn them over and move them to and fro; and when also (as reported by Piaget, 1955) the infant moves his head to and fro towards and away from an object he holds in his hands. Thus the continuous pattern of impressions obtained from moving objects is schematized, and their identification depends, not upon a single stationary impression, but on this integrated schema. It is probable also that the child's spatial schemata – his impressions of the three-dimensionality of objects and of continuous space – are closely integrated with the movements of the body and of objects. Several experiments have suggested that even in adult perception movement can give the impression of depth, three-dimensionality and size constancy when these are lacking with stationary stimulus patterns.

Although immediate perception of movement develops so early, assessment of speed of movement is not made correctly until a much greater age. Indeed, throughout life estimates based on immediate perception are subject to the same type of inaccuracy as we noted earlier in connexion with visual illusions in the perception of shapes and their dimensions. Thus assessments of speed are affected by the nature of the objects in movement and by the surrounding visual field. Large objects seem to move more slowly than do small ones. Movement across a narrow field or a homogeneous background appears relatively slower than movement across a wide field or a heterogeneous background. But although adults perceive these effects, they can usually correct them if they are asked to make accurate judgements, because they know that speed is a function only of distance covered in a given time. Children do not know this, and are apt to base estimates of distance and speed on immediate percepts, which may lead to judgements which to us appear absurd. Thus Piaget (1946) found that children up to 6–7 years tended to say that the ascending movement of a funicular 'goes further' than the descending movement because more effort is involved. In comparing the movements of two objects, children of this age took into account only the end points of these movements; one object was said to move further if its movement ended ahead of that of the other, no matter where they started nor how far they travelled. Again, an object which passed another was thought to move faster, irrespective of the paths of movement, or where they began. If one object came to a stop behind the other, it was said to have moved more slowly, whereas if the two objects stopped opposite to one another, they were judged to have moved at the same speed. Lovell *et al.* (1962) repeated some of Piaget's tests and substantiated his results, showing that children below the age of 7–8 years could hardly ever make correct judgements of these phenomena; and it was not until about 10 years that all could do so. Thus we have further examples of overdetermination by the immediately perceived situation, which requires correction in the light of logical judgement; and the younger children are incapable of this.

4. *Perception of causality*

It appears that particular types of movement may become 'schematized' or associated with particular types of event. Michotte (1946) carried out extensive investigation of the type of movement which has the appearance of 'mechanical causality'. He argued that we have an innate tendency to perceive certain associated movements of objects in terms of 'mechanical causality'; and that this can be demonstrated by an arrangement in which, for instance, a black square moves across a background until it touches a red square, at which point the red square moves in turn across the background. Although no actual causal event has occurred, yet the red square appears to have been caused to move by the impact of the black square. Now if the tendency to perceive causality were indeed innate, it might be supposed that children would perceive it without prior experience. Yet Piaget (1955) demonstrated that infants gradually develop an understanding of causal relations between movements of real objects during the first year of life. With arrangements such as those of Michotte, Olum (1956) found that children of about 7 years perceived causality significantly less often than did adults; many of the children reported instead that one square passed the other. However, Fisher (1964) has suggested that language difficulty in describing these phenomena may be a relevant factor. Piaget and Lambercier (1958) also showed that children of 6–8 years perceived the causal phenomena less readily than did adults. The adults reported causality even when the first object did not quite touch the second, but the children did not. Thus it seems probable that as age increases children develop certain schematic categories of perceived movement as the result of experiences they obtain with moving objects; and that the category of 'mechanical causality' becomes increasingly compelling in circumstances where there is the appearance of causality but not necessarily the reality.

5. *Summary*
    There may be an innate capacity to perceive objects as situated in three-dimensional space, though it is uncertain exactly what cues are utilized by young children. But the ability to assess distances accurately develops gradually, through experience. Inferential judgements as to far distances and the nature of spatial relations are not perfected until about 10 years.
    Perception of movement also appears to be innate, but judgements of movement and speed of movement and perception of causality in movement again are acquired through learning.

VIII. PERCEPTION OF SYMBOLIC MATERIAL

1. *Interpretation of pictures*
An integral part in the education of children is played by teaching them to perceive forms not merely as meaningless shapes, but as more or less indirect representations of objects and events. The simplest material of this kind, which children begin to understand long before they go to school, is constituted by representational pictures of real objects. In the early stages, such pictures usually consist of the outline drawings of single objects, seen in a familiar aspect, with a few simple interior details. Children are able to say what such drawings represent at the age of 2–3 years (Terman and Merrill, 1937). It might seem that this

ability depends on frequent experience in looking at pictures and having them named and described. But Hochberg and Brooks (1962) found that a child of 19 months, who had seen only a few pictures and had never heard the objects in them named, could nevertheless identify pictures of familiar objects by name as well as he could identify the objects themselves.

This is indeed surprising, when one considers that an outline drawing is physically entirely dissimilar from the object it is supposed to represent. It is possible, however, that the tactile handling of objects in infancy may emphasize the contours which are reproduced in pictures.

But any lack of clarity in outline makes it more difficult for young children than for adults to recognize what the pictures represent. Identification of objects drawn with incomplete outlines, such as those shown in Figure 7, improves steadily from 3–5 years; the 5-year-olds did not differ significantly from adults (Gollin, 1960). Again, with pictures obscured by cross-hatching, the number identified during a four-second exposure increased from one at 3 years to five at 5 years (Gollin, 1956). The ability to identify blurred pictures of familiar objects shown for ten seconds each improved even up to 9 years (Draguns and Multari, 1961). It seems possible that children require clearer and less ambiguous information than do adults to enable them to select those aspects of the drawings on which to base identification. But it was apparent also in the last experiment that the younger children were less careful in making their judgements; that is to say, they showed less perceptual activity. Moreover, Bruner (1964) found that as the pictures gradually became less blurred, children of 6 years put forward a succession of quite unrelated hypotheses as to what the pictures represented. It was not until 12 years that logically related hypotheses appeared leading to a single conclusion.

Figure 7

By the age of $3\frac{1}{2}$ years children are able to identify objects the representations of which are included in complex pictures (Terman and Merrill,

1937). This does not mean that the children can, like adults, interpret the manner in which the objects and people in the picture are related to each other, nor what is supposed to be happening to them. Binet (1905) found that children of 3 years merely enumerated in succession the more obvious objects in the picture; but by 7 years they could give some description of what was happening. Craumussel (1924) considered that children of 2–3 years did not attempt to observe a picture as a whole, but looked first at one object and then at another, without any attempt to relate them together (as did Piaget's 5-year-olds with the visual illusions).

According to Binet, a real understanding of the meaning of the whole picture does not develop until about 15 years. But in Burt's revision of the Binet-Simon test (Burt, 1921), the age at which Binet's pictures could be interpreted is given as 12 years; that is to say, at this age the child can go beyond a mere description of what is shown, and say what is happening, what the people depicted are doing, etc. Clearly, the actual age depends on the obviousness of the meaning, and with simpler pictures interpretation develops earlier. It was observed by the author (Vernon, 1940) at about 10 years, and by Amen (1941) even as early as 4 years. But with pictures, as with meaningless shapes, the children were often unable to discover the significant features, those on which depended the essential meaning of the picture; they centred on unimportant details. It seems therefore that in the educational use of pictures, for instance in teaching children to read, there is a danger that they may not notice the main features with which words are associated. And children may fail to understand the meanings of pictures of historical events or of scenes in foreign countries, which depict occurrences quite unfamiliar to them.

Pictorial charts are often used in teaching which are semi-diagrammatic and not directly representational. Pictures of people and objects are grouped in such a way as to show sequences of historical events or of manufacturing processes. These often attempt to present too much information in a confined space. Moreover, their use presupposes that the children can go beyond the immediate representational meaning of the pictures, and can understand that the charts depict a succession of events over time or space. The difficulty of this was demonstrated in an experiment in which children of 10–14 years were shown a process-chart of the passage of wheat through a flour-mill, and asked to mark the point of entry, direction of flow and point of exit of the wheat (Malter, 1947). Only 25 per cent were able to do this correctly; and although the older children performed better than the younger, only about 40 per cent of the eldest were completely correct. Performance improved when appropriate labels were inserted; but there were still numerous errors, and many children ignored the labels completely. Probably they regarded the chart simply as a picture, and could not understand its symbolic meaning.

2. *Interpretation of diagrams*

Children are gradually introduced to diagrammatic material which is purely symbolic and has no pictorial relation to the events it presents. In the natural and social sciences, quantitative data are often shown in the form of graphs and histograms. The educated adult finds these valuable in that they present to a single view the relationships between quantitative data, and do so more quickly and clearly than do tables of figures. But considerable experience is required to grasp the significance of these diagrams. The author (Vernon, 1946) showed that grammar school children and even training college students often found this difficult. They perceived that the diagrams consisted of lines and curves which were intended to present some kind of quantitative data, but they could understand neither the nature of the data nor their precise relationships. It should also be noted that even adults may be unaware that trends in data may be distorted by manipulating the scales on which they are plotted; for instance, that by using particular scales, curves may be made to rise and fall so steeply as to suggest very sharp increases and decreases.

Quantitative data are sometimes shown in a form called the 'pictogram', which attempts to utilize pictorial representation. Frequencies of men, goods, money, etc., are presented in drawings of men, objects, etc., each of which corresponds to a given quantity, the total quantity then being symbolized by the numbers of these drawings (see Figure 8). It has been supposed that these 'pictograms' are relatively easy to understand because they are semi-pictorial. However, the author (Vernon 1946) found that even though the 'pictograms' may arouse curiosity and attention, they are no easier to understand and interpret than are conventional diagrams. Indeed, in so far as conflict may be aroused between pictorial representation and symbolic meaning, the 'pictogram' may be even more confusing than is the ordinary graph or histogram. It is quite clear that even adults may require training and experience before they can fully understand and use 'pictograms' with facility, and these are no more suitable for the uneducated than are ordinary graphs.

3. *Perception in reading*

Finally, we must consider the perception of material which is entirely symbolic in meaning, namely writing and print. In the early development of writing, shapes were employed in picture writing which were pictorial representations of particular objects and events. The Chinese 'characters', which symbolize words, retain some trace of this representation, but from alphabetic writing it has entirely disappeared. The

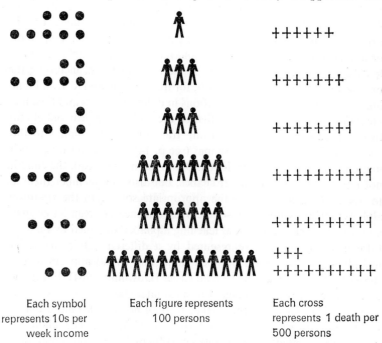

Each symbol represents 10s per week income	Each figure represents 100 persons	Each cross represents 1 death per 500 persons

Figure 8. Population, Income and Mortality

association between written and sounded letters is almost completely arbitrary (though possibly the letter 'o' might be thought to signify the rounded mouth). In our alphabet, this association is not even regular and consistent, since vowels are sounded differently according to the words in which they are contained. To a child, also, the sound of a sequence of letters may differ considerably from the sound of the word in speech context. Finally, both the sounded and the written word of course symbolize an object, event or some relationship between them. We do not know how man originally developed the capacity to signify and describe objects and actions in speech. But in early life, the infant learns to do this by modifying his spontaneous babbling sounds, through imitation and trial-and-error, until they approximate to the sounds spoken by adults. Learning to read and write, however, is a much slower process.

When he is first confronted by printed material, the young child perceives a set of shapes far more complex than any he is likely to have encountered before, and without representational meaning. In some methods of teaching, he may be required to associate the shapes, parrot fashion, with the names of objects shown him in pictures. This is a process as laborious as learning the Chinese 'characters'. Thus sooner or later he has to learn to perceive and remember the shapes of separate letters, observing the essential characteristics of these, including their orientation (in order to distinguish, for instance, 'b' and 'd'), and ignoring the inessentials, such as variations in different scripts and type faces. Now Gibson *et al.* (1962) investigated the ability of 5-year-old children to discriminate letters from certain 'transformations' similar to those used with their meaningless shapes (see p. 14), and found this discrimination to be fairly well developed. But in learning to read, the child has not only to discriminate letter shapes, but also to remember them and to associate each one with the appropriate sound. In the traditional alphabet, there is no one-to-one correspondence between letter shapes and sounds. But in the 'initial teaching alphabet' designed by Sir James Pitman, each sound is represented by a different letter shape. This unambiguous association between shape and sound appears to make the early stages of learning to read easier (Downing, 1964). But it is not certain whether the advantage persists at later stages.

A possible reason for this is that reading necessitates more than the association between shapes and sounds of letters. The child must analyse the printed word into its constituent letters, and combine the sounds of these to make the sound of the whole word. This necessitates perceiving and remembering the exact order of letters in words; and the concept of order is one which children do not develop fully until the age of about 7 years (Piaget and Inhelder, 1956). Moreover, the synthesis of letter sounds to produce total word sounds often seems to cause difficulty. The sequence of letter sounds are not easy to identify with the whole word patterns of sound as the child is accustomed to speak them. Finally, he must grasp the meaning of a series of words in a whole phrase or sentence; and these again may appear to the child as integrated wholes, not easily analysable into separate words, and therefore difficult to equate with the latter.

It is indeed remarkable that the majority of children are able to acquire all those difficult processes at so young an age, and not surprising that some may fail to do so. Many of these failures appear to be due to inadequate teaching (Morris, 1966). But it does seem that some children fail through a constitutional disability, which may be linked to slow maturation (Vernon, 1957, 1962). Some of these cases exhibit a general linguistic retardation; others, an inability to analyse complex visual shapes correctly. With the latter, understanding of order and direction may also be defective, and they may produce mirror writing and/or reading. That maturation is retarded is suggested by the fact that often they grow out of their difficulties and become normal readers, especially if given suitable teaching. Other more severe cases may recover less easily; and in these the cause may be an inability to perform the complex reasoning processes described above.

4. *Summary*

There are several skills which children have to acquire in which an accurate perception of shapes must be followed by the analysis and resynthesis of the perceptual data and the association of these with some form of representational or symbolic meaning. Of these, the simplest is the understanding of pictures; but though this begins to develop at an early age, it is not fully acquired until many years later. Reading and the interpretation of diagrammatic material are more advanced skills, in which the processing of the initial perceptual data is largely controlled by symbolic thought processes.

IX. CONCLUSIONS

What then may we conclude as to the origin and development of perception in children? Although many of the physiological processes involved in perception are well developed at birth, or mature very early in life, they operate mainly in simple reflex responses. But these do not appear in the main to lead directly to more highly developed perceptions. We may discover the origins of these in the infant's exploration of his environment, first through undirected and wandering gaze and movements, but later with increasing attention, control and awareness. Although in early months sensations from the internal organs may be paramount, tactile and visual sensation become increasingly important, and finally visual sensation plays the predominant part. But sensory impressions especially in the tactile and visual modes are co-ordinated together in schemata corresponding to particular objects and events, which are further modified and extended through the infant's intentional movements and explorations. Memories of past experiences are involved in these schemata, which enable the child to identify the principal features of his environment.

However, it is as impossible as it is undesirable to attend to and perceive every environmental stimulus. Certain objects are perceived in preference to others; and later, certain aspects or characteristics of these objects. In early infancy, the qualities of intensity (brightness and loudness) and of movement seem to be the main determinants of what is perceived; to which must be added certain emotion-provoking qualities such as pleasingness and painfulness. A little later, shape and colour are also taken into account; but the really important aspect is that for many years the child tends to select and perceive what has some significance for him personally, or what happens to catch his attention at the moment; and to overlook or ignore other aspects of the field which should be considered if it is to be perceived veridically. He develops only slowly the capacity for perceptual activity, that is to say, the systematic deployment of attention to all relevant aspects of the field, and the careful objective assessment of all its significant features.

The absence of such perceptual activity was apparent in the perception of simple shapes, complex figures and pictures; and in the formation of abstract concepts of number, quantity, etc. However, it seems possible that this absence of perceptual activity may be due in some cases to lack of interest or of understanding how to set about the task; or to lack of verbal ability, the employment of which is essential to identification at this stage and to the formation of concepts. But we must agree with Piaget that the efficient performance of these tasks involves more than the immediate primary perceptions, and is dependent in part upon the modification and guidance of perception through intelligent reasoning. On the other hand, perception in many cases cannot afford to be too deliberate and selective; it is still the means by which we quickly obtain those impressions of the environment which are necessary for survival. Thus we can understand why in making a rapid selection of the most significant events, preparatory to effective action, our immediate perceptions are never completely reliable. But when accurate judgement is required, when abstract concepts or symbolic meaning are involved, then immediate percepts must be carefully considered and the evidence they give weighed intelligently in the light of knowledge. To do this, children may need more, and more unambiguous, information than do adults.

We have also seen that as the child grows his perceptual schemata in themselves become modified by the assimilation of new perceptual data. The principal schemata are based upon classification of objects, and include class characteristic of shape, colour, tactile impressions, spatial position, movement and activity, and associations of use. These are the schemata upon which are based our knowledge of the environment and our ability to react to it appropriately. Thus the child learns to disregard or compensate for unimportant variations in these characteristics, as in the perception of the 'constancies'.

Now it seems reasonable to suppose that these developments in perception proceed in close conjunction with the child's maturation. Clearly this is true of early infancy; developments in sensitivity, in direction of attention and in co-ordination of sensory data within schemata must depend on maturation, since the infant is incapable of profiting by his experience until these developments have taken place. There is evidence also which suggests that simple discrimination depends mainly on maturation. Thus it has been found in adults that discrimination between shapes is unaffected by experience of these shapes; it is no more difficult to judge that two unfamiliar meaningless shapes are the same or different than to make the same judgement with pictures of familiar objects (Robinson *et al.*, 1964). But the latter can be identified more quickly than the former. And there can be little doubt that in children identification, based upon object schemata, must to a great extent be a function of the child's experience in exploring and manipulating his environment.

Again, the emergence of perceptual activity seems to depend on maturation; but it would appear unlikely that the child could employ his perceptual activity in perceiving accurately complex shapes and the relationship between their parts without experience in so doing. Maturation also seems to be involved in the perception of a shape such as that of the diamond. For it was found that mentally defective children could match a diamond shape among a number of figures which deviated from it better than normal children of equal mental age, though less well than children of equal chronological age (Nelson, 1962). On the other hand, size constancy in mental defectives corresponded to chronological age and not to mental age (Jenkin and Feallock, 1960). Thus although it presumably cannot appear before a certain stage in maturation, its full development seems to depend on experience. Again, it might be inferred from the experiment by Walk and Gibson (1961) that some ability to estimate distance exists initially without prior experience of that particular type of situation. Yet the behaviour of a man who recovered his sight at the age of 52 years through a corneal graft suggests that spatial schemata and judgements of distance are not adequate without the necessary experience (Gregory and Wallace, 1963).

Perhaps we may conclude that certain degrees of maturation are essential before certain types of perception can develop at all; but that at each stage adequate and relevant perceptual experiences are necessary for complete development.

REFERENCES

AHRENS, R. (1954). Beitrag zur Entwicklung des Physiognomie und Mimikerkennens. *Zeit. f. Exper. u. Ange. Psychol.* **II**, 412 and 599. Quoted by Ambrose, J. A.

AMBROSE, J. A. (1961). The development of the smiling response in early infancy. In Foss, B. M. (ed.), *Determinants of Infant Behaviour*, **II**. London: Methuen.

AMEN, E. W. (1941). Individual differences in apperceptive reaction. *Genet. Psychol. Monogr.* **23**, 319–385.

AMES, J. B. *et al.* (1953). Development of perception in the young child as observed in responses to the Rorschach Test Blots. *J. Genet. Psychol.* **82**, 183–204.

BABSKA, Z. (1965). The formation of the conception of identity of visual characteristics of objects seen successively. In *Monographs of the Society for Research in Child Development*, **30**, No. 2.

BINET, A. (1905). Interpretation. *Ann. Psychol.* 11.

BIRCH, H. G. (1963). Dyslexia and the maturation of visual function. In Money, J (ed.), *Reading Disability*. Baltimore: John Hopkins Press.

BOWER, T. G. R. (1965). Stimulus variables determining space perception in infants. *Science*, **149**, 88–89.

BRUNER, J. S. (1964). The course of cognitive growth. *Amer. Psychol.* **19**, 1–19.

BRUNSWICK, E. (1965). *Perception and the Representative Design of Psychological Experiments.* University of California Press.

BURT, C. (1921). *Mental and Scholastic Tests.* London: P. S. King.

CANTOR, G. N. (1955). Effects of three types of pre-training on discrimination learning in pre-school children. *J. Exp. Psychol.* **49**, 339–342.

CHASE, W. P. (1937). Color vision in infants. *J. Exp. Psychol.* **20**, 203–222.

COOK, W. M. (1931). Ability of children in color discrimination. *Child Developm.* **2**, 303–320.

CRAUMUSSEL, E. (1924). Ce que voient les yeux d'enfants. *J. de Psychol.* **21**, 161.

CRUIKSHANK, R. M. (1941). The Development of visual size-constancy in early infancy. *J. Genet. Psychol.* **58**, 377.

DOWNING, J. A. (1964). *The Initial Teaching Alphabet.* London: Cassell.

DRAGUNS, J. G., and MULTARI, G. (1961). Recognition of perceptually ambiguous stimuli in grade school children. *Child Developm.* **32**, 541–550.

FANTZ, R. L. (1958). Pattern vision in young infants. *Psychol. Rep.* **8**, 43–47.

FANTZ, R. L. *et al.* (1962). Maturation of pattern vision in infants during the first six months. *J. Comp. Physiol. Psychol.* **55**, 907–917.

FISHER, G. H. (1964). Experimenting with young children. *Research Bull.*, No. 2. Department of Psychology, University of Newcastle-upon-Tyne.

FISHER, G. H. (1965). Visual and tactile-kinaesthetic shape perception. *Brit. J. Educ. Psychol.* **35**, 69–78.

FRANCÈS, R. (1962). *Le développement perceptif.* Paris: Presses Universitaires de France.

GARNER, W. R. (1962). *Uncertainty and Structure as Psychological Concepts.* New York: Wiley.

GELLERMAN, L. W. (1933). Form discrimination in chimpanzees and two-year-old children. *J. Genet. Psychol.* **42**, 28–50.

GESELL, A. *et al.* (1949). *Vision: Its Development in Infant and Child.* New York: Hoeber.

GHENT, L. (1956). Perception of overlapping and embedded figures by children of different ages. *Amer. J. Psychol.* **69**, 575–587.

GIBSON, E. J. *et al.* (1962). A developmental study of the discrimination of letter-like forms. *J. Comp. Physiol. Psychol.* **55**, 897–906.

GIBSON, J. J. (1950). *The Perception of the Visual World.* Boston: Houghton Mifflin.

GOLLIN, E. S. (1956). Problems of developmental psychology. *Child Developm.* **27**, 223–235.

GOLLIN, E. S. (1960). Developmental studies of visual recognition of incomplete objects. *Percept. Motor Skills.* **2**, 289–298.

GRAHAM, F. K. *et al.* (1960). Development in pre-school children of the ability to copy forms. *Child Developm.* **51**, 339–359.

GREGORY, R. L., and WALLACE, J. G. (1963). Recovery from early blindness: a case study. *Exp. Psychol. Soc. Monogr.* No. 2.

HALPERN, E. (1965). The effects of incompatibility between perception and logic in Piaget's stage of concrete operations. *Child Developm.* **36**, 491–497.

HERSHANSON, M. (1964). Visual discrimination in the human newborn. *J. Comp. Physiol. Psychol.* **58**, 270–276.

HETZER, H., and TUDOR-HART, B. (1927). Die frühesten Reaktionen auf die menschliche Stimme. *Quelle u. Stud. z. Jugendk.* **5**, 103–124.

HOCHBERG, J., and BROOKS, V. (1962). Pictorial recognition as an unlearned activity. *Amer. J. Psychol.* **75**, 624–628.

INHELDER, B., and PIAGET, J. (1964). *The Early Growth of Logic in the Child.* London: Routledge & Kegan Paul.

JENKIN, N., and FEALLOCK, S. M. (1960). Developmental and intellectual processes in size-distance judgement. *Amer. J. Psychol.* **73**, 268–273.

KAILA, E. (1932). Die Reaktionen des Sauglings auf das Menschliche Gesicht. *Ann. Univ. Aboensis.* B. Humaniora. Quoted by Ambrose, J. A.

KATZ, P. A. (1964). Effect of labels on children's perception and discrimination learning. *J. Exper. Psychol.* **66**, 423–428.

LAMBERCIER, M. (1946). La configuration en profondeur dans la constance des grandeurs. *Arch. de. Psychol.* **31**, 287–324.

LING, B. C. (1941). Form discrimination as a learning cue in infants. *Comp. Psychol. Monogr.* **17**, No. 2.

LIUBLINSKAYA, A. A. (1957). The development of children's speech and thought. Simon, B. (ed.). In *Psychology in the Soviet Union.* London: Routledge and Kegan Paul.

LOVELL, K. (1960). A follow-up study of some aspects of the work of Piaget and Inhelder on the child's conception of space. *Brit. J. Educ. Psychol.* **29**, 104–117.

LOVELL, K. *et al.* (1962). The growth of the concept of speed: a comparative study. *J. Child Psychol. Psychiat.* **3**, 101–110.

LURIA, A. R. (1961). *The Role of Speech in the Regulation of Normal and Abnormal Behaviour.* Oxford: Pergamon.

MACCOBY, E. E., and BEE, H. L. (1965). Some speculations concerning the lag between perceiving and performing. *Child Developm.* **36**, 367–377.

MALTER, M. (1947). The ability of children to read a process-diagram. *J. Educ. Psychol.* **38**, 290–298.

MEYER, E. (1940). Comprehension of spatial relations in pre-school children. *J. Genet. Psychol.* **57**, 119–151.

MICHOTTE, A. (1946). *La Perception de la Causalité.* Louvain: Publications Universitaires de Louvain.

MORRIS, J. M. (1966). How far can reading backwardness be attributed to school conditions? In Downing, J. A. (ed.) *The First International Reading Symposium.* London: Cassell.

NELSON, T. M. (1962). A study comparing visual and visual motor perceptions of unimpaired, defective and spastic cerebral palsied children. *J. Genet. Psychol.* **101**, 299–332.

OLUM, V. (1956). Developmental differences in the perception of causality. *Amer. J. Psychol.* **69**, 417–423.

OSTERRIETH, P. A. (1945). Le test de copie d'une figure complexe. *Arch. de Psychol.* **30**, 206–356.

PIAGET, J. (1946). *Les notions de mouvement et de vitesse chez l'enfant.* Paris: Presses Universitaires de France.

PIAGET, J. (1951). *Play, Dreams and Imitation in Childhood.* London: Heinemann.

PIAGET, J. (1952). *The Child's Conception of Number.* London: Routledge and Kegan Paul.

PIAGET, J. (1955). *The Child's Construction of Reality.* London: Routledge and Kegan Paul.

PIAGET, J. (1961). *Les mécanismes perceptifs.* Paris: Presses Universitaires de France.

PIAGET, J., and INHELDER, B. (1956). *The Child's Conception of Space.* London: Routledge and Kegan Paul.

PIAGET, J., and LAMBERCIER, M. (1951). La comparaison des grandeurs projectives chex l'enfant et chez l'adulte. *Arch. de Psychol.* **33**, 81.

PIAGET, J., and LAMBERCIER, M. (1958). La causalité perceptive visuelle chex l'enfant et chez l'adulte. *Arch. de Psychol.* **36**, 77–201.

PIAGET, J. et al. (1954). La résistance des bonnes formes à l'illusion de Müller-Lyer. *Arch. de Psychol.* **34**, 155–201.

PIAGET, J., and STETTLER-VON ALBERTINI, B. (1954). Observations sur la perception des bonnes formes chez l'enfant par actualization des lignes virtuelles. *Arch. de Psychol.* **34**, 203–242.

PIAGET, J., and VINH BANG (1961). Comparaison des mouvements oculaires et des centrations du regard chez l'enfant et chez l'adulte. *Arch. de Psychol.* **38**, 167.

ROBINSON, J. S. et al. (1964). Tests of effects of past experience on perception. *Percept. Motor Skills.* **18**, 953–956.

SALZEN, E. A. (1963). Visual stimuli eliciting a smiling response in the human infant. *J. Genet. Psychol.* **102**, 51–54.

SKEELS, H. M. (1932). A study of some factors influencing form-board accomplishments of two and three-year-old children. *J. Genet. Psychol.* **40**, 375–395.

SMEDSLUND, J. (1961). The acquisition of conservation of substance and weight in children. *Scand. J. Psychol.* **2**, 71–84.

SMITH, O. W. and SMITH, P. C. (1966). Developmental studies of spatial judgments by children and adults. *Percept. Motor Skills.* **22**, 3–73.

SPEARS, W. C. (1964). Assessment of visual preference and discrimination in the four-month-old infant. *J. Comp. Physiol. Psychol.* **57**, 381–386.

STIRNIMAN, F. (1944). Über des Farbemfinden Neugeborener. *Ann. Paediat.* **165**, 1. Quoted in Carmichael, L. (ed.) (1946), *Manual of Child Psychology*, New York: Wiley.

TERMAN, L. M., and MERRILL, M. A. (1937). *Measuring Intelligence.* London: Harrap.

THOMAS, H. (1965). Visual fixation responses of infants to stimuli of varying complexity. *Child Developm.* **36**, 629–688.

VERNON, M. D. (1940). The relation of cognition and phantasy in children. *Brit. J. Psychol.* **30**, 273.

VERNON, M. D. (1946). Learning from graphical material. *Brit. J. Psychol.* **36**, 145–158.

VERNON, M. D. (1957). *Backwardness in Reading.* Cambridge: Cambridge University Press.

VERNON, M. D. (1962). Specific dyslexia. *Brit. J. Educ. Psychol.* **32**, 143–150.

VURPILLOT, E. (1963). *L'organisation perceptive: son rôle dans l'évolution des illusions optico-géometriques.* Paris: J. Vrin.

VURPILLOT, E., and BRAULT, H. (1959). Étude expérimentale sur la formation des schèmes empiriques. *Ann. Psychol.* **59**, 381–394.

WALK, R. D., and DODGE, S. H. (1962). Visual depth perception in a 10-month-old monocular human infant. *Science.* **137**, 529–530.

WALK, R. D., and GIBSON, E. J. (1961). A comparative and analytical study of visual depth perception. *Psychol. Monogr.* **75**, No. 15.

WEIR, M. W., and STEVENSON, H. W. (1959). The effect of verbalization in children's learning as a function of chronological age. *Child Developm.* **30**, 143–149.

WELCH, L. (1939). The development of discrimination of form and area. *J. Psychol.* **7**, 37–54.

WERTHEIMER, M. (1961). Psychomotor coordination of auditory and visual space at birth. *Science*, **134**, 1692.

WHITE, B. L., and CASTLE, P. W. (1964). Visual exploratory behavior following post-natal handling of human infants. *Percept. Motor Skills*. **18**, 497–502.

WHITE, B. L., CASTLE, P. W., and HELD, R. (1964). Observations of visually directed reaching. *Child Developm*. **35**, 349–363.

WOHLWILL, J. F. (1960). A study of the development of the number concept by scalogram analysis. *J. Genet. Psychol*. **97**, 345–377.

WOHLWILL, J. F. (1962). The perspective illusion: Perceived size and distance in fields varying in suggested depth in children and adults. *J. Exp. Psychol*. **64**, 300–310.

WOHLWILL, J. F., and LOWE, R. C. (1962). Experimental analysis of the development of conservation of number. *Child Developm*. **33**, 153–167.

WOHLWILL, J. F., and WIENER, M. (1964). Discrimination of form orientation in young children. *Child Developm*. **35**, 1113–1125.

WÜRSTEN, H. (1947). L'évolution des comparaisons de longueurs de l'enfant à l'adulte. *Arch. de Psychol*. **32**, 1.

ZEIGLER, H. P., and LEIBOWITZ, H. (1957). Apparent visual size as a function of distance for children and adults. *Amer. J. Psychol*. **70**, 106–109.

2

Social Learning and Identification

H. R. SCHAFFER

I. INTRODUCTION

IT is possible to maintain that all human learning is really of a social nature, for the acquisition of any skill or item of knowledge is dependent on the cultural values, attitudes, and social relationships which surround both the act of learning and its content. The term *social learning*, however, has come to signify a particular area in developmental psychology, and in this chapter we shall accordingly use it to refer to the acquisition of those behaviour patterns which specifically enable the individual to function as a member of a social group.

In many lower species of animals, such as bees or ants, quite complex forms of social behaviour have been found to occur from the beginning without any previous learning experience. In the human child, however, the part which experience plays is far greater. His innate equipment provides him with certain potentialities, but before he can use these in order to help him to function as a member of society a learning process must take place which will determine the precise manner in which these potentialities are used. All children, for instance, reach a stage at about the beginning of the second year when they are maturationally ready to begin to communicate with others by means of the spoken word, yet whether they do so, the language they use, their enunciation, and to some extent also the richness of their vocabulary and the complexity of their sentence structure is largely a function of the particular social environment in which they are living. The socialization process is thus a vital determinant of personality development and its analysis an important task of psychology.

Two things are involved in such an analysis. In the first place, an effort must be made to recognize those aspects in the child's environment which are influential in shaping his behaviour. Does birth order matter? Do breast-fed babies develop differently from bottle-fed babies?

42

What is the role of the father? In the second place, one must understand the manner in which the child responds to these forces and how he retains their influence, i.e. study the learning process itself whereby a child develops from an essentially a-social state to full membership of a society to whose rules of conduct he has learned to conform. Although our knowledge of this progression is still woefully inadequate, it does seem evident that it is in the earliest years of life that a child's most important learning experiences take place. For this reason, and also because the phenomena of social learning are rather more clear cut at this period, we shall give special emphasis in this chapter to the earliest stages of development.

II. THE BEGINNINGS OF SOCIABILITY

From the early weeks on an infant is equipped with a number of behaviour patterns which link him to other human beings. The sucking reflex, for instance, enables him to respond to and accept the maternal breast, by crying he can summon help for the alleviation of discomfort, and his smile has the effect of evoking pleasure and loving behaviour in those responsible for his care. These responses are part of the infant's inheritance and their biological purpose is to ensure his survival. Initially helpless and entirely dependent on others, they provide him with means of signalling his requirements and of responding to their caretaking activities.

Yet at first these responses are by no means truly social in nature, for they are linked to far more primitive aspects of the environment than other human beings as such. Investigations of the infant's smile have made this point clear (Spitz and Wolff, 1946), for they have demonstrated that between the ages of 2 and 6 months it does not require the whole human face to evoke smiling in a baby but merely certain quite crude characteristics such as a pair of eye-like dots. A mask containing nothing but such dots will evoke the smile in a young infant as surely as his mother's face bending over him. Narrowing down to the socially 'correct' object takes place only gradually in the course of development, and it is not till the second half of the first year that the smile loses its reflex character, requires the full human face before it is shown, and is used in a selective manner to only certain familiar individuals. Similarly with other responses found in interpersonal situations: sucking is at first elicited by any nipple-shaped object, and an infant's crying becomes a purposive social tool only after a period during which it is automatically activated by certain internal conditions.

The reflex-like nature of these forerunners of social behaviour does not, however, mean that these responses are entirely rigid and invariable. Even at this very early stage it is possible for the environment to shape and modify their course and for experience to produce lasting adjustment, thus providing examples of some of the earliest forms of learning. It has been shown, for instance, that from the very beginning the mother's mode of handling and physical characteristics can produce adaptations in the infant's feeding responses which are retained in his behavioural repertoire (Call, 1964; Gunther, 1961). An experiment performed by Marquis (1941) illustrates this point. Two groups of infants were observed during the first ten days of life. One group was on a four-hour feeding schedule throughout this period, whereas the other group was on a three-hour schedule for the first eight days and was then shifted to a four-hour schedule. Continuous records of bodily activity were obtained from each infant, and in this way it was possible to demonstrate that, within a few days following birth, both groups showed a gradual rise in restlessness before their respective feeding times. This rise became particularly marked when the infants previously fed on a three-hour schedule had to wait the extra hour for their feed. Learning, it may be concluded, had taken place and the first steps in socialization had been taken.

There are, it appears, two ways in which an infant's responsiveness to his social environment may be shaped by the actions of other people at this early stage of development. The first is illustrated by an experiment which set out to demonstrate that the smiling response of 4-months-old infants is subject to environmental reinforcement (Brackbill, 1958). In this study the occurrence of each smile was immediately 'rewarded' by the experimenter, the reward consisting of smiling back at the infant, patting him and briefly picking him up. It was found that the use of this procedure made it possible not only to increase the rate of smiling but also to extinguish the response subsequently by withholding the reward. A similar effect was observed in a study of vocalization (Rheingold, Gewirtz and Ross, 1959): again the rate of the infants' response could be increased by following each vocalization with a social act on the part of the experimenter and decreased by no longer rewarding it in this way. In both studies a particular response was singled out and a reward given contingent on its occurrence. A very specific kind of learning was thus fostered.

The other way in which the environment affects infantile behaviour is of a more general kind. Not only does an infant require specific types of stimulation (things to suck, things to manipulate, etc.), but he must also be provided with a certain over-all quantity of stimulation in order to maintain an optimum degree of alertness. Infants reared in certain kinds of institutions, where they receive only a minimal amount of care and experience little opportunity for social interaction with adults, tend to show a general lag in development and sometimes marked social apathy. We shall review the relevant studies below in our discussion of deprivation, but here an experiment by Rheingold (1956) may be quoted in which the opposite effect was attained, i.e. social responsiveness was increased by providing extra stimulation. In this study the experimenter played the role of mother to eight institutionalized infants, aged six months, for a period of eight consecutive weeks. Each day she fed, changed, and played with the babies and generally provided them with a far greater amount of stimulation and care than that given to other infants in the same institution receiving only the routine amount of attention. Observations and tests showed that, as a result of their special treatment, the mothered infants showed much more social responsiveness than the normally treated infants, this being not only manifested to the experimenter herself but also generalized to other people.

These demonstrations of environmental control over behaviour must not, however, lead one to the conclusion that all individual differences between infants are solely due to learning experiences. This 'tabula rasa' conception of the child, i.e. the notion that the infant is initially a kind of blank, featureless slate on which others may write at will, cannot be sustained in the face of the increasing evidence that profound constitutional differences exist which play an important part in determining the behaviour of even very young babies (Wenar and Wenar, 1963). There are, for instance, some infants who, from the early weeks on, show a very considerable need for social stimulation, who cannot be left alone without immediately evoking intense protests and who demand an almost continuous supply of excitation. There are others who, on the contrary, make few demands for attention and who are content even when left to their own devices for lengthy periods. It is not easy to apportion individual differences such as these between heredity and environment respectively, yet there are strong indications (Schaffer and Emerson, 1964a) that some part at any rate is of an innate origin. Thus the tendency to seek stimulation from social sources may, on account of constitutional factors, be stronger in some

c

children than in others and therefore result in greater demands being made on the environment for the provision of relevant learning opportunities. The overdependent child, for instance, is not necessarily one who has been 'spoilt' by his mother: this popular notion is based on the automatic assumption that a child's behaviour is entirely a function of maternal practices and does not allow for the influence of factors inherent in the child. Although we are still largely ignorant about the precise nature of these constitutional factors, some indications are just beginning to emerge about their identity. Thus it has been claimed (Chess *et al.*, 1959), on the basis of repeated observations of children throughout their first two years, that there are certain intrinsic reaction patterns which appear in the early months and persist thereafter in stable form. Sensory threshold, activity pattern, and regularity of response are among such characteristics which appear to be relatively fixed and resistant to change. One of these in particular, namely, activity pattern, which has repeatedly been claimed as of constitutional origin (Fries, 1953; Mittelmann, 1954), has in several studies been found to exercise an influence on the manner in which social development proceeds (Escalona, 1963; Schaffer and Emerson, 1964b): a hyperactive, tense infant will seek to interact with his social partners in a very different way from that of a placid, inactive infant, and the respective effects of these two patterns on the mothers will in turn help to establish very different life experiences for these infants.

A complex form of interaction between the two sets of forces, environmental and constitutional, is indicated. The interaction between the child and his social environment is not one-way but two-way, and the characteristics of the child as well as those of his caretakers must be taken into account when tracing the development of his behaviour. The influence of environmental forces may be enormous, but their ability to mould behaviour is by no means unlimited and must be related to the individual's inherent nature.

III. THE FORMATION OF THE FIRST SOCIAL RELATIONSHIP

When a baby in the early weeks of life is separated from his mother (because, for instance, of hospitalization) and handed over to the care of others, he will not protest at the loss and show no aversion to being handled by strangers. A child of 12 months, on the other hand, will generally be most distressed in this situation and continue his protests until once more restored to his mother. The older child shows by his behaviour that he has now formed a definite emotional bond with a particular individual, and it is this first relationship which many believe to be the most important influence a child is ever likely to encounter in the course of his development. How is this bond formed? When does it first emerge? What factors underlie its appearance?

A number of views have been advanced to answer these questions. According to one school of thought (e.g. Miller and Dollard, 1941) the child forms an attachment to his mother because he has learned to associate her presence with the alleviation of physical needs such as hunger and pain. Mother love is thus basically cupboard love, or, in the language of learning theory from which this notion has been derived, is a secondary and not a primary drive. Originally, the theory states, the child is interested only in the alleviation of physiological tension states, but as the mother is always the agent of tension reduction her presence gradually becomes associated with a state of well-being until finally, through a process of generalization, she acquires reward value in her own right. Emotional dependence, according to this view, develops on the basis of physical dependence.

This theory has of late come under attack. For one thing, it has been shown that strong emotional bonds can be formed by an infant to people who have had no part in his physical care (Ainsworth, 1963, Schaffer and Emerson, 1964a). For another, studies with monkeys have indicated that there are innate mechanisms other than hunger which bind mother and child together (Harlow, 1958). A young monkey, it appears, is far more influenced in his choice of social object by the property of 'contact-comfort' than by food-giving capacity, and it is therefore the need to cling and the resulting tactile stimulation which provide the innate basis for the development of the relationship with the mother. Although observations of human infants (Schaffer and Emerson, 1964b) suggest that this contact need may not have the same overriding importance there as in lower primates, it does seem that children can learn to love their mothers for reasons other than food.

Congruent with these findings, a hypothesis has been proposed by Bowlby (1958) which challenges the learning theory view. According to this notion the dynamics underlying the tie formed by the child to his mother are dependent on five instinctual responses: smiling, crying, sucking, clinging, and following. These behaviour patterns are at first relatively independent of each other; in due course they become integrated and are focussed on a single mother figure. Social behaviour, according to this formulation, is not a secondary phenomenon, derived from the satisfaction of other needs, but is primary in that the infant starts off life equipped with certain innate behaviour patterns, the biological purpose of which is to promote the tie with the mother. Learning takes place in that the infant gradually finds out that one and the same person is always available as the object of the initially separate instinctual responses, and the process of their fusion into the need for the mother thus takes place as the inevitable result of the child's rearing experiences in his family environment.

Yet another view arises from empirical investigations of the manner in which infants in the course of the first twelve months respond to loss of the familiar adult – either for long periods, as in hospital (Schaffer, 1958), or for only brief periods, as when the mother merely leaves the room (Schaffer and Emerson, 1964a). One question at least can be answered with a fair degree of certainty as a result of this work, namely that concerning the age when the primary social relationship is first manifested. It is not until approximately seven months of age that the majority of infants first show a need for the presence of some specific individual rather than being satisfied with attention from anyone: before then the infant will be oriented towards the common attributes of people rather than to the people themselves, and though he may gradually have learned to distinguish familiar individuals from strangers and be prepared to smile or coo more readily at the former than the latter, he shows as yet no distress at the loss of his mother if other people are prepared to take over her caretaking activities. From about seven months on, however, signs of a specific attachment suddenly emerge, and it is thus at this crucial period that the first real social relationship may be said to come into existence.

Even prior to this point, however, infants show a strong need for the proximity of other people. If left entirely alone, the majority of infants will sooner or later show signs of distress despite being neither hungry nor in pain – distress which is generally alleviated only by the presence of other people. Protests in the everyday separation situations which occur in the lives of all babies can be found from the early weeks on and may often give rise to considerable problems to parents who regard this type of crying as not stemming from a 'genuine' need. Yet it may be concluded that we have evidence here of one of the earliest and most basic attributes of the human child, namely his need for the proximity of other people. Initially this biologically extremely important need exists in an indiscriminate form and can be satisfied by attention from anyone, but in the second half of the first year it becomes narrowed down and linked to just one or two well-known individuals. The phase of indiscriminate social attachments is thus followed by a phase of specific social attachments, and the evidence indicates that the time of change-over is maturationally determined as long as the right learning opportunities exist at the crucial time, i.e. the child is cared for by one or two familiar individuals able and willing to give him the necessary amount of attention. If at this time he is looked after by a large and constantly changing number of caretakers who can provide him with only a very limited amount of attention, the proper conditions for the attainment of this milestone of development are not present and the transition will then not take place (Schaffer, 1963).

Does this mean that the need for the proximity of other human beings is necessarily inborn in the child? As previously indicated, in the early months an infant is oriented only towards certain superficial human-like attributes and not to other people as such. A bottle will satisfy his need to suck as well as the maternal breast, and a mask will elicit a smile as effectively as the human face. Similarly, when a child in the first few months cries after being left alone it appears that he does not, to begin with, require specifically *social* stimulation but that any form of stimulation can quieten him. Most mothers are intuitively aware of this requirement and will accordingly lay on a supply of 'stimulators': rattles, beads, passing traffic, music from the radio, curtains blowing in the wind, patterned wallpaper and other such devices all serve the function not only of giving the child experience of certain specific objects in his environment but also that of providing him with that quantity of general stimulation which he must have in order to maintain a state of alertness (Casler, 1961).

According to this formulation, then, early social development takes place in three stages. In the first, the infant is motivated to obtain stimulation in general and will actively strive to satisfy this aim by emitting the necessary signals (usually crying). In due course, however, he learns that certain objects in his environment, namely other human beings, are particularly interesting from this point of view: for one thing, they possess a far greater range of stimulation-giving properties than the inanimate part of the environment (Rheingold, 1961), for another they provide specific kinds of stimulation which are especially satisfying to the infant, and furthermore they are usually the agents who provide even inanimate stimulation. Thus, through a learning process, a narrowing down takes place and people are sought in their own right.

This stage is finally succeeded by the third stage when social attachments are formed to only certain specific individuals.

The mechanisms underlying the transition to the third stage, i.e. the processes responsible for the formation of the first real social relationship, are not yet understood. In animals a similar phenomenon has been observed although its appearance is more sudden and dramatic. In many lower species the appearance of the primary social relationship has been found to take place within a quite sharply delimited period of development. In dogs, for instance, the critical period of maximal susceptibility for the formation of the first social bond extends from the age of 3 to 10 weeks (Scott, 1958). Only during this time is it possible for the animal to establish this relationship, and if no opportunity to come into contact with others exists at this crucial period, the animal may remain unsocialized for the rest of its life and for ever unable to form attachments to other members of the species. Lorenz (1937), who was one of the first to draw attention to this phenomenon, referred to it as 'imprinting' and demonstrated (mainly with birds) that an animal can become imprinted to a wide range of such 'incorrect' objects as boxes or human beings if it was exposed to these during its critical period rather than to the socially 'correct' object, namely its parent.

At one time it was believed that imprinting involved a qualitatively distinct type of learning which differed from other types in (a) being rigidly confined to certain restricted periods early in life; (b) having irreversible effects on the individual's behaviour; and (c) becoming linked with behaviour patterns (such as the sexual or the parental function) which, at the time of the original learning, are not yet functional. All these criteria have, in fact, been challenged (Thorpe, 1962), and it is now doubted whether imprinting depends on learning mechanisms fundamentally different from those underlying other forms of learning. What this work has done, however, is to draw attention to the importance of the timing of learning experiences in relation to the developmental phase reached by the individual. Although the evidence regarding the human child is still scant, it does seem that there are critical periods of development during which the individual is at his most susceptible to certain kinds of experience, and that, if the right kind of learning opportunity is not forthcoming, it will be very much more difficult for him to acquire the requisite skills subsequently. At each developmental stage the child requires certain quite specific types of stimulation from his environment and, conversely, is also highly vulnerable to particular kinds of noxious experiences. In the case of social development, for example, the period from 6 months on is crucial for the formation of the primary relationship but also makes the child highly susceptible to separation from the mother. What holds for social behaviour is also applicable to a wide range of other functions, and it seems likely that in the ensuing notion of 'organismic readiness' we have a concept of far-reaching importance in understanding child development and its relation to particular environmental happenings.

IV. THE COURSE OF SOCIAL DEVELOPMENT

Once the child has formed its primary attachment, the course of further social development in childhood revolves mainly around the manner in which his emotional dependence on others is expressed, the extent to which this need is met, and its replacement, in due course, by an increasing tendency towards independence. In the first two or three years a child's sense of security is entirely linked to the availability of his loved ones, and the nature of these primary relationships, it is believed, sets the tone for all future relationships. If his mother handles him gently and sensitively he will develop an expectation that the world is a good place and can be approached confidently, and in this way, on the basis of his earliest experiences, develop what one writer (Erikson, 1950) believes to be one of the most important heritages of early childhood – a sense of trust. Satisfaction and security in the relationship with the mother will, according to this formulation, generalize to other social situations.

The mother has, of course, the prime responsibility for the child's socialization in the early years, and it is therefore not surprising that socialization studies have in the past concerned themselves almost exclusively with the mother-child relationship. The most commonly held view is that the child in the typical Western family will form his first social relationship with only one person, that this person is always his mother, and that other, quite subsidiary relationships are only formed when this first bond has become firmly established. The development envisaged is thus like the growth of a tree, with the trunk representing the relationship to the mother and the later-appearing and smaller branches representing the child's other relationships.

There are indications, however, that this view may be too simple and that a misleading impression may be given by isolating the child's relationship to his mother from the rest of his social behaviour. Schaffer and Emerson (1964a), for example, found that some infants form multiple attachments from the very beginning of the phase in which ties to specific individuals emerge, and that in all other instances such multiple attachments are manifested within a relatively brief period. Of the sixty infants studied by them, 29 per cent already showed multiple attachments during the first month of the specific phase, and by the age of 18 months all but 13 per cent of the sample directed their attachment behaviour at more than one person. Moreover, relationships to individuals other than the mother often assume a form every bit as intense, if not more so, than the relationship with the mother – despite the fact that these other individuals are less often available to the child and that they may take no part in feeding or the satisfaction of other physical needs. Therefore it looks as if the process of fixing on an attachment object is a function of several variables. The total amount and type of stimulation accruing to the child in the course of interaction with each individual may be more important than his (her) availability or the fact that he (she) acts as principal caretaker. An under-stimulating mother would thus take second place to a father who is less frequently seen but who is willing to provide an optimal amount of stimulation on the occasions when he does interact with the child. Moreover, the child can learn from the beginning that different people are prepared to give him satisfaction to various degrees in different situations, so that a diversified, bush-like rather than tree-like, model may be envisaged. To what extent degree of diversification of early social ties is a handicap to mental health or, as has also been argued (Mead, 1962), a furtherance, remains unsettled. On the one hand it can be maintained that an exclusive and intense parent-child relationship is essential for developing the kind of personality which we value in our society; on the other hand one may regard a system of multiple mothering as a kind of insurance policy against loss and, furthermore, point to studies of community-reared children (such as those brought up on the Kibbutzim of Israel (Spiro, 1958) which have failed to find any signs of gross pathology. What does seem certain is that diversification of social objects is a function of the social setting in which the child is reared: whether, for instance, he is brought up by one exclusive mother-figure with few opportunities for other interpersonal contacts, or whether he is the member of a family in which child-care is distributed amongst a relatively large number of aunts, grandmothers, older siblings and neighbours. His learning opportunities in such different settings will, of course, vary accordingly, and understanding of a child's social behaviour consequently involves some knowledge of all his interpersonal contacts and not just an exclusive preoccupation with the maternal relationship.

The manifestation of a child's emotional dependence may take many forms. In the first year crying will be his most effective means of securing the adult's presence, but the development of locomotion and speech then brings about a far greater range of overt expressions. In a study of nursery school children (Beller, 1955) five behavioral components of dependence were distinguished, namely seeking help, physical contact, proximity, attention and recognition. These five components were found to be closely related, so that children differed consistently from one another in their dependence scores. As the child gets older, however, physical manifestations are more and more replaced by verbal manifestations. Thus Heathers (1955), in a comparison of the behaviour of 2- and 5-year-old children in a nursery school, found that seeking reassurance and affection from adults tend to decline in the early years of childhood relative to the seeking of attention and approval. Dependence on other children, however, remained high, though it took a much more active and assertive form.

The rate at which dependence diminishes as the child gets older and independence takes its place is a function of a number of factors, of which the mother's mode of behaviour has been particularly singled out for study. The extent to which this apparently natural development can be blocked by a mother's distorted attitude has been graphically illustrated by Levy (1943), who presented a number of detailed case histories to describe the syndrome of 'maternal over-protection'. This consisted of excessive contact, prolongation of infantile care and prevention of independent behaviour, the combination of which successfully kept the children fixated at an early stage of social growth and resulted in infantile, over-dependent and over-demanding behaviour.

Levy's study was a purely descriptive one, but there have been many further research efforts to isolate those components in maternal behaviour which bear an aetiological relationship to the child's social dependence. Thus it has been shown that the intensity of a child's demands on his mother will depend on the extent to which she punishes him for such dependent behaviour (Sears *et al.*, 1957): punishment of dependence, it appears, actually *increases* the likelihood of its occurrence, and similarly rejection can produce heightened dependency (Yarrow, 1948).

Another series of studies investigated the effects of early infant training procedures, in the belief that the antecedents of dependency could be found in the extent to which the child in the very earliest period of life learned to regard his mother as a gratifying or frustrating individual. According to this theory (which stemmed mainly from Freud), the infant is at first concerned only with immediate satisfaction of all his needs and desires and cannot tolerate frustration. Socialization, however, inevitably involves some degree of frustration, and therefore the child's first encounter with restraints imposed upon him is likely to have lasting effects on the type of relationship established with the restraining agents. Much of the work on this subject has, however, produced confusing and conflicting results. Thus Sears *et al.*, (1953) found that frustration in infancy expressed through rigidity of feeding procedures and severity of weaning was related to the degree of later dependency but that severity of toilet training was not so related. In a subsequent study, however, Sears *et al.* (1957) were unable to confirm these findings, in that no general connexion between early socializing practices in the feeding situation and later dependence could be consistently established. This is in line with the general failure to determine firm connexions between specific techniques of infant training and subsequent personality characteristics (Orlansky, 1949) as a result of which it has now been concluded that the infant's personality is too plastic an organization to be permanently and invariably affected by one particular event occurring at a particular phase of development. Knowledge of one isolated socializing technique cannot, by itself, help one to predict a child's future behaviour, for the same technique may be employed for different reasons by different mothers. Instead, attention must be given to the total context of the mother-child relationship within which these techniques occur.

As a result, much effort is now devoted to the isolation from the great welter of maternal behaviour of meaningful attitudes such as warmth, punitiveness, indulgence, etc. – attitudes which will transcend the expression of particular behaviour patterns and form an all-pervasive background to the parents' relationship with the child. Various scales have been perfected to measure these characteristics (Baldwin, *et al.*, 1945, Schaefer and Bell, 1958), and efforts are being made to establish correlations with different aspects of child behaviour. This work, however, is still in its beginnings, for the complexity of interacting forces in social relationships is such that no quick answer can be expected.

Birth order and sex are two further factors the influence of which have been investigated in relation to social development. Many previous investigations have failed to find any consistent effects of birth order, but according to one writer (Schachter, 1959) this factor does play a part in determining an individual's behaviour in stressful situations. Under such conditions persons who were first-born or only children were found consistently to prefer the company of other people whereas later-born individuals tended to face their worries alone. This difference, which emerged clearly only under anxiety-provoking conditions, was not related to family size but only to absolute order of birth and was believed to reflect the strength of the 'affiliative needs' of the individuals concerned. The explanation of this phenomenon was thought to lie in the different attitudes which parents adopt to their first born child as compared with subsequent children: with the former they are more inclined to be oversolicitous and anxious, and as a result of this treatment the child is more likely to develop strong habits of dependence which will emerge whenever the individual is subjected to stress. Later-born children tend to receive rather less care, learn to be less dependent on others, and will consequently, as adults, prefer to deal with their troubles alone.

As to sex, there are many ways in which boys and girls respectively are expected to learn to behave according to certain culturally prescribed norms. Some of these we shall mention in the next section, but here we may note that this appears to be one influence on the manner in which a child's dependence is gradually replaced by independence. In our society it is regarded as more important that boys show independence and learn to stand on their own feet as early as possible. Socialization pressures geared to this aim are therefore more likely to be heavy in the case of boys than girls. It is this, presumably, which accounts for the greater stability of dependent behaviour in girls as compared with boys which was found in a study where appropriate measures were taken periodically between the ages of 3 and 14 (Kagan and Moss, 1962).

V. IDENTIFICATION

Having formed a strong bond to certain selected individuals, the child will inevitably wish to conform to their standards of behaviour and avoid their disapproval of inappropriate conduct. He does so by becoming like them – by incorporating their standards and thus identifying with them.

The task of socialization is at first almost entirely in the hands of the child's family. This is the primary social group in which he is introduced to the mores of society and which helps him to acquire the basic skills necessary to cope with the environment. In so far as social learning is a function of social contagion, i.e. the extent to which the individual comes into contact with others, the family is likely to provide the most powerful formative influence on personality development, for in the early years, at the time of maximum susceptibility, the child will be in almost continuous contact with family members. On an overt level, their influence manifests itself in the child's tendency to imitate their ways of behaviour and consequently to become more and more like them in speech, dress, eating habits and other personal characteristics. Habits of imitation can, in fact, be learned if the child is suitably rewarded for doing so (Miller and Dollard, 1941). However, imitation is not merely conditioned by overtly given rewards and instructions but depends on the total parent-child relationship and the powerful, though often subtle, feelings which a child develops towards those on whom he is emotionally dependent. The whole process that leads the child to think, feel and act as though the characteristics of another person were his own is called identification. The person with whom the child identifies is known as the model, and identification may thus also be regarded as the wish to be the model. Two qualifications must, however, be added: in the first place, a child need not necessarily identify with the whole model but may do so with only certain of its parts or attributes, and in the second place this tendency can be a wholly unconscious process.

Most of the difficulties of studying identification arise from this latter point. Freud, to whom much of the credit must be given for drawing attention to this process, was mainly concerned with it as a defence mechanism, i.e. as a way of dealing with the anxiety which the child experiences as a result of the feelings of hostility that parental frustrations engender. Afraid of losing the parents' affection as a result of these hostile feelings, the child solves the conflict by repressing his aggression and instead adopts the safer course of himself, as it were, becoming the aggressor through incorporating the parents' characteristics. The Freudian theory thus views identification as being mainly based on the child's negative feelings towards his parents and in this way differs from the learning theory account, which proposes instead that the child's wish to be the parent arises from his past experiences of feelings of gratification and pleasure associated with the presence of the parent, as a result of which he adopts his characteristics in order, so to speak, to supply his own rewards.

Whichever view is the correct one, the process is clearly a very important one in making the child into an acceptable member of society. Most of the research dealing with it has investigated it in relation to two areas: sex-typing and the development of conscience.

From a very early age on boys and girls are expected to behave differently. Already at 3 and 4 years of age children have formed definite and sex-appropriate preferences when asked to choose from such toys as guns, dolls, kitchen utensils and soldiers (Hartup and Zook, 1960), and the strength of these sex-linked preferences tends to increase with age. To some extent learning the appropriate role is due to direct training procedures employed by the parents, but there is evidence suggesting that it is also a result of identification with the same-sex parent. The little boy is expected to be 'like daddy' and to engage in masculine activity like hammering in nails and kicking footballs, while the little girl is similarly encouraged to imitate her mother's interests in cooking, knitting, etc. Society thus guides the child towards the appropriate model and gives him or her the opportunity to form the relevant identification with it. This process involves, of course, not merely the imitation of certain interests and hobbies but also the incorporation of more basic personality characteristics. Aggression, for instance, is regarded as being a mainly masculine trait and therefore fostered in boys by contact with their father. In one investigation (Sears, 1951) pre-school boys whose fathers were away on military service were found to have developed less aggression than boys whose fathers were at home. No such difference was found between father-present and father-absent girls of the same age.

Many attempts have been made to ascertain those characteristics in a child's family environment which foster strong sex-identifications. There is general agreement that the quality of the relationship with the parent is the most decisive factor in this respect. In a study of 5-year old boys (Mussen and Distler, 1959) a test was administered to measure strength of masculine identification. The scores were then compared with the boys' perception of their fathers (as obtained from the endings which the children supplied to incomplete stories), and it was found that boys with high male identifications tended to see their fathers as warmer and more affectionate than boys with low male identifications. Similar evidence has come from another study (Payne and Mussen, 1956), this time on adolescent boys and using 'test similarity' as a criterion of father-identification: again the strength of identification and the perception of the father as warm, helpful and kind were related. The same finding also applies to girls, for those with high femininity scores on sex-role tests have been found to have warmer relationships with their mothers than girls with low scores. It is thus the rewarding, positive qualities of the parents that promote identification rather than their negative, fear-arousing characteristics.

Another parental quality which encourages the child to model himself on the parent can be described as the latter's 'power'. In the study of 5-year olds quoted above the boys with high male identifications described the father not only as warm but also as strong, powerful and competent: clearly all qualities which aroused the child's incentive to be like the father. Similarly, the parent's interest in the child and the amount of time spent with him promoted identification, suggesting that it is primarily those variables which describe the parent's salience in the child's experience that affect this process.

A child's parents will usually, of course, exercise the most decisive influence on the nature of his identifications. They are, however, by no means the only individuals who will serve as models, and indeed identifications may subsequently be formed with groups and institutions as well. In the case of sex-identification, a study by Koch (1956) shows the importance of family members other than parents. Girls who have older brothers, it was found, tend to be more 'tomboyish' than girls with older sisters, and likewise boys with older sisters have a some-what higher proportion of feminine traits than boys with older brothers.

Whether sex-linked behaviour is, in fact, solely a function of social learning, as so many writers seem to assume, or whether constitutional factors do not also play a part, remains as yet an unsolved problem. Certainly anthropological material concerning the very different conceptions of sex-roles found in other societies indicates that behaviour regarded by us as 'natural' may turn out to be a product of socialization rather than inheritance. Yet in the area of sex-linked behaviour above all the assumption of the '*tabula rasa*' child ought to be avoided until more data have been gathered to enable us to make more precise statements regarding aetiology than we can make at present.

The other main area in which the process of identification has been studied is the development of conscience. The learning of moral standards and prohibitions starts early in life in relation to such mundane things as feeding, elimination and aggression, and it is here rather than on the lofty plane of morality and ethics that the foundations of conscience are laid. At first 'right' and 'wrong' are, from the child's point of view, purely arbitrary notions that are imposed on him by external agents. Sooner or later, however, he learns that these agents will follow 'right' actions with praise and 'wrong' actions with punishment and withdrawal of love. In order to avoid the latter consequences he begins to incorporate the rules of behaviour expected of him, so that his conduct is no longer exclusively governed by sanctions employed by other people but becomes increasingly regulated by the feeling of guilt which he experiences after all transgressions. Thus, in the adequately socialized child, the tendency to model his behaviour after that of his parents results in the incorporation of adult moral standards and the capacity for self-punishment.

The progression from external to internal regulation of behaviour takes a long time and may, in some individuals, never be completed. Again, a satisfactory relationship with the parents appears to be an essential prerequisite for such a development, for children with a highly developed conscience have mostly been found to have warmer, more accepting parents than children of the same age with less well developed consciences. A further influence, however, has also been isolated, namely the actual technique which parents employ in order to impose conformity. In general, withdrawal of love has been found far more effective in producing a strong conscience than physical punishment, deprivation of privileges, or the giving of tangible rewards (Sears, Maccoby, and Levin, 1957). However, this relationship only holds in those cases where the parents are also generally warm and affectionate towards the child, for otherwise, presumably, there would be less love to take away and the child would not be as affected by the threatened loss as a child who has a rather more affectionate relationship with his parents. Thus the children most advanced in conscience development appear to be those whose parents are relatively warm towards them but who make their love contingent on the child's willingness to conform to their demands.

Once again one must remember, however, that parents are not the only models a child encounters. Influences outside the home also play their part in shaping conscience: a conclusion borne out by an interesting finding on boys with criminal fathers (McCord and McCord, 1958). This investigation showed that such boys are less likely to become criminals themselves if accepted by their fathers than if rejected by them. Where the parent model is found by the child to be opposed to society's norms, parents' acceptance may actually operate against identification.

Just in what way identification is to be differentiated from imitation is still an open issue. Some writers distinguish between these terms on the basis of the degree of specificity of the behaviour pattern which is learned; others consider that identification presupposes the existence of an attachment to the model, whereas this is not a necessary precondition in the case of imitation; and still others believe that imitation is a process that requires the model's presence at the time, whereas identification refers to the performance of the model's behaviour in the latter's absence. However, one recent body of research stemming from the work of Bandura and Walters (1963) has proceeded from the assumption that the two terms refer in fact to the same set of behavioral phenomena and to the same learning process, and that no useful purpose is served by making any distinction between them. Both terms, according to these writers, apply to the manner in which patterns of social behaviour are acquired through a process that may most suitably be labelled as *observational learning*. Whereas previous theories had stressed the need for rewards to be made available if imitation is to occur, these investigators have shown that, through simple exposure to a model and the opportunity to observe him perform certain activities, children will acquire new responses that match those of the model and which can, moreover, be reproduced not only at the time but also be replicated at a later date. Thus, in a typical experiment (Bandura, Ross, and Ross, 1963), nursery school children watched a model behaving aggressively in a play situation by showing, for instance, a number of unusual hostile responses towards a large inflated rubber doll. When the children were subsequently allowed to play in the same situation it was found that they showed precisely matching responses and tended to behave far more aggressively than children who had not previously been exposed to a model. Moreover, there was no difference in the extent of imitation between children who had observed a real-life model and children who had observed a filmed model, suggesting not only that exposure to aggression can heighten and also shape the nature of children's aggressive reactions, but also that this influence can be exerted by means of pictorial as well as real-life stimulation.

From experiments such as these Bandura (1962) concludes that social behaviour is typically acquired by means of imitation, that this may take place merely on the basis of 'sensory contiguity' (i.e. the opportunity to observe and attend to the activities of others), and that such learning usually involves the imitation of large segments of behaviour or whole sequences of activities rather than proceeding through the slow, gradual acquisition of isolated responses, each of which must be differentially reinforced by a suitable programme of

ewards and punishment. However, imitation is by no means conceived
of as a purely passive process, as exposure of an individual to a set
of stimuli is no guarantee that he will attend to and learn the relevant
cues. It is, however, a virtue of this conceptual approach that it is
possible, through a variety of laboratory experiments (cf. Bandura,
1965) to isolate the conditions under which imitating does occur and
thus to specify both the environmental and the subject factors which
make for optimal susceptibility to the influence of social models. In
this way those adult-child similarities of behaviour, which have given
rise to the concept of identification in psychodynamic theories, can be
studied empirically and traced back to their developmental origins.

There can be little doubt that identification is an extremely complex
process and that it as yet little understood despite the growing amount of
research into it. This is partly because of the rather crude techniques
that have been used to investigate it: for instance, parental identifications have been measured by the relative amounts of handling of father-
dolls and mother-dolls in structured doll-play situations, yet the validity
of this technique remains unknown. Similarly in research on moral
development the choice of criteria for conscience, such as the type of
endings which a child supplies to uncompleted stories, is not based on
any established association with actual behaviour. Nevertheless, this area
does represent an earnest attempt to find out how society impinges on
the growing child and the manner in which it shapes and canalizes his
behaviour. At present our theories about identification may be rather
more impressive than their empirical underpininngs, but at least they
serve to draw attention to some of the more subtle forms of interaction
between the child and his social environment and to the wide range of
variables which may influence any one behavioural activity.

VI. DEPRIVATION AND ITS EFFECTS

Finally, what of those children where social development takes an
abnormal course? There are many reasons why this can occur, some
inherent in the child (seen at their most extreme in psychotic children),
others stemming from peculiarities of the environment. Amongst the
latter, distorted parent-child relationships are particularly potent
sources, but these assume so many complex and ill-understood forms
that we shall have to confine ourselves to those cases where children
are brought up without any mother-figure at all and reared instead
under impersonal (usually institutional) conditions.

Much work has been done on the effects of maternal deprivation, and though there is still disagreement as to the precise effects on personality development and particularly their permanence (O'Connor, 1956), it does appear that this experience can, under certain conditions, have far-reaching consequences. A series of studies by Goldfarb (1943, 1945, 1955) gives some indication of the possible effects. Goldfarb compared orphans who had been reared in a highly depriving institution for the first three years of their lives before being transferred to foster homes with a matched group of children who had been brought up in foster homes from the beginning. The differences between these two groups assumed many forms. The institution-reared children, even at adolescence, remained mentally backward as revealed by intelligence tests and tests of reasoning, concept formation, and abstract thinking. Language and speech difficulties were particularly marked among them, and behaviour problems were frequently reported. Most serious, however, was their emotional shallowness, for these children were found to be incapable of forming affectionate personal attachments. Though they made many demands for attention and unnecessary help, they remained emotionally aloof from their foster parents and apparently capable of only the most superficial interpersonal relationships.

Goldfarb's study gives some indication of the wide range of possible effects of deprivation in the early years, but also draws attention to the importance of the timing of social learning experiences in relation to the child's developmental status. His institutionalized children had, by the time he saw them in late adolescence, spent most of their lives in the company of a mother-figure who gave them every opportunity of forming a meaningful social relationship. Yet, because the first three crucial years had been spent in an environment that gave them no such opportunity, they were unable to make this developmental advance.

It should not be thought, however, that the effects just quoted are necessarily typical for all cases of maternal deprivation. For one thing, this term covers a wide range of conditions all of which can affect outcome (Yarrow, 1961). Thus the child's age at the time of onset of the period of deprivation, the length of this period, the conditions of care during it, the relationship with the mother prior to it, the reasons for the separation as they impinge on the child: these and many other variables shape his reactions and make it necessary to avoid sweeping generalizations. For another thing, constitutional factors also appear to play a role, for given the identical experience different children will react in a variety of ways. Though we know little yet about the nature of these constitutional factors which make for differential 'toughness' in the face of this experience, it is clearly necessary to take these into account and eventually to isolate and describe them (Stott, 1962).

Of all the various factors mentioned the child's age is one of the most important. Thus it has been shown that the same experience (hospitalization) will affect a child of 6 months quite differently to a child of 12 months (Schaffer, 1958). Because the social attachments of the latter are no longer indiscriminate, he is deeply affected by the separation from his mother. The younger child has different needs and will be affected mainly by those elements which involve the perceptual deprivation that is so often the consequence of institutional care and which is brought about by lack of toys, insufficient opportunities to explore the environment and inadequate attention. This can, under extreme circumstances, result in a serious lag of development affecting all aspects of the child's behaviour (Dennis and Najarian, 1957), and though this condition can be readily reversed in young infants when suitable stimulation is supplied once more (Schaffer, 1964), the outcome can, according to some writers (Spitz, 1945), assume the form of mental deficiency if no intervention is forthcoming in time.

Inadequate mothering may thus affect intellectual development in a number of ways through the failure to provide the young child with that optimum of over-all stimulation which interchange with a mother-figure normally brings about. The acquisition of a wide range of skills (perceptual, motor, and verbal) has been shown by these studies not merely to represent an automatic unfolding of maturational processes but to depend intimately on the nature of the child's social environment. Most attention, however, has been given in the literature on maternal deprivation to the effects on social behaviour. Children brought up under purely impersonal conditions can, it appears, develop a number of deviant response patterns in interpersonal relationships (Yarrow, 1961). Social apathy is one of these, manifesting itself in a complete lack of social responsiveness and withdrawal in the face of any approach from another person. Another has been described as 'affect hunger' and is characterized by incessant and insatiable, but also quite indiscriminate, seeking of affection. These two, apparently very different, patterns have one fundamental characteristic in common, for they both indicate the child's inability to establish a close and permanent relationship to other individuals. The failure to form a specific attachment at the usual time, because of the absence in the environment of any person prepared to give the child the necessary stimulation, may thus leave him unable to form such relationships in the future – a condition labelled by Bowlby (1946) as the 'affectionless character.'

Lack of close social ties with other people in the early years can also be expected to affect identification. The child who has no model, or who on the contrary has too many models and thus gets confused by their inconsistencies, at best, forms only weak identifications with groups rather than individuals. There is, however, little objective evidence relating to this point. Clinical studies (Goldfarb, 1955) suggest that the deprived child's sense of self-identity is poorly developed, with resulting defects in impulse controls and low achievement motivation. It has also been suggested that lack of conscience development is brought about by deprivation, which may thus be regarded as an aetiological factor in the explanation of delinquency (Bowlby, 1946). This hypothesis, however, remains to be substantiated.

There are two reasons why the topic of maternal deprivation is important. In the first place, by drawing attention to the conditions under which some children are reared and the effects of these conditions on their personality development, mental health workers have brought about a considerable amelioration in the care of children in institutions and hospitals. In the second place, and nearer to our concern in this chapter, studies of deprived children are able to point to some of the requisites and needs of children in general. Deviant forms of behaviour can only be understood against a background of knowledge of normal development, but in its turn abnormality can frequently highlight those conditions which govern the growth and development of all children.

REFERENCES

AINSWORTH, M. (1963). The development of infant-mother interaction among the Ganda. In Foss. B. M. (ed.), *Determinants of Infant Behaviour*, **II**. London: Methuen.

BALDWIN, A. L., KALHORN, J., and BREESE, F. H. (1945). Patterns of parent behaviour. *Psychol. Monogr.* **58**, No. 268.

BANDURA, A. (1962). Social learning through imitation. In M. R. Jones (ed.), *Nebraska Symposium on Motivation*. Lincoln: U. of Nebraska Press.

BANDURA, A. (1965). Behavioral modification through modeling procedures. In Kradner, L., and Ullmann, L. P. (eds.), *Research in Behaviour Modification*. New York: Holt, Rinehart and Winston.

BANDURA, A., ROSS, D., and ROSS, S. A. (1963). Imitation of film-mediated aggressive models. *J. Abnorm. soc. Psychol.* **66**, 3–11.

BANDURA, A., and WALTERS, R. H. (1963). *Social Learning and Personality Development.* New York: Holt, Rinehart and Winston.

BELLER, E. K. (1955). Dependence and independence in young children. *J. Genet. Psychol.* **87**, 25–35.

BOWLBY, J. (1946). *Forty-four Juvenile Thieves, their Characters and Home Life.* London: Bailliere, Tindall & Cox.

BOWLBY, J. (1958). The nature of the child's tie to his mother. *Internat. J. Psycho-Anal.* **39**, 350–373.

BRACKBILL, Y. (1958). Extinction of the smiling response in infants as a function of reinforcement schedule. *Child Developm.* **29**, 115–124.

CALL, J. D. (1964). Newborn approach behaviour and early ego development. *Internat. J. Psycho-Anal.* **45**, 286–294.

CASLER, L. (1961). Maternal deprivation: a critical review of the literature. *Monogr. Soc. Res. Child Developm.* **26**, No. 2.

CHESS, S., THOMAS, A., and BIRCH, H. (1959). Characteristics of the individual child's behavioural response to the environment. *Amer. J. Ortho-psychiat.* **29**, 791–809.

DENNIS, W., and NAJARIAN, P. (1957). Infant development under environmental handicap. *Psychol. Monogr.* **71**, No. 436.

ERIKSON, E. (1950). *Childhood and Society.* New York: Norton.

ESCALONA, S. (1963). Patterns of infantile experience and the developmental process. *Psychoanal. Study Child.* **18**, 197–244.

FRIES, M. E. (1953). Some hypotheses on the role of the congenital activity type in personality development. *Psychoanal. Study Child.* **8**, 48–62.

GOLDFARB, W. (1943). Infant rearing and problem behaviour. *Amer. J. Orthopsychiat.* **13**, 249–265.

GOLDFARB, W. (1945). Effects of psychological deprivation in infancy and subsequent adjustment. *Amer. J. Psychiat.* **102**, 18–23.

GOLDFARB, W. (1955). Emotional and intellectual consequences of psychologic deprivation in infancy: a re-evaluation. In Hoch, P., and Zubin, J. (eds.) *Psychopathology of Childhood.* New York: Grune and Stratton.

GUNTHER, M. (1961). Infant behaviour at the breast. In Foss, B. M. (ed.) *Determinants of Infant Behaviour.* London: Methuen.

HARLOW, H. F. (1958). The nature of love. *Amer. Psychol.* **13**, 673–685.

HARTUP, W. W., and ZOOK, E. A. (1960). Sex-role preferences in three and four-year-old children. *J. consult. Psychol.* **24**, 420–426.

HEATHERS, G. (1955). Emotional dependence and independence in nursery school play. *J. Genet. Psychol.* **87**, 37–57.

KAGAN, J., and MOSS, H. (1962). *Birth to Maturity.* New York: Wiley.

KOCH, H. (1956). Attitudes of young children towards their peers as related to certain characteristics of their siblings. *Psychol. Monogr.* **70**, No. 19.

LEVY, D. M. (1943). *Maternal Overprotection.* New York: Columbia University Press.

LORENZ, K. (1947). The companion in the bird's world. *Auk.* **54**, 245–273.

MCCORD, J., and MCCORD, W. (1958). The effect of parental role model in criminality. *J. Soc. Issues.* **14**, 66–75.

MARQUIS, D. B. (1941). Learning in the neonate: the modification of behaviour under three feeding schedules. *J. exp. Psychol.* **29**, 213–282.

MEAD, M. (1962). A cultural anthropologist's approach to maternal deprivation. *W.H.O. Public Health Papers.* No. 14, 45–62.

MILLER, N. E., and DOLLARD, J. (1941). *Social Learning and Imitation.* New Haven: Yale University Press.

MITTELMANN, B. (1954). Motility in infants, children, and adults. *Psychoanal. Study Child.* **9**, 142–177.

MUSSEN, P., and DISTLER, L. (1959). Masculinity, identification and father-son relationships. *J. abnorm. soc. Psychol.* **59**, 350–356.

O'CONNOR, N. (1956). The evidence for the permanently disturbing effects of mother-child separation. *Acta. Psychol.* **12**, 174–191.

ORLANSKY, H. (1949). Infant care and personality. **66**, 1–48.

PAYNE, D. E., and MUSSEN, P. (1956). Parent-child relations and father identification among adolescent boys. **52**, 358–362.

RHEINGOLD, H. L. (1956) The modification of social responsiveness in institutional babies. *Monogr. Soc. Res. Child Developm.* **21**, No. 63.

RHEINGOLD, H. L. (1961). The effect of environmental stimulation upon social and exploratory behaviour in the human infant. In Foss. B. M. (ed.) *Determinants of Infant Behaviour.* London: Methuen.

RHEINGOLD, H. L., GEWIRTZ, J., and ROSS, H. W. (1959). Social conditioning of vocalisations in the infant. *J. comp. physiol. Psychol.* **52**, 68–73.

SCHACHTER, S. (1959). *The Psychology of Affiliation.* Stanford University Press.

SCHAEFER, E. S., and BELL, Q. (1958). Development of a parental attitude research instrument. *Child Developm.* **29**, 339–361.

SCHAFFER, H. R. (1958). Objective observations of personality development in early infancy. *Brit. J. med. Psychol.* **31**, 174–184.

SCHAFFER, H. R. (1963). Some issues for research in the study of attachment behaviour. In Foss, B. M. (ed.) *Determinants of Infant Behaviour*, **II**. London: Methuen.

SCHAFFER, H. R. (1964). Changes in developmental quotient under two conditions of maternal separation. *Brit. J. soc. clin. Psychol.*

SCHAFFER, H. R., and EMERSON, P. (1964). (a) The development of social attachments in infancy. *Monogr. Soc. Res. Child Developm.* **29**, No. 94.

SCHAFFER, H. R., and EMERSON, P. (1964) (b). Patterns of response to physical contact in early human development. *J. child Psychol. Psychiat.* **5**, 1–13.

SCOTT, J. P. (1958). Critical periods in the development of social behaviour in puppies. *Psychosom. Med.* **20**, 42–54.

SEARS, P. S. (1951). Doll play aggression in normal young children: influence of sex, age, sibling status, and father's absence. *Psychol. Monogr.* **65**, No. 323.

SEARS, R. R., MACCOBY, E. E., and LEVIN, H. (1957). *Patterns of Child Rearing*. New York: Harper & Row.

SEARS, R. R., WHITING, J. W. M., NOWLIS, V., and SEARS, P. S. (1953). Some child-rearing antecedents of aggression and dependency in young children. *Genet. Psychol. Monogr.* **47**, 135–236.

SPIRO, M. (1958). *Children of the Kibbutz*. Harvard University Press.

SPITZ, R. (1945). Hospitalism. *Psychoanal. Study Child.* **1**, 53–74.

SPITZ, R. and WOLFF, K. (1946). The smiling response. *Genet. Psychol. Monogr.* **34**, 57–125.

STOTT, D. H. (1962). Abnormal mothering as a cause of mental subnormality. *J. child Psychol. Psychiat.* **3**, 79–92.

THORPE, W. H. (1962). *Learning and Instinct in Animals*. London: Methuen.

WENAR, C., and WENAR, S. C. (1963). The short term perspective model, the illusion of time, and the tabula rasa child. *Child Developm.* **34**, 697–708.

YARROW, L. J. (1948). The effect of antecedent frustration on projective play. *Psychol. Monogr.* **62**, No. 293.

YARROW, L. J. (1961). Maternal deprivation: toward an empirical and conceptual re-evaluation. *Psychol. Bull.* **58**, 459–490.

3

Experimental Approaches to Concept Development in Young Children[1]

MARION BLANK

I. INTRODUCTION

DESPITE a major increase in research on concept development within the last two decades, any conclusions are extremely tenuous since the field remains vague and unco-ordinated. This disorder has arisen for many reasons not least of which is the fact that concept formation is a vast area intimately related to, but not identical with, such complex psychological processes as thinking, learning, problem solving, language development, and symbolic representation. The difficulty in disentangling these interrelated phenomena is immediately demonstrated by the fact that there is not so much as an agreed definition of the term 'concept'. Almost all investigators would agree that a concept reflects some abstraction which unifies stimuli that are not identical but which share a common element. For example, on a very elementary level, all round objects, whether a ball, an orange or a wheel, can be seen as sharing a common characteristic in that they can be rolled about. By contrast, on a more advanced level, a man working, a generator operating and the sun shining can be seen as illustrating various forms of the concept of dissipation of energy. These two examples indicate some of the many difficulties in this area. In the former example, the concept is derived from the perceptual properties of the stimuli themselves (they are all round) and from the simple unifying action that can be performed on all (they can all be rolled). In the latter example, the stimuli are perceptually quite dissimilar and the 'activities' involved seem entirely different; yet, they can be unified by the highly abstract concept of energy. Because of the marked differences in the levels of abstraction

[1] The writing of this chapter was supported by United States Public Health Service Grant No. K3 MH 10,749.

used it is debatable whether it is reasonable or even advantageous to give a seeming unity to such divergent levels by labelling them under the common term of concept. The lack of an accepted definition of the term 'concept' is also unfortunate in that each researcher conducts his work using a definition which he never makes explicit. For some investigators a concept refers to the ability to label different objects with a common name (e.g. pear and banana as 'fruit'); for others it refers to the use of relational thinking (e.g. being able to compare objects as to size – bigger, smaller); for others it refers to the ability to select out the relevant physical dimensions in problem solving (e.g. size, form, colour). Thus each investigator seems to define a concept by limiting himself to the operations he requires the subject to perform. By applying the same term 'concept' to these disparate phenomena, it looks as though a common issue is being discussed when in fact different types and mechanisms of problem solving may be involved.

Beyond the question of definition of terms, an additional difficulty is introduced by the differing theoretical or philosophical frameworks of the investigators. The theories in this area, while numerous, tend to fall into two major groupings; those posited by the experimentalists (behaviourists) *v.* those posited by the cognitive theorists. Each of these two groups has come to the area of concept development with different backgrounds, different aims and different techniques. Philosophically, the experimentalists have approached the problems of psychology from the empiricist tradition. Wherever possible, an attempt is made to trace the development of behaviour to 'variables . . . outside the organism, in its immediate environment and in its environmental history'. They believe that such variables 'have a physical status to which the usual techniques of science are adapted, and they make it possible to explain behaviour as other subjects are explained in science' (Skinner, 1953, p. 31). Thus the experimentalists have avoided using 'mentalistic' phenomena as explanatory constructs since they feel that such phenomena cannot be subjected to 'scientific analysis'. Given this prohibition against mental events, concept formation can only be inferred through overt behaviour. Since even overt behaviour can involve complex sequences which are difficult to quantify, the experimentalists have tended to restrict their analysis to controlled laboratory situations. As a result, these investigators have developed sophisticated experimental techniques that have produced theoretical formulations based on the analysis of discrete units of behaviour.

Methodologically, this approach has had important implications since it has led the behaviourists to use animals more readily than humans in their research. Animals permit the behaviourists to fulfil the dual aims of adopting rigid experimental controls as well as avoiding 'mentalistic' phenomena which are so tantalizing in subjects who can verbalize. It was only much later with the recognition of the possible importance of language in problem solving that the experimentalists began to emphasize the need to work with humans and, in particular, children. Even in their work with children, however, the experimentalists have tended to use the same theories, constructs, and techniques derived from animal behaviour. Up to comparatively recent times, the bulk of the research on concept formation in English-speaking countries has been in the behaviourist tradition.

As in any dichotomy, the cognitive theorists represent the antithesis of this viewpoint. These theorists, influenced by the philosophical approach of rationalism, have tended to trace the development of behaviour at least in part to the structure of the subject's mind which allows him to perceive the world in certain ways and not in others. One of their major concerns is with the growth of knowledge in man and, in particular, with how he uses what they believe are his unique cognitive and language skills to expand his understanding of his environment. Man, therefore, is the focus of their interests and they are not concerned with formulating theories that encompass the abilities of both animals and man. As a result, they deal freely with introspective thought processes (mental events) since they feel that these are major determinants in human development. For these theorists then, thought processes are themselves explanatory constructs. With this orientation, the cognitive theorists are less interested in restricting behaviour to controlled laboratory situations involving limited numbers of variables. Instead, they emphasize the observation of children in actual situations or in complex laboratory situations which closely resemble the child's 'normal' environment. In child psychology, an outstanding exponent of the non-behaviourist tradition is Piaget.

A significant feature of this experimental-cognitive dichotomy is the fact that different experimental questions are asked by investigators in the two groups. Since the questions asked in research largely determine the answers to be obtained, the findings of the different investigators are often not interpretable or meaningful from one orientation to the other. For example, the cognitive theorists' discussion of the concept of mental imagery would be meaningless to an experimentalist. Because these theoretical approaches exert such influence, the material that follows will not focus on particular findings but rather on illustrating the most representative approaches used by these different theorists. The major portion of this chapter will be directed towards understanding the work of the experimentalists. However, the work of the cognitive theorists will also be briefly considered in the latter part of the chapter, primarily to offer an indication of an alternative approach to the orientation put forth by the experimentalists.

II. EARLY EXPERIMENTAL WORK

Before presenting a detailed account of the work of the experimentalists, it seems worthwhile to set forth a few guide-lines. First, as noted above, in the study of concept formation the behaviourists have emphasized not the internal thought processes of the subject but rather the manipulation of external variables which can be rigidly controlled by the experimenter. This goal was stated quite explicitly by one of the leading behaviourists, 'Abstraction, too, is not a form of action on the part of the organism. It is a narrowing of the control exercised by the properties of stimuli. The controlling property cannot be demonstrated upon a single occasion. In other words, a single instance of an abstract response will not tell us very much about its "referent". The controlling relation can be discovered only through a survey of a large number of instances.' (Skinner, 1953, p. 135.)

This statement, in essence, describes the format used by the experimentalists in much of the work that follows. It states that the basis for the development of a concept is to be found (*a*) in the properties of the stimuli and (*b*) through a history of differential reinforcement of these properties; differential reinforcement referring to the fact that the organism's selection of instances of the concept is rewarded, while selection of non-instances of the concept is not rewarded. (*c*) The use of the term 'instances' of necessity implies that the organism must have a number of opportunities to respond to the concept; otherwise it will not be possible to determine whether any particular successful choice occurred because of chance or because of a true recognition of the concept. Usually, the experimenter establishes criteria which he feels are sufficient to justify any conclusions about the organism possessing the concept. For example, he may require that the subject makes nine correct responses out of ten trials or that he maintain an 80 per cent correct response rate for fifty trials. A further common test of the possession of the concept is the subject's demonstration of transfer – i.e. a 'savings' (in time, number of trials, etc.) in learning from one problem to another.

The following example will serve to illustrate these techniques. A subject may be presented with a problem involving the concept of number – e.g. one *v.* two. On the first problem he may be shown two squares *v.* one square, and he will be required to make some sort of response to one of these stimuli (e.g. he may have to press a lever under one of the stimuli). If the concept of 'two' is being reinforced, the organism will receive a reward (e.g. food) every time he presses the lever under the two squares and he will never receive a reward if he presses the lever under the one square. After learning this problem to criterion (e.g. 9 out of 10 trials correct) he may be *transferred* to a new instance of the concept of one and two; e.g. this time he may be shown one *v.* two circles. The transfer or savings from the first problem to the second problem will then be determined. A variety of controls are also necessary to evaluate the transfer that has occurred. For example, did the subject have some concept of number or did he improve simply because of having practice in making visual discriminations? Basically this question asks whether the subject would have improved on the second number problem had he been trained initially not on a number discrimination (i.e. 'one', 'two') but rather on an 'unrelated' discrimination such as form (e.g. triangle *v.* rectangle). To control for this factor, another set of subjects may be given problems without a unifying concept (e.g. form then number). Their performance on the second problem will then be compared with that of the subjects who had a consistent concept from one problem to another (e.g. both 'number' problems). If the latter group performs better than the former, it will be concluded that they have grasped the concept of number, at least at the level of complexity used in these problems. The experimental designs can become much more complex and sophisticated than in this simple illustration. However, this example serves to illustrate the basic format used in much of the experimental work that follows.

Using these techniques, a basic question asked by the experimentalists is: by what stages and at what ages does the child pass from simple concepts to more abstract and general ones? A second question of importance is: by what mechanisms does this development occur and in particular, what role does language play? It will become clear from the evidence that follows that the first question tended to dominate the early work and the second question has become increasingly important in more recent work. This difference in emphasis is one of the major reasons for separating the early work from the more recent studies. A second reason is that the early research is important in setting the background for many of the significant issues in concept formation studies today. It should be kept in mind, however, that this separation according to dates is in part artificial since many of the studies in the early work are highly sophisticated and are of direct relevance to the work being conducted at present.

The early experimental work, directed at outlining the growth of complex concepts in children stemmed, like so many concerns in both past and present day psychology, from Darwinian theory. One legacy of this theory in psychological research has been a major concern with the question of qualitative *v.* quantitative developments in evolution. The particular expression of this issue in concept formation research has been the question as to whether the superior intellectual ability of man is qualitatively or only quantitatively different from the intelligence of other animals. This question has led to much of the research on the cognitive skills of children since childhood is the transition period between an organism functioning on the sensori-motor level (as in animals) and an organism functioning on the more cognitive level of the human adult. A dramatic illustration of this concern is the study in which an ape and a child were reared together mainly to determine the limitations of intelligence in non-human primates (Kellogg and Kellogg, 1933).

Consistent with Darwinian influence, some of the first attempts at answering the qualitative *v.* quantitative question consisted of applying to children direct adaptations of experimental techniques developed with animals. Some of the leading experiments in this vein in the 1930s were those on insight (sudden grasp of a solution) developed by the Gestalt psychologists in their work with apes. In these problems the task generally required that a novel solution be devised to overcome an obstacle in order to reach a desired reward (e.g. putting together two short sticks so as to make a long stick needed to reach food.) Since insightful learning was believed to represent one of the highest forms of reasoning, it was almost inevitable that these problems be extended to studying concept development in young children (Alpert, 1928; Matheson, 1931). In these studies insight was found to be highly correlated with verbalization of the solution. However, as might be expected from the successful insight performance of non-verbal animals, some children solved these 'insight' problems without verbal awareness.

This finding, however, serves to illustrate an important point; namely, if animals have succeeded with an experimental technique, such a technique, when applied to man, cannot be expected to yield qualitative differences between animals and man. Since animals are known to succeed on these tasks, the most that children can do is to perform somewhat more efficiently, but not qualitatively differently. If different levels of cognitive functioning are to be shown to exist, it will be necessary to devise far more complex means of assessing learning than the simple but commonly used measures such as success or failure on a problem or the number of trials to criterion.

One aspect of these insight studies did suggest such a measure. In contrast to the performance of animals, immediate insightful solution occasionally occurred in children after a delay in which the child had been away from the as yet unsolved problem (Alpert, 1928). This finding suggests that problem solving in young children is facilitated by a consolidation process involving representation of previously perceived material. It will be seen later that such inner representation plays a significant role in Piaget's formulation on the development of thinking and language.

In contrast to the work of the Gestaltists on insight, much of the experimental work in the 1930s was based on the idea that concepts are first and foremost a way of grouping classes of stimuli having a common element. Language, therefore, became an easily favoured explanation for concept development since a common label can easily unify many different stimuli. For example, a pear, banana and pineapple though quite different perceptually can be unified by the concept of 'fruit'. Thus the common element unifying diverse discrete objects was the verbal sign or symbol.[1]

Since concepts and symbols are closely related and there is a tendency to equate them, it is important to remember that they are not equivalent. A symbol can represent a specific object without necessarily representing a class of objects as does a concept. For example, a child may learn to label a particular spherical object with the verbal symbol of 'ball'; this symbol, however, is not a concept until the child learns that all members belonging to that spherical class bear the common designation of 'ball'. Thus, a symbol may exist without a concept; whether a concept can exist without a symbol is another problem and one which

---

[1] It should be noted that various investigators define these terms differently. For purposes of simplicity in this introductory statement, the term symbol will include what is generally intended by both signs and symbols.

leads to a major dispute in this area. Some investigators go so far as to say that 'Abstraction, therefore, appears to have become possible only with the development of verbal behaviour'. (Skinner, 1953, pp. 135–36.) Others would disagree strongly with attributing the origin of abstract concepts entirely to the conventions of language (Piaget, 1952; Harlow, 1959).

Because of the importance of language, however, a great deal of research was done to determine the significance of language in concept formation. A common way of studying this problem experimentally has been to teach children to associate nonsense syllables with stimuli (e.g., labelling) and then to study how these labels are grouped into higher order concepts such as classes. The work of Welch and his associates is among the most frequently cited of this period (1939, a, b, c; 1940a,b; Welch and Long, 1940) and the techniques evolved then have continued into present day research as exemplified by the work of Spiker and his associates (Spiker, 1963).

Welch assumed that the ability of children to learn a name reflects the degree of generality of the category; i.e. object names such as 'mummy', 'daddy' are easier to learn than first-order hierarchies such as parent. Whether in fact language concepts are learned in this way – from the particular to the general – is a matter of considerable dispute. Werner and Kaplan (1963) in discussing the growth of the symbolic function describe how children initially apply words very generally to all objects bearing some association to each other. Only later do they slowly begin to differentiate and apply the words specifically to particular objects. Thus in contrast to Welch's assumption, there seems to be excessive generalization initially so that the name for single object represents a whole class of objects.

Examination of the problem suggests that this contradiction arises largely because of a failure to define terms adequately. In trying to understand a child's growth in this area, it is worthwhile to remember that a child finds it easier to label a single object with a particular word rather than label a group of seemingly unrelated objects with the same word, e.g. it is difficult for the child to learn to say 'furniture' to such entirely different objects as a table, bed, and bookcase, while he can learn the names for the individual objects fairly readily. Once he learns the individual names, however, he is liable to generalize them readily to any objects that look alike or serve the same function e.g., if he had learned the word 'bed', he may call a sofa a 'bed' since you can lie down on both. If he had been taught to say 'furniture' for a bed, however, he would say it as well to sofa. His degree of abstraction would be no greater, however, than the child who had learned the word 'bed'. It is therefore important to keep in mind that the label itself does not tell you the degree of abstraction of the child's thinking. This point was emphasized by Brown in his statement that the order of language acquisition is not necessarily a function of the child's thought processes, but rather that, 'the child's vocabulary is more immediately determined by the naming practices of adults' (1958, p. 18); e.g. the adult teaches 'mummy' rather than 'parent'. In those cases where the adult uses the more abstract class word rather than the specific label, e.g. 'fish' is more commonly used than are names like 'perch' and 'bass', then Brown states that the usual order of concrete to abstract in children's language development will be reversed.

Welch used labelling not simply as a means of studying language development, but also as an index for assessing young children's ability to categorize (e.g. what sorts of objects would they group under the same label). Welch (1939a) however, also devised means for studying categorization without language and he was therefore able to study this ability in very young children. For example children were asked to solve a series of discrimination problems which shared a common category or dimension (e.g. they had to consistently select square as opposed to rounded shapes). This work is still of importance since it involves some of the few experimental studies of generalization in children as young as twelve months. Welch found that discrimination learning of size and form occurred as early as fourteen months. Children below this age may also have these capacities, but they could not be studied because of their lack of motivation on the stereotyped, repetitive tasks required.

One of the most famous studies conducted on categorization in young children was that of Gellerman (1933) who compared the performance of chimpanzees and two-year-old children on form discrimination problems. This comparison of sub-human primates with humans illustrates again the Darwinian inspired interest in the qualitative *v.* quantitative differences controversy. In the Gellerman study, the problems involved the concept of 'triangularity' (i.e. the subjects had to respond to the triangular shapes even though the shapes were presented in increasingly different ways so that size, background, orientation, outline, etc., all could be varied). In later sections, it will be seen that assessing the capacity to generalize to stimuli which bear increasingly less physical similarity is a basic technique still used by the experimentalists in testing for concept formation. Because of the few subjects involved in the Gellerman study and the constant retesting of the same subjects, this study did not offer conclusive findings. However, potentially significant differences between children and other primates emerged which have since proven to be recurrent themes in work on concept formation. In general, the children learned in many fewer trials than did the chimpanzees. The latter also displayed a much narrower range of equivalence of cues (e.g. failed to recognize the triangular forms if there were variations in size, background, etc.), suggesting that chimpanzees respond more to specific properties and generalize less readily than do children. Thus, to return to an earlier example, while the child's calling a sofa a 'bed' may not represent a recognition of the higher order concept of 'furniture' it may represent the beginning of higher level cognitive functioning in that the child can now recognize similarities in increasingly different situations. Most significantly, Gellerman attributed the children's superior performance to their use of verbalization to direct their behaviour. An interesting sidelight of this experiment is that on some complex discriminations the chimpanzees succeeded when they traced the visual stimulus with their 'fingers'. This observation was a forerunner of more recent findings that (see section IV – Reversal Learning) discrimination is facilitated when more information is obtained from a stimulus either through increased attention and/or an increase in the number of cues available.

Gellerman's studies were in keeping with a large group of studies at this time directed towards determining the differential development of various concepts; e.g. is colour easier to learn than size; is size easier than form, etc., Although at first glance this problem seems easy to resolve, it is extremely difficult because of the numerous variables involved. This problem is useful, however, as an illustration of the methodological difficulties in working in concept formation. First, it raises the question of the equivalence of different stimuli in the various dimensions. For example, it might be found that the discrimination of a large *v.* a small figure (size dimension) is easier than that of a black *v.* a white figure (brightness dimension). However, the question remains as to whether this would hold true for other sizes and other brightnesses or whether it is an artifact of the particular problem. The answer to this seemingly simple question would require testing many children on a large number of problems dealing only with those two dimensions. Similarly, determination of the difficulty of each 'concept' within a

D

dimension (e.g. redness, triangularity, roundness, etc.) would require additional extensive testing. Thus the results of studies asking these kind of questions tend to be inconclusive because the task difficulty depends in large measure on the particular variations introduced in the stimuli. Another methodological difficulty is the question of whether children would maintain their response to a particular dimension if different testing procedures were employed (e.g. *matching* stimuli by placing identical stimuli together *v.* consistently *selecting* one of a group of stimuli). These methodological considerations are important in indicating that one cannot be certain how general and inclusive a concept is until it has been tested under a wide variety of conditions and procedures.

A common way that these problems have been handled has been to rephrase the question so as to ask, 'At what age can children make discriminations of form, colour, brightness, etc.?' In most of the early studies done in this vein the samples were fairly small and the results were reported for individual subjects with few tests of statistical significance for the overall results. The findings are nevertheless useful for indicating the relative difficulty a child experiences on various concepts. For example, Thrum (1935) in working with concepts of magnitude found no differences in performance on various concepts according to age in children 2 to 4 years old. This result is in accord with the work of Welch (1939a, 1939b) who found that although over wide age ranges there was a relationship between age and conceptual ability, within any particular narrow age range this correlation was not found. There appear instead to be sudden spurts in the development of a concept and then a plateau of performance is maintained until the next jump forward. Thrum also found that these young children were able to select big and little objects when verbally instructed to do so, but had great difficulty in selecting a middle sized object. Interestingly since there were only three objects and the children knew the big and little ones, they theoretically could have chosen the middle one by elimination. This sort of logical problem solving strategy may not be available to young children.

These results using concepts such as magnitude were significant not so much as an indicator of a limitation of children's thinking as they were a spur to much additional research in this area. Discrimination of stimuli which differ according to a concept such as magnitude strongly implies an ability to recognize quantitative differences in objects on the same stimulus dimension. Therefore such a discrimination appears to tap a complex relational response (e.g. bigger, smaller) which requires a simultaneous comparison of a group of stimuli. The possible significant implications of this kind of problem led to one of the most popular and enduring experimental paradigms in testing concept development – namely, the paradigm of transposition learning.

III. TRANSPOSITION LEARNING

As indicated in the discussion of Gellerman's work, possession of a concept is commonly tested by giving children a series of problems where the stimuli are quite dissimilar from one problem to another, but where they share a common category such as form, number, etc. A difficulty in all this work is the problem of physical generalization; that is, the subject may transfer not because he sees the essential similarity in spite of the difference, but rather because he fails to see that the stimuli are different from one problem to the next (e.g. the subject may be reinforced for selecting a square *v.* a circle, on the next problem the same figures may be present against a different background; the subject may continue to select the square not in spite of the background change, but because he never noticed the background at all). Thus the experimentalists have consistently tried to devise paradigms which would overcome the problem of physical generalization by making the stimuli so markedly different that transfer could occur only because of the possession of a concept. Transposition learning appeared to be one answer to this search since it is a specific form of discrimination learning requiring a relational rather than an absolute response to stimuli. For example, on a brightness discrimination problem a subject may be trained to select the grey object in a white-grey choice and then be transferred to a grey-dark grey discrimination. If in the transfer task he selects not the previously positive grey object, but rather the new dark grey one, he is said to be responding on a relational basis (i.e. selecting the 'darker' one). In this instance, a simple stimulus-response (S-R) model would have predicted an absolute choice; i.e. the subject should have selected the grey object since it was the previously rewarded one. It was thus believed that this design overcame the problem of physical generalization since the stimulus identical to or most like the previously rewarded one is no longer correct.

Another type of transposition task that is commonly employed is the intermediate size problem. In contrast to the two-choice task outlined above, the intermediate size problem requires the subject to select the middle-sized object of three stimuli. In later problems, he must then transfer the response by selecting the middle-size object regardless of the absolute dimensions of the stimuli.

Cognitive theorists became interested in these problems since the relational response appeared to support their theory as opposed to an S-R model. In particular, they believed it indicated a need to postulate an intervening mediating mechanism to explain the transposition phenomenon (e.g. an inner mental representation of the concept of 'greater' or 'lesser'). A counter explanation to the cognitive model was offered, however, when Spence proposed a theoretical S-R explanation for the transposition phenomenon (Spence, 1936, 1937, 1942). This explanation is too complex to be dealt with at length in this chapter. In brief, Spence stated that the rewarded stimulus would have a generalization curve of excitation surrounding it resulting in the negative stimulus having some positive valence. In the transfer task, this previously negative stimulus would therefore have more positive valence than the new stimulus since it is closer on the dimension to the previously positive stimulus. As a result, in the transposition test when the subject selects the previously negative stimulus it will appear that a relative judgement is being made. In Spence's view, however, the subject is merely choosing the stimulus with the greater excitatory potential. Spence in this formulation is thus stating that contrary to its major aims the transposition paradigm has not overcome the problem of physical generalization but rather any transposition that occurs is a reflection of the existence of physical generalization. In effect, Spence denies that the animal has any awareness of the relational properties of the stimuli. As a test of this hypothesis, Spence predicted that animals would show transposition only to stimuli which lie close on the physical dimension to the training stimuli ('near' transposition) due to the fact that the generalization gradient is limited to a restricted range of stimuli. Transposition would therefore not be expected with stimuli which are physically distant from the training stimuli ('far' transposition). This phenomenon has been termed the 'distant effect'. These hypotheses have been important in setting off a chain of research to confirm or refute Spence's postulations.

A major step in the confirmation of Spence's theory was an experiment by Kuenne (1946) on nursery school children. She predicted and found that pre-verbal children would behave like animals and display only 'near' transposition; however, verbal children who had the mediating concept (e.g. 'smaller', 'lighter') would display both 'near' and 'far' transposition. She also found that verbalization was highly correlated with success, supporting her 'far transposition' prediction. Kuenne's study was also important in that it distinguished among stages of verbal development (e.g. from having words but not using them to guide behaviour to verbalization directing thinking and problem solving). For many of the experimentalists, language was often synonymous with labelling (i.e. giving a name to an object or action) and Kuenne's distinction between levels of language development was an important step in expanding the experimentalists' view of language.

Alberts and Ehrenfreund (1951) confirmed Kuenne's results in a study which included not only the 'near' and 'far' tests, but also several intermediate stages. They found that in older children transposition was achieved no matter how discrepant the stimuli. For the younger children, however, the degree of transposition depended upon the stimuli used; the nearer the test stimuli were to the training stimuli, the greater the transposition. The facilitation of transposition through application of a verbal label in nursery school age children has been confirmed by Spiker and his associates (Spiker and Terrell, 1955; Spiker, Gerjuoy, and Shepard, 1956).

These studies suggested that language was required for 'far' transposition. A study by Johnson and Zara (1960), however, indicated that the latter could also be achieved through appropriate non-verbal training techniques such as training on two, rather than one, stimulus pairs. In a similar study, employing the intermediate size problem, Gonzalez and Ross (1958) used two widely separated sets of stimuli in the training task. Then contrary to Spence's hypothesis, they obtained transposition to stimuli which were intermediate between the two training sets, but which exceeded the range of the stimulus generalization curves.

These last two studies exemplify a series of investigations demonstrating the role of the training tasks in determining whether a relative or an absolute choice is made in the transposition task. In general, these studies have indicated that the more readily the training stimuli are discriminated from the test stimuli, the more will absolute rather than relative transposition be obtained. Among the factors that aid discrimination of the stimuli are such things as overtraining on the initial task and greater physical differences between the stimuli (e.g., a size ratio of 1 : 4 as opposed to a ratio of 1 : 2). This finding has been confirmed in many studies that have manipulated a wide range of parameters

(Jackson, *et al.*, 1938; Rudel, 1957, 1960; McKee and Riley, 1962; Reese, 1961, 1962a).

These studies suggest that transposition may paradoxically result both from failure to recognize that the test stimuli are different from the training stimuli (e.g. in the 'near' transposition) and from a much more highly sophisticated recognition, through either verbalization and/or specialized training, that although the stimuli are physically different, they share a common attribute (e.g. 'larger', 'brighter', etc.). This seeming paradox highlights the ever present problem of determining whether generalization and equivalence represent a failure to discriminate or conversely the ability to recognize essential similarities while nevertheless differentiating among the individual stimuli. According to Rudel (1960), whether or not an organism will show transposition will depend upon the degree to which perceptual differentiation has proceeded; with no differentiation, relative responses occur; as differentiation begins, absolute responses tend to occur; then as differentiation develops further, relative responses begin to re-emerge.

An interesting technique used to aid differentiation is successive as opposed to simultaneous presentation of the stimuli. In the former, the stimuli are presented separately, one after the other; while in the latter, the stimuli are presented together in juxtaposition to one another. Jackson and Jerome (1940, 1943) found that the successive method resulted in more absolute as opposed to relative choices. These authors suggest that in contrast to the simultaneous technique, the successive method requires the subject to attend more carefully to the stimuli and retain a clear impression of them if he is to succeed. They also suggest that the different results obtained with the simultaneous *v.* successive technique argue against Spence's hypothesis which would have predicted no difference since the curves of generalization are the same under the two procedures.

Jackson and Jerome offer an alternative 'patternedness' hypothesis stating that in the simultaneous method an 'irreducible pattern' is perceived resulting in transposition on 'near' problems. Interestingly, this 'patternedness' construct has been adopted by followers of the Spencian theory (Berman and Graham, 1964; Graham *et al.*, 1964). It is now maintained that the organism does not respond to the stimuli as individual units, but rather that the relationship between stimuli serves as a stimulus in the transposition phenomenon. This construct is a major revision of the early traditional S-R approach and one which acknowledges some of the original claims of the cognitive theorists.

Similarly, cognitive theorists have moved closer to the S-R position in that they recognize that both absolute and relational processes may coexist (Stevenson and Bitterman, 1954). One reason for this 'merger' of the two views is that the results of many experiments fail to clearly support one theory or the other. One of the more recent theories proposed to explain transposition, the ratio theory, has also failed to receive definitive substantiation (Zeiler, 1963a, 1963b).

The limitations and ambiguities of the transposition technique have led investigators in this field to seek other experimental paradigms. One of the most popular in use today is that of reversal learning. In trying to understand the research on reversal learning, it is well to keep in mind the language – v. – non-language based hypotheses put forth in the transposition work. As will be seen below, in essence this same controversy arises again as investigators seek mechanisms to explain the findings they obtain.

IV. REVERSAL LEARNING

In reversal learning, a subject must in a first task learn to select one of two (or more) stimuli, He is then required in a second task to select one of the previously incorrect choices; i.e. he must learn to reverse his response to a particular situation. It should be noted that, just as with transposition, a major purpose of the reversal learning paradigm is the hope that it would overcome the problem of physical generalization (i.e. since the correct choice must be reversed, the subject cannot succeed by selecting the object that looks like the previously correct object). In addition, since the ability to reverse enables an organism to meet new demands in an altered situation, it also seems to be a highly adaptive mechanism for functioning in the real world and not simply in an artificial laboratory setting.

Within the past few decades reversal learning has specifically attracted researchers interested in the role of language in concept development. These investigators believe that language is the key factor in providing the flexibility and abstraction required for reversal learning, i.e. the child learns not to select a particular stimulus (such as black) but rather through language can with facility select any one of the whole range of stimuli sharing a common dimension (such as black, white, grey on the brightness dimension). In this view, reversal learning is therefore thought to be a useful technique for assessing the age and the way in which language begins to influence and to direct behaviour.

In particular it has been postulated that it is not until about the age of five years that children develop a verbal mediating response. This verbal mediation deficiency hypothesis (Reese, 1962b) states that before a certain age children are deficient in their ability to use verbal mediation to direct their behaviour and as a result have difficulty in reversal learning.

Since the experimental situation is so important, the methodology of the reversal studies will be discussed in some detail. In one investigation (Kendler and Kendler, 1959), kindergarten children (5–6 years) were trained on a discrimination problem with two pairs of stimuli which differed both in size (e.g. large *v*. small) and brightness (e.g. black *v*. white). Only one stimulus within a specific dimension was correct (e.g. the large stimulus in the size dimension); the stimuli in the other dimension (e.g. both brightness stimuli) were irrelevant to the solution of the problem. After solving this problem, the children were required to solve a second discrimination in which they either had to *reverse* their previous choice (e.g. select small) or shift to the previously irrelevant dimension (e.g. select black rather than either large or small). The former is termed a reversal shift; the latter a nonreversal shift. A single unit S-R theory, which the Kendlers believe applicable to non-verbal animals, would predict that it would be easier to respond to the previously irrelevant dimension (which was partially rewarded) than to select the previously negative stimulus (which was never rewarded). With the kindergarten children neither shift was favoured. However, when the children were divided into fast and slow learners, based on their first task performance, it was found that the fast learners mastered the reversal shift better than the nonreversal shift while the opposite was true for the slow learners. To explain these results, the Kendlers invoke the idea of a mediational link between the traditional S-R connexion. Unfortunately, this mediational link is never clearly defined so that the hypothesis can never be subjected to a critical test. For example in the above problem, the link might serve to unite the discrete stimuli large and small under the concept of 'size is relevant'. The Kendlers further hypothesize that the difference obtained in the shift performance between fast and slow learners is caused by the fact that 5-6 years is the transitional point at which verbal mediation appears; therefore, children who had not yet learned to mediate would be the slower learners and would find it difficult to reverse. Conversely children who had learned to mediate would be the fast learners and would find it easy to reverse. Although this explanation has numerous unproven assumptions (e.g. slow learners need not be non-mediators; there is no clear demonstration that mediation occurred, etc.), it has aroused considerable interest because it has broadened the range of the phenomena normally encompassed by S-R theory.

As a means of verifying these hypotheses, pre-kindergarten age children were then tested (Kendler, Kendler and Wells, 1960) since at this age most children should be premediational and therefore show better nonreversal than reversal shifting. Again using the dimensions of size and brightness, the authors report verification of their hypothesis. However, in this study in contrast to the one cited above, the training task involved only a single dimension (e.g. brightness) with no irrelevant dimension present. Therefore, the two studies may not be comparable. In the first (Kendler and Kendler, 1959), the children may have learned to avoid the irrelevant cue (e.g. avoid size when brightness was correct) and thus found nonreversal shifting difficult since they then had to select this previously negative dimension. In the second study, however, (Kendler, Kendler, and Wells, 1960) nonreversal shifting may have been easy not because the children were younger but rather because they could have no bias against the dimension used in the second task. That dimension had not been present in the first task and thus the children had no opportunity to learn to avoid it. In the author's view the role of the irrelevant cue may prove to be a crucial variable in studies of the relative difficulty of reversal *v.* nonreversal shifting. For example, it may be found that nonreversal shifting is more difficult than reversal shifting when the nonreversal shift contains a dimension which had been previously irrelevant. Learning of the first task will then be facilitated if the subject learns to avoid the irrelevant dimension while his learning of the second nonreversal shift task will be hampered since the irrelevant dimension now becomes relevant.

Such discrepancies in design illustrate the difficulties in drawing valid conclusions in this area. For example, in some studies the same stimuli are used for training and reversal; in other studies new stimuli are used in the reversal task but they employ the same relevant dimensions as in the training task; sometimes there is an irrelevant cue and other times not; sometimes a physical dimension such as size or colour is reversed, while at other times, position responses are reversed, and these may be qualitatively different problems (Bitterman, 1965).

Even without questioning the design of the reversal experiments, however, there is doubt as to whether mediation and in particular verbal mediation need be invoked to explain reversal learning. O'Connor and

Hermelin (1959) conducted a size discrimination experiment on mental defectives and normal children, both groups with a mental age of about 5 years. They found that the defectives, who are known to be weak in verbal development, were able to reverse more easily than the normal children. The authors attribute this result to the fact that the defectives did not use language and so had no mediating response to conflict with the new learning in the reversal problem. When the defectives were taught the relevant verbalization, their reversal performance was significantly poorer. It was hypothesized that the previously appropriate verbal response (e.g. 'pick the big one') persisted in the reversal situation (e.g. when 'small' was now correct) and thus misguided the subjects. A mediational hypothesis need not be altered by the finding that language when used in a specific, rather than general way (e.g., 'big' rather than 'size') can function to misdirect behaviour. However, this explanation can not readily account for the better performance of the defective children in the first part of the study when language was not used.

The results of studies on reversal learning in non-verbal animals pose an even more serious argument against the verbal mediation hypothesis. As that hypothesis would predict, most studies on animals have found reversal learning to be more difficult than nonreversal learning (Kelleher, 1956; Mackintosh, 1962; Lawrence and Mason, 1955). However, with overtraining, many although not all studies report a facilitation of reversal learning in animals, including easier reversal than nonreversal shifting (see review article by Paul, 1965). The explanation for this phenomenon is still in dispute. This finding in organisms who are obviously non-verbal nevertheless raised serious questions about the necessity for a verbal mediation construct to explain reversal learning. While verbal mediation may well facilitate, it seems unlikely that it is required for the reversal phenomenon.

The question then arises as to how facilitation of reversal learning is achieved with overtraining, but without language. A common factor in the hypotheses that have been advanced is that overtraining allows better discrimination of the stimuli and/or the stimulus situation (Reid, 1953; Capaldi and Stevenson, 1957; Brookshire, Warren, and Ball, 1961; Mackintosh, 1962). This hypothesis has been variously stated as 'switching in of the analyser for the stimulus dimension' (Mackintosh, 1962; Sutherland, 1959), 'observing responses of the stimulus dimension' (Zeaman and House, 1963), and 'acquired distinctiveness of cues' (Lawrence, 1949, 1950). In other words, the overtraining encourages the discrimination process so that the organisms both differentiate the stimuli more readily (e.g. in a large-small discrimination, they discern the size difference more clearly) and also recognize more readily when a change in reinforcement has occurred (e.g. because of the consistent reinforcement received during overtraining, they are readily aware when the reward changes from the large to the small stimulus).

Since these investigators are interested in the subject's ability to handle stimuli sharing the same dimension, they have broadened the experimental question so as to study not simply reversal-nonreversal shifting but also to include shifting *within* as opposed to *across* stimulus dimensions (i.e. intradimensional shifting, such as from one set of colours *v.* extradimensional shifting such as from colours to forms). In this framework it should be noted that reversal learning can be considered one specific form of intradimensional shifting (the stimuli are in the same dimension, but the reward is reversed). According to investigators in this area, the attention theory model that is used to explain intradimensional learning can therefore explain reversal learning; no verbal mediation hypothesis need be invoked. Unfortunately, the studies conducted on children to test this hypothesis have used subjects with mental ages over 6 years (Youniss and Furth, 1964, a, b; Furth and Youniss, 1964; House and Zeaman, 1962). Since children at this age readily use verbal mediation, these experiments do not offer a means of differentiating between the predictions of the verbal *v.* the attentional mediation theories.

The fact that these theories make few differential predictions probably reflects also weaknesses in their construction. But it also reflects the fact that many major changes in thought and behaviour occur at about 5–6 years. The child at this age is not simply characterized by a sudden growth in control of behaviour by language, but also by better attention, greater ability to delay, growth of different conceptual categories, greater frustration tolerance, etc. Until much more carefully controlled experiments are devised which will separate these factors, it seems premature to attribute facility in reversal learning to any one of them.

V. LEARNING SET

In many of the previously cited experiments, the problems involved discrimination learning, i.e. learning to select which of two (or more) stimuli is consistently rewarded. Investigators in concept formation used this technique to determine whether an organism could apply a unifying concept across a variety of problems (e.g. always selecting 'the bigger one', 'the brighter one' of physically disparate stimuli). Therefore, the focus of interest was not simply to determine how easily a problem was learned (intraproblem learning) but rather how easily it was learned relative to a previous problem (interproblem learning).

This latter type of learning deals with increasing facility in coping with successive problems and forms the basis of the phenomenon of 'learning set' (LS). As defined by Harlow (1959), the term learning set does not refer to all transfer in problem solving situations, but rather to a specific type; i.e. . . . 'The transfer between many problems of a single class instead of the more commonly studied transfer between problems of disparate classes or transfer between a few problems of a single class' (p. 494). Learning sets may be further identified by the class of problems used in establishing the set. Thus, there can be discrimination learning sets (a different pair of stimuli is used in each problem), reversal learning sets (the correct response varies from one stimulus to the other on every problem), oddity learning sets (selecting the odd stimulus of three stimuli)' etc.

Reese (1963) in a review article on learning set in children refers to all non-learning set transfer as 'performance set' or 'learning to learn'. In other words, the improvement is not specific to a particular class of problems but rather to general improvement in dealing with all problems (e.g. learning to attend, learning how to manipulate the stimuli, lessening of anxiety in the situation, etc.).

Since learning set refers to the specific improvement in dealing with a class of related problems, it implies the utilization of a unifying principle and is thus of obvious interest to researchers in concept formation. Harlow in fact states that 'all concepts such as triangularity, middle-sizedness, redness, number and smoothness evolve only from LS formation' (1959, p. 510).

A criticism of this formulation lies in the problem of differentiating between 'learning set' and 'performance set' since both refer to interproblem learning and the same learning process(es) may underlie both. However, the distinction is consistently made and numerous controls are often instituted in an attempt to separate these two types of learning. The criterion used is that ultimately one-trial learning is achieved in the former, but not in the latter. One-trial learning means that after one exposure to the stimuli, the subject will thereafter be consistently able to select the correct stimulus; i.e. if he was wrong on the first trial, he will change his response on the second trial; if he was correct on the first trial, he will continue to respond to that stimulus. Different training methods have been used to achieve learning sets or one-trial learning; sometimes a set number of trials on each problem is given regardless of whether solution is achieved on the individual problems. In other cases criterion must be reached on each problem before the next problem is presented, etc.

Of particular interest is the fact that the curve of interproblem learning is similar to that of intraproblem learning; i.e. the percentage of correct responses on the first few problems is similar to chance or what has been termed trial and error performance at the start of intraproblem learning. Performance, however, slowly improves from chance until one-trial learning occurs. Thus, in both intra and interproblem learning the initial number of correct responses is at chance, but shows a gradual rise until almost perfect performance is attained. However, if one looks at the intraproblem learning curves of the *later* learning set problems (i.e. when the learning set is established), the curve does not look like a normal continuous learning curve. Rather it resembles that of insightful learning where there is an immediate rise to near perfect performance from trial one to trial two. Thus, in this system, insight is the result of having developed learning sets prior to the particular situation in which insight is demonstrated.

The learning set phenomenon was originally found in non-human primates but its application has since been extended both downwards and upwards in the phylogenetic scale. There are many interesting studies dealing with differences among species in the facility with which they acquire learning sets (see Harlow, 1959). Generally, it may be stated that the ability with which learning sets are developed correlates with the evolutionary status of a species; that is, the higher up the evolutionary scale, the more easily are learning sets formed.

This finding is of importance to those interested in the issue of whether the cognitive abilities of various species are qualitatively or quantitatively different (see Bitterman, 1965). Advocates of learning sets have generally taken the stand that since non-human primates easily form such sets, there is nothing qualitatively different between the abilities of man and other primates. As a result, studies with humans have been concerned not with whether language or complex thought processes uniquely influence learning sets, but rather with defining test and subject variables which influence how rapidly a learning set is formed.

In particular, the factors studied in children have been concerned with external aspects such as the number of trials per problem and the kinds of stimuli used, or with subject variables such as IQ, chronological age, mental age, etc. (see review article by Reese, 1963).

Most of the aspects of the learning set phenomenon found in animals have been confirmed in humans. However, the single most important difference is that if normal children of about 5 years are trained to criterion on a first problem involving simple object discrimination, then by the second problem one-trial learning is established. It should be noted that by no means all learning sets in children are formed this quickly. However, the rapidity, at least under certain conditions, of the formation of learning sets in humans and never in sub-humans suggests a striking, and perhaps qualitative, difference in the problem solving capacities of humans *v.* other primates. The factors that account for this difference (e.g. language, greater attentiveness, better memory, etc.) remain to be determined.

Although learning set studies have not added significantly to our knowledge of children's learning, the theory proposed to account for the phenomenon may be of importance in understanding children's problem solving capabilities. The theory, termed the 'error factor theory' (Harlow, 1959), is unique in that it places its emphasis not on the learning of the positive (reinforced) stimulus, but rather on learning to avoid the negative (nonreinforced) choices. This theory therefore states that learning occurs due to a progressive elimination of errors. Harlow identifies four error factors: 1. stimulus-perseveration (repetitive choice of the incorrect stimulus object); 2. differential-cue (distinguishing the inappropriate cue when several cues are rewarded; e.g. recognizing whether the position or the object in that position is the relevant cue); 3. response shift (the tendency to respond to both stimuli in an object-discrimination task so that one stimulus is not consistently chosen); 4. position-habit errors (consistently preferring one position, such as the left side, so that learning of the correct object is hampered since its position varies from trial to trial). Although not as systematically studied as the above, other error factors can be present to hamper learning (e.g. anxiety, inattentiveness, lack of motivation, etc.).

In effect, this theory postulates that all the relevant problem solving strategies are present in the organism from the outset and learning is merely a matter of selectively reinforcing some, or rather of inhibiting all but one. The theory leaves out completely any explanation of the way in which the subject learns to select out significant components of a situation and thus it cannot stand as a general theory of learning[1]. Nevertheless, error factor theory may offer a unifying explanation for a variety of phenomena. For example it may be relevant to the facilitation of reversal learning by overtraining, i.e. the more training, the more the suppression of error factors. Therefore in the overtraining reversal situation, the increasing suppression of error factors produces positive transfer. Although learning set had not been extensively explored with children, the error factor theory may also prove useful in understanding their behaviour. Many difficulties that young children have in learning may be based not simply upon a failure to learn the appropriate stimuli, but rather on the fact that they adopt inappropriate hypotheses which then govern their behaviour. In addition, especially in very young children with low frustration tolerance, if these 'hypotheses' fail to be rewarded, the children may become distressed and fail to learn. It may be important, therefore, that the teaching methods with young children be directed not simply towards teaching the appropriate responses, but also towards controlling inappropriate response tendencies in the child. The most appropriate techniques for suppressing error factors in children, however, remain to be determined.

VI. EVALUATION OF EXPERIMENTAL TECHNIQUES

Common to the various theoretical models thus far discussed was the hope that carefully controlled experimental conditions would provide a clear understanding as to the nature of children's thinking and the mechanisms underlying it. Yet, despite these attempts, two reviewers of children's learning have made the following contradictory claims:

1. 'There are no learning processes which are unique in children, as opposed to animals or adults' (White, 1963, p. 196).

2. 'It appears, then, that two learning-set theories are needed; to account for learning sets in infra-human subjects, a theory might be based on traditional stimulus-response learning theory; and to account for learning sets in older children and human adults, a theory of verbal learning and mediation is adequate' (Reese, 1963, p. 138–9).

Thus, despite the use of stringent experimental procedures, no clear-cut understanding of concept formation in young children has been obtained. In addition to this confusion, a variety of questions arise concerning the limitations of the methods developed by the experimentalists. One of the first questions that arises concerns the issue as to

---

[1] See also Vol. I, Chapters 4, 5, for a fuller discussion. (E.A.L.)

whether these paradigms, restricted as they are to discrimination learning, reflect the way in which concepts, or even any significant group of
concepts, are learned. In many animal studies, it is assumed that the
animal does not possess the concept (e.g. 'redness', 'roundness', 'big-
ness') before the experiment, but rather learns it through exposure to
and/or reinforcement of the relevant stimuli. In studies with children,
however, they generally do possess the concept before the experiment
and their experimental task is to recognize which variables determine
the correct solution (e.g. position, colour, size, etc.). It might be argued
that even though children possess the concept before testing, they learned
it in their natural environment in much the same way as animals learn
it in the experimental setting. This question remains to be investigated.

As noted in the introduction, a question also arises as to whether the
differences among concepts are quantitative or rather qualitative, and
as such should not be grouped as one entity. Even if discriminations
of physical properties, such as colour and size, are considered to be
concepts, do they involve the same cognitive processes as do much higher
level concepts such as mathematical symbols, disjunctive concepts, the
concept of a concept, etc.? In the former case the concepts are clearly
tied to physical properties which can be fully illustrated by example; in
the latter case although examples containing the concept may be pointed
out, there are no precise physical dimensions which contain the concept.
As a result, these latter concepts involve a much higher order of
abstraction and are increasingly removed from specific physical stimuli.

Some experimenters have attempted to bypass this issue of levels of
conceptualization by replacing 'the question of whether animals can
acquire concepts' by 'questions about what species can acquire what
concepts, and under what conditions' (Kendler, 1961, p. 462). In
practice, however, as witnessed by the comments above of Reese, White
and Bitterman, this question has not been resolved since the conceptual
limitations and capacities of various species remain in dispute.

Even if one accepts Kendler's orientation, there still remains the need
to account for the more complex concepts (e.g., the more abstract and
relational concepts) attained by children as opposed to animals. Factors
such as attention, verbalization, and the ability to delay are here brought
into account for the growth in conceptual skills in children. Language in
particular has been selected as important by many theorists since it is
characteristic of human beings. Other animals may possess communication systems; language, however, in its complexity of structure, meaning and verbalization is a uniquely human phenomenon (see Chapters 5

and 6). It seems obvious to many theorists that such a significant feature should exert a major influence on thinking and problem solving. However, in many of the studies where language was invoked as an explanation for children's behaviour, it seemed a reasonable, but not a necessary hypothesis. Other hypotheses, such as attentional mechanisms, offered equally good explanations. As a result, there is little decisive evidence demonstrating the significance or lack of significance of language on thought. The ambiguity of this situation has produced a range of interpretations where at one end of the scale the structure of language is believed to determine man's thoughts and concepts (Whorf, 1956) to the other end of the scale where language is believed to have no 'direct, general, or decisive influence on intellective development' (Furth, 1964, p. 145).

An additional weakness of much of the experimental work is the way in which language has been defined. Language is frequently viewed as a label which is evoked by a particular response; it is thereby seen as a response-produced cue that is linked up to the traditional S-R framework. As such, it has advantages over a simple S-R connexion; i.e. it can be evoked in the absence of physical stimuli ('self-signalling'); it can be applied to a range of phenomena thus encouraging generalization, etc. The experimentalists have also recognized levels in the use of language ability indicating an awareness of the complexities of a verbal system (e.g. verbalization accompanying a response but not serving to direct the response, spontaneous verbalization *v.* elicited verbalization, etc.) (Kendler, 1963; Spiker, 1963; Kuenne, 1946; Luria, 1957).

Other theorists such as psycholinguists (e.g. Miller) and Gestaltists (e.g. Werner) would argue that the experimentalists still have a much too simplified view in that language, both in its origins and development, functions in much more complex ways. For example, they would claim that viewing language in terms of labels restricts concepts to the classification of objects and thus fails to explain the higher level concepts. This argument concerning the experimentalists' view of language is basically similar to the criticisms raised against other of their formulations; namely, that the present restricted laboratory techniques do not permit an adequate understanding of the full range of children's thinking nor of the psychological processes involved. In particular questions are raised concerning whether the full range of children's abilities could have been tapped through the use of experimental paradigms which were based on techniques developed for sub-human animals. As stated by Bitterman (1965), 'The simplest problems would not serve to reveal distinct modes of intelligence and different neural mechanisms at work in various animals' (p. 92). Therefore a basic question must be asked as to whether the experiments cited above truly tested concept formation in young children.

In analysing the bulk of the experimental work reviewed here, it is apparent that the study of conceptual development has been confined to a quite narrow range of phenomena – in particular, categorization (applying nonsense syllables), selection of a physical attribute or dimension (size, colour) or a relational response (bigger, brighter). The aim underlying these varying techniques was that of trying to have a child unify physically different stimuli through the application of a common category or mediator. Many investigators feel that this cannot be a full measure of concept formation. Entire areas of concept development seem to have been neglected – for example, the role of imagery in thinking, the processes that allow language to develop, the development of creative thinking, the pre-verbal conceptualization of the child, the role of logical and illogical processes in thinking, etc. As noted in the introduction, the behaviourists would say that many, if not all, of these questions cannot be investigated scientifically, at least for the present, and therefore they should not be considered. Yet this answer seems very inadequate since from both a practical (e.g. education) and a philosophical viewpoint, these areas pose intriguing and important questions. It is precisely because Piaget has grappled with these issues in a provocative manner that his theory of mental development has attracted such interest. It is not within the scope of this chapter to outline the work of Piaget. However, some particular points of contrast in both theory and methodology will be outlined so as to indicate an approach different from that put forth by the experimentalists. A major point to keep in mind in comparing these two approaches is that the refusal of Piaget to accept the theoretical and methodological assumptions and limitations of the experimentalists was a key factor in permitting him to build a markedly different formulation of concept development in the child.

VII. AN ALTERNATIVE APPROACH: THE WORK OF JEAN PIAGET

As emphasized earlier, the experimentalists in their investigations of concept development devoted much of their efforts to overcome non-concept based transfer (e.g. physical generalization). They tried to devise situations in which the label or category was not bound to a particular physical characteristic, but rather represented an abstraction of some aspect of the situation. The abstraction could then be dissociated from the particular stimulus and applied to any relevant situation. This type of design was in large measure responsible for the development of the transposition and reversal paradigms. However, the prototype used in all these experiments, namely that of discrimination learning, is by definition tied to restricted physical properties (e.g. colour, form, size, etc.). The binding to physical characteristics makes it extremely difficult, if not impossible, to design discrimination tasks which *force* the use of a truly abstract formulation. Certain concepts do begin to tap this kind of abstraction; for example, time (past, present), space (near, far, under, over) and causality (sequences of actions and their consequences). These concepts are more abstract in that no direct or single physical referent can exist which clearly demonstrates the concept. In fact most of them require an evaluation and comparison of several factors and they cannot be illustrated through the standard type of perceptual discrimination in which only two or three stimuli are present.

Examination of Piaget's work makes it immediately apparent that these are precisely the sorts of concepts in which he is interested. In addition, Piaget, did not restrict himself to a limited methodology and was therefore able to explore such abstract concepts as space, time, permanence, velocity, number and movement. It is apparent that Piaget has been influenced by the physical sciences and the development of concepts which proved fruitful in these sciences. The behaviourists, as indicated earlier, were also influenced by the physical sciences. In the case of behaviourists, however, the example of the physical sciences led them to conclude that anything not quantifiable was not capable of being studied scientifically; they adopted the methodology of science. By contrast, the scientific influence on Piaget led him to pose questions as to how scientific concepts develop within the individual to lead to a more accurate grasp of reality; he focussed on the development of scientific concepts.

Implicit in this developmental emphasis is Piaget's marked concern with understanding and delineating the constant cognitive changes that are occurring in the growing child. His work in child development is unique in that it provides a comprehensive theoretical system which documents the capacities of the normal child at each stage of development from birth through adolescence. By contrast, although the experimentalists have shown an increasing awareness that the intellectual functioning of children differs from that of adults, they have not carefully documented the myriad developmental changes that the children undergo. Some implicit recognition of these changes is evident from the fact that, in testing concept formation, the experimentalists give more difficult problems to older as compared to younger children. However, the selection of appropriate problems has usually been determined empirically and not on the basis of any theoretical developmental framework.

Piaget is contrasted to the experimentalists not only in his delineation of developmental changes but also in his emphasis on the fact that these developmental capacities and limitations determine the type of reality that the child will experience. For example, the concept of time will be different for a five-year-old child and one aged nine. It will be different not because of the presence or absence of a single factor such as language, but rather because the entire mental structure of the young child will prevent him from having concepts as sophisticated as that of an older child (i.e. he has limited experience, he has difficulty in retaining objects in mind when they are absent from view, he cannot simultaneously compare several objects or events, etc.).

By contrast, the experimentalists believe that the child develops an awareness of the concept through repeated exposure to a variety of instances of the concept; the stimulus must be 'stamped in' for the concept to be attained. The child is therefore essentially regarded as a passive participant in the learning process. Piaget, however, views the child as playing an active role in understanding reality; the child *from birth* constantly seeks to adapt to and impose an order on the reality confronting him. An inevitable conclusion from Piaget's theory is that some sort of primitive concepts develop during the early pre-verbal period (sensori-motor era – 0 to 2 years). However, the young child's behaviour is quite limited and so a problem exists as to how to determine what concepts are available to him. Here too, Piaget is in marked contrast to the experimentalists in that he takes single instances of behaviour and freely interprets what these behaviours may represent in terms of the mental processes of the child. Piaget particularly stresses the role of mental imagery (i.e. the child's retaining mental impressions of what has occurred in his world) in accounting for the development of conceptual behaviour. This imagery is seen as the basis for the growth of a primitive non-verbal representational system (e.g. gestures); the latter, in turn, is seen as prerequisite for the development of language itself. Although Piaget sees language as the most effective vehicle for higher symbolic activity, he does not see it as being required for all symbolic activity. In addition, even when language develops, he does not believe that it alone can account for a complete understanding of mature symbolic activity; such an understanding requires a delineation of the whole range of types of reasoning and problem solving that are available to the child (e.g. not simply language, but imagery, logical reasoning, gestural symbols, imaginative thinking, developmental changes in classificatory behaviour, etc.). In essence, then, Piaget is concerned not with establishing a theory for any particular or limited set of concepts or mechanisms involved in conceptual development but rather in establishing a theory for the total conceptual capabilities of the child.

A question logically arises as to how to determine the various mental mechanisms available to the child. The issue of methodology again offers a sharp contrast between the work of Piaget and that of the experimentalists. Piaget's techniques are noteworthy in that he frequently does not use standardized procedures. In fact, his analysis of the sensorimotor period (i.e. 0–2 years) is based on his observations of his own three children in the simple problem solving situations he created for them. Many of his interpretations of early language behaviour are similarly based on observations of children in natural settings. With slightly older children (e.g. about 4 years) who are more testable, Piaget does use some experimental intervention. In contrast to the experimentalists who have tended to search for 'the paradigm' indicative of concept formation, Piaget has used a variety of less well-controlled techniques. In particular, he uses a modified clinical approach where questioning by the experimenter is often central as well as varied according to the child's individual responses. By contrast, the experimentalists apply the identical method to all subjects and any questioning that occurs takes place after the experiment as a supplement to the results.

As is inevitable in any system as complex and extensive as that of Piaget, there are areas of weakness. These weaknesses, however, do not detract from the fact that this theory remains a major and singular achievement in ascertaining the complex mental development of the normal child.

SUMMARY

Concept formation in young children is a complex area of psychological research which has been approached differently depending upon the theoretical orientation of the investigator. Two of the major orientations in present day research are those of the experimentalists (behaviourists) and those of the cognitive theorists. Each group has its own questions, methods, and interpretations in dealing with the data in this area. The experimentalists, strongly influenced by the methodology of the physical sciences, have attempted to develop a science of cognitive ability based solely upon quantifiable behaviour. A second influence, namely that of evolutionary theory, has led them to an interest in such questions as whether children's thinking is qualitatively or only quantitatively different from that of animals. They are particularly concerned with defining the role of language in children's concepts since complex language is unique to man. The experimentalists have relied upon controlled laboratory situations where the range of possible behaviour is, of necessity, limited. In particular, they have developed specific paradigms which they believe to be experimental models of the way in which concepts develop. Illustrative of this approach has been the work on transposition, reversal learning, and learning set. This work has yielded sophisticated experimental designs and analyses, but it has failed to yield unequivocal answers to the questions to which it was directed. The ambiguity seems to have developed in part from the fact that the paradigms used dealt with limited situations which could tap only physical dimensions (e.g. colour, form, size) rather than broader conceptual categories. The paradigms therefore may not have reflected the total range of the child's capacities nor the way in which concepts develop in his normal environment.

The work of the cognitive theorists, as illustrated by that of Jean Piaget, differs sharply in many respects from that of the experimentalists. Generally this work is not concerned with the 'animal-human' controversy, but rather with the developmental changes that occur in thinking and concept formation *within* the human organism. The major interest is directed towards what is occurring in the mind of the child, particularly with reference to such broad conceptual areas as space, time, causality, mathematical relations, etc. This interest results in a strong emphasis on observation, questioning, and verbalization of children in a naturalistic setting. The experimental methods tend to be much less standardized and are readily adapted to meet the individual responses of each child. While Piaget's approach has tended to describe behaviour, rather than to experimentally alter it in any way, it has been extremely productive and unique in offering a unified, comprehensive theory of mental development in the normal child.

REFERENCES

ALBERTS, E., and EHRENFREUND, D. (1951). Transposition in children as a function of age. *J. exp. Psychol.* **41**, 30–38.

ALPERT, A. (1928). *The Solving of Problem-situations by Preschool children: An analysis.* New York: Teacher's College Contr. Educ.

BERMAN, P. W., and GRAHAM, F. K. (1964). Children's response to relative, absolute and position cues in a two-trial size discrimination. *J. comp. physiol. Psychol.* **57**, 393–397.

BITTERMAN, M. E. (1965). The evolution of intelligence. *Scientific Amer.* **212**, 92–100.

BROOKSHIRE, K. H., WARREN, J. M., and BALL, G. G. (1961). Reversal and transfer learning following overtraining in rat and chicken. *J. comp. physiol. Psychol.* **54**, 98–102.

BROWN, R. (1958). How shall a thing be called? *Psychol. Rev.* **65**, 14–21.

CAPALDI, E. J., and STEVENSON, H. W. (1957). Response reversal following different amounts of training. *J. comp. physiol. Pyschol.* **50**, 195–198.

FLAVELL, J. H. (1963). *The developmental psychology of Jean Piaget.* Princeton, New Jersey: Van Nostrand.

FURTH, H. G. (1964). Research with the deaf: Implications for language and cognition. *Psychol. Bull.* **62**, 154–164.

FURTH, H. G., and YOUNISS, J. (1964). Effect of overtraining on three discrimination shifts in children. *J. comp. physiol. Psychol.* **57**, 290–293.

GELLERMAN, L. W. (1933). Form discrimination in chimpanzees and two-year-old children. *J. Genet. Psychol.* **42**, 3–27.

GONZALEZ, R. C., and ROSS, S. (1958). The basis of solution by preverbal children of the intermediate-size problem. *Amer. J. Psychol.* **71**, 742–746.

GRAHAM, F. K., and BERMAN, P. W. (1964). Learning of relative and absolute size concepts in preschool children. *J. exp. Child Psychol.* **1**, 26–36.

HARLOW, H. F. (1959). Learning set and error factor theory. In S. Koch (ed.) *Psychology: A Study of a Science. Vol. 2. General Systematic Formulations, Learning and Special Processes.* New York: McGraw-Hill.

HOUSE, B., and ZEAMAN, D. (1962). Reversal and nonreversal shifts in discrimination learning in retardates. *J. exp. Psychol.* **63**, 444–451.

HUNT, J. MC V. (1961). *Intelligence and experience.* New York: Ronald Press.

JACKSON, T. A., and JEROME, E. (1940). Studies in the transposition of learning by children: IV A preliminary study of patternedness in discrimination learning. *J. exp. Psychol.* **26**, 432–349.

JACKSON, T. A., and JEROME, E. A. (1943). Studies in the transposition of learning by children: VI Simultaneous *v.* successive presentation of the stimuli to bright and dull children. *J. exp. Psychol.* **33**, 431–439.

JACKSON, T. A., STONEX, E., LANE, E., and DOMINGUEZ, K. (1938). Studies in the transposition of learning by children: I Relative *v.* absolute response as a function of amount of training. *J. exp. Psychol.* **23**, 578–600.

JOHNSON, R. C., and ZARA, R. C. (1960). Relational learning in young children. *J. comp. physiol. Psychol.* **53**, 594–597.

KELLEHER, R. T. (1956). Discrimination learning as a function of reversal and nonreversal shifts. *J. exp. Psychol.* **51**, 379–384.

KELLOGG, W. N., and KELLOGG, L. A. (1933). *The ape and the child.* New York: McGraw-Hill.

KENDLER, T. S. (1961). Concept Formation. *Ann. Rev. of Psychol.* **12**, 447–472.

KENDLER, T. S. (1963). Development of mediating responses in children. In J. C. Wright and J. Kagan (eds.) Basic Cognitive Processes in Children. *Monogr. Soc. Res. Child Developm.* **28**, 33–48.

KENDLER, T. S., and KENDLER, H. H. (1959). Reversal and nonreversal shifts in kindergarten children. *J. exp. Psychol.* **58**, 50–60.

KENDLER, T. S., KENDLER, H. H., and WELLS, D. (1960). Reversal and nonreversal shifts in nursery school children. *J. comp. physiol. Psychol.* **53**, 83–88.

KUENNE, M. R. (1946). Experimental investigation of the relation of language to transposition behaviour in young children. *J. exp. Psychol.* **36**, 471–490.

LAWRENCE, D. H. (1949). Acquired distinctiveness of cues: I Transfer between discriminations on the basis of familiarity with the stimulus. *J. exp. Psychol.* **39**, 770–784.

LAWRENCE, D. H. (1950). Acquired distinctiveness of cues: II Selective association in a constant stimulus situation. *J. exp. Psychol.* **40**, 175–188.

LAWRENCE, D. H., and MASON, W. A. (1955). Systematic behaviour during discrimination reversal and change of dimensions. *J. comp. physiol. Psychol.* **48**, 1–7.

LURIA, A. R. (1957). The role of language in the formation of temporary connections. In Simon, B. (ed.) *Psychology in the Soviet Union.* London: Routledge and Kegan Paul.

MACKINTOSH, N. J. (1962). The effects of overtraining on a reversal and a nonreversal shift. *J. comp. physiol. Psychol.* **55,** 555–559.

MATHESON, E. (1931). A study of problem solving behaviour in preschool children. *Child Developm.* **2,** 242–262.

MCKEE, J. P., and RILEY, D. A. (1962). Auditory transposition in six-year-old children. *Child Developm.* **33,** 469–476.

O'CONNOR, N., and HERMELIN, B. (1959). Discrimination and reversal learning in imbeciles. *J. abnorm. soc. Psychol.* **59,** 409–413.

PAUL, C. (1965). Effects of overlearning upon single habit reversal in rats. *Psychol. Bull.* **63,** 65–72.

PIAGET, J. (1926). *The language and Thought of the Child.* London: Routledge and Kegan Paul.

PIAGET, J. (1928). *Judgment and Reasoning in the Child.* London: Routledge and Kegan Paul.

PIAGET, J. (1929). *The Child's Conception of the World.* London: Routlege and Kegan Paul.

PIAGET, J. (1930). *The Child's Conception of Physical Causality.* London: Routledge and Kegan Paul.

PIAGET, J. (1950). *The Psychology of Intelligence.* London: Routledge and Kegan Paul.

PIAGET, J. (1951). *Play, Dreams and Imitation in Childhood.* London: Heinemann.

PIAGET, J. (1952). *The Origins of Intelligence in Children.* London: Routledge and Kegan Paul.

REESE, H. W. (1961). Transposition in the intermediate-size problem by preschool children. *Child Developm.* **32,** 311–314.

REESE, H. W. (1962). (a) The distance effect in transposition in the intermediate size problem. *J. comp. physiol. Psychol.* **55,** 528–531.

REESE, H. W. (1962). (b) Verbal mediation as a function of age level. *Psychol. Bull.* **59,** 502–509.

REESE, H. W. (1963). Discrimination learning set in children. *Adv. in Child Developm. and Behav.* **1,** 115–145.

REID, L. S. (1953). The development of noncontinuity behavior through continuity learning. *J. exp. Psychol.* **46,** 107–112.

RUDEL, R. G. (1957). Transposition of response by children trained in intermediate-size problems. *J. comp. physiol. Psychol.* **50,** 292–295.

RUDEL, R. G. (1960). The transposition of intermediate size by brain-damaged and mongoloid children. *J. comp. physiol. Psychol.* **53,** 89–94.

SKINNER, B. F. (1953). *Science and Human behaviour.* New York: Free Press.

SPENCE, K. W. (1936). The nature of discrimination learning in animals. *Psychol. Rev.* **43,** 427–449.

SPENCE, K. W. (1937). The differential response in animals to stimuli varying within a single dimension. *Psychol. Rev.* **44,** 430–444.

SPENCE, K. W. (1942). The basis of solution by chimpanzees of the intermediate size problem. *J. exp. Psychol.* **31,** 257–271.

SPIKER, C. C. (1963). Verbal factors in the discrimination learning of children. In Wright, J. C., and Kagan, J. (eds.) Basic Cognitive Processes in Children. *Monogr. Sec. Res. Child Developm.* **28,** 53–69.

SPIKER, C. C., GERJOUY, I. R., and SHEPARD, W. O. (1956). Children's concept of middle-sizedness and performance on the intermediate size problem. *J. comp. physiol. Psychol.* **49,** 416–419.

SPIKER, C. C., and TERRELL, G., Jr. (1955). Factors associated with transpositional behaviour of preschool children. *J. genet. Psychol.* **86,** 143–158.

STEVENSON, H. W., and BITTERMAN, M. E. (1954). The distance effect in the transposition of intermediate size by children. *Amer. J. Psychol.* **67,** 251–255.

SUTHERLAND, N. S. (1959). Stimulus analysing mechanisms. In *Proceedings of a Symposium on the Mechanisation of Thought Processes.* London: H.M.S.O. **2,** 575–609.

THRUM, M. E. (1935). The development of the concepts of magnitude. *Child Developm.* **6,** 120–140.

WELCH, L. (1939) (a). The development of size discrimination between the ages of 12 and 40 months. *J. genet. Psychol.* **55,** 243–268.

WELCH, L. (1939) (b). The development of discrimination of form and area. *J. Psychol.* **7,** 37–54.

WELCH, L. (1939) (c). The span of generalization below the two year age level. *J. genet. Psychol.* **55,** 269–297.

WELCH, L. (1940) (a). A preliminary investigation of some aspects of the hierarchical development of concepts. *J. genet. Psychol.* **22,** 359–378.

WELCH, L. (1940) (b). Genetic development of associational structures of abstract thinking. *J. genet. Pyschol.* **56,** 175–206.

WELCH, L., and LONG, L. (1940). The higher structural phases of concept formation of children. *J. Pyschol.* **9,** 59–95.

WERNER, H., and KAPLAN, B. (1963). *Symbol Formation*. New York: John Wiley.

WHITE, S. H. (1963). Learning. In Stevenson, H. W. Kagan, J., and Spiker, C. (eds.) *Child Psychology: The Sixty-second Yearbook of the National Society for the Study of Education*. Chicago: Univ. of Chicago Press.

WHORF, B. L. (1956). *Language, thought and reality*. New York: John Wiley.

YOUNISS, J., and FURTH, H. G. (1964) (a). Reversal learning in children as a function of overlearning and delayed transfer. *J. comp. physiol. Psychol.* **57**, 155–157.

YOUNISS, J., and FURTH, H. G. (1964) (b). Reversal performance in children as a function of overtraining and response conditions. *J. exp. child Psychol.* **1**, 182–188.

ZEAMAN, D., and HOUSE, B. J. (1963). An attention theory of retardate discrimination learning. In Ellis, N. R. (ed.) *Handbook of Mental Deficiency: Psychological Theory and Research*. New York: McGraw-Hill. 159–223.

ZEILER, M. D. (1963) (a). New dimensions of the intermediate size problem: Neither absolute nor relational response. *J. exp. Psychol.* **66**, 588–593.

ZEILER, M. D. (1963) (b). The ratio theory of intermediate size discrimination. *Psychol. Rev.* **70**, 516–533.

4

Skill

G. F. REED

I. INTRODUCTORY NOTE

THE basic aim of this chapter is to introduce the reader to some of the ideas produced by psychologists investigating human skilled behaviour, and to outline some relevant findings. For the practical application of these to teaching, the reader is warmly recommended to read two admirably lucid books by Knapp (1963) and Holding (1965).

II. 'SKILLS' AND 'SKILL': PSYCHOLOGICAL APPROACHES

The first problem to be faced in any general discussion of the present topic is that the word 'skill' has different meanings for different people. In its lay sense it is in common use, but with varying connotations. We speak of a schoolchild 'acquiring the basic skills'; pressed for further examples we might cite such divergent activities as gymnastics and embroidery or rugby football and chess. Here we imply the definition of 'skills' in terms of apparently circumscribed abilities, tasks or pursuits. Or we can refer to a statesman as having 'skill in negotiation', or to an orchestral conductor's 'skill in interpretation'. We may refer approvingly to one person's 'skill in handling students' or, less approvingly, to another's 'skill in avoiding work'. In such examples we are using the word 'skill' as an evaluator of performance, suggesting that the individual has attained a high *level* of ability in a given activity.

Within the field of scientific psychology the usage of the term 'skill' is no less confusing at first sight. In one sense it has a much more specific application. Most psychologists could assemble a list of their colleagues who are regarded as being investigators of 'skill' as opposed to the much larger group who are concerned with 'learning' in general. Many textbooks have separate sections or chapters on 'skill' as well as on 'learning'. Clearly the two have considerable overlap; the crucial

104

feature of skilled performance is that it involves learning. But there is no general agreement as to whether skill should be regarded merely as one sort of learning, whether it is best considered as a separate entity or whether the difference is merely one of terminology. To make matters more complicated it may be argued that, far from being a limited subject of academic study, skilled behaviour provides the key to learning or, indeed, to all adaptive existence. The student attempting to acquire a balanced knowledge of the subject may be seriously misled in his perspective, or merely bewildered, when faced with texts written at different periods with varying semantic presuppositions and theoretical standpoints. For this reason it may be of value to sketch some changes in psychological approach which may be borne in mind when consulting relevant texts.

As a specialized area of psychological investigation, the study of 'skill' has traditionally been delimited, although concepts, methods of approach and fields of application have changed considerably. The reasons or precipitants for these changes are mainly ones of historical accident not directly related to the science of psychology but rather to social demands. Thus, military requirements during the Second World War demanded new psychological techniques and their application to specific, practical and usually complex problems. Post-war developments in the study of skill were led by a generation of experienced experimental psychologists whose training and interests had been in research related to such problems as the selection of aircrews, the training of bombers and anti-aircraft gunners and the effects of fatigue upon radar operators. Their concepts and experimental approaches owed a great deal to engineering and did not always relate readily to those of pre-war investigators. As Kay (1957) has pointed out, research in skills up to about 1940 was primarily concerned with *responses* or 'output'. Post-war skill research has also studied stimuli and environmental factors or 'input'. The influence of engineering concepts is discernible in contemporary theories which view the human operator as a link, component or 'channel' in a system which includes input and output. Meanwhile, other investigators have continued to use the 'response' approach in traditional types of experimental learning situations such as rote-learning or mirror-drawing. But nowadays they would be regarded in psychological circles as studying 'learning' rather than 'skill'. The latter term is currently reserved for the work of investigators using the concepts, terminology and techniques of the postwar group referred to above. In other words, the term 'skill' in psychology reflects professional usage rather than classificatory precision. Partly for this reason no formal definition of the term seems as yet to have received unanimous acceptance within the discipline.

The lack of a standard definition also reflects changes in ideas about the scope and implications of the specialized study of skill. At one time psychologists used the term only in reference to *motor* performance. Subsequently the realization of an essential interrelationship in many activities was indicated by the introduction of the term '*perceptual-motor* skills'. And, finally, it is becoming increasingly accepted that the same concepts and methods which have been applied to the study of perceptual-motor skills may well prove useful in the study of language development, concept-formation and problem-solving. This view is paralleled by another discernible trend in skill psychology. In the first paragraph above a distinction was made between 'skills' as tasks and 'skill' as a level of performance. It is fair to say that most contemporary psychologists are concerned with the latter rather than the former. Earlier theorists tended to analyse the characteristics of particular activities such as swimming or archery, which were taken to be 'typical skills'. This involved attempts to define what were 'skills' and what were not, or to distinguish between 'high grade' and 'low grade' skills. To most modern skill psychologists such classification would be a red-herring endeavour, which is avoided by studying the nature of the development or acquisition of *skilled behaviour* rather than the task as such. From this point of view, not only fencing and football, but walking, talking and using a knife and fork are germane to skill study. For the same reason the plural form 'skills', with its connotation of specific, self-contained tasks or abilities is becoming less prevalent in psychological publications. It is being replaced by the singular form 'skill', by 'skilled performance' or by similar terms which are neutral as regards the specific nature of *tasks* themselves, but have reference to *level of performance*.

It is perhaps not surprising that few investigators have ventured to formulate a categorical definition of 'skill', despite the fact that, as Irion (1966) puts it, they 'develop an intuitive feeling for what is, and what is not properly to be considered a part of the skills field'. One way out of the difficulty is to propose an operational definition (stressing *what* is done, rather than *how* it is done) as does Knapp (1963) in her very interesting discussion of this very problem:

'. . . skill is the learned ability to bring about predetermined results with maximum certainty, often with the minimum outlay of time or energy or both.' (Knapp, 1963, p. 4.)

But more acceptable to skill psychologists, because it high-lights what seem to be the crucial psychological problems involved, is the statement by Fitts (1964), who defines a skilled response as:

'. . . one in which receptor-effector-feedback processes are highly organized, both spatially and temporally.' (Fitts, 1964, p. 244.)

Probably the majority of contemporary investigators of skill would agree with Fitts that the central problem is how such *organization* or patterning takes place. For the most profitable approaches to the subject have been those which emphasize selection, organization and integration. Such approaches imply a rejection of the view that skill should be studied in terms of habit-formation or simple stimulus-response chains. But before proceeding to examine this issue it will be as well to summarize some of the common features of skilled activity.

III. THE CHARACTERISTICS OF SKILLED PERFORMANCE

In what way does the performance of a skilled person differ from that of the beginner? This is a much more difficult question than it appears at first sight, and psychologists are not yet agreed on the nature of the answer. It seems clear that the solution cannot be expressed merely in terms of the *end result* of the skilled activity. The achievements of the skilled arithmetician, seamstress or athlete cannot be attained by the beginner. But there are many activities, usually of a less complex type – for instance, sorting tasks, and maze-learning – where the beginner achieves the correct result though with less consistency. There are others, such as puzzle-solving, where he may well succeed, given time. The important changes with increasing skill seem to occur not in terms of result alone but in the way in which the result is accomplished.

In many skilled activities improvement is assessed in terms of *speed* and it is commonly assumed that the overall time taken to complete any activity reflects the level of skill. But in absolute terms this is not necessarily so. In some skills the overall time may not decrease with improved ability; in others, the overall time may decrease but the time taken for each individual movement may not. As Woodworth (1938) pointed out, expert performance is not merely that of the beginner executed more rapidly. The changes which are associated with improved skill seem to be reflected not in the overall speed but in the *relative rates* of component activities. Thus, skill in motor activities is characterized by the absence of fuss or hurry, and the skilled exponent's performance seems relaxed, graceful and unhurried. Clearly this is the outcome of the temporal reorganization of sequential movements rather than mere speed. Bartlett (1947) stresses the central importance of '*timing*' as opposed to '*time*' in the consideration of skilled activity.

One way in which unhurried performance is achieved is by the elimination of surplus movements, activities or processes, or what Bartlett calls 'the suppression of flourishes'. In motor skills such as learning to ride a bicycle or play golf this is clearly discernible. To some extent such surplus movements may be due to faulty co-ordination. But it is also likely that in the early stages the learner may be maximizing feedback cues (to his posture, balance and control) which become unnecessary as he improves. Similarly, in mental tasks he learns to ignore inessentials, and no longer needs as many mental checks as he did initially. Thus at this, and other levels, the learner utilizes active *inhibition* in his selection of the responses available to him. In fact, one aspect of most skill development is that the subject becomes able to carry out the task with less information (be it sensory, perceptual, cognitive or social) because he is better able to comprehend and benefit from such cues as he does select.

This is reflected at the conscious level by increasing *confidence*, and a diminution in the need for checking and reassurance. At the same time the actual process of checking becomes more reliable. The skilled subject becomes able to detect and eliminate errors in his performance more effectively and speedily. This may be seen in terms of what Welford (1958) refers to as the building up of 'rules' in the translation process between perception and action. Indeed, Bartlett has suggested that the speed with which errors are detected and thrown out is 'the best single measure of mental skill'. Certainly in many tasks, both mental and bodily, an overall increase in speed with improved skill may be due not to any increase in speed of component activities but to a reduction in the time spent on checking.

Related to this heightened comprehension of data about the task is the development of *anticipation*. As the subject learns to interpret and schematize data appropriately he becomes able to anticipate forthcoming data. He can 'think ahead' so that his responses become less and less individual components and progressively more patterned and integrated temporally as well as spatially. Similarly the actual size of 'units' of performance increases with skill. In many activities this may be observed as a decrease in jerkiness and the development of grace. Thus the golfer develops a 'good' swing and the tennis player not only masters a stroke but learns to position himself tactically after making the stroke. The classical examples of anticipation and of the enlarging of units of performance occur in telegraphy and typewriting where the skilled operator becomes more able to 'copy behind' i.e. to receive larger chunks of message before actually writing.

With improved skill there comes an *automatization* of response. Introspectively this is reported as a diminution of conscious control. The skilled performer does not have to 'think about what he is doing'. Experienced car drivers often report driving long distances and under varied conditions without being aware of some portion of the journey so that they 'wake up' to find they are miles farther on than they had realized. The skilled games player will carry out intricate activities 'instinctively'. (It is clear, of course, that skilled behaviour is not 'unconscious' at all levels; the operator or subject's perceptual functioning must be heightened during performance.) This automatization is presumably associated with the development of larger work 'units' and, as Welford has suggested, with the virtual elimination of uncertainty in performance. So that it is not surprising that relative diminution in skill, as when task difficulty is radically increased, is accompanied by de-automatization. The operator becomes aware of aspects of his behaviour and the task which he had previously 'taken for granted'. The car driver entering a patch of fog notices his own movements and becomes uncomfortably aware, for instance, of muscular stiffness, lack of ventilation and the sound of his engine.

One further important characteristic of skilled behaviour which may follow automatization is its *reliability* as compared with the learner's performance. The latter may reach a level where his end result appears to be as speedy and accurate as that of a highly skilled person. But his performance will be less resistant to unfavourable conditions. Thus the seasoned observer will suspend assessment of an up-and-coming young athlete until he has seen him perform under pressure. The skill of a pilot has finally to be judged in terms of his ability to retain his abilities in an emergency. The top rank golfer or chess player is not necessarily *always* better than the competent club player; the point is that his performance is more *consistent*. His skill level is less likely to disintegrate in distracting or disturbing situations.

E

IV. SKILL AND HABITS

Skill and habits clearly have much in common. Both involve learning and are developed over time, both are characterized by the automatization mentioned in the preceding section. But this should not mislead us into equating the two, despite the fact that a traditional approach to the study of skill has been through the analysis of habit formations. At one level, these certainly play their part in the development of skilled behaviour. But, as Guthrie (1952) puts it, habits can be good or bad whereas in a sense skilled behaviour is always taken to be 'good'. For the more fixed a habit is, the less adaptive it is to environmental demands. Skilled behaviour, on the other hand, is not only directed towards some criterion but, as has been noted, one mark of increased skill is that the learner becomes progressively more capable of adjusting to changes, external and internal. It follows that acquiring skill involves not only simple habit formations but a dynamic process of selective response reinforcement and generalization. This implies the progressive and hierarchical integration of a whole repertoire of habits, not all of which are required to be in operation at any given phase of the activity. The selective process demands active *inhibition* as well as arousal.

Thus few investigators now believe that skilled performance is to be regarded in terms of strings or assemblies of discrete habits. (On the other hand, for teaching, as well as for experimental purposes, it is often convenient to break a performance down into sequential components). It seems unlikely that skill in complex activities can fruitfully be studied in terms of simple 'chained' responses, useful as such an approach may be in the study of more elementary learning. On the contrary, the most promising lines of research seem to have stemmed from an awareness that skill depends upon an active temporal/spatial organization which is responsive to, and continually regulated by, discrepancies between activity and intention. The cues which indicate such discrepancies may come from within the organism or from the environment (which may or may not present changing features) or from a combination of both. Thus the gymnast's actions are guided by proprioceptive and kinaesthetic feed-back whereas the footballer's skill, beyond a certain level, is determined by his anticipations of, and adjustment to, a variety of social factors. Poulton (1957) has made the useful distinction between 'closed' skills where external requirements are minimal, closed skills with predictable external requirements (e.g. diving), and 'open' skills which demand adjustment to unpredictable or exacting environmental requirements. In all types of activity, however, skilled responses are those which are continually modified to correct discrepancies from a 'model' which sets criteria for performance and which itself is modifiable as a result of experience or changing circumstances. This emphasis on dynamic organization stems largely (in this country at least) from the influence of Sir Frederick Bartlett. In his classical work *Remembering* (1932) he decried the theory of static but fading 'traces' and propounded a dynamic theory which made use of the neurologist, Sir Henry Head's concept of the 'schema'.

' "Schema" refers to an active organization of past reactions, or of past experiences, which must always be supposed to be operating in any well-adapted organic response. That is, whenever there is any order or regularity of behaviour, a particular response is possible only because it is related to other similar responses which have been serially organized, yet which operate, not simply as individual members coming one after another, but as a unitary mass. . . . [All incoming impulses] have to be regarded as constituents of living, momentary settings belonging to the organism, or to whatever parts of the organism are concerned in making a response of a given kind, and not as a number of individual events somehow strung together and stored within the organism.' (Bartlett, 1932, p. 201.)

Bartlett goes on to give as an example the making of a stroke in tennis or cricket, which depends on the relating of new, usually visual experiences to other immediately preceding visual experiences, and to a balance of postures which is the result of a whole series of earlier movements.

'When I make the stroke I do not, as a matter of fact, produce something absolutely new, and I never merely repeat something old. The stroke is literally manufactured out of the living visual and postural "schemata" of the moment and their interrelations.'
(Bartlett, 1932, p. 202.)

Oldfield (1959) neatly points this up in saying that what we learn at tennis is not a set of strokes, but how to make strokes appropriate to the moment. He summarizes Bartlett's differentiation between skills and habits:

'. . . habit demands conformity to a prescribed, standard sequence of motor acts, while in skilled behaviour the same act is, strictly speaking *never* repeated . . . in a skill the effectiveness of the behaviour is *dependent* upon the absence of stereotyping.'
(Oldfield, 1959, p. 34.)

This viewpoint suggests, then, that most light will be shed on skilled behaviour if it is examined in terms of the development of dynamic *strategies* which direct the selection and integration of tactical procedures. The individual procedures (responses and habits) are themselves of less interest than the way in which they are *organized*, the manner in which *matching* takes place and the degree to which *discrepancies* are identified and corrected.

V. THEORETICAL MODELS

What sort of theoretical models can allow for the interpretation of data in terms of selection, organization, matching and discrepancy-correction? It must be admitted that no completely satisfactory model has as yet been devised. A relatively recent field of study has, however, suggested analogues or constructs which psychologists have found helpful. This field is that of cybernetics, a name suggested by Wiener (1948) for the scientific study of control and communication systems. An excellent introduction to the subject and its influence on psychology has been provided by Sluckin (1954).

The most well-known control system principle is that of *feedbacks* which is employed in such self-regulating devices as the thermostats in heating systems and domestic refrigerators, and which is an essential consideration in radio design. The main point here is that the instrument or machine must be constructed to detect differences between its current state and some standard. Machines capable of achieving operating stability in this way are known as 'servo-mechanisms', the classical example being the steam engine governor. There is, of course, nothing new about the general principle involved, but such a model was not fully exploited by psychologists for the study of skill until the Second World War, when Cambridge researchers were influenced by engineering concepts. Such psychologists as Craik (1947, 1948) saw that it was possible, by regarding man as a 'black box' of unknown circuitry, to study the human operator as part of a control system which included tools, apparatus or test manipulanda. By analysing the input and output of such a system it is possible to find analogues with engineering systems which suggest how the human 'black box' component may be functioning, or even to design instrumental analogues to replace the black box in certain situations.

An important analytical method employed in the design and study of servo-mechanisms is that of *transfer function*, which has been used to describe and quantify human performance. Transfer function is the mathematical expression of the ratio of output to input, or the prediction of the former from the latter, given particular conditions. Differential equations have been proposed (by, e.g. Fuchs, 1962) which can substantially fit data from human performance on 'tracking' tasks. They utilize constants analogous to error amplitude, error ratio, and reaction time to predict the operator's performance. (Such equations have not only been shown to fit performance data; they have been used to provide analogue computer's models of behaviour. In tracking tasks these can match the human operator performance so well that when the computer's output is substituted for the human's, without his knowledge, up to half a minute may elapse before he is aware of the change.)

Clearly, the control concept ideas outlined above, do not, as they stand, allow for the development of learning of skill. They may shed light on the nature of skilled behaviour but not on the *changes* involved in its acquisition. To improve our performance in skilled activities we must be able to profit by experience. This includes the effects of practice and the recalling of errors as well as successful performances. Furthermore, we must usually have some idea of what we are aiming to achieve, an overall conspectus of optimal performance. Within this conspectus are a variety of responses and 'sub-skills'. Improvement is geared to the mastery of these components and, as discussed above, the ability to utilize or inhibit them according to the requirements of the overall aim as modified by changing conditions. The attainment of skill thus involves memory, adaptation and hierarchical organization. Theoretical models which encompass these processes have been evolved under the title of '*adaptive system models*'. The best-known of these is the stored-programme data-processing system. The computer's stored programme is its 'memory' whilst hierarchical organization is represented by 'executive' programmes as well as sub-routines. The latter are modified by the 'executive' programme in accordance with both stored and in-coming information.

Control system models are concerned with the feeding-back of information about performance to improve or stabilize subsequent performance. This is achieved by the matching or comparison of 'output' with 'input', which involves '*information processing*'. Thus skill psychologists have drawn upon the concepts of 'information theory'. This was originated by telecommunication engineers who needed methods for the statistical determination of the optimal amounts of information in telegraphic messages, allowing for losses during trans-mission. Information is taken to be that which diminishes uncertainty by excluding alternatives, so that crucially it is concerned with the probable occurrence of alternative 'events'. The *amount* of information is measured by the number of alternatives excluded, and the conven-tional unit of measurement is that which allowed a decision to be made between two equally probable events. This is termed a binary unit, or 'bit' for short. One bit of information is conveyed by the answer to such questions as 'Should I take the right or the left fork in the road?' or 'Is it a boy, doctor?' Generally, the amount of information contained in a signal or event is given by the logarithm (to the base of two) of the number of alternatives. The probability of an event is inversely pro-portional to this number. So the amount of information conveyed by a signal (event) is the negative logarithm of the probability of its occurrence.

If H is the amount of information and P is the prior probability of an event, then

$$H = -\log_2 P \text{ bits}$$

Clearly, where there are no alternatives there can be no information ($P = 1$, and $-\log_2 1 = 0$). The more certain some outcome or event is (the higher its probability) the less information can be conveyed. Con-versely, the lower the probability of a signal the more information it conveys.

From the informational point of view a signal may include 'redun-dancies' or, of a sequence of signals, some may be redundant. Thus, to the first question above, an answer of the form 'Turn right. Do not turn left' contains one bit of information whilst the remainder is redundant.

Signals are conveyed physically by '*communication channels*', each of which has a 'capacity' indicated by the number of bits per second that it can carry. For optimal transmission the effect of 'noise' must be allowed for, signals must be coded and de-coded in the most efficient manner, and redundancies of signal content must be minimized. And when input at any time exceeds the carrying capacity of the channel there must be some method of selecting or 'filtering' out the most signi-ficant information. Ideally also, there should be some way of 'storing' material until it can be handled at various points in the system.

In human performance it has long been known that when two stimuli (e.g. lights) are presented in rapid succession the time taken to respond to the second stimulus is delayed. For instance, in a well-known experi- ment by Vince (1948), it was found that a subject who is required to trace a moving line through a slit in a screen shows delay in responding to a changed position of the line if the change occurs within about half a second of the previous change. This was at first presumed to be evidence of a 'psychological refractory phase'. However, Welford (1952) argued that such results were explicable if the central processes involved in the organization of each response stimulus could not overlap in time with each other, nor with response feedback information. In other words, the human nervous system can to some extent be regarded as a single communication channel of limited capacity.

Broadbent (1958) has argued convincingly for the acceptance of this approach, and has proposed an information-flow model of the organ- ism where the incoming sensory signals are sampled and held in a 'short term store' before filtering, when selection is made in terms of certain of their properties and various states of the organism. After passing through the channel, information may be returned to temporary store or may go into a long-term store. This adjusts internal coding to the probabilities of prior events and thus modifies the filtering process. Using this model Broadbent has been able to offer plausible explana- tions for a number of problems in the study of learning and skill.

The models outlined above allow for coding, matching, the correc- tion of discrepancies and the selection and inhibition of responses. Selection is also crucial at the receptor stage. In Broadbent's model, input is condensed by peripheral filters which reject much incoming data. Presumably skill involves increased discrimination, so that the skilled person has learned what to 'pay attention' to, and what not. He can simplify his performance by rejecting redundant or irrelevant signals and thus gain the necessary amount of information from fewer events. The learner, on the other hand, does not yet know how to dis- tinguish between a confusing mass of incoming stimuli. Of necessity, he will at first tend to give equal attention to all of them. He is undertaking, therefore, in a very real sense, a much harder task than the skilled person. Thus the *perceptual* aspect of skilled performance has aroused considerable interest. If analysis of the significance of incoming signals is to be regarded in terms of pattern-matching or recognition (Cross- man, 1964) then the receptor system must have access to a store of 'patterns' accumulated throughout life. 'Perceptual learning' has been shown to be of immediate importance in the acquisition of skills (Belbin, 1958) but little is known of the processes involved.

VI. MATURATION AND LEARNING

Evidently the successful acquisition of many skills presumes an appropriate level of neuro-muscular, perceptual and cognitive development. It would be foolish to expect a 3-year-old to learn the Western Roll or the intricacies of billiards. On the other hand 3-year-olds can be taught to swim, and circus children, highly motivated and intensively trained from their earliest years, may demonstrate advanced skill in balancing, tumbling and juggling feats. Teachers and parents often admit puzzlement as to whether maturation or learning is the more important. But expressed in this way this is not a soluble problem.

In formal education this confusion was reflected, for instance, by the concept of 'reading readiness' which preoccupied investigators for over a decade. In 1930 it took the simple form of a question: 'At what age are children ready to begin learning to read?' Numerous researches were interpreted as indicating that, other things being equal, a mental age of at least 6 was a prerequisite for effective learning to read. It was suggested that premature teaching was not only ineffective but might actually be associated with subsequent difficulties in learning. The whole question became confused with opposing ideologies and such 'progressive' theories as 'free education'. The proponents of reading readiness produced abundant experimental data. Its opponents saw it as dangerously fatalistic and as a desertion of the teacher's central responsibility. Much misunderstanding was due to a lack of definition of terms, so that 'reading' meant different things to the protagonists and there was a failure to disentangle the various levels and types of skill involved. Some balance was introduced when it was recognized that any effort to measure reading readiness must begin by inquiring 'Ready to read what?' and 'Ready to read how?' The controversy is not yet dead although, characteristically enough, there are signs that the pendulum is beginning to swing in the opposite direction. In fact experimental attempts are being made to teach children to read as early as possible.

The stress upon 'maturation' or 'readiness' as opposed to learning holds an interesting place in this history of scientific ideas. Basically it represents a modification of the 'instinct' theories which predominated at the beginning of the century but which were discredited and to some extent replaced by the behaviourist outlook in the twenties. Evidence which would be interpreted as supporting the maturational viewpoint was forthcoming in the thirties and has more recently received impetus because of the interest shown by psychologists in the findings of etholo-gists stimulated by the classical studies of Lorenz and Tinbergen.

The baby animal or bird seems to be endowed with a whole reper-toire of instinctive response behaviours which may be elicited only by an appropriate stimulus. (Ethologists term such stimuli 'Innate Releasing Mechanisms' or I R Ms.) Responses can not be elicited except by the presentation of appropriate stimuli at the appropriate periods of development. I R Ms are triggered off by perceptual characteristics of the environment which are species-specific. In many cases these 'sign-stimuli' have been identified and shown to be precise and objective. Thus the robin's territorial defence responses are elicited by the posturing of a rival. But experiments have shown that it is not the overall appearance of the other bird that releases defence behaviour, but the red breast feathers alone. A stuffed robin with its red breast painted brown fails to elicit a response whereas a simple bunch of red feathers on a wire will do so (Lack, 1939). Similarly, many birds show instinctive escape behaviour in response to predatory birds passing overhead. The same escape be-haviour may be elicited by the presentation of models which may have relatively little resemblance to predators but do possess certain specific features of movement and 'shortness of neck' (Tinbergen, 1951). These dominant features are capable of releasing behaviour patterns which are unlearned and unreinforced, i.e. the behaviour is immediately elicited in young birds which have had no experience of predators.

So it appears that young organisms are endowed with instinctive pre-dispositions to behave, or learn to behave, in certain ways, but these behaviours are released only by *appropriate stimuli*. Furthermore, to be fully effective, the stimuli must be presented during certain phases of development or *'critical periods'*. A survey of relevant studies has been made by Scott (1962). In the present context the evidence regarding critical periods for learning is of central importance. Brief mention of a few representative studies may be made here.

It has long been known that some songbirds have to learn their characteristic song from others of the same species. Thorpe (e.g. 1961a) demonstrated the existence of critical periods in the song-learning of the chaffinch. If the fledgling male chaffinch is kept in isolation he can learn to sing only an incomplete song. He seems to be endowed, in fact, with a specific singing pattern, but this lacks certain features which in nature are learned from older birds. Thorpe showed that if the isolated bird is allowed to hear an adult singing when he is 2 or 3 weeks old, before he can himself sing, he will produce, the following spring, the 'full' chaffinch song. In nature again, further refinements are learned during a period of a few weeks at about a year of age when the birds compete over territory.

Hebb (1947) and the Forgays (1952) are among those who have shown that young rats reared in a stimulating environment, in which they have opportunity for exploration and spontaneous learning, perform better on experimental learning tasks than do animals confined to an unfurnished cage. This effect is most observable when the period of differential upbringing has commenced between 20 and 30 days of age.

It seems clear that for the optimal development of social relationships and the acquisition of skills of many types the young organism must experience appropriate stimulus conditions during appropriate phases of its development. These phases, or 'critical periods', vary according to the response or skill concerned, but for each such response the critical period is of a limited duration. Stimulus conditions which are effective when presented within the critical temporal limits may be ineffective if presented outside these limits. Conversely, if the young organism is deprived of the stimulus conditions during the critical period it will fail to develop the appropriate response or do so less effectively.

It will be seen that this concept of 'critical periods' is of crucial relevance to the question of educational 'readiness' which was outlined at the beginning of this section. The question is to what extent it is permissible to generalize from ethological findings to human development and training. What evidence is there of similar findings with human subjects? If 'critical periods' can be demonstrated in human development are they of such precise duration as those found in birds and animals? Do they apply to learning of such disparate skills as, for instance, walking and reading?

It is generally accepted that there are different periods in human infancy when children most readily learn, e.g. to listen, to imitate sounds, to walk and to control their sphincters, the acquisition of these abilities being closely related to maturation of the nervous system. A few observations suggest also (Thorpe, 1961b) that there may be brain mechanisms which, if not properly activated at the appropriate time, cannot be activated subsequently. Thus, children who are prevented, by physical defect or faulty environment, from learning to speak or to read at the usual ages, find it very difficult to learn to do so subsequently and may, in fact, never fully 'catch up'. How far can these observations be applied to the formal *instruction* of children? The most widely cited experimental studies of relevance to educationalists are those of Gesell and Thompson (1929) and McGraw (1935). In each case the co-twin method of study was used, one of a pair of twins being given special training in a number of simple skills prior to the time at which these would normally have been mastered. Thus at the age of 46 weeks, Gesell and Thompson's identical twins were regarded as being about to start climbing and cube building. One twin was now given a daily ten-minute session of intensive training in these activities. Six weeks later the other twin was introduced to training. After two weeks she could perform as well as her sister had done after six weeks. The authors concluded that training could not be shown to speed up the emergence of skills of the types studied. Similarly McGraw exercised one twin, Johnny, in a number of motor activities from the age of 21 days to 22 months, whilst his brother Jimmy was confined to a crib during the experimental sessions but was tested at intervals during the programme. As he grew older Johnny was introduced to, and given practice in additional activities ranging from crawling up a slope to riding a tricycle and roller-skating. Johnny became superior to Jimmy in some activities but not in others. McGraw concluded that the extent to which skills could be improved by practice depended upon their type. Those activities which children must acquire to function normally in our culture – such as sitting up, standing, walking, etc. – were least subject to modification. Those which are not strictly necessary – such as swimming and roller-skating – may be accelerated.

In general, both these well-known studies and others like them seem to offer evidence that training or practice in many basic skills is ineffective if it is introduced prematurely. The child must have reached an appropriate level of development to benefit fully from practice. At that point he will 'take to it naturally' and rapidly catch up with another child who has received more, but premature, training.

One or two sour notes mar the clear harmony of evidence from these studies. Understandably, they have not received the same attention as the outlines given above. Firstly, in both studies the trained twin proved subsequently to be more successful than the control in a variety of motor activities. Gesell and Thompson's trained twin was reported to be more mobile and adventuresome as long as 24 weeks after her control had received her two weeks' training. And McGraw, who followed up her twins over a period of years, found subsequently that Johnny was superior to his brother in motor co-ordination. Secondly, it was later found that McGraw's twins were not, in fact, identical but merely fraternal. Thus the presumption of equivalent maturational development in the boys cannot be maintained and the importance of the study from the present viewpoint is to some extent vitiated. Thirdly, although Johnny was found to be unable to ride a tricycle any earlier than other children, he could roller-skate before he was two. As both these activities come under McGraw's second category (which she termed *ontogenetic* as opposed to *phylogenetic*) her generalizations are not clearly supported in this respect.

A few other studies have tended to confirm the general results of the classic pair. Thus Hilgard (1932), using the method of equivalent groups, showed that a control group of pre-school children, after one week's practice at such skills as cutting with scissors and ladder-climbing, achieved almost the same level as the experimental group who had been given practice during the *twelve* previous weeks. Similar results have been reported by Hicks (1930), Strayer (1930), Hilgard (1933), and Mirenva (1935). Such findings seem to support the maturational standpoint in general and the idea of 'critical periods' in particular.

The work of Mattson (1933) offers some evidence that improvement of unpractised groups is related to the difficulty of the test material. Unpractised children, he claimed, are at a distinct disadvantage on more complex tasks compared with matched children who have received practice. Mattson's tasks were three rolling ball mazes of increasing difficulty. A theoretical problem here, as in many other studies, is that without data on the precise stage in infant development at which specific types of skill are about to be mastered it is difficult to know whether findings are relevant to the maturational controversy. In many studies relative improvement in performance is gauged by differences between initial tests and retests administered days or weeks later. In the interval one group receives training or practice whilst the other does not. To consider any improvement shown by the unpractised group is indicative of *maturation* is unwarranted. The effect could be due to reminiscence, mental practice or other factors. Clearly, all such studies offer important evidence about *learning*. But whether they are all relevant to the consideration of maturation and 'critical periods' is a matter of interpretation.

It must be remembered also that the evidence to date refers only to infants. We do not know to what extent the concept of critical periods can usefully be employed with children of school age. The practical application of the concept to teaching practice must await normative data for every particular skilled activity considered. And it is probably imprudent to draw the flat conclusion that training which is developmentally premature is quite ineffective and to infer from this that it is a waste of time to 'push children along'.

On balance, however, the available findings are reconcilable with the Piagetian view of development proceeding step-wise. The acquisition of skilled behaviour may be seen as contingent upon the level of hierarchical organization already achieved and integrated. In other words, new responses cannot be thought of as though they are intact and self-sufficient *additions*, like beads on a string. Rather must they be considered as the dynamic *productive* expressions of existing schemata. Thus the level of complexity of skill which can be attained depends upon the level of complexity of the schema into which it must be integrated.

VII. TRANSFER OF TRAINING

How far, if at all, can the learning of one activity carry over to performance in another? This question, with its long and classically stormy history is of crucial importance in education. Formal education itself is valued partly because it is assumed that the training received by pupils will carry over or transfer to life outside school, and subsequently to adult living. Central to educational theory for many years was the belief that the mind could be trained, just as the musculature can be strengthened, by practice. Just as the body builder uses particular exercises to strengthen particular muscle groups, so it was (and still is) believed that certain subjects should be taught for their transfer effects on particular 'faculties of the mind'. Thus algebra was thought to be necessary because its study would benefit reasoning, and Homer was learned by heart to improve the faculty of memory. At a somewhat different level the study of Latin and mathematics was regarded as beneficial for 'mental discipline'. The pendulum of intellectual folk belief has now swung in the opposite direction, but like many other folk beliefs the classical view seems to have had at least some validity, although the idea of 'faculties' has long been discredited. There are some tasks in which learning may be speeded up or facilitated by previous training. But there are others in which the new learning may be hindered or modified, and in many no effects whatsoever can be discerned.

The facilitatory effects of previous training or experience may be observed in many everyday situations which we take for granted. Once we have learned to ride a fairy cycle we can readily learn to balance on other two-wheeled vehicles; when we are familiar with one library index system we find it relatively easy to learn to use another; if we know the rules of rugby union we find it easier to understand those of rugby league. These are all examples of *positive transfer*.

On the other hand our very familiarity with one specific activity may inhibit or interfere with our performance on another. This is termed *negative transfer*. It is likely to occur whenever we are called upon to produce a new or changed response to an old stimulus. A dramatic example cited by Underwood (1949) is that of a trans-oceanic Lockheed Constellation which, having landed at Shannon Airport, was about to taxi to the unloading zone. On the pilot's command of 'Flaps up!' the co-pilot automatically pulled a lever on the left side of his seat. The *wheels* retracted and the aircraft dropped seven feet to the runway, being badly damaged. The investigation revealed that the co-pilot's training had been on another type of transport plane, the flap-up lever of which had been in the position of the Constellation's wheels-up lever. The earlier learned response to the old stimulus of the command 'Flaps up!' had displaced the new response of pulling the appropriate lever.

Some learning situations may involve both positive and negative transfer. Thus, while competent lawn tennis players are often equally good at table tennis, such differences between the two games as wrist action may initially hamper the experienced table tennis player who takes up lawn tennis. Similarly the long stroke and follow through practised by the lawn tennis player may cause him difficulty when he takes up squash. Again, the similarity of technique between the violin and viola enables a violinist to become proficient on the viola much more rapidly than if he had started to learn that instrument from scratch. Positive transfer facilitates his learning. But he will experience *more* difficulty than the beginner in learning to read the alto clef in which viola music is written. This represents negative transfer because his familiarity with playing violin music, which is written in the treble clef, puts him in the position of having to execute different responses to what are perceptually the same stimuli. Furthermore the switch involves *interference effects* which do not necessarily involve negative transfer. The viola is larger than the violin so that slightly larger intervals between the fingers are required. In the initial stages of mastering the viola the ex-violinist may find that if his attention wanders, or if he is under stress, his fingering reverts to the old patterns and his intonation flattens. A common example of such interference occurs when one drives a new car with slightly different controls.

As long ago as 1901 Thorndike and Woodworth examined the idea of 'mental discipline' experimentally by training subjects in tasks such as the estimation of areas of geometrical figures, guessing weights and lengths, and cancelling figures. Training did not carry over consistently and sometimes hindered learning in similar activities. Thorndike and Woodworth concluded that training in one activity transfers positively to the performance in another *only* if both activities include *identical elements*. For instance, in a direct examination of the alleged value of studying Latin, Thorndike and Ruger (1923) found that the only relative improvement shown by students of Latin in their use or understanding of English was where English words with Latin roots were concerned. Thorndike's work was valuable in disposing of the cherished doctrines of 'faculties of the mind' and 'mental discipline'. His theory was the first systematic attack on the nature of transfer and it, or modifications of it, can be made to fit many factual findings. Unfortunately it is descriptive rather than explanatory because he never made clear what constituted an 'element'. Basically he defined this in terms of the 'bond' or connexion between stimulus situation and response. But these could involve practically any level of experience, so that 'elements may be words, ideas, methods, materials, attitudes or environmental stimuli. The very inclusiveness of the concept makes the application of the theory to any given learning situation a matter of individual interpretation.

In opposition to the theory of 'identical elements' was that of '*transfer of principles*'. In Judd's (1908) famous experiment a group of boys was taught the principle of refraction of light entering water. They and an uninstructed control group were given practice in throwing darts at a target under twelve inches of water, the performances of the two groups being equally good. The target depth was then reduced to four inches. The control group showed very little transfer; they approached the task in a random trial and error way, as though they were doing it for the first time. But the instructed group adapted quickly by correcting their aim to allow for the changed target conditions.

The crucial weakness of most interpretations of the theory of 'identical elements' has been the assumption that learned behaviour consists of features (responses, stimuli or connexions) which can be considered in isolation. As discussed above, skill is more profitably regarded in terms of *organization*. The 'transfer of principles' approach goes some way towards recognizing this. A principle, after all, is not a stimulus or a response, but a system of organization. Unfortunately, however, some discussions of the topic imply that a principle is itself a sort of element. Ironically enough, evidence for the organizational nature of behaviour was to be found in the very field which had excited the first observations on transfer, that of *bi-lateral transfer*. The ability to carry over performances learned with one hand to the other had been commented upon long before the turn of the last century. Subsequent controlled experiments by Bray (1928) and Cook (1933), who examined performances on mirror tracing, also demonstrated transfer from hands to feet and from feet to hands on the same or opposite sides of the body. As Thorndike had acknowledged, the fact of bilateral transfer indicates that central processes are responsible for the behaviour. But furthermore, is clear that what is important is not the responses themselves, but their interrelationship.

Neglect of the above considerations may well account for the confusion which exists in the literature of transfer. A vast number of investigations have been reported, but interpretation or comparison of their findings is often difficult. Thus Gagné *et al.* (1948), in their survey of relevant studies, found them difficult to compare because of the varying ways used to measure 'amount of transfer'. Similarly, Chambers (1956) prefaces his bibliography with the complaint that exceedingly few studies have dealt with the 'exercise of established skills in new or altered situations. On the contrary, the vast majority of experiments ring the changes on relatively simple stimulus-response situations.' It seems possible that the study of transfer has raised a series of false problems because investigators have tended to regard the skilled performance of different tasks as distinct, unchanging summations of unchanging elements. In other words, in some theorizing, skilled activities have been given the status of separate clusters of habits. As pointed out above, such an assumption misses what seems to be the most important aspect of skilled behaviour – that it is primarily a matter of strategy, response selection, and temporal/spatial organization.

However this may be, what does seem clear is that in practice transfer is most effective and consistent when learning emphasizes the understanding of relationships and concepts rather than the acquisition of discrete responses or items of factual knowledge. This sort of approach, which is now often referred to as '*learning to learn*', has long appealed to many educationalists, whilst experimental evidence for its effectiveness in the classroom has been provided by several well-known studies. For instance, in a study of arithmetic learning, Swenson (1942) found that an emphasis on the interrelations of facts led to better results than intensive drill on the actual arithmetic task. The same sort of differential teaching was used by Katona (1940) in a study of transfer in problem-solving, which stressed 'meaningful' as opposed to 'senseless' learning. Between the initial and final tests (which utilized the same principles) one group of students was told to memorize the solutions to the original problems and was given repeated practice. Another group was instructed in the principles involved. This latter group subsequently showed considerably more transfer than both the 'memorization' group and a control group.

'Learning to learn' involves insight into methods or modes of attack. Munn (1932) gave children practice in a game of catching a ball in a wooden cup from which it was suspended by a string. These children then performed better with their other hands than did unpractised children. The transfer seemed to be due to the children's working out of techniques, such as watching the ball rather than the cup. In other studies subjects have been instructed in the necessary techniques. Woodrow (1927) found that a group of students given special training in effective methods of memorizing, subsequently showed greater improvement in tests of memory than both an unpractised control group and one which had engaged in undirected memorizing. Indeed, explicit instruction in methods of attack, or the calling of attention to significant features in the task seems to produce high positive transfer. Bartlett (1951) considers that:

> 'The most fundamental thing about transfer is that if it is desired it must, as rule, be sought and prepared for in the style of instruction or teaching. So long as the emphasis is upon the particular material or problem that is to be studied the scales are weighted against any positive transfer.'
>
> (Bartlett, 1951, p. 118.)

By now the reader may have an uneasy feeling that the wheel has come round full circle. He might be forgiven if he expressed some dubiety as to whether some of the studies referred to above should properly come under the heading of 'transfer of training' or under one of 'teaching methods' or merely 'learning'.

VIII. KNOWLEDGE OF RESULTS

Common sense suggests that attempts to practise a skill without information as to the efficiency of one's actions is unlikely to be effective. A person learning to play darts, for instance, tries to modify his throwing in the light of the result of his last attempt. In this example the task itself provides the learner with knowledge of results. In other situations, such as mastering of the correct style of making a tennis stroke or a swimming action, he is dependent upon extrinsic information such as that provided by a coach. Again, the 'feedback' may be provided by reference to the end result of the activity or in the course of the activity itself. Strictly speaking only the first is 'knowledge of results'. The second is often termed 'knowledge of performance'.

Miller (1953) distinguished between 'learning feedback' and 'action feedback'. The first of these corresponds to activities like dart-playing and to the design used in many learning experiments, where the subject is given information about what he has just achieved. This enables him to modify his subsequent responses. Action feedback is contained in cues received by the subject as he is actually engaging in his task. During serial activity he is thus enabled to correct his current responses. It has been shown that the type of feedback can modify the subject's learning. (Learning feedback is believed to lead to a slower increase in skill than action feedback, but to a slower fall off in performance after the removal of feedback). In practice many instances of overlap may be observed. For example, the amateur violinist tunes his 'A' string by adjusting it until it is in tune with a concert pitch standard such as a tuning fork or the note played by his teacher. After each adjustment he compares his note with the criterion and his teacher may make some such comment as 'You're a little sharp'. Thus he receives learning feedback. With advancing listening skill and confidence he may acquire the ability to 'carry the A in his head' and adjust his instrument to concert pitch without the necessity of an external auditory criterion. Tuning in this way may be regarded as utilizing action feedback. But an intervening level of ability (and one at which the majority of musicians remain) is that where he bows the string continuously whilst adjusting the tuning peg until the note produced coincides with the criterion. Here both forms of feedback may well be operating. But in any case the use of action feedback in this situation is usually preceded by a period where learning feedback is necessary.

Knapp (1963) has pointed out that whilst action feedback may make for better performance on any given trial it may prove detrimental to the long-term development of style. In many sports the learner's adjustments or improvisations in response to such feedback may gradually build up an unsatisfactory pattern of movement. For instance, a last second wrist adjustment when serving in tennis may be necessary as an emergency measure. It may succeed in keeping the ball in the court, whilst being in general an inelegant and inefficient movement. The danger is that its effectivity on the first occasion may reinforce its subsequent use so that it becomes a habit.

It seems possible, then, that 'knowledge of results' or learning feedback is of more relevance and effect during the acquisition of skill, whilst 'knowledge of performance' or action feedback determines the actual performance when a working level of skill has been achieved.

Psychologists have gained some insights by depriving subjects of feedback information. The dart-player who is artificially prevented from seeing where his darts strike may well improve the *consistency* of his throwing. But without information regarding his scores he will not be able to improve his *aim*. Indeed, in some respects it is possible that his ability will deteriorate.

It has been reported (Lindsley, 1943) that radar operators who were not given information as to their progress became less and less accurate in successive practice trials. There is laboratory evidence, too, that improvement is closely related to the degree of precision of the information. The classical demonstration of this principle is that of Thorndike (1927). Two groups of blindfolded subjects were instructed to draw lines of 3, 4, 5 or 6 inches in length during a series of trials. One group were given knowledge of results, being told simply 'right' or 'wrong' according to whether or not each of their attempts was correct to within a quarter of an inch. The performance of this group showed considerable improvement in accuracy. The second group, on the other hand, were allowed no knowledge of results. After several days of practice they were drawing less accurately than they had at the beginning.

Trowbridge and Cason (1932) repeated Thorndike's experiment, using different sorts of information. Their results confirmed those of Thorndike, but it was also shown that subjects who were told the exact extent and direction of each error improved much more than those who were merely informed whether the line drawn was 'right' or 'wrong'.

To be most effective, knowledge of results needs not only to be precise but to be accessible as soon as possible after the practice activity. Ammons (1956), after surveying relevant studies formulated the following generalizations:

(*a*) The more specific the knowledge of performance, the more rapid the improvement and the higher level of performance.

(*b*) The longer the delay in giving knowledge of performance, the less effective is the given information.

Knowledge of results has been discussed above in terms of its informational importance for the learner. Without information as to which of his responses are incorrect the learner is unable to determine and 'stamp in' an effective response pattern. When informed which of his responses are incorrect he can speed up his task of finding effective responses, and then concentrate on producing them consistently. But knowledge of results also seems to improve performance in quite a different way by acting as a motivator. Thus, stars, 'mark ladders', and achievement graphs in the classroom are employed by teachers because of their known efficiency as incentives rather than for purely informational purposes. This aspect of knowledge of results as an inducer of competitiveness has not been ignored in experimental studies. Thorndike regarded his 'rights' and 'wrongs' as rewards and punishments rather than as information-givers. Arps (1917) required his subjects to repeatedly lift weights with one finger, a task which demands no extrinsic information. The subjects' persistence in this tiring and unrewarding activity was maintained by allowing them to see a continuous performance graph. A neat example of the de-motivating effect of the removal of feedback was provided by MacPherson, Dees and Grindley (1948). They found that subjects' performance on line-drawing deteriorated as soon as they were told that no knowledge of results would be provided during the next series of trials. The deterioration occurred *before feedback was withheld*.

It is possible that similar affective factors are partially responsible for the phenomenon of 'signal redundancy' in aircraft control. Several investigators such as Fritz and Grier (1954) have examined the information transmitted between pilots and control towers during aircraft take-off and landing. Such complex operations demand meticulous attention to informational feedback. Yet investigators have discovered that surprising amounts of apparently redundant signals are passed, and pilots are reported to welcome these and to feel uneasy if deprived of them. Annett and Kay (1957) interpret the redundant information as providing a 'safety margin'. But it seems equally valid to regard such redundancy as reflecting the pilots' need for personal contact and reassurance.

On the other hand, a not implausible case can be made for the interpretation of studies concerned with *incentives* in terms of knowledge of results. The classical experiment on praise and reproof was Hurlock's

(1925) study of arithmetic learning. She selected four groups of 9 and 11-year-old schoolchildren carefully matched for ability in arithmetic. The members of the first group were consistently praised before the class for their work, the members of the second criticized harshly, whilst the work of the third group was not commented upon. The fourth was a control group which was isolated in a different classroom. Changes in performance were dramatic. The praised and reproved groups both showed improvement immediately of 35 per cent to 40 per cent, twice as much as the ignored group. During the five-day experiment both the reproved and ignored groups slowed down, but the praised group continued up to a 79 per cent improvement. The isolated group showed no improvement throughout. Hurlock concluded that over a short period praise and reproof are equally effective as motivators, but that reproof becomes less effective as time goes on. Such a 'motivational' finding may be considered also from the 'information' standpoint. Praise following a correct response or result (answer, method, etc.) generally contains more information about that result than does reproof following an incorrect one. For in most performances there is only one 'right' outcome, but many possible wrong ones. The statement 'correct' identifies one strategy, that being the one desired. The statement 'wrong' (or 'You should be ashamed of yourself', etc.) identifies a strategy also, but only slightly raises the probability of identification of the one desired. Some such account would fit with Hurlock's data, but it is possible that 'reproof' which detailed the nature of each error would be more effective than the general criticism used by Hurlock. (Clearly, the learner's reactions would depend a great deal on his personality, his previous experiences and his relationship with the teacher. In fact, as Schmidt, 1941, has shown, the personality of the incentive-giver is far more important than the incentive itself). The interaction between 'knowledge of results' and 'motivation' has not yet been fully examined. But at least it can be said that in the acquiring of skill one often acts in the same way as the other.

IX. THE TEMPORAL ORGANIZATION OF LEARNING

Practice seems to be essential for the acquisition of skill, but practice as such does *not* necessarily make perfect. Firstly, if the general strategy is wrong, practice of tactical components will not improve overall performance. Secondly, inappropriate practice will obviously not lead to the desired ends. Thirdly, too much or ill-rewarded practice may defeat its own ends by de-motivating the learner. And fourthly, the effect of practice seems to be related to its deployment over time. This last consideration will be the main topic of this section.

1. *Learning curves and 'plateaux'*

Early psychologists devoted a great deal of energy to the production of learning curves for various activities. A learning curve is derived by plotting the serial performances of subjects as practice continues. Measures used may be scores, times or decreases in error. As might be expected, such graphs typically show increments of improvement which gradually taper off as an upper limit of achievement is reached. However, such a curve is seldom smooth in the way they were at one time reported. Regular, smooth curves are usually only found when the average scores of numbers of subjects are plotted. An individual's progress is much more jerky, because it is affected by all sorts of personal factors. The shape of the curve will also vary with the nature of the task. Thus, despite early hopes, it is not possible to draw any general conclusions or make precise predictions about the learning curve derivable from any given individual's progress.

The development of skill, especially in complex activities which are mastered over a long period, is sometimes marked by periods where no improvement seems to take place. The learning curve will show a temporary flattening-out, followed by another spurt of improvement in performance. Such 'plateaux' were first reported by Bryan and Harter (1897) in their study of learning the Morse code. Bryan and Harter suggested that a 'plateau' occurred when the learner had mastered various lower-order skills and now had to integrate them into higher-order skills. Thus, their subjects learned to receive individual letters with steady progress. A 'plateau' occurred when they had to receive letters combined in words. Book (1925) in his study of learning to typewrite, noted failures of improvement at the stage between letter habits and word habits. But he ascribed this to failures in attention and motivation due to discouragement. Bryan and Harter's study has been criticized, but their view of the hierarchical nature of skilled behaviour has considerable merit and accords well with much everyday experience.

2. *The distribution of practice*

If seven hours are available for learning some activity, is it better to spend the time in one concentrated session or to spend one hour a day for a week? This question of 'massed' versus 'spaced' or 'distributed' practice has been intensively studied for many years. The weight of evidence has been in favour of the distributed practice method, but the question is not such a simple one as it might appear. Many variables are involved, including the actual lengths of practice session and inter-trial intervals (to which the present account will be limited), the nature and complexity of the task, varieties of inter-practice activity and individual learner differences in motivation and fatigue.

A much-quoted experiment by Lorge (1930) provides a neat illustration of the basic phenomena to be considered. Lorge studied the effects of practice on performance in code substitution, mirror-reading and mirror-drawing. Each of his three groups of subjects was allowed to practise for twenty trials. But the first group were encouraged to use their allocation of trials in continuous (i.e. 'massed') practice. The second group received a 'rest period' of one minute between each trial, whilst the third group received rest periods of one day. The improvement shown by both the distributed practice groups was consistently greater over the series than that of the massed practice group. The results are representative of the majority of findings concerned with the learning of simple tasks, or, as in this case, ones of moderate difficulty. But the feature of Lorge's experiment which has most interested investigators is that there was very little difference between the results of the two distributed practice groups. Rest periods (or 'inter-trial intervals') of a minute were almost as effective as ones lasting a day. Several experimenters have subsequently examined the relative effectiveness of different *lengths of rest period*.

Kientzle (1946) examined the improvement of her subjects in printing the alphabet upside down. She held the practice periods constant at one minute's duration but varied the groups' rest periods from 0 to 90 seconds (in 15 second steps) with one group receiving an interval of seven days. Her results showed that there was a considerable increase in the effect of short intervals over no rest at all, but that this levelled off at about 45 seconds. Beyond this length of interval little seemed to be achieved by lengthening the rest period. Oddly enough the improvement shown by the seven-day interval group was not significantly less than that of the one-minute interval group. Other studies have supported the suggestion that improvements in learning related to distributed practice is a negatively accelerated function of the duration of the rest period. But the levelling-off point, which may be taken as indicating the most economical length of interval, varies according to the task employed and the conditions of practice.

There is some evidence that the *length of the practice period* is more crucial than the length of the rest period. As has been seen, the most important point about distribution of practice is that any spacing is better than no spacing at all. If the duration of the rest interval is increased after the levelling-off point no advantage will be gained. But almost any change in the duration of the practice or work period seems to modify the rate of learning. Thus Travis (1939) found that in using the manual pursuit oscillator 2-minute practice sessions were more effective than 4-minute sessions. For his subjects much of the practice in each 4-minute session was a 'waste of time and actually deleterious to learning of this type'.

So far as the evidence goes, it would seem that, for rote learning and motor skills, distributed practice using a combination of short practice periods and short rest intervals is most effective in the facilitation of learning. But whether this applies to complex mental activities is not known. Indeed, the work of Riley (1952) suggests that distributed practice itself is not so clearly effective where verbal learning is concerned.

Why should massed practice be inferior to distributed practice? First of all, fatigue and boredom limit the amount of time which may usefully be spent in practice at any one session. If boredom or frustration sets in, prolongation of practice may indeed have negative effects, as Travis suggested. The good teacher avoids this by introducing different activities or modes of attack during each teaching period. The good lecturer who, conventionally, has to demand his students' uninterrupted attention for anything up to an hour, will at least change the pace and rhythm of his discourse. Awareness of feedback from his audience enables him to 'distribute' his attack by the introduction of, e.g. lively illustrations or teaching aids. Secondly, the intervals between trials in distributed practice have a positive effect, inasmuch as some sort of learning goes on. The 'rest period', in fact, is not merely a respite from work, as many investigators seem to have presumed. On the contrary, it allows for continued rehearsal in the form of *'mental practice'*. At the same time it may also allow for the 'forgetting' of negative features of the previous practice session. Of the several types of theory proposed to account for the superiority of distributed practice (see, e.g. McGeoch and Irion, 1952) that which is currently most popular among psychologists stresses this last point. Theories of this type are based on the concept of differential *'extinction'*. For instance, Underwood (1961) concludes that distributed practice allows for 'successive extinctions of error tendencies' which build up during actual performance, because of 'interference occurring in the response-learning phase'. He assumes that during massed practice error tendencies are suppressed rather than extinguished. The same sort of argument can be expressed in a different way by approaching the whole matter in terms of the establishment of schemata instead of in terms of discrete responses, errors and error tendencies. As argued above, skill is to be seen as the organization and interrelationships of responses. The provision of rest intervals allows for the consolidation of the modification to the schema. Interference occurring during practice sessions will hamper performance but will not necessarily hinder the development of the schema itself. The danger is that gross interference or faulty assumptions about the task requirements may mask what should be learned. The learner may then evolve an inappropriate strategy and develop the 'wrong' schema.

So far, this account has considered only the results of short-term experiments. Of more importance for 'real life' skill learning is what happens over a long period. If, for instance, any of the investigators referred to above had tested their subjects a fortnight or six months later, would the differences between group performances still be apparent? In fact, had they simply carried on their experiments over longer periods would the differences between group learning rates have been maintained? A large number of studies have attacked these problems in recent years (see Bilodeau and Bilodeau, 1961) and it is difficult as yet to assess and reconcile the new evidence. However, it does seem clear that differences produced by distributed or massed practice tend to decrease or disappear with the passage of time. This is due to relative improvement on subsequent sessions by subjects who have had massed practice. Such improvement is an example of the phenomenon known as '*reminiscence*'.

Reminiscence, in its technical sense, is defined as an increment in the performance of a partially learned activity after a period without practice. Thus, under certain conditions, subjects who have had a rest recommence practice at a higher level of performance than that which they had attained at the end of the previous session. The phenomenon was first observed in studies of rote verbal learning but has since been reported in many experiments concerned with psychomotor skill. Its significance for the present topic is that it occurs more after massed practice. When massed and distributed practice groups are re-tested, the massed group may show a distinct initial improvement over its previous final level. The distributed practice group, on the other hand, will typically show some decrement at first. Its subjects have forgotten a little during the inter-session interval and need to 'warm up' before they can 'get back into their strides'. During the rest of the session they will again show better rates of learning than the massed practice subjects, whose performance may even decline slightly during the session. But over protracted series of sessions the distributed practice group's rate of learning will eventually flatten out so that the difference between the learning curves of the two groups disappears.

What is not known is how far these findings apply to tasks of different complexities. It seems possible that in skilled tasks of great complexity, the establishment of schemata occurs over such a long period of time that the actual allocation of practice within that period assumes less significance. Given that it takes several years to learn to play the bassoon, the question of massed or distributed practice in terms of minutes can scarcely be of crucial importance. On the other hand, most instructors would insist on daily practice rather than weekly, whilst if total practice time is to be held constant sessions of massed practice are exhausting. Even the reluctant bassoon learner can manage half an hour per day, whereas three and a half hours on a Sunday would prove intolerable. But this may not apply in other tasks. The student attempting to master 'games theory' or matrix algebra may arrive at points where it is wiser to keep going 'until the penny drops'. At such a stage a rest interval might be quite frustrating. In such instances progress seems to be related to problem-solving and the experience of insight. These themselves are dependent upon a pre-existing schema and the strategies the learner has at his command.

Such questions as that posed at the beginning of this section are not, in fact, ones to which a general answer is possible. The optimal lengths of practice sessions and inter-practice intervals will depend upon the task in question, the individual learner and his stage in the acquisition of skill.

3. *'Whole' versus 'part' learning*

In the development of skill, is it more effective to tackle the activity as a whole or to break it down into smaller units which can be learned individually? For instance, should the budding batsman be shown the footwork for each type of stroke and perfect that before going on first to shoulder and then to wrist action? Or should he be encouraged to acquire the complex interrelated actions simultaneously as he will subsequently use them in striking the ball? Should the swimmer learn the component actions of a given stroke by land drill? Or, having watched demonstrations, should he be required to carry out the whole stroke from the start, whilst actually in the water? A highly relevant example in a field crucial to basic education is that of infant reading methods which have aroused wide interest and heated debate for many years. The weight of opinion has swung from 'whole' to 'part' to 'whole' and to 'part' again. In the seventeenth century Comenius introduced a 'whole' method using words and pictures. In the latter half of the nineteenth century 'part' methods – the alphabetic and phonetic – became highly developed. In reaction against some aspects of the phonetic method – the artificiality of some primers, the drudgery of the drill, and the dubiety of this approach to such an irregular language as English, the 'whole' approach gained in favour in the form of 'look and say' methods. Currently the tide has changed again and various mixed phonetic methods are in favour.

A more esoteric but equally heated controversy was that of 'Orthodox' versus 'Fairbairnism' in the training of oarsmen. The 'orthodox' method is a classical example of 'part' learning, the rules of instruction being laid down by the famous Eton coach R. S. de Havilland at the turn of the century. Conventionally the budding oarsman starts his training in a 'tub' which is fixed to the river bank. He learns, one by one, the series of movements which constitute rowing action. Then he is taught to carry these out in series by numbers on the command of his coach, pausing between each movement. Subsequently his serial movements are speeded up. Only then is he allowed to train in a racing four or eight where the whole crew carry out training programmes which again, in the initial stages, involve 'actions by numbers'. In 1904 Steve Fairbairn, an Australian, rocked the rowing world's boat by introducing a revolutionary 'whole' procedure. In his view rowing action could not be broken down into separate movements. The oarsman learned by building up the strength of his back and legs and then getting into the boat and making it move. 'I get him to concentrate his attention on his blade and leave Nature to work his body in unconscious response.' The criterion of whether the individual oarsman's style was effective was the 'bell-note' produced by the blade 'taking' the water at the most effective angle. Orthodox coaches were aghast at this slipshod approach. But Fairbairn crews reached the head of the river at Cambridge and won the Grand Challenge Cup at Henley.

In many skills, of course, some forms of groundwork are clearly beneficial. For instance, the stronger the tennis player's wrists before he actually starts to play, the more readily can he acquire the skills required. But appropriate wrist exercises constitute *prelearning* – in this case the development of physical attributes which will facilitate optimal performance when learning has actually commenced. Similarly the infant's subsequent attainment of reading can be facilitated by 'pre-reading' activities including oral work and shape discrimination. Pre-learning activities are generally very valuable; but they are not of direct relevance to the question we are trying to answer here, which refers to the learning process itself.

In brief the proponents of the 'part' approach would say that it is safer and ultimately more efficient to 'learn one thing at a time' and learn it well. The subsequent learning of further 'things' is then cumulative; building is continued upon a sure foundation. Meanwhile, the learner's interest is maintained because each 'part' or unit is individually easier to master than the whole. This approach has long been reflected in educational practice. The opposing viewpoint is that this is a 'piecemeal' approach which stresses routine efficiency at the expense of an integration of knowledge and skill and which is apt to mar the final objective of the training by a blind insistence upon 'method'. On this argument it is far better to take a 'global' view of learning, to tackle the new skill as far as possible by encouraging the pupil to engage in the activity itself rather than in artificially-determined 'parts' of the whole. This enables the pupil to see the point of what he is doing, gives him quick success, even if at a low level of achievement, and thus maintains his interest. To this the 'parts' adherents may reply by claiming that the quickness is artificial and the success illusory. Such an approach, it may be claimed, is inefficient because it enables the pupil to acquire bad habits. In the long run more time may be spent on attempting to eradicate these than would have been required to teach each part effectively in the first place. Thus the tennis player who is trained on a global approach may indeed achieve some initial satisfaction but at the expense of acquiring a poor style. By inventing, of necessity, some idiosyncratic strokes in the early stages he is precluded from attaining any higher level of ability. Similarly the 'sentence method' reader may show apparently quicker results than the child who is subjected to a conventional phonic approach. But his spelling may subsequently be atrocious and his ability to handle new words haphazard.

The trouble with this controversy is that the examples are seldom as clear-cut or as relevant as some disputants believe. Few teachers have ever used a 'pure' phonic method or a 'pure' sentence method. Few rowing coaches, apart from Fairbairn himself, have ever relied solely upon his method, whilst 'orthodox' coaches have often paid little more than lip-service to the classical drill. Furthermore, as far as our present interest is concerned the general argument merely confuses the issue. Examples cited involve activities at different levels of complexity or ones which would not generally be regarded as skilled at all. At one time, possibly as a reaction against over-formal 'drill' methods of instruction, experimental evidence was interpreted as giving support to the 'whole' approach. But the reported results of controlled laboratory experimentation are open to various interpretations. This confusion is probably due to the equation of results of rote-learning experiments, which are concerned with the amount of material recalled after a given period, with those from experiments in skill training. Here the only recall required of the subject is that of a few simple instructions, and his task is to improve his speed and/or accuracy in a series of perceptual-motor responses. It may be premature to assume that the same processes are involved in motor and symbolic learning.

In some cases experimenters have been crude in their division of tasks into 'parts' or 'wholes' in merely temporal and spatial terms, regardless of psychological variables. As Annett and Kay (1956) pointed out – 'the very obviousness of the nomenclature has been its undoing since in most experiments on part-whole learning the independent variable has never been adequately defined'. To take an absurd instance – it would be foolish to examine improvement in performance of the high jump by comparing subjects practising the whole with subjects practising 'parts' which consisted of each yard of the run-up distance. There have, however, been a few reasoned analyses of this problem. Seymour (1954) examined part-whole training in the operation of a capstan lathe and found that where the task cycles contained some hard and some easy elements it was more economical to learn the hard ones separately. No difference between the methods was found for speed of acquisition of a 'simple' task where movement predominated and where perceptual requirements were limited. Where a higher level of perceptual discrimination and coordination was demanded, the part method proved to be superior because it enabled greater attention to be concentrated on the difficult elements. In the whole method, practice of the difficult perceptual elements involves wasting time on the simple elements which have already been mastered. This coincides with everyday observation and practice. The teacher will draw his pupil's attention to his weaknesses and ensure that relatively more time is spent on correcting these. Seymour concluded that the outcome of his experiment was not that part methods of training are more effective than whole methods but 'rather that the terms "part" and "whole" are misleading and inadequate in these discussions'.

Like many other questions in psychology, it would appear that the 'whole versus part' controversy has suffered from over-simplification and over-generalization. We know now that the answer is again of the 'it all depends' variety.

X. SUMMARY

From the psychological viewpoint 'skill' is characterized by the relatively complex organization of receptor-effector processes. It is the nature of this *organization* – both temporal and spatial – which currently stimulates research and speculation, rather than the component responses themselves. In skilled behaviour an effective response is not a discrete event, nor is it merely a reflex or habit. It reflects the active relating of new signals to the dynamically organized mass of previous experiences to which Bartlett applied the term 'schema'. The relevance of this approach to developmental psychology is clear. It receives vivid support from the work of Piaget and is reconcilable with ethological observations.

Skill is now being examined in terms of the development of strategies which direct the selection and integration of tactical procedures. On the effector side this selection involves not only facilitation but inhibition of some of the responses available to the individual. It also presupposes the matching of on-going activity with strategic criteria, and the functioning of 'feedback' in the identification and correction of discrepancies. On the receptor side the process is presumed to include selective attention, coding, storage and the organization of perceptual criterion 'patterns' drawn from a repertoire acquired throughout life. Research has been stimulated and findings placed more clearly in theoretical frameworks by the use of models drawn from the fields of engineering and cybernetics. Concepts which have proved fruitful include those of negative feed-back, information-processing, filtering systems and communication channels.

Skilled performance is the outcome of hierarchical interactions and may be considered at a number of levels, according to the complexity of the task in question and its degree of 'openness'. Thus, car-driving might be studied at the level of tactical procedures; for instance, the accuracy, timing and co-ordination of the movements involved in changing gear. At a more strategic level, the integration of such procedures might be considered; for instance, the combination of cue-assessment, changing to a lower gear, positioning and signalling involved in turning off a main road. At a yet higher level, performance over a protracted period under widely varying stimulus conditions might be examined in terms of the selection, modification and integration of procedure patterns. Not all such levels have yet been examined experimentally, whilst it is often difficult to determine the level to which findings bear most relevance. The literature is further confused by references to the results from studies of rote-learning, by terminological differences and by the relative absence of studies of the acquisition of skill over long periods. Furthermore, there has been a conventional tendency for studies of skill to be more concerned with what has been learned than with learning itself. Nevertheless, skill research has demonstrated that complex activity is amenable to experimental analysis, whilst its emphasis upon organization may prove crucial for developments in other fields of psychological study.

REFERENCES

AMMONS, R. B. (1956). Effects of knowledge of performance: a survey and tentative theoretical formulation. *J. gen. Psychol.* **54**, 279–299.

ANNETT, J., and KAY, H. (1956). Skilled performance. *Occup. Psychol.* **30**, 112–117.

ANNETT, J., and KAY, H. (1957). Knowledge of results and 'skilled performance'. *Occup. Psychol.* **31**, 69–79.

ARPS, G. F. (1917). A preliminary report on work with knowledge versus work without knowledge of results. *Psychol. Rev.* **24**, 449–455.

BARTLETT, F. C. (1932). *Remembering.* Cambridge: C.U.P.

BARTLETT, F. C. (1947). The measurement of human skill. *Brit. med. J.* No. 4510, 835–838 and No. 4511, 777–880.

BARTLETT, F. C. (1951). *The mind at Work and Play.* London: George Allen and Unwin.

BARTLETT, F. C. (1958). *Thinking.* London: George Allen and Unwin.

BELBIN, E. (1958). Methods of training older workers. *Ergonomics.* **1**, 207–221.

BILODEAU, E. A., and BILODEAU, I. McD. (1961). Motor-skills learning. *Ann. Rev. Psychol.* **12**, 243–280.

BOOK, W. F. (1925). *Learning to Typewrite.* New York: Gregg.

BRAY, C. W. (1928). Transfer of learning. *J. exp. Psychol.* **11,** 443–467.

BROADBENT, D. E. (1958). *Perception and Communication.* Oxford: Pergamon.

BRYAN, W. L., and HARTER, N. (1897). Studies in the physiology and psychology of the telegraphic language. *Psychol. Rev.* **4,** 27–53.

BURNETT, I., and PEAR, T. H. (1925). Motives in acquiring skill. *Brit. J. Psychol.* **16,** 77–85.

CHAMBERS, E. G. (1956). Transfer of training: a practical problem. *Occup. Psychol.* **30,** 165–168.

COOK, T. W. (1933). Studies in cross education: I. Mirror tracing the star-shaped maze. *J. exp. Psychol.* **16,** 144–160.

CRAIK, K. J. W. (1947). Theory of the human operator in control systems: I. The operator as an engineering system. *Brit. J. Psychol.* **38,** 56–61.

CRAIK, K. J. W. (1948). Theory of the human operator in control systems: II. Man as an element in a control system. *Brit. J. Psychol.* **38,** 142–148.

CROSSMAN, E. R. F. W. (1964). Information processes in human skill. In Summerfield, A. (ed.), Experimental Psychology. *Brit. Med. Bull.* **20,** No. 1.

FAIRBAIRN, S. (1951). *Steve Fairbairn on Rowing.* Fairbairn, I. (ed.). London: Nicholas Kaye.

FITTS, P. M. (1964). Perceptual-motor skill learning. In Melton, A. W. (ed.), *Categories of Human Learning.* New York: Academic Press.

FORGAYS, D. G., and FORGAYS, J. W. (1952). The nature of the effect of free-environmental experience in the rat. *J. comp. physiol. Psychol.* **45,** 322–328.

FRITZ, E. L., and GRIER, C. W. Jr. (1954). Pragmatic communication. In Quastler, H. *Information Theory in Psychology,* Glencoe, Illinois: The Free Press.

FUCHS, A. H. (1962). The progression-regression hypotheses in perceptual-motor skill learning. *J. exp. Psychol.* **63,** 177–182.

GAGNÉ, R. M., FOSTER, H., and CRAWLEY, M. E. (1948). The measurement of transfer of training. *Psychol. Bull.* **45,** 97–130.

GESELL, A., and THOMPSON, H. (1929). Learning and growth in identical infant twins. *Genet. Psychol. Monogr.* **6,** 1–124.

GUTHRIE, E. R. (1954). *The Psychology of Learning* (Rev. Ed.). New York: Harper.

HEBB, D. O. (1947). The effects of early experience on problem-solving at maturity. *Amer. Psychologist.* **2**, 306–307.

HICKS, J. A. (1930). The acquisition of motor skill in young children. *Child Developm.* **1**, 90–105.

HILGARD, J. R. (1932). Learning and maturation in preschool children. *J. Genet. Psychol.* **41**, 36–56.

HILGARD, J. R. (1933). The effect of early and delayed practice on memory and motor performances studied by the method of co-twin control. *Genet. Psychol. Monogr.* **14**, 493–567.

HOLDING, D. H. (1965). *Principles of Training.* Oxford: Pergamon.

HURLOCK, E. B. (1925). An evaluation of certain incentives used in school work. *J. educ. Psychol.* **16**, 145–159.

IRION, A. L. (1966). A brief history of research on the acquisition of skill. In Bilodeau, E. A. (ed.), *Acquisition of Skill.* New York: Academic Press.

JUDD, C. H. (1908). The relation of special training to general intelligence. *Educ. Rev.* **36**, 28–42.

KATONA, G. (1940). *Organizing and Memorizing.* New York: Columbia University Press.

KAY, H. (1957). Information theory and the understanding of skills. *Occup. Psychol.* **31**, 218–224.

KIENTZLE, M. J. (1946). Properties of learning curves under varied distribution of practice. *J. exp. Psychol.* **36**, 187–211.

KNAPP, B. (1963). *Skill in Sport.* London: Routledge and Kegan Paul.

LACK, D. (1939). The behaviour of the robin: I and II. *Proc. Zool. Soc. Lond. A.* **109**, 169–178.

LINDSLEY, D. B. (1943). Cited by Wolfle, D. (1951). Training. Chap. 34 in Stevens, S. S. (ed.), *Handbook of Experimental Psychology.* New York: John Wiley & Sons.

LORGE, I. (1930). The influence of regularly interpolated time intervals upon subsequent learning. *Teach. Coll. Contr. Educ.* No. 438.

MCGEOCH, J. A., and IRION, A. L. (1952). *The Psychology of Human Learning.* New York: Longmans, Green & Co.

MCGRAW, M. B. (1935). *Growth: A Study of Johnny and Jimmy.* New York: Appleton Century.

MACPHERSON, S. J., DEES, V., and GRINDLEY, G. C. (1948). The effect of knowledge of results on performance: II Some characteristics of very simple skills. *Quart. J. exp. Psychol.* **1**, 68–78.

MATTSON, M. L. (1933). The relation between the complexity of the

F

habit to be acquired and the form of the learning curve in young children. *Genet. Psychol. Monogr.* **13**, 299–398.

MILLER, G. A., GALANTER, E., and PRIBRAM, K. H. (1960). *Plans and the Structure of Behaviour.* New York: Henry Holt.

MILLER, R. B. (1953). *Handbook on Training and Training Equipment Design.* Wright Air Development Center. Tech. Rep. 53–136. Dayton, Ohio: U.S.A.F.

MIRENVA, A. N. (1935). Psychomotor education and the general development of preschool children. Experiments with twin controls. *J. Genet. Psychol.* **46**, 433–454.

MUNN, N. L. (1932). Bilateral transfer of learning. *J. exp. Psychol.* **15**, 343–353.

OLDFIELD, R. S. (1959). The analysis of human skill. In Halmos, P., and Iliffe, A. (eds.), *Readings in General Psychology.* London: Routledge and Kegan Paul.

POULTON, E. C. (1957). On prediction in skilled movements. *Psychol. Bull.* **54**, 467–478.

RILEY, D. A. (1952). Rote learning as a function of distribution of practice and the complexity of the situation. *J. exp. Psychol.* **43**, 88–95.

SCHMIDT, H. O. (1941). The effects of praise and blame as incentives to learning. *Psychol. Monogr.* **53**, No. 240.

SCOTT, J. P. (1962). Critical periods in behavioural development. *Science.* **138**, 949–958.

SEYMOUR, W. D. (1954). Experiments on the acquisition of industrial skills. *Occup. Psychol.* **28**, 77–89.

SLUCKIN. W. (1954). *Minds and Machines.* (Rev. Ed. 1960). Harmondsworth: Penguin.

STRAYER, L. C. (1930). Language and growth: The relative efficacy of early and deferred vocabulary training, studied by the method of co-twin control. *Genet. Psychol. Monogr.* **8**, 215–317.

SWENSON, E. J. (1942). Generalization and organisation as factors in transfer and retroactive inhibition. *Proc. Indiana Acad. Sci.* **51**, 248–255.

THORNDIKE, E. L. (1927). The law of effect. *Amer. J. Psychol.* **39**, 212–222.

THORNDIKE, E. L., and WOODWORTH, R. S. (1901). The influence of improvement in one mental function upon the efficiency of other functions, I, II and III. *Psychol. Rev.* **8**, 247–261, 384–395, 553–564.

THORNDIKE, E. L., and RUGER, G. J. (1923). The effect of first-year Latin upon knowledge of English words of Latin derivation. *Sch. and Soc.* **18**, 260–270.

THORPE, W. H. (1961) (a). *Bird-Song.* Cambridge: C.U.P.

THORPE, W. H. (1961) (b). Sensitive periods in the learning of animals and men: a study of imprinting with special reference to the induction of cyclic behaviour. In Thorpe, W. H., and Zangwill, O. L. (eds.), *Current Problems in Animal Behaviour.* Cambridge: C.U.P.

TINBERGEN, N. (1951). *The Study of Instinct.* Oxford: O.U.P.

TRAVIS, R. C. (1939). Length of practice period and efficiency in motor learning. *J. exp. Psychol.* **24,** 339–345.

TROWBRIDGE, M. A., and CASON, H. (1932). An experimental study of Thorndike's theory of learning. *J. gen. Psychol.* **7,** 245–260.

UNDERWOOD, B. J. (1949). *Experimental Psychology.* New York: Appleton-Century-Crofts.

UNDERWOOD, B. J. (1961). Ten years of massed practice on distributed practice. *Psychol. Rev.* **68,** 229–247.

VINCE, M. A. (1948). The intermittency of control movements and the psychological refractory period. *Brit. J. Psychol.* **48,** 149–157.

WELFORD, A. T. (1952). The 'psychological refractory period' and the timing of high speed performance – a review and a theory. *Brit. J. Psychol.* **43,** 2–19.

WELFORD, A. T. (1958). *Ageing and human skill.* Oxford: O.U.P.

WIENER, N. (1948). *Cybernetics, or Control and Communication in the Animal and the Machine.* New York: Wiley.

WOODROW, H. (1927). The effect of type of training upon transference. *J. Educ. Psychol.* **18,** 159–172.

WOODWORTH, R. S. (1938). *Experimental Psychology.* New York: Henry Holt.

5

Language and Mental Development

M. M. LEWIS

TO UNDERSTAND the relations between the language and the general development of children we must first look briefly at language as we find it in adult life. Much of what we can say about children's language can only be by way of inference from what we observe; but we can be helped by comparing it with our direct experience of our own language and its relations with our general behaviour.

I. CHARACTERISTICS OF A LANGUAGE

What is a language? There is no easy answer. The best we can do is to describe those of its characteristics which most clearly seem to mark it off from other forms of behaviour. And this, in fact, is doing no more than giving names to what we have all long experienced. A description which has been found to provide a good starting-point is that a language is a system of symbols; we then have to say what we mean by the terms 'system' and 'symbol'.

1. Signs, signals and symbols

To begin with *symbol*. Language is obviously a special instance of social interchange in which one person produces a pattern of behaviour to which another person responds. What specifically marks out language from other kinds of social interchange is the nature of the response.

The broadest general distinction is this. In much social intercourse what is produced evokes a response to this in itself; for instance, when I place a chair for someone; when I pass him a dish, at table. But on other occasions a person produces a pattern of behaviour which evokes a response not to this in itself, but rather to the situation in which it occurs. Instances are: beckoning, facial expression and vocal utterance. We may say that each of these is a *sign* to the respondent, evoking from him behaviour relevant to the situation in which it occurs.

Now, among signs are some which, in the course of social inter-

144

change have acquired functions which bring them a step still nearer to language. These are of a kind which can be made to evoke behaviour not only relevant to the situation in which the sign appears, but also relevant to a situation, not now present, in which the sign has previously appeared. We may call this the production of, and response to, a *signal*. A railway 'signal' is an example. Set at 'danger', it does not draw the attention of the driver to the section in which he is at this moment travelling; it puts him in readiness to engage in behaviour relevant to a situation which for him is still in the future. It is able to evoke the appropriate response from him in virtue of his previous experience – including 'training' – by which the 'signal' has become a signal of a coming section of the line.

We are still outside the realm of language. We come nearer to it when we notice that some signals have the peculiar characteristic that, in making the signal, the producer is himself responding to it. This kind of signal we may call a *symbol*, following such workers as Miller and Dollard (1941) and C. W. Morris (1946), who themselves follow G. H. Mead. For him, an utterance becomes a symbol when it has 'the same effect on the individual making it as on the individual to whom it is addressed' (Mead 1934, p. 46). Here the word 'same' is obviously open to question – as, in fact, Mead himself recognizes.

Some signals are clearly not symbols. If, for instance, I frown, this may be a sign or a signal for another person, evoking a response either to the present or to an absent situation. It becomes a symbol if, in frowning, I am myself also responding to my own frown. A railway signal is usually a symbol; since it means to the signalman very much what it means to the engine-driver.

Yet a railway-signal though a symbol is still beyond the realm of language. When do symbols become linguistic? The answer brings us back to our first definition. A symbol is linguistic when it forms a *system* with other symbols.

2. *A language is a system*

It would be agreed that any human utterance that we recognize as linguistic must have systematic relations with other such utterances. By a system we mean a constant pattern of regularities. A language is a system of interlocking systems. Broadly these are of two kinds. First, the utterances of which the language is made up have structures which can be formulated as the phonology or the grammar of a language – these are the subject of a good deal of recent linguistic study, as by

Chomsky (1957) and Strang (1962). Then there are semantic regularities, that is, regular relationships between structures of the language and the responses which they evoke – as studied, for instance, by Ullmann (1962). Useful terms for these two aspects of the system of a language are given by Osgood and Miron (1963), following Jakobson and Halle (1956). They speak of the internal structures of a language as syntagmatic; and of the systematic relations between the forms of a language and their contexts, linguistic and non-linguistic, as paradigmatic.

It is clear that the progressive mastery of these systems is the task that lies before every child; but before we turn to this let us look a little further at the syntagmatic and paradigmatic aspects of language as they occur in adult life, in order to see more clearly what are the specific problems that face the growing child.

3. *Language as social behaviour*

When two people are in linguistic communication with each other, it is obvious that in utterance and in comprehension the behaviour of the speaker and the listener largely consists of the operation of habitual procedures. That is, when a person speaks in a particular situation he is likely to use forms which he has learnt to utter in similar situations. Again, the response of a person to speech in a situation is likely to be by behaviour which has become habitual to him in similar situations.

The linguistic habits are, of course, highly complex. Each occasion of utterance and response demands choice from among the regular patterns of the language: lexical – that is, the choice of particular words; their phonemic qualities; their intonation and stress; their accidence and their syntax, including their order. For the speaker these features are determined by his intention; for the listener they determine his response. In every language there are regularities of usage, in utterance and response, which can be formulated as generalizations – 'rules' – and which can be a guide, for instance, to an adult attempting to acquire a language not his mother tongue.

It need hardly be said that in everyday life, in uttering and responding to the mother tongue, we are for the most part unaware of rules. The speaker and the listener each brings to the present situation a disposition to behave in accordance with a pattern of his behaviour in a relevant situation in the past. In psychology today, a widely-accepted picture of this process is the hypothesis of the *schema*, defined by Bartlett as 'an active organization of past reactions, or of past experiences . . .

operating in any well adapted organic response' (Bartlett 1932, p. 201). The hypothesis is particularly apposite to the consideration of linguistic behaviour, since it was in the interpretation of phenomena of aphasia that Henry Head, whom Bartlett has followed, found the hypothesis illuminating. Today, over a wide field the hypothesis, under one name or another, has proved fruitful. Piaget, for instance, uses the term in Bartlett's sense; Osgood, again, who postulates a 'mediation process' underlying linguistic utterance and response, at one point explicitly identifies this with 'schema' (Piaget 1953, p. 416; Osgood 1953, p. 627).[1]

If adults are normally unaware of their linguistic schemata, it is also surely true that a child's mastery of the regularities of the mother tongue proceeds – in the early stages at any rate – not so much by his aware-ness of rules as by the establishment of linguistic habits, under social approval, and their operation in familiar situations. As time goes on he may formulate some of the rules for himself or he may accept them when formulated for him – by his teacher or his grammar-book or his dictionary. But for a child or an adult the chief value of a linguistic rule is not that it reinforces a habit but rather than it enables a person to test its application to an unfamiliar situation. One of the chief needs in human behaviour is the ability to deal with what is unfamiliar; and linguistic intercourse constantly makes demands – perhaps the most important – upon this ability to effect 'transposition' to a new situation.

In the development of his language the growing child needs not only to perform habitual linguistic acts in habitual situations, but also to adapt his linguistic behaviour to unfamiliar situations. This is true both of the syntagmatic and the paradigmatic aspects of the mother tongue. A child, for instance, accustomed to adding -*ed* or -*t* to indicate action in the past, now says *I thinked*. He receives a response which makes him aware of a new situation: that the pastness of *I think* is to be indi-cated by *I thought*. Or again he hears *sheep* and recognizes that this is intended to draw his attention not to a single animal but to several. Or, again, seeing a picture of a fox he says *doggie*. In all these instances, if he acts in unchanged accordance with established schemata, the response he receives tells him he is 'wrong'. To be right – that is, to receive social approval, reinforcement of his behaviour – he has to modify schemata.

Habitual language, then, is the operation of unchanged schemata; unfamiliar situations demand problem-solving, the adaptation of schemata. Thus a child's success in acquiring a language is likely to be related to his ability to perceive and manipulate relationships in

[1] See also Vol. 1, Ch. 4, for a fuller discussion of the concept of 'schema.' (E.A.L.)

unfamiliar as well as familiar linguistic situations; in other words, the exercise of his intelligence upon the syntagmatic and paradigmatic characteristics of the language.

4. *Language as personal behaviour*

So far we have been speaking of a language as a form of social behaviour. We have now to turn to what is no less important: the non-social – what we may call the personal – functions of a language.

Evidently, whenever a language is used socially, it has also personal functions for the speaker. For, as we have said, it is one of the distinguishing characteristics of a language that a speaker tends to respond to his own utterance. If what I say tends to evoke thought, feeling and physical activity in another person it also tends to evoke them in myself.

These personal effects are of course more marked when I am communicating not with another person but with myself. I keep a diary; I make notes as memoranda; I write in order to clarify my ideas or express my feelings; I speak to myself when I am thinking out things. These are primarily personal uses of language but they are also potentially social – that is, they could be perceived by another person. My diary and my notes could be read: and even in my silent speech the movement of my vocal apparatus could be recorded and to some extent interpreted.

All these uses of a language are, then, actually or potentially overt. We now come to very important uses of language which are not even potentially overt. These occur when I am thinking in linguistic terms, when I am imagining linguistic forms in the course of my mental processes. This kind of linguistic behaviour may be called 'inner' in contrast to 'overt'; my linguistic thinking is not open to the perception of any other person. I can to some extent symbolize my thinking through the medium of words: it is these that then become the medium of communication; it is these, not my private thinking, that evoke responses in other people.

It is clear that this inner language is likely to be present whenever I use language, whether socially or personally: when I am in communication with another person, when I am communicating with myself in speech or writing, as well as when I am 'thinking' in linguistic terms. And this 'thinking', it will be seen, may comprise the whole range of my mental processes, cognitive and orectic. Inner language may occur in the course of perceptual and conceptual activity, in imagining, in remembering and in reasoning, and in the orectic aspects of all these – 'states of mind' to which we give such names as interest, attitudes and emotions,

This inner language has important functions in the behaviour of any person, to the extent that it permeates his mental processes. By symbolizing a cognitive or orectic pattern, language gives it a certain specific objectivity, enabling us to 'carry it in the mind' more readily, and so bring it more readily into relation with subsequent experience. Words help to sharpen and direct our awareness in our perceptual thinking, in imagining, remembering and reasoning; they promote a person's awareness of his interests, attitudes and emotions. The process by which this awareness is then carried forward to a subsequent situation has been described by Bartlett in a picturesque phrase: language enables us to 'turn round upon our own schemata' and so bring them more readily into relation with a situation (Bartlett 1932, p. 206, p. 225; 1958, p. 83). It need hardly be said that non-linguistic symbols ('non-verbal images') may also have these functions: only, as Bartlett says, language generally provides the most effective symbols. This, we may add, is because language is systematic and because human behaviour is permeated by language. Most, if not all, the social situations we encounter owe some of their characteristics to the fact that they are presented to us by speakers.

5. *The process of communication*

We can now outline the main features of what occurs when two persons are in linguistic communication. First, as to the speaker, whose behaviour is both inner and overt. Of his inner behaviour perhaps the most important feature is what we call his intention to evoke a relevant response in the listener; and this intention will normally have both cognitive and orectic characteristics.

The overt behaviour of the speaker will consist mainly of the production of linguistic patterns acting as symbols to evoke the listener's response. At the same time the speaker may engage in non-linguistic behaviour which may provide signs and signals for the listener – for instance, gestures, facial 'expression', bodily posture – and evoke responses from him.

The response of the listener is therefore likely to be complex. What is evoked will include inner behaviour, which will probably have cognitive and orectic characteristics and which will tend to be permeated by linguistic forms. The overt behaviour of the listener is also likely to be both non-linguistic and linguistic. His non-linguistic behaviour may include 'doing something' – that is, engaging in a task; he may also exhibit gestures, facial expression, posture. His linguistic behaviour may consist in 'saying something' in reply to the speaker.

Finally we may note an important distinction in the sequential behaviour of a listener. We have said that he may engage in a task, that is, he may attempt to produce some change in the existing situation. Instances of overt tasks are handing something to the speaker; performing particular acts; in general terms, manipulating the physical situation. The listener may also engage in inner tasks; when, for instance, his response leads towards the solution of a problem – what we call reasoning and may here speak of as the manipulation of inner processes. In all these cases, overt and inner, we may say that language has had *manipulative* effects.

But often enough the listener does not engage in any task. What is evoked by the speaker's utterance is no more than a complexity of cognitive and orectic responses to the utterance itself; if there is any overt behaviour it will consist in manifestations, linguistic and non-linguistic, of these responses. Common instances are responses to conventional greetings: *Good morning; How do you do?* We may call these effects of language *declarative* – where the effect of the speaker's utterance is to achieve rapport with the listener and the response of the listener promotes this rapport.

Our recognition of the declarative functions of a language owes much to what Malinowski called 'phatic communion' (Malinowski 1923, p. 153). In studying the behaviour of societies and observing that a language is an important instrument in the performance of social tasks, it became clear to him that a language had another function no less important in the life of a society: phatic communion, which he defined as 'a type of speech in which ties of union are created by a mere exchange of words.'

Following Malinowski we see that phatic communion is only a part of a very wide field of linguistic functions which extends from the mere interchange of greetings to such far-reaching and profound modes of human behaviour as sexual love, imaginative literature and religion. It is for this wider field of language which is primarily non-manipulative that I have proposed the name declarative.

Declarative utterance may, of course, fail of its intention, evoking not rapport but disharmony, not communion but disruption. The lover's declaration may disgust, the dramatist's tragic intention seem merely comic, the language of liturgy absurd. But all these are still instances of an intention primarily declarative, as distinct from a primarily manipulative intention.

Malinowski observed that the establishment of phatic communion was often the necessary preliminary to the promotion of social tasks as well as a powerful aid in maintaining these tasks and carrying them through to success; and again that, in turn, the performance of social tasks helped to promote phatic communion. In everyday communication, these are the complex inter-relationships of declarative and manipulative language, between the intention of the speaker and the evoked behaviour of the listener. The speaker may have primarily a manipulative intention, the listener respond declaratively; or the declarative intention of the speaker may have manipulative effects in the behaviour of the listener. Most frequently, perhaps, the utterance of the speaker is both manipulative and declarative in intention, the response of the listener more or less relevant to this intention.

From this general summary of linguistic communication in adult life we may now go on to see how a child's progress towards it may be fostered, or, indeed, impaired.

II. THE BEGINNINGS OF UTTERANCE AND RESPONSE AND THEIR FUNCTIONS

1. *Complexity of origin*

Inevitably we bring to the observation of infants a picture of language in adult life, and this certainly helps us to recognize the beginnings of linguistic behaviour. But it also has its dangers. We may fail to see that the apparently simple rudiments are already complex; on the other hand we may credit them with characteristics which occur only in a mature language.

On the complexity of the rudiments: it is doubtful whether even today, after some decades of the close study of infant behaviour, we have an adequate grasp of the complex processes that combine in the emergence of language. Systematic observations are still astonishingly sparse, in view of the resources now available for the recording of spoken communication in its contexts. We have still to rely on what seem to be the hypotheses that best fit the data we have.

The first and fundamental generalization is this: that language has its roots both in the child himself and in his social environment – and that both these factors are evident from the very beginning. From the child himself there come his primary sound-making and his primary responses to the human voice. From his social environment there comes speech to the child; there come the responses of others to the child's own sounds; and the responses of others to the child's responses to their speech. It is from the constant inter-action of these diverse influences that linguistic development takes its course.

Probably everyone who attempts to describe this development recognizes the convergence of personal and social factors. But perhaps because the process is seen mainly as the 'acquisition' of language, there is a notable tendency to emphasize the primacy of the environment. Langer, for instance, in the course of her masterly study of the functions of language, maintains that language begins for a child as a process of imitation; he learns to see a relationship between what is said to him and its context and so comes to imitate the heard speech in similar situations (Langer, 1951, Chap. V; Mowrer, 1950, p. 700 and 1960, p. 73). Skinner takes a more balanced view; still emphasizing the role of environment, he suggests that the beginnings of language are not primarily in the sounds which we 'elicit' from the child. The main process is, rather, this: in a given situation a child 'emits' a sound, which we reinforce by changing the situation (Skinner, 1957, p. 31). Where Skinner falls short, as critics such as Church have pointed out, is in his inadequate attention to the sources of emitted sounds (Church 1961, p. 80). But Skinner does, in fact, go so far as to speak of the relationships between a child's emitted sounds and his internal states (Skinner 1957, p. 45).

A complete description must include all these aspects of a child's behaviour. We must look at his early vocalizations, their forms and their functions; at the various kinds of social reinforcement of his emitted sounds; at the manner in which sounds are elicited from him in imitation. And throughout we must see the beginnings of language not only as a many-sided process but as a continuous development; in which there is progressive adaptation, with its duality of accommodation and assimilation as recognized by Piaget; and in which there cannot fail to be the operation of pre-linguistic schemata on subsequent linguistic behaviour.

2. *Early utterance*

If we look at the earliest utterances and the situations in which they occur we find certain broad regularities in all children alike. Almost immediately after birth 'crying' begins; that is, high-pitched, vowel-like sounds often interspersed by consonant-like sounds which are formed by lips, tip and blade of tongue and gum-ridge. Roughly rendered, typical forms are *meh . . . meh* and *neh . . . neh*. After some weeks the child begins to utter sounds in states of contentment, for instance, satiety after food, mostly front consonant-like sounds, but not nasalized, together with some back sounds. Typical forms are, roughly, *beh . . . beh, deh . . . deh* and *gu . . . gu*. The specific phonetic characteristics of the discomfort-cries and of the comfort-sounds can be shown to be the distinctive vocal aspects of the child's complex response to one internal state or the other. In particular, they include speech patterns formed by sucking-movements, in hunger or satiety, made during vocalization. (Here we can give only the broadest outline; detailed accounts are in Irwin, 1947, 1948; Leopold, 1947; Lewis, 1951.)

Discomfort-cries and comfort-sounds soon evoke distinctive responses from those who 'mother' the child. The discomfort-cries tend to have manipulative effects – that is, they bring the child's mother to relieve his discomfort; they probably also have some declarative effects in evoking her concern for him. The comfort-sounds in general tend to have declarative effects; that is, they are taken by his mother as signals of his contentment, evoking 'pleasure' – and her expression of this, which in turn may reinforce his contentment.

We must now distinguish between two kinds of utterance in states of comfort. In addition to the comfort-sounds, the vocal manifestations of states of contentment, a new kind of utterance emerges, often as early as the sixth week. This consists of characteristically regular repetitive, rhythmical and intonational vocal patterns. We may call this 'babbling', in contrast to 'expressive' comfort-sounds; the child appears to us to find satisfaction in the act of utterance itself. It is difficult to account for babbling except by saying that it is vocal play – and this, of course, is a description not an explanation. But the hypothetical description has this validity, that it brings babbling into line with the wide range of activity that we call play and accept as a characteristic form of infant behaviour. It also throws light upon other aspects of the child's pre-linguistic and linguistic development.

First, babbling tends to evoke a vocal response from others, just as we tend to join in with any of his play. As the child babbles we often imitate him and so stimulate him to further babbling (Lewis, 1951, p. 74 and references there). This becomes very important for the progress of the child's adaptation of his utterance to the phonemic repertory of the mother tongue. Some of his babbling sounds are reinforced as he hears sounds that approximate to his own. These he repeats in his babbling and receives social approval of his 'imitators'. Social approval stimulates him to further repetition of the sounds and so an English child is led to 'practise making English sounds'.

Further, since a main characteristic of babbling is a child's attention to the forms of his own utterance, it may well offer him a rudimentary aesthetic attitude, a delight in the patterns of speech. This is important not only for the intrinsic value of the child's aesthetic development but because it may also promote his instrumental uses of language. A child whose awareness of the forms of speech is sharpened is to that extent likely to use speech more effectively in communication – more likely to understand and make himself understood.

In recognizing the importance of babbling, there are implications for the linguistic education of children whose primary vocal activity is impaired from one cause or another. These implications we shall look at in Section IV.

3. *The child's responses to speech*

From a very early age the child responds to the sound of a human voice. Within the first month children frequently cry at the sound of others crying; and often as early as this the sound of his mother's voice will reduce a crying child to silence. It is possible that these responses are the maturation of innate tendencies. It is clear that in any case other factors are likely to be present; heard cries may – like some other noises – evoke a state of discomfort and so its vocal manifestation, crying; the cessation of crying, in responses to his mother's voice, may obviously result from the child's repeated experience of the relief that she brings.

As time goes on the child begins to make specific responses to specific vocal patterns. Thus the word *milk* uttered by his mother as she brings him milk becomes first a sign, later a signal, of the situation of being fed. It is a sign for him when he responds to it only in the presence of the milk; a signal for him when he responds in the absence of the milk. His responses are likely to be non-vocal and vocal. Non-vocal are his state of discomfort and his urgent bodily reactions if the milk is delayed; or his contentment and relaxation on receiving the food. Vocal responses are likely to be discomfort-cries in the former case; comfort-sounds in the latter. Already, therefore, even at this early stage a pattern of heard speech has rudimentary manipulative and declarative effects in the child's behaviour.

After this there is normally progress in the 'imitation' of speech patterns. This again is far from being a simple kind of response which is to be explained by calling it 'imitation'; it is a complicated process of development, a description of which must still be somewhat hypothetical. We have seen that rudimentary imitations tend to occur in the course of adult intervention in a child's babbling. These become less frequent – indeed, usually disappear – in the latter part of the first year, as the child is making progress in responding to the specific situations in which he hears speech-patterns. We say that he is 'understanding more of our words.' Out of this there grows vocal behaviour of the kind that we normally recognize as imitation; an approximation of the child's speech-patterns to some heard by him and then uttered by him in situations similar to those in which he has heard them. Less cumbrously – and less exactly – we say that 'he is now using words correctly.' (Details in Lewis, 1951, Chapter VI; briefly in Lewis, 1963, p. 22.)

This account of imitation is meant to emphasize the process of progressive approximation, as Skinner (1957, p. 30) calls it; or the process by which, in Piaget's terms, the child accommodates his own speech-patterns to those that he hears and assimilates heard speech to his own (Piaget, 1953, p. 291). It is by attending to the facts of the child's progressive adaptation that we see his linguistic development as a process of change from his earliest utterances. And it is from neglect of these facts that some workers are able to conclude that a child's early vocalizations have nothing to do with his 'acquisition' of the mother tongue.

Mowrer, for instance (1950, p. 700) maintains that early vocalization is random and autistic, having no instrumental, that is, communicative, effects; that it is only when the child takes over a word from the mother tongue that he begins to speak instrumentally.

Against this we have to set a different picture. A child's early discomfort-cries and comfort-sounds are, of course, 'without communicative intention'. But if we look closely at the changes that take place, we find that it is out of this early expressive utterance that there emerge, by progressive approximation, some of the most important of a child's uses of speech-patterns of the mother tongue, with their functions.

Take, for instance, a typical discomfort-cry: *meh . . . meh . . . meh* or the like. As we have said, this is not a random utterance. It is the vocal aspect of a child's urgent behaviour when hungry. It evokes responses from others. It is difficult to believe that even as early as six months, with repeated experiences of these responses, the child utters his cry without some rudimentary response in himself to the situation in which he cries, and to what follows his crying. Now, when his mother comes to him she is likely to say something like *mama* (*. . . is coming*) – itself a traditional approximation to infantile utterance. If the child replies with something between *meh* . . . *meh* and *mama*, he receives approval; so gradually his approximation to the adult speech-pattern, in form and function, is reinforced.

Take, again, an instance from comfort-sounds. Among the earliest 'words' of children recorded in different countries is *didda* on seeing and hearing a clock (Lewis, 1951, p. 285). This again is not a random utterance: it is typical of the forms spoken in contentment. A child in such a state of relaxation, his urgent needs being satisfied, may attend to the clock – or have his attention drawn to it; his contentment now includes his orectic response to the clock; and *didda* expresses this contentment as well as reinforcing his attention to the clock. His mother, hearing him, may well say *tick-tock* – again a traditional approximation to infantile speech. If he then responds with something between *didda* and *tick-tock* he wins approval and so, here again, his approximation to the adult speech-pattern, in form and function, is reinforced.

It is clear that these transformations must owe much to the willingness of others to adapt their speech-behaviour to the child's, as well as to his responsive willingness towards them. Sooner or later, in greater or less degree, he may come to direct his own behaviour, so that instead of progressive approximation by short steps, he may attempt leaps and bounds – from *mama* to *mother*; from *tick-tock* to *clock*. How far this happens to any one child can only be known by detailed observation.

4. *Social response to the child's speech*

In describing a child's response to adult speech we have inevitably had to emphasize adult response to his speech. Indeed there is no stage in linguistic development which can be adequately described except as convergence between the child and his social environment.

There is a constant influence upon the child by which his attention, in speaking and in listening, is drawn to particular features of the current situation. If at first his *mama* is the vocal behaviour of his condition – distress, then relief, with perhaps some dim awareness of food and the person who brings it – certainly as time goes on social influence canalizes his attention towards the person of his mother. Broadly speaking, there is a progressive emergence of cognitive and objective responses – that is, directed to the situation – from earlier responses which were orectic and subjective.

What others do and say in reply to him also constantly strengthen the manipulative and declarative effects of his speech; and so foster his growing awareness of the effects of his vocal behaviour. When, if ever, is it valid to speak of his manipulative or declarative *intention*? It would seem that no complete description of linguistic behaviour can dispense with the assumption. Thus Skinner, who proposes to make 'no appeal to hypothetical explanatory entities', nevertheless has to take account of 'what is called intention' by maintaining that in general it 'may be reduced to contingencies of reinforcement' (Skinner, 1957, pp. 12, 41). In other words, when the child seems to be directing his own linguistic behaviour, this fact is being directed by reinforcing features of the situation. But we feel bound to say here that the child not only becomes aware of these contingencies but also comes to direct his behaviour so as to bring about changes in them. So, sooner or later, in distress he says *mama* in order to cause his mother to relieve his discomfort; in contentment he says *mama* in order to cause her to share his contentment. We have to maintain that the phrase 'in order to cause' is a minimal description of something that does happen. It is obvious that those in communication with a chiild, by what they do – still more, by what they say – foster behaviour in him which can only be described in some such phrase as this.

They are also constantly influencing the forms of his speech. Ultimately he achieves 'correct' renderings of the patterns of the mother tongue; but in the meantime the process of approximation shows itself in a characteristic repertory of speech-forms that we call baby-language.

5. *Basic and secondary baby-language*

In this we can distinguish two stages. At first basic baby-language; a collection of speech-patterns which are the relatively unchanged forms of discomfort-cries and comfort-sounds. Typically they are mainly of six kinds: *mama, nana, papa, baba, tata, dada*. We recognize these at once as the limited repertory which, with local variations in forms and functions, are used by children over a very wide area of the globe, perhaps universally, as their earliest 'words'.

Secondary baby-language is a repertory of speech-patterns which are transformations of the basic forms, as influenced by the child's verbal community. *Didda*, already mentioned, is a typical instance; other forms of this recorded of children in different countries are *dida, titta, titit*. All of these have affinities with children's basic utterances; all of them also owe something to the linguistic behaviour of those in communication with a child, drawing his attention to a feature of the current situation. Only people, not clocks, say *tick-tock*; only people say *bow-wow, quack-quack, cocorico, puff-puff*. For many children this baby-language is a bridge to the adult mother-tongue.

During this transitional period, and to some extent later, the language of a child may seem to be studded with 'bizarre forms' and 'odd meanings' for conventional words. The bizarre forms can be explained by the phonological analysis of the processes of the approximation of speech-patterns; these cannot be detailed here (Lewis, 1951, Chapter X). But something must be said about the 'odd meanings' – the functions for the child of words that he takes over from the mother tongue; for a study of these illuminates not only his language but his general development. From the beginning, as we have seen, there are intimate reciprocal relationships between language and the cognitive and orectic aspects of behaviour. We must now look at these relationships in a child's further growth.

III. LANGUAGE AND GENERAL DEVELOPMENT

1. *The place of cognition in linguistic development*
We have said that every step forward is likely to be a combination of habit and problem-solving. But even the habits have often begun as the solution of problems, situations that demand the ability to learn. This means that a child's progress in language must largely be determined by cognitive abilities.

From the beginning, both aspects of language – the syntagmatic and the paradigmatic – present their own problems: the syntagmatic, in the relations which constitute the patterns of the language; the paradigmatic, in the relations between the linguistic patterns and their contexts in the current situations. The child is called upon to manipulate these relationships on every new occasion of communication; and this may demand, partly the kind of ability required in non-linguistic as well as in linguistic problems – what we call 'general intelligence'; and partly a special linguistic ability. There would seem to be good evidence – obtained, it is true, from the study of older children – of this special ability. As might be expected, it is thought to be a product of innate potentialities and environmental conditions (Vernon, 1950, pp. 17, 32).

Now, even in the early approaches to the mother tongue both general cognitive and special linguistic abilities are probably called into play. Take, for instance, the case of a child of eleven months who makes a relevant response to *doggie* (Lewis, 1951, p. 336). Syntagmatically, this is a pattern of auditory relationships; paradigmatically, a pattern of relationships between this auditory experience and the child's perception of his mother holding up a toy dog. We can infer that at this stage he is responding to these relationships if we notice what occurs more clearly in his subsequent development. For, a year later this child is saying *doggie* on seeing a real dog as well as his toy dog. The form of the word – an adaptation of the child's own schemata – shows an awareness of the auditory syntagmatic pattern; the extension of the word's application shows an attention to its paradigmatic function.

In saying that the child responds to relationships we take it that in the earliest stages he may well do so without being aware of them; and that if later he does become aware of them, this itself is partly a result of his further linguistic development – words having become for him a means of symbolizing relationships.

The syntagmatic development of children demands further study. Although we can map out the course we cannot yet say with any certainty how children progress from point to point. Berko and Brown have summarized experimental methods of inquiry (Berko and Brown, 1960). The results so far indicate that normally within a few years a child's language, in utterance and response, comes to include the whole range of the structures of the mother tongue. Systematic observation enables us to estimate how long this takes for particular children. Templin, for instance, has shown that American children are normally acquainted with most of the structures of spoken English by the age of 8 (Templin, 1957, p. 134). After this, further progress in the mastery of the syntagmatic aspects of the language would be by way of extending the scope of each of the structures within the child's usage.

Progress in the paradigmatic aspects of the mother tongue is a much more complex and far-reaching development – what in everyday terms we call the growth of meaning. What begins as a response to speech as a sign of a situation, changes into a response to speech as a signal and so to the symbolizing function of language. In the course of this development the child comes to use and to respond to speech-patterns in their contexts more effectively, to the extent that his abilities to perceive, to think conceptually, to remember, to imagine and to reason are more and more at his command.

But the development of these cognitive abilities is itself largely a product of the child's linguistic development. We must now look at this side of the nexus of language and behaviour: the place of language in such activities as we normally name perceptual and conceptual thinking, remembering, imagining and reasoning. A complete picture must, of course, include their constant orectic aspects – emotion, motivation – and also the non-linguistic behaviour which is always part of cognitive activity. But for our immediate purpose we narrow our attention to the part played by language in their development.

2. *The place of language in cognitive activities*

Common everyday observation makes it clear that throughout a child's development, language is a permeative influence in all his behaviour. For his cognitive activities it is more than this – it is a prime condition of their functioning.

Here it is possible to give only the briefest of accounts, with some references to detailed studies. And we confine ourselves to the beginnings, partly because it is the later stages that are more usually described, partly because the beginnings afford us some insight into the manner in which language enters into non-linguistic behaviour.

Take first perceptual discrimination. How soon the human voice influences an infant's perceptual distinction between one situation and another we can hardly say. But as early as the end of the first year there is pretty clear evidence of this from systematic observations in experimental conditions. Some Russian workers, for instance, studied children learning to choose between two containers only one of which held a sweet. One group of children were made to hear a specific speech-pattern, *red*, at every correct choice; these were notably quicker than the rest and their discriminative perception was more ready and more stable on subsequent occasions (Simon 1957, p. 198; Luria, 1961, p.10). In other words, the auditory speech-pattern helped the establishment of a scheme of discriminative perception and its revival later. Evidence of this kind suggests a caveat in accepting Piaget's characterization of behaviour in the first two years of life as completely pre-symbolic and sensori-motor.

The beginnings of conceptual thinking again are seen in the manner in which children normally extend a pattern of linguistic behaviour from one specific situation to others – and subsequently limit this extension to particular situations. An instance is a child of 20 months who, already in the habit of saying *pay* on seeing an aeroplane, now says this on seeing a kite (Lewis, 1951, p. 191, where other examples are given). The record of this child suggests that his utterance of the word *pay* occurs when his total response – non-linguistic and linguistic – to a previous situation is now evoked by a new situation. To say that the aeroplane and the kite are similar to the child is another way of saying that they evoke similar responses from him. If his use of the word *pay* on both occasions receives social approval (*Clever boy!*), this helps to stabilize his production of the response to both situations. Later, by a further social interchange, he comes to use *kite* and *pay* for two different groups of situations.

This is the kind of evidence upon which Skinner bases his account of the formation of concepts under social reinforcement (Skinner 1957, p. 127). Russian studies, relying upon 'objective' data in the form of measurable physiological changes, have shown that a specific involuntary response may be evoked from a child in a wide range of situations (Luria, 1963, pp. 180–192).

Thus the study in detail of the development of conceptual thinking brings home the fact that this is an elaboration, largely under social control, of perceptual discrimination. The perceptual basis of conceptual thinking has, of course, long been recognized. In the traditional terms of logic, the process was formulated many years ago by Stout in the pithy statement that the universal is implicit in the percept (Stout, 1896, II, p. 174). What has been added by recent workers is an increased emphasis upon the importance of social interchange in promoting the linguistic symbolization which aids the 'abstraction' that is involved in conceptual thinking.

We could then speak of the beginning of 'abstract thinking', except that the term does not command agreed usage in psychological discussion. To enter into this would take us too far afield. We need only say that here we are using the term to name the process by which a child comes, with the aid of symbolization, to attend to what is general to a number of situations. This implies that the process has a basis of non-linguistic behaviour, that it usually develops through linguistic intercourse, but that it is not exclusively a linguistic product. It also implies that the terms 'concrete' and 'abstract' cannot be used to indicate either simple opposition or mutual exclusion; we must say, rather, that abstract thinking is behaviour of a higher degree of generality than concrete, made possible by the aid of language.

Support for the hypothesis of the dependence of 'abstract thinking' upon language comes from general studies such as those of Mead (1934), Skinner (1957), Luria (1961), and Vygotsky (1961, 1962); from experimental work with normal children, (summarized in Lewis 1963); and from the study of children in whom language is impaired; this we refer to in Section IV.

When we turn to the place of language in remembering, we see that this also is fundamentally the extension of a specific speech-pattern from one situation to another – in this case, from past to present. Instances from the record of a child in his second year show that sometimes the process occurs without social aid. The child's spontaneous linguistic behaviour in a particular situation today includes utterances evoked on a 'similar' occasion yesterday. Certainly his listeners may powerfully reinforce this process. They supply words and they question him, in these ways helping him to symbolize his present experience as belonging to the past. We say then that the child is referring to the past. What happens appears to fit Bartlett's picture of language as a means of turning back upon one's own schemata. Whatever non-linguistic symbolization may enter into the process of remembering, for most people it is undoubtedly language which helps to make recall more specific and more accurate.

In very similar fashion what we call imagining is already at an early stage promoted by language. Basically, it begins as an elaboration of remembering, and comes to be a recombination and transposition of symbolized past experiences. In Bartlett's words, again: in remembering a person 'constructs on the basis of one schema', in imagining he 'freely builds together events, incidents and experiences that have gone to the making of several different schemata'. (Bartlett, 1932, p. 205). The symbolizing behaviour, the imagining, is freed from its bonds with the past; the symbolized ('imagined') situation is treated as merely absent – whether temporally linked with the past, or the present, or the future, or as having no time-reference at all.

The beginnings of this are seen in the early, non-linguistic, anticipatory behaviour of an infant, where the present situation evokes a response appropriate to what is yet to come; the rudiments are present as soon, indeed, as a hungry child looks towards the door through which his food normally appears. That this can be explained as an instance of learning, or even of conditioning, does not rob it of its potentialities for developing into imagining. The advent of language into the process again fosters development. An observed child, at 17 months, said *ha* (his customary word for honey) one morning at breakfast when the usual honey was absent from the table, at the same time 'seeking', 'looking for' the honey. This is pretty clearly manipulative speech in the attempt to secure social aid in satisfying a need; but it also is, or will soon become, a symbolization of the absent honey. Soon we can say that the child is 'imagining the honey'.

How social co-operation fosters this process is instanced by a record of a dialogue with the same child five months later. While being wheeled in his pram he says, *Home!* His mother: *Whom do you want to see?* Child: *Ganny!* Through speech the adult is reinforcing what the child is already doing: attending to an absent situation and symbolizing it (Lewis, 1951, pp. 355–8).

This brings us to what is probably the most powerful factor in promoting all the cognitive activities we have so far mentioned – conversation. We evoke speech from the child by speaking to him. A specialized form of this is the question: a form of utterance to which the expected response is speech. Or again, when the child speaks we answer him; so he learns to use the interrogative speech-pattern as an effective means of evoking a linguistic response. It is worth noticing that an interrogative intonation may appear in a child's pre-linguistic vocalizations. His questions, of course, gain potency when they take the form of conventional phrases.

We have left the place of language in reasoning until now because all the other cognitive activities we have mentioned come into it: perceptual and conceptual thinking, remembering, imagining. We need only make the briefest reference to all the various processes that enter into this complicated activity that we call reasoning, because these are treated more fully in other chapters. There is little doubt that the course of genetic development is broadly in accordance with the schematic series of stages pictured by Piaget – from the sensori-motor stage, through pre-operational behaviour to concrete operations and so to formal reasoning.

Further – and this is Piaget's main theme – the development of a child's reasoning, up to its highest forms, depends upon his intercourse with others: 'L'échange de pensée' (Piaget, 1950, p. 195). Where, strangely enough, his formulation falls short is in his comparatively inadequate recognition of language as a continued factor throughout the course of development; in particular, as we have indicated, he underestimates the importance of linguistic intercourse between the child and members of his community. Certainly Piaget himself makes full use of language as the main instrument of his 'clinical' method; but it is fair to say that he tends to neglect the functions of questions – as, indeed, of verbal interchange generally – in promoting, or hampering, the development and the exercise of reasoning.

Other workers, before and since, have done much to make up the deficiency. To mention a few: in England, Susan and Nathan Isaacs

(Isaacs, 1930); in U.S.S.R., Luria and Galperin (Simon, 1957); in U.S.A., Osgood (1953) and Skinner (1957). Nevertheless, although from the early days of Child Study much has been written about children's questions, there are still gaps in our knowledge of the place of questions, by and to the child, in his general growth.

Even so, what is abundantly emphasized today is the primacy and ultimate importance of a child's interchange with his linguistic community at every stage of his cognitive development.

3. *Language and orectic development*

By a child's orectic development we mean the emergence of his personality, the growth of his social life, the differentiation of his aesthetic attitudes and his ethical development. We use the term ethical in its everyday sense, and at its widest, to mean conduct that is subject to the value-judgements of a moral code.

These are all closely interrelated and related to language. All spring from roots in earliest infancy when, as we have seen, a child's orectic states are expressed by his own rudimentary utterances or evoked by the speech of others. Then, as he comes to respond more specifically to speech and as his own discomfort-cries and comfort-sounds are modified, supplemented and replaced by the forms of the mother tongue, social influence continues. Language becomes the means by which personal, social, aesthetic and ethical attitudes and conduct are differentiated and fostered. By permeating much of a child's non-linguistic behaviour, language promotes the formation of habitual patterns of attitudes and conduct and, ultimately, the hierarchical organizations of these into what we see as a person with a characteristic social life, taste and ethical conduct. Meanwhile language also enables him to become aware of himself as a person with these orectic characteristics.

Of the three communities in which a child normally grows up – his family, his school and his peers – the third plays a larger part in his orectic than in his cognitive development. Broadly speaking, while his elders present him with the ultimate patterns of adult life, his daily intercourse with his peers strongly influences his immediate habitual conduct and attitudes, which may or may not be at variance with the adult patterns. Thus the adolescent is not simply an immature adult; he has a distinctive personality and a marked way of life, more or less precariously stable.

Anything approaching a detailed account of the long and complex course of orectic development through language is impossible here; a fuller statement to which we may refer is still only a summary (Lewis, 1963). Here we can only point to the main landmarks.

One of the earliest of these is the beginning of response to a verbal signal of adult disapproval – to *No!* The rudiments of this may occur within the first year. For instance, in the record mentioned above (Lewis, 1963, pp. 43–46), a child in his tenth month responded with some regularity to his father's *No!* by inhibiting an incipient act. It would seem probable that at this early stage the child is responding not so much to the phonemic pattern of the word as to intonation and intensity as well as to the speaker's facial expression and posture. Ultimately, of course, it is the abiding phonemic pattern ('the word *No*') which evokes the inhibitory behaviour.

Not until a year later did this child begin to respond to *Yes!* It is not surprising that as early as possible we train a child to respond appropriately to *No!* so that we exercise 'remote control' upon him. Then there comes a time – in the child cited, at 20 months – when he himself says *No!* and inhibits his own incipient act. How long it is before this becomes internalized we can hardly say; but there can be no doubt that it is among the most important developments in a child's life.

An advance beyond *No* and *Yes* is the beginning of the use of specific words to differentiate orectic attitudes. The child cited above used, during the latter part of his second year, *pretty, nice, dirty, naughty*, with some appropriateness and reference to the situation (Lewis, 1963, pp. 62–64). Detailed records show that there is no simple answer to the question, Which comes first, the word or the attitude? Sometimes a child expresses an attitude for which another person supplies a word; sometimes the attitude appears to be evoked only as a result of hearing a word. Certainly, as time goes on, it is through the enlargement of his discriminative vocabulary that a child's orectic attitudes are differentiated.

4. *The growth of self-awareness*
The verbalization of approval and disapproval also fosters self-awareness. The child hears words such as *nice* and *naughty* applied to his own acts; and, again, when he himself uses them for other people, they often evoke approval or disapproval from listeners. From repeated experiences of this kind a child must in time begin to be aware of his own acts and attitudes as set beside those of other people.

Meanwhile, in other ways he is also becoming aware of himself. Non-linguistically, he experiences co-operation and resistance in his dealings with others; all this again brings him to see himself as distinct from others – in a rudimentary fashion the object of their behaviour. Language sharpens this awareness.

Something of this, it should be noticed, occurs long before he has begun to symbolize himself by his name or *I* or *me*. When, for instance, he repeatedly responds to *No!* by inhibiting an incipient act, he must in time begin to see himself as acted upon by other persons; when, again, he says *No!* and inhibits an incipient act, he must come to see himself as acted upon by himself. Much of his manipulative speech must have the same effect. When, instead of merely naming what he wants – for instance, chocolate – he begins to symbolize his need, *Want it!*, this must bring with it some awareness of his attitude and behaviour, as distinct from their object. Ultimately he symbolizes himself by such forms as *John want it* or *I . . .* or *Me. . . .*

Such a phrase at the same time must strengthen and accelerate his possessiveness and dawning awareness of ownership; closely connected with this is the symbolization and awareness of being able to direct his own behaviour, *I do this self.* (In one case, both phrases in first quarter of third year; Lewis, 1963, pp. 72–73).

It need hardly be pointed out that as a child moves from non-linguistic manifestations of self-assertion to verbalization of them, they become much more specifically the targets of the behaviour of other people, and that all this must again enhance his self-awareness.

5. *Social and ethical growth in a community*

Thus, inseparable from the development of self-awareness is the increasing differentiation, through language, of social relationships and ethical attitudes and conduct. For self-awareness, as we have said, implies awareness of others; and this grows out of, and further fosters, awareness of relationships between the child and others, and among these others.

In the course of this growing social awareness through language, ethical attitudes and conduct – the child's own and others' – are also verbalized and so emerge for him with increasing clarity. Much of this will spring from the daily give-and-take within the family circle; but it receives a marked impetus and enlargement as a child begins to live with other children in a community extending beyond his home. For while there can be no doubt of the enormous importance of adult influence upon a child's ethical development, his immediate actual attitudes and conduct are subjected to the severity of testing and trial as he has to find a way of life with other children, whose problems are more nearly his while their solutions tend to be nearer to his understanding and abilities.

As children grow out of infancy, their social life in community is characterized by a pervading ethical principle termed the rule of mutuality by Piaget (1932, p. 18), and reciprocity by Susan Isaacs (1933, p. 276). The basis of the special ethos of the group lies within the group itself, demanding acceptance by the members of the group and reciprocity in their mutual behaviour. Piaget asked how this is sustained, and could find no adequate answer. Susan Isaacs noted the concurrence of a 'secret language' among children of ten to twelve years of age. But it was left to the careful recording of the sub-language of children by I. and P. Opie (1959) to bring home to us in full force that a sub-language, more than any other feature of the group life of children, evokes and sustains their ethical attitudes towards each other (Lewis, 1963, Chap. XI).

Here is a field that remains to be explored; and this must be done if we are to understand not only the ethical life of children but also what follows from it; the nature of the ethical life of adolescents, about which we – and probably they themselves – are today so bewildered.

IV. CAUSES AND EFFECTS OF LINGUISTIC RETARDATION

Much of what we know of the place of language in normal development is confirmed by the study of children with impaired language. This again is a field relatively unexplored until recently and in which more remains to be done.

The causes of linguistic impairment are many, and though they are not yet completely surveyed we can summarize them as of four kinds, brain damage not producing auditory loss; dysphasia orectic in origin; deafness; environmental inadequacy. These are not mutually exclusive.

1. *Brain damage*

The neurological bases of dysphasia in infancy and childhood are still largely undetermined. The language disorders may be general or specific. General dysphasia, that is, impairment over a wide field of linguistic development, is recognized as a result of damage which impairs cognitive functioning in general and therefore, inevitably, the development of language – as in mongolism and other forms of general mental deficiency.

In other cases, the linguistic disorders are more specific and more limited: impairment of the reception or execution of speech in communication; later, dysgraphia, dyslexia or dyscalculia. Often these are combined. On the neurological bases of these specific disorders there are two schools of thought. The first of these relates each disorder to a corresponding specific neurological condition – not necessarily closely localized in the brain (for instance, dyslexia, by Critchley, 1964). The second view is that a specific dysphasic disorder is the manifestation of a more general organic deficiency, which results in an impairment of particular forms of cognitive functioning not confined to language; for instance, ability to deal with spatial or temporal relationships. Evidence for this view is adduced by Luria and his associates (Luria, 1963); and it is perhaps not too much to say that there is a notable trend of opinion in this direction.

The issue is further complicated by the undoubted fact that a child's actual linguistic functioning due to organic damage is always influenced by environmental conditions: those which affect his physical well-being, his cognitive and orectic development and, more immediately, his acquisition of the forms of the mother tongue.

2. *Orectic dysphasia*

When we turn to language disorders which are thought to be orectic in origin and are given such names as autism and elective mutism, we find that here again diagnosis and treatment are uncertain. In a group of children all presenting a picture of autism there is likely to be a diversity of conditions – not excluding organic damage or deficiency. Where the children are alike is in the weakness of their relationships with other people. Autistic children are distant, shut off, apparently indifferent to other human beings. When this manifests itself early in infancy, is seen in other social relationships than linguistic interchange and is unaccompanied by marked auditory impairment, it is diagnosed as orectic in origin (Renfrew and Murphy, 1964).

3. *Deafness*

The children we characterize as deaf are those who, while they again present a variety of conditions, all suffer auditory impairment to a degree that demands special treatment in their linguistic development. Deafness in infancy is generally specified as of three kinds: conductive, perceptive or neurological, although we have still much to learn about each of these, especially the third, and about their possible combination in any one case. Their sources, again, may be hereditary, or non-hereditary; congenital, peri-natal or post-natal. In very many cases the evidence is insufficient to enable us to identify the causal conditions.

What is clear is that deafness may exist without any primary impairment of mental functioning, where an infant – so long as language itself is not involved – manifests the range of mental abilities of normal hearing children of the same age and similar general background. In many cases, however, deafness is accompanied by another handicap, which may be general mental deficiency with or without dysphasia.

Here again, environmental conditions remain an ultimate influence on actual linguistic functioning. This is, of course, most evident where a child, otherwise normal, is subject to only a minor degree of auditory impairment. But experimental work now going on shows that even in some of the severest cases special educational treatment may promote linguistic development (Ewing, 1957; Ewing and Ewing, 1964). The importance of beginning this treatment as soon as possible is now recognized. It is strongly urged by some skilled observers that the early vocalizations of a deaf infant must not be allowed to lapse. In particular, he must be stimulated to maintain his babbling (Taylor, 1960, p. 3; Tervoort, 1964, p. 46).

4. *Language deprivation*

Finally we come to the effects of environmental conditions on normal children; that is, normal in general mental ability and potential linguistic development and whose hearing is physically unimpaired. These unfavourable environmental conditions include institutions in which children are segregated from ordinary family life; unduly large families; and homes in which the economic or mental resources of the family are inadequate to promote the linguistic development of the children.

Institutional upbringing has been shown to have an adverse effect on language development even at very young ages. Brodbeck and Irwin compared infants in an orphanage with those from a similar parental background. Already in the first six months the orphanage infants were inferior in the range and frequency of vocalizations, by statistically significant measures (Brodbeck and Irwin, 1946). Other investigations have shown that residence in an institution may retard linguistic development throughout infancy and childhood (Pringle and Tanner, 1958; earlier work is summarized by McCarthy in Carmichael, 1954).

The inference from these studies is that in an institution children are relatively deprived of the intimate daily relationships with adults so necessary, as we have seen, for the promotion of their linguistic development.

Children, again, who are members of large families may suffer some linguistic retardation. A common explanation of this fact has been that large families are characteristic of the poorest homes, which tend to be at the least intelligent strata of a society and that this handicap naturally retards the development of language. But it is a measure of our growing knowledge that we can now see a different pattern of relationships. We consider what occurs when we correlate the linguistic attainment of children with the size of their families, excluding – statistically or actually – the effect of socio-economic level. Nisbet, in a study of some 5,000 children, has shown that, irrespective of the socio-economic level, to be born into a large family may still have a retarding effect on linguistic development (Nisbet, 1953). We must conclude with him that this occurs because in a large family a child may be relatively deprived of adequate linguistic intercourse with adults.

The adverse effects of a poverty of economic and mental resources have long been recognized and a great deal of confirmatory evidence accumulated. (Instances are: Stern, 1907; Descoeudres, 1927; Hetzer and Reindorf, 1928; Irwin, 1948; Templin, 1957). The sources of this retardation are likely to be both hereditary and environmental. It is possible that potential linguistic ability – through organic structure – is inherited; what is quite certain is that daily life in the home must also play its part, since language development always depends on a linguistic community.

In another, less obvious, but very important way, familial environment may effect linguistic development. As Bernstein has recently suggested – and to some extent confirmed by evidence – a child's language may be limited in its range by the occupations and interests, and therefore the conversation, of his parents. Comparing 'working-class' with 'middle-class' homes, he finds the language of the former more concrete and more likely to rely upon non-linguistic communication such as gestures, than upon verbal elaboration. One far-reaching result of this may be that their children are so much the less well fitted for the more academic aspects of education which demand verbalization, especially in the symbolization of abstract relationships (Bernstein, 1958, 1960).

In all these cases of linguistic impairment there are complex relationships. Cognitive and orectic immaturity affect each other; both may retard language development and the retardation may in turn show itself in cognitive disability and orectic immaturity. These, then, may have non-linguistic causes; but it is also clear that often they are the direct result of poverty of linguistic experience.

The cognitive effects have been demonstrated by many investigations. On organic damage, it is a main theme of Luria – following Pavlov and Vygotsky – that the resulting disability in linguistic symbolization, 'the second signalling system', leads inevitably to deficiency in abstraction and generalization (Vygotsky, 1961, Luria, 1963). Of the effects of autism we know less, because of the difficulties of diagnosis and because of the comparatively short period in which this condition has been studied. Certainly in some cases there is a deficiency in cognitive functioning, and it is difficult to believe that this is not due, in part at any rate, to the characteristic poverty of language of the autistic child (Renfrew and Murphy, 1964).

The cognitive disabilities of deaf children are, on the other hand, well known. Many investigations (summarized, for instance, by Ewing, 1957) have found that these children tend to show immaturity and distortion of reasoning, not only where language is directly involved, but even where a problem is not verbally presented nor demands a verbal solution; for example, in tests in diagrammatic or pictorial form.

The cognitive retardation of children in an unfavourable social environment is likewise well established – children in an institution, a large family or a home culturally poor. Here, in particular, there may be non-linguistic influences upon development; but many investigators concur in the view that the cognitive disabilities are also a reflection of linguistic retardation (summary in Lewis, 1963, pp. 75–9, 198–202).

In orectic development, again, immaturity, instability and maladjustment are also held to arise sometimes from linguistic impairment. In all the special conditions we have mentioned – organic damage, autism, deafness, deficient social life – we find a tendency for some children to be immature and disturbed in their orectic development towards a stable personality, well adjusted in social life and mature in ethical attitudes and behaviour. Detailed studies show remarkable similarities in the orectic deficiencies of children under quite different adverse conditions; for instance, deafness and life in an institution (Lewis, 1963, p. 76). While these orectic characteristics may be directly due to a child's personal defects, the adversities of his social life, or his cognitive disabilities, investigators are led to the conclusion that in many cases the orectic disturbances may also arise from linguistic shortcomings consequent on these conditions (summary in Lewis, 1963, 157–9).

Thus the systematic observation and experimental study of normal and of defective children, living in favourable or unfavourable social conditions, combine to demonstrate the intimate relationships between their progress in language and their general development.

REFERENCES

BARTLETT, F. C. (1932). *Remembering.* Cambridge: Cambridge University Press.

BARTLETT, F. C. (1958). *Thinking.* London: George Allen and Unwin.

BERKO, J., and BROWN, R. (1960). Psycholinguistic research methods. In Mussen, P. H. (ed), *Handbook of Research Methods in Child Psychology,* 517–575. New York: Wiley.

BERNSTEIN, B. (1958). Some sociological determinants of perception. *Brit. J. Soc.* **9,** 159–174.

BERNSTEIN, B. (1960). Language and social class. *Brit. J. Soc.* **11,** 271–276.

BRODBECK, A. J., and IRWIN, O. C. (1945). The speech behaviour of infants without families. *Child Developm.* **17,** 3.

CARMICHAEL, L. (ed.) (1954). *Manual of Child Psychology.* (Third edn.) New York: Wiley.

CHOMSKY, N. (1957). *Syntactic Structures.* The Hague: Mouton.

CHURCH, J. (1961). *Language and the Discovery of Reality.* New York: Random House.

CRITCHLEY, M. (1964). *Developmental Dyslexia.* London: Heinemann.

DESCOEUDRES, A. (1927). *Le Développement de l'Enfant.* Geneva and Neuchatel: Delachaux and Niestlé.

EWING, A. W. G. (1957). *Educational Guidance and the Deaf Child.* Manchester: Manchester University Press.

EWING, A. W. G., and EWING, E. C. (1964). *Teaching Deaf Children to Talk.* Manchester: Manchester University Press.

FREUD, S. (1891). *On Aphasia.* Trans. E. Stengel. London: Imago.

FURTH, H. G. (1966). *Thinking without Language.* New York: Free Press.

HEAD, H. (1926). *Amphasia and Kindred Disorders of Speech.* Cambridge: Cambridge University Press.

HETZER, H., and REINDORF, B. (1928). Sprachentwicklung und Sociales Milieu. *Z. f. Angew. Psychol.* **29.**

IRWIN, O. C. (1947). Infant speech. *J. Sp. Dis.* **12.**

IRWIN, O. C. (1948). The effect of family occupation status and of age on the use of sound types. *J. Sp. Hear. Dis.* **13.**

ISAACS, S. (1932). *Social Development in Young Children.* London: Routledge and Kegan Paul.

JAKOBSON, R., and HALLE, M. (1956). *Fundamentals of Language.* The Hague: Mouton.

LANGER, S. (1951). *Philosophy in a New Key.* Cambridge, Mass: Harvard University Press.

LEOPOLD, W. F. (1947). *Speech Development of a Bilingual Child: a Linguist's Record* (4 vols.) Evanston, Illinois: Northwestern University Press.

LEWIS, M. M. (1951). *Infant Speech: A study of the Beginnings of Language* (2nd revised edn.) New York: Humanities Press.

LEWIS, M. M. (1963). *Language, Thought, and Personality in Infancy and Childhood.* London: Harrap.

LURIA, A. R. (1961). *The Rôle of Speech in the Regulation of Normal and Abnormal Behaviour.* Oxford: Pergamon. *

LURIA, A. R. (ed.) (1963). *The Mentally Retarded Child.* Oxford: Pergamon.

MALINOWSKI, B. (1923). In Ogden, C. L., and Richards, I. A. (eds.) *The Meaning of Meaning.* London: Routledge and Kegan Paul.

MEAD, G. H. (1934). *Mind, Self and Society.* Chicago: University of Chicago Press.

MILLER, N. E., and DOLLARD, J. (1941). *Social Learning and Imitation.* New Haven: Yale University Press.

MORRIS, C. W. (1946). *Signs, Language, and Behaviour.* New York: Prentice Hall.

MOWRER, O. H. (1950). *Learning Theory and Personality Dynamics.* New York: Ronald.

MOWRER, O. H. (1960). *Learning Theory and the Symbolic Processes.* New York: Wiley.

NISBET, J. D. (1953). *Family Environment: A Direct Effect of Family Size on Intelligence.* London: Cassell.

OPIE, I., and OPIE, P. (1959). *The Lore and Language of Schoolchildren.* Oxford: Clarendon.

OSGOOD, C. E. (1953). *Method and Theory in Experimental Psychology.* New York: Oxford University Press.

OSGOOD, C. E., and MIRON, M. S. (1963). *Approaches to the Study of Amphasia.* Urbana, Illinois: University of Illinois Press.

G

PRINGLE, M. L. K., and TANNER, M. (1958). The effect of early deprivation on speech development. *Language and Speech.* **1,** 4.

PIAGET, J. (1932). *The Moral Judgement of the Child.* London: Routledge and Kegan Paul.

PIAGET, J. (1950). *The Psychology of Intelligence.* London: Routledge and Kegan Paul.

PIAGET, J. (1951). *Play, Dreams and Imitation in Childhood.* London: Heinemann.

PIAGET, J. (1953). *The Origin of Intelligence in the Child.* London: Routledge and Kegan Paul.

RENFREW, C., and MURPHY, K. (1964). *The Child who does not Talk.* London: Heinemann.

SIMON, B. (ed.) (1957). *Psychology in the Soviet Union.* London: Routledge and Kegan Paul.

SKINNER, B. F. (1957). *Verbal Behaviour.* New York: Appleton-Century.

STOUT, G. F. (1896). *Analytic Psychology.* In Muirhead, J. H. (ed.), Library of Philosophy, Third Series. London: Sonnenschein.

STRANG, B. (1962). *Modern English Structure.* London: Edward Arnold.

TAYLOR, I. G. (1960). Basic problems in mental health of children during pre-school years. In Ewing, A. W. G. (ed.), *The Modern Educational Treatment of Deafness.* Manchester: Manchester University Press.

TEMPLIN, M. C. (1957). *Certain Language Skills in Children: Their Development and Inter-relationships.* Minnesota: University of Minesota Press.

TERVOORT, B. TH. (1964). Speech and language development in early childhood. *T. Deaf.* **62,** 37–57.

ULMANN, S. (1962). *Semantics: An Introduction to the Science of Meaning.* New York: Barnes and Noble.

VERNON, P. E. (1950). *The Structure of Human Abilities.* London: Methuen.

VYGOTSKY, L. S. (1961). Thought and speech. In Saporta, S. (ed.), *Psycholinguistics, a Book of Readings.* New York: Holt, Rinehart and Winston.

VYGOTSKY, L. S. (1962). *Thought and Language.* New York: Wiley.

6

The Experimental Psychology of Grammar and its Relevance to Children's Language Learning

P. HERRIOT

I. INTRODUCTION

1. *Rationale of the chapter*

THE VERY limited purpose of this chapter is to describe and evaluate experiments showing that the units and rules of language discovered by linguists are relevant to the psychology of language. The writer presupposes that an adequate description must be given of fully developed language behaviour before its development can be meaningfully discussed. It is therefore proposed to divide the chapter in the following way:

i. The descriptions of language offered by the linguists will be surveyed.

ii. Attempts to apply these descriptions to the language behaviour of adult language users will be discussed.

iii. Analyses of children's language learning in linguistic terms will be evaluated.

2. *The nature of linguistics*

Linguists study language as a system; they distinguish language from speech, which is the series of sounds produced by the language user. They obtain their evidence about the nature of language from the responses of informants who are native speakers of the language being investigated. These informants tell the linguist, for example, whether a word is the same after certain substitutions have been made in its sound patterns; or whether a sentence is grammatical or not. Linguistic analysis occurs at different levels, dealing with units of different size. It results, for example, in the isolation of *phonemes* which are inferred

175

units; the substitution of one phoneme into a word for another realizes a different word. *Morphemes* are minimal meaningful forms; 'house' is a morpheme, and so is the second 's' in 'houses'. Grammatical analysis deals with the ways in which morphemes are connected to form sentences. The major difference between grammatical analysis and the lower levels of analysis is that it allows the production of novel combinations of morphemes which are still grammatically acceptable. One can create a novel sentence, but one cannot create a novel phoneme.

3. *Constituent analysis*

The grammatical analysis of a sentence has traditionally employed the technique of constituent analysis. This allows the sentence to be sub-divided into subject and predicate, and these units in turn to be subdivided into smaller units, until the lowest level, the morpheme, is reached. The units at different levels of this hierarchy may be isolated by the linguist substituting items for the hypothesized unit; the informant agrees that these items perform the same function as the deleted unit. Constituent analysis is applied to particular sentences; a new development is the phrase-marker tree (Chomsky, 1957), which expresses constituent structure in terms of symbols. (e.g. S (sentence), NP (noun phrase), V (verb)). These symbols allow the generative nature of sentence construction to be made clear; the larger grammatical units are subdivided into smaller by means of re-write rules, and the individual morphemes are only allocated to the sentence structure after the re-write rules have been applied.

4. *Transformational grammars.*

Until recently, it was clear that linguists were concerned with the language system, psychologists with the language user's behaviour and inferences from it about his functioning. Psychologists distrusted the linguists' use of informants because it smacked of introspection, but welcomed their isolation of grammatical units, since these could be treated as hypothetical response classes. However, Chomsky (1957, 1965) has introduced many new concepts, which emphasize the generative aspects of grammar; he maintains that the ability of language users to deal with novel sentences is what needs to be explained.

Chomsky distinguishes competence from performance. Competence is the knowledge of his language that the language user has; it consists of a linguistic description of language in terms of various components. Performance is the language user's behaviour, which reflects his competence only indirectly; this is because the physical limitations of the human organism prevent the infinite potentiality of the linguistic rules from being realized. Chomsky also distinguishes deep from surface structure. Sentences may have the same logical subject and object but have different constituent structure (e.g. active and passive types of sentence); or they may have the same constituent structure but different logical subject and object (e.g. 'John is eager to please' and 'John is easy to please'). It is therefore necessary to hypothesize a deep structure, consisting of strings of morphemes in the form of subject and predicate or main verb and object. The sentences we speak are generated from these deep structure strings partly by means of transformational rules. These include the rules for the formation of sentences with subordinate clauses, and of negative, interrogative, or imperative types of sentence. It is supposed that the negative element (for example) is chosen in the deep structure, and then obligatory rules are applied to produce a negative sentence.

It must be emphasized that these are linguistic, not psychological theories. Inferences are made about the nature of language on the basis of informant's responses and linguists' intuitions. Neither traditional nor generative linguists assume that their theory is a psychological one. However, Chomsky does maintain that his theory must be a part of a model of the language user. But he stresses that the language user's behaviour is a very indirect reflexion of the theory. Clearly, this raises the basic problem of whether the linguists' intuitions or the subject's behaviour are the ultimate criteria. The linguists assume that the experimental techniques for investigating behaviour are at fault, because they do not reveal the effect of competence on performance.

II. THE PSYCHOLOGY OF GRAMMAR

1. *The planning of language*

This basic conception of the planning of language behaviour by the language user according to rules is elaborated by Miller *et al.* (1960). A stimulus-response theory of language production, they maintain, is inadequate. If a sentence is a response, then there is no possibility of my ever having learned the sentence I am now writing; for I have probably never written it before, and therefore there has been no opportunity for reward or learning. A more sophisticated learning theorist might support an information theory approach. This would suggest that previous utterances produce self-stimulation to which subsequent utterances are responses; for information theory supposes that a new state of the speaker is produced by each item of language output, and that this new state generates the next item, which in its turn gives rise to a new state; and so on, till the sequence is completed. Aborn *et al.* (1959) showed that this conception is inadequate by proving that when any word in a passage was omitted and had to be guessed, less guesses were required when five previous and five subsequent words of context were given than when ten previous words were given. This experiment concerned the input (decoding) aspect of language behaviour. The study of pausal phenomena by Goldman-Eisler (1961) and Maclay and Osgood (1959) indicates that the same applies to language output (encoding). Goldman-Eisler showed that when subjects were given a cartoon, there were more pauses in their speech when they were explaining it than when they were merely describing it. Moreover, the pauses occurred before words which required most guesses by other subjects when omitted from a transcript of the recording. Maclay and Osgood also found that pauses occurred before lexically difficult words and before syntactic units. The conclusion is inescapable that subjects were planning their output during the pauses. Such a conclusion invalidates any theory of language which maintains that only previous context determines present utterance. One must therefore abandon a simple learning theory or information theory approach; for apart from its unwarranted assumption that words are the basic unit of language behaviour, information theory cannot embrace the planning of future utterances.

However, this does not imply that the acceptance of the generative linguists' model of language as a psychological model is necessary. They are assuming that their description of language, derived more from their own intuitions than from informants' responses, is also a description of the language user's competence. The psychologists' job, they say, is to investigate performance and isolate the characteristics of the human organism which make performance such a bad reflexion of competence. They assume that their intuitions are correct and must be incorporated into the psychological model of the language user. The difficulties of this view become clear when the behaviour of experimental subjects does not conform to predictions based on the competence model. The linguist claims that this is because the performance is only an indirect reflexion of competence; many psychologists would say that it is because the competence model is not empirically justified as an intervening variable. If results do not support an hypothesis, then the hypothesis, not the experimental method must be discarded. The linguists' theories are therefore to be regarded as fruitful sources of experimental hypothesis. Experiments show that human beings do use some linguistic rules, and can analyse down to deep structure; but there is no need to put a little linguist in every brain. A general theory of behaviour which can embrace language behaviour must be found.

2. *Transformations*

Psychological hypotheses demand the use of psychological techniques to test them. The question psychologists must ask is whether different transformations are functionally different, that is, whether the language user deals differently with each of them. Whether or not transformational syntax is an adequate description of the language is not their concern. Miller (1962), in an important experiment, found that different transformations took students different times to perform. He supposed that performing transformations was part of the planning behaviour of language users, and therefore in a sense was experimentally assuming the process he was hypothesizing. He found that, as transformational grammar would predict, affirmative to negative transformations took less time than active to passive ones, and affirmative active to negative passive took approximately the sum of the times of the two simpler transformations. It was left to other experimenters, for example Mehler (1963), to show that subjects recalled sentences they had learned with greater or lesser success according to their transformational type, and to conclude that they recalled the affirmative sentence plus a grammatical 'tag' noting which transformation to perform.

However, the difficulty of isolating syntactic variables of this sort from semantic variables was demonstrated by Slobin (1966). He found that the transformation from affirmative to negative was more difficult than that from active to passive when the task was evaluating the truth or falsehood of a sentence by referring to a picture of the event described in it. As soon as the subjects were required to relate language to a state of affairs, the grammatical expectation that passive transformations would be more difficult than negative is refuted. Semantic variables had added complications to syntactic predictions, with the result that the greater simplicity of the rules for negative transformations did not lead to a greater ease in relating negative statements to states of affairs.

Wason (1965) has also found this semantic difficulty in negativity. Marks and Miller (1964) have started the complex task of analysing this interaction of syntax and semantics; they produced syntactic nonsense by randomizing word order and semantic nonsense by mixing words between their experimental sentences. Thus the normal sentence 'Healthy young babies sleep soundly' became the syntactically confused 'Sleep young soundly babies healthy', and the semantically anomalous 'Colourless green ideas sleep furiously'. They found that both semantic and syntactic structure aided recall, and that syntactic confusion led to different types of error from semantic confusion. Miller and Isard (1963) found that normal grammatical sentences were perceived more accurately in noise than semantically anomalous but grammatically correct sentences, and that these in turn were perceived more accurately than strings of words. This indicates that syntactic and semantic factors are relevant to the perception of input as well as the planning of output, a conclusion not necessarily to be inferred from experiments demanding memorizing and recall.

3. *Constituent analysis*

Constituent analysis may also provide psychologically important rules and units. Concentration on transformational syntax has led to a disregard of the possibility that phrase units are psychologically basic, and that in the adult language user transformations may be so automatic as to take up little planning time. Instead, the production of sequences of phrase units connected by the requisite markers and fitted to the communication requirements might be the hardest task for the speaker.

Ladefoged and Broadbent (1960) had subjects listen to a passage, and placed click noises in the middle of words and of phrase units. When subjects were afterwards asked to recall where in the sentence these clicks had occurred, they tended to place them before the word or phrase in the middle of which they had in fact occurred. However, the possibility arose that the clicks were drawn to the beginning of units because there was an acoustic pause there, not because of the psychological importance of the phrase units. Nevertheless, Fodor and Bever (1965) confirmed the Ladefoged and Broadbent results in essence, and found that more correct recalls occurred when the clicks were in fact placed at the constituent junctions than when they were not.

Johnson (1965) found that when sentences were learned and recalled, transitional errors occurred more frequently at phrase junctions than within phrases. A transitional error is defined as passage from a correct word to an incorrect word. Furthermore, within the phrases themselves, transitional errors were more likely to occur when the transition was near the stem of the phrase-marker tree than when it was near the periphery. In other words, the larger the constituent units between which the transitions existed, the higher the probability of transitional error; for example, in the sentence 'The tall boy saved the dying woman', transitional errors were more likely to occur between 'saved' and 'the' than between 'the' and 'dying', and more likely between the latter two than between 'dying' and 'woman'. This result supported the hypothesis that sentences are planned in a hierarchical way, from larger to smaller units, and that these units are those isolated by constituent analysis. Johnson (1966a and 1966b) produced added experimental evidence. He found (1966a) that subjects who had previously learned adjective-noun pairs made less transitional errors when they learned sentences including those pairs than subjects who had not previously learned the pairs. However, the same improvement did not occur in the case of subjects who had learned noun-verb pairs. In the sentences he used, the adjective-noun pairs occurred within phrase units, the noun-verb pairs between them. Johnson also found (1966b) that sentences of greater Yngve depth (see II, 4) gave rise to a higher transitional error probability in recall than sentences of a lower depth. However, this result may not be due so much to the grammatical complexity of the sentences (as indexed by Yngve depth) but to differential familiarity of the subjects with the sentence frames used. One would expect subjects to be more familiar with the sentence frames used in the sentences of lesser depth, e.g. 'The parent who spoke with me is old', than with the frames used in the sentences of greater depth, e.g. 'The parent with me who spoke is old'. Semantic variables, also, may have confounded results.

An interesting technique aimed at excluding semantic variables as far as possible was introduced by Epstein (1961). He generated strings of seven nonsense words, e.g. 'erenstan cate elendi edom ept ledear ari'. Then he added function words, e.g. 'The erenstan cate elendi the edom ept with ledear and ari'; finally, inflexions were added, e.g. 'The erenstany cates elendied the edom eptly with ledear and aris'. Epstein found that the strings with function words and inflexions added required less trials to a criterion of perfect recall than the strings with function words only; and both types required less trials than when their word-order was randomized. The reason for these results may well be that the added grammatical structure, provided by the function words and inflexions acting as markers, allowed subjects to group the strings into

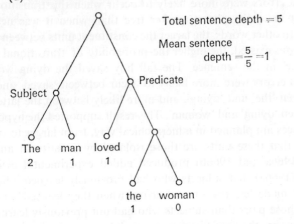

(a) The man loved the woman

Total sentence depth $= 5$

Mean sentence depth $= \dfrac{5}{5} = 1$

Predicate

Subject

The   man   loved
2   1   1

the   woman
1   0

(b) The man with the wooden leg loved the woman with the horrible squint

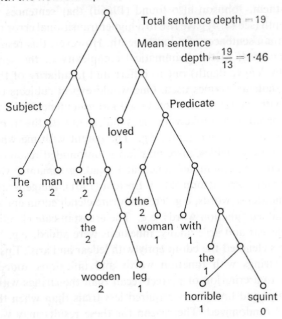

Total sentence depth $= 19$

Mean sentence depth $= \dfrac{19}{13} = 1 \cdot 46$

Subject   Predicate

loved
1

The   man   with
3   2   2

the
2

the
2

woman   with
1   1

wooden   leg
2   1

the
1

horrible   squint
1   0

Figure 1. Yngve analysis. Numbers under each word indicate its depth.

phrase units. A further possibility is that the grammatical structure by itself, apart from the words fitted to it, provides semantic reference. Agents, an action, a sufferer, a method, and instruments are all implied in the above 'nonsense' sentence. These hypotheses remain to be experimentally validated.

4. *Yngve analysis*

Perhaps the most important application of constituent analysis to psychology appears in the work of Yngve (1962). Yngve suggests that the depth of any word in a sentence is the number of left branches leading to it in a binary phrase-marker tree (see Figure 1.). Thus in the simple sentence 'The man loved the woman', the word 'The' has a depth of two. The sentence as a whole has a mean depth of one, calculated by dividing the sum of the depth of the words by the number of words. In the sentence 'The man with the wooden leg loved the woman with the horrible squint', the mean sentence depth is 1·46. More important, the mean depth of the phrase 'with the wooden leg' is 1·75, that of the phrase 'with the horrible squint' 0·75. This is because the former is structurally embedded between the subject and the predicate, while the latter is tagged on to the end of the predicate. The notion of depth is psychologically important both to output and to input; to output, because it indicates to the speaker how many grammatical commitments he has let himself in for; and to input because it indicates to the listener how much grammatical complexity he may expect. In the example 'The man loved the woman', the word 'The' leads to two commitments, first, to utter a noun, and secondly, to utter a predicate. Similarly, in the longer example quoted above, the phrase 'with the wooden leg' has a greater depth than 'with the horrible squint' because the speaker has continually to bear in mind his commitment to utter a predicate. These commitments and expectations need to be stored in the short-term memory while the sentence is being spoken, at least until each has been fulfilled. Thus a valuable theoretical connexion is made with findings in the field of short-term memory. If the depth of any item is more than seven, it is improbable that the immediate memory has the capacity to retain the commitments involved. Miller (1956) showed that seven chunks of information, (plus or minus two) was the capacity of short-term memory. Add to this the need to store semantic as well as syntactic commitments, and one is left with the hypothesis that a practicable limit to the depth of any word in a sentence should be much less than seven.

Yngve emphasizes the planning aspect of grammar to such an extent that he neglects the need, when a sentence is being uttered, to remember not only the grammar that is going to be used, but also the grammar that has already been used. The earlier parts of any sentence contain the most information (when information is defined as the uncertainty of any item as indexed by the number of guesses taken by the adult language user to guess that item when it is omitted). This is obviously true, since there is little or no context at the beginning of a sentence to reduce uncertainty, whereas at the middle and end of a sentence there is maximum context. It is reasonable to assume that grammatical structure as well as semantic content follow this rule. One would therefore find the maximum need to memorize the earlier parts of the sentence, since they contain the most information. Uncertainty as to the large-scale structure of a sentence decreases as the sentence progresses. However, it might be argued that this only indicates that there would be a heavy load on memory if there were the need to store the earlier part of the sentence, but that this is still unproven; it may on the contrary be true that the language speaker need only remember his commitments for as long as they are unfulfilled; once he has fulfilled each commitment, there is no need to remember either the commitment, or the word (e.g. 'The' in Figure 1) whereby he committed himself. This may be true of the speaker, although it is difficult to believe that he can afford to forget such large scale structures as the subject; but what of the listener? Yngve does not clearly bring out the possible distinctions between speaker and listener. The speaker may have planned his utterance at all levels of the hierarchy, from subject and predicate down to morphemes; but the listener cannot perceive in such large units until he has discovered what those units are in any given sentence. It is not known at what point in a sentence the listener succeeds in making this transition from the small units which he must deal with at first to the larger units. However, it may be surmised that the phrase-markers, such as tense suffixes and function words, have an important cue function for the listener in indicating where the phrase boundaries are; and it must also be supposed that the listener must retain the early items of any sentence in his short-term memory, at least until he knows how those items are organized into larger units. This need for the perceiver of language to store the previous context in memory is perhaps exemplified in the greater length of written than of spoken sentences; one can re-read the beginning of a sentence in a book, but it is annoying for a speaker to be asked to repeat what he has just said. One is left with the hypothesis that speakers plan hierarchically from larger units to smaller, while listeners structure their perception from smaller units to larger; and that therefore memory of what is past is more important to the listener than to the speaker. An additional complication is the part played by semantic content. Can the speaker forget his previous semantic context? Or do semantic and syntactic commitments function in different ways? It might be supposed that previous semantic context has a greater constraint on subsequent utterance than previous syntactic context; there may be many ways of finishing a sentence grammatically, but only a few of finishing it so that it is being used appropriately (this should not be taken as a definition of semantics!).

However, Yngve's hypothesis has great explanatory power. It deals, for example, with the result which transformational grammar on its own cannot explain; that sentences of the same transformational type, length, and word frequency are nevertheless recalled with different degrees of accuracy. Martin and Roberts (1966) found that sentences with the above variables controlled, but differing in mean Yngve depth, were differentially recalled. Thus, for example, 'They were not prepared for rainy weather' has a mean depth of 1·29, and was more efficiently recalled than 'Children are not allowed out after dark' (depth 1·71). Martin and Roberts also found a significant effect of transformational types of sentence, and an interaction effect between sentence type and mean depth. An analysis of errors revealed that some errors were grammatical in nature, and consisted of a transformation of the sentence actually presented; sometimes the sentence produced in error was of a lesser depth than the sentence presented; only when the presented sentence was of a depth of 1·71 was this so. In other words, the depth of the more complex sentence proved too much for subjects, who tried to simplify the structure as a result. One may question this inference on the grounds that it is fairly difficult anyway to generate a sentence of a depth less than 1·29. However, the results do indicate the need to take the grammatical complexity of any sentence into account regardless of its type; they further show that the results attributing difficulty of recall to complexity of transformational type (e.g. Mehler, 1963) may be partly explained in terms of complexity of constituent structure. Indeed, Martin and Roberts succeed in explaining Mehler's results solely in terms of the differing mean depths of his sentences, which he failed to control. Furthermore, a valuable quantitative index of grammatical complexity has been derived, and a theoretical connexion made with another field of experimental psychology.

III. LANGUAGE LEARNING

Granted the premiss that linguistic rules are psychologically important, the questions remain in what way, at what age, and in what order do children acquire these rules necessary for generating grammatical output. The acquisition of a rule does not, of course, imply its conscious adoption; merely the regular use by the child of language predictable by some of the rules found necessary to predict adult language.

There is a danger of tacitly assuming that learning processes, whether of a reinforcing or an inductive type, are the only processes at work. Lenneberg (1964) argues that there are critical periods during the development of the central nervous system in which rules of language have to be learned by the child; and, indeed, that there are aspects of this development which favour the learning of certain rules of language and not that of others.

A regular development of morphemic rules has been distinguished by Berko (1958). She found that when children were shown drawings of strange creatures and actions which were given nonsense names (e.g. 'wug', 'glinging'), they successfully added 's' to form the plural when two such wugs were shown, and 'ed' to form the past tense when past action was implied. Plural 's' occurred earlier than possessive ''s', and in both these cases and that of the past tense, the consonant form ('s') occurred at an earlier age than the syllabic form ('es'). It has also been found, by Ervin and Miller (1963), that such rules are generalized to all occasions, disregarding the irregular forms (e.g. 'bringed' for 'brought'). From such failures to produce irregular forms, the existence of regular rules (albeit over-inclusive ones) may be inferred. The importance of inflexions in providing structure was indicated in the earlier discussion of Epstein's (1961) work; it may be surmised that the growth of some morphemic rules is a necessary condition for the growth of more than a minimal phrase grammar. If this is so, it indicates that an Yngve analysis of children's speech needs the previous formation of morphemic rules by the child as well as the learning of the subject-predicate distinction. These learning factors are also qualified by the added physiological factor of short-term memory capacity.

The Berko experiment has been cited first as an example of work in this field. It solves one of the major problems; how to indicate that a child has mastered a rule. Like any concept, mastery is only evidenced by the application of a rule to a new instance, new, that is, in the experience of the child. If nonsense words and unfamiliar referents had not been used, the child could merely have been repeating or reducing an adult's utterances which he had heard.

However, Berko's experimental technique requires the use by the child of regular adult rules. Other workers (e.g. Brown and Fraser, 1963) have recorded children's spontaneous speech in their homes. Their utterances have then been analysed as though they were a novel language, and special grammars written to describe them. It has been found that the earliest two-word utterances consist of two classes of words, pivot and open. Pivot words occupy a fixed position in the utterance and are few in number; the open class contains many different items from the child's vocabulary. 'Plane gone', 'Car gone', 'Daddy gone' are typical early two-word sentences. Children start producing such utterances at about 18 months.

Later developments show that children's grammar approximates more and more closely to adult grammar. One of the earliest stages is the differentiation of the pivot class; articles, demonstrative pronouns, adjectives, and possessive pronouns all become used with the pivot word. As a result, the child utters a phrase, substitutable for the original pivot class. However, such utterances as 'A dirt', 'A hands' and 'A Jimmy' show that the rules acquired are still over-generalized when compared with adult grammar; the rule NP $\rightarrow$ Art+N has been mastered, but the distinction between mass, count, and proper nouns has not been acquired.

At a later stage still, the child is in the process of mastering the more complex transformational rules (Menyuk, 1964). Such utterances as 'No wipe fingers', 'I not crying', 'It's doesn't fall out' indicate different stages of mastery of the negative transformation. McNeill (1966) suggests that transformations are acquired to ease the cognitive load of remembering the different possible placements of the negative morpheme.

Considerable controversy centres on the acquisition process. Generative linguists consider that there is a considerable innate component involved. They cite the speed of acquisition as evidence, and, more important, they allege that the deep structure of language and not its surface structure has been acquired at an early stage. They claim that the earliest child utterances reflect the rules of deep structure; for example, the distinction between pivot and open classes is taken to reflect the child's embryonic application of the deep-structure distinction between subject and predicate. It is claimed that the utterances of young children are so different from those of adults that the learning component is minimal and the contribution of innate factors is considerable. These theorists therefore favour a very specific critical period theory in which language heard by the child serves only to trigger off the innate components. These components are taken (by Chomsky, 1965), to be the linguistic universals, that is, those features of deep structure common to every known language.

Many suggestions have been made as to possible learning processes involved. Fraser and Brown (1963) note the 'telegraphic' nature of children's utterances. Function words are omitted, content words retained. It is suggested that children imitate what they hear said, but that they cannot repeat the whole utterance because of memory limitations. They therefore select the basic elements and omit the function words. The process may be reversed, it is suggested, by the parents expanding the child's telegraphic utterance, though still using simplified forms (Spradlin and Rosenberg, 1964). The child may then imitate the expanded version. Generative theorists criticize this theory on the grounds that children's utterances are so different from those of adults; the order of the words is often reversed (e.g. 'All gone milk', 'Put on it'). This objection is also applied to learning theorists who attempt to explain the pivot and open class in terms of position, supposing that the child succeeds in establishing a pivot class by hearing the pivot word used in a certain position in adult sentences. Further evidence cited against the imitation hypothesis is the report of Ervin (1964) that imitations by children of adults were no more grammatically complex than their ordinary utterances.

It may well be concluded that the imitation – expansion cycle is not by itself an adequate explanation. It must be supposed that the child has more abstract principles of production than would be predicted from the imitation hypothesis. However, it does not follow that these principles must be highly specific and innately based. The fact that the child hears many elliptical and ungrammatical utterances while learning is taken to support the generative hypothesis; for, it is argued, the successful acquisition of language by the child could not occur using such faulty models for learning. However, the ungrammatical and elliptical nature of adult speech could be the reason for some of the child's faulty generalizations and unusual utterances; he might say 'All gone milk' because he has heard the words 'All gone' and 'Milk' in isolation. The general success of children in developing a hierarchical productive mechanism may be innately based, but the hierarchical nature of other skills allows this to be considered a general rather than a specifically linguistic maturational feature.

The fact that older children have successfully grasped the functional nature of form classes is clear from the many findings (e.g. Ervin, 1961) that their responses in a word-association task are paradigmatic while those of younger children are syntagmatic. That is, older children respond with a word which might be substituted for the stimulus word in a sentence, while those under 7 or 8 respond with words which would follow the stimulus word in a sentence.

One of the main shortcomings of the generative linguists' approach is that they do not consider the non-linguistic context of the child's utterance when recording data; they merely apply a grammatical analysis to the transcriptions of their recordings. However, this appears to omit the important feature of comprehension. Fraser, Bellugi, and Brown (1963) showed that 3-year-old children could comprehend, for example, the past-tense and plural morphemes when presented with two utterances which differed only in that specific grammatical feature. Comprehension was indicated by the correct selection of one of two pictures differing only in the relevant feature. Imitation was found to be easier than comprehension, which in its turn was easier than production. It is possible that comprehension is a necessary condition for meaningful production. Children may have learned to assign deep-structure functions to certain word classes and grammatical constructions on the basis of each class or construction being used of a particular type of referent. For a young child, nouns are associated with objects, verbs with actions, and so on.

It may be said in conclusion that the application of linguistics to psychology is of vital significance. It allows the experimental investigation of language in forms at least reasonably like natural language. It offers an explanation for the planning behaviour of language users, allowing full importance to future as well as to past linguistic events. It provides the concepts of rules and grammars, and thereby a rationale and techniques for investigating children's language learning. However, linguistics cannot be expected to solve problems that are basically psychological in nature. It remains to be discovered how grammatical rules are learned; how the different levels of rules interact; whether different principles are involved in the perception and production of language; and what are the complex relationships between syntax and semantics.

REFERENCES

(J.V.L.V.B. = Journal of Verbal Learning and Verbal Behaviour.)

ABORN, M., RUBENSTEIN, H., and STERLING, T. D. (1959). Sources of contextual constraint upon words in sentences. *J. exp. Psychol.* **57,** 171–180.

BERKO, J. (1958). The Child's learning of English Morphology. *Word.* **14,** 150–177.

BROWN, R., and FRASER, C. (1963). *The acquisition of syntax.* In Cofer, C. W., and Musgrave, B. S. (eds.), *Verbal Behaviour and Learning,* 158–209. New York: McGraw-Hill.

CHOMSKY, N. (1957). *Syntactic Structures.* The Hague: Mouton.

CHOMSKY, N. (1965). *Aspects of the Theory of Syntax.* Cambridge, Mass: M.I.T. Press.

EPSTEIN, W. (1961). The influence of syntactical structure on learning. *Amer. J. Psychol.* **75,** 121–126.

ERVIN, S. M. (1961). Changes with age in the verbal determinants of word association. *Amer. J. Psychol.* **74,** 361–372.

ERVIN, S. M. (1964). Imitation and structural change in children's language. In Lenneberg, E. H. (ed.), *New Directions in the Study of Language,* 163–190. Cambridge, Mass: M.I.T. Press.

ERVIN, S. M., and MILLER, W. R. (1963). Language development. In *Child Psychology.* (Yearbook of Nat. Soc. Stud. Educ.) Chicago: University of Chicago Press, 108–143.

FODOR, J., and BEVER, T. (1965). The psychological reality of linguistic segments. *J.V.L.V.B.,* **4,** 414–420.

FRASER, C., BELLUGI, U., and BROWN, R. (1963). Control of grammar in imitation, comprehension, and production. *J.V.L.V.B.* **2,** 121–135.

GOLDMAN-EISLER, F. (1961). Continuity of speech utterance, its determinants and its significance. *Language and Speech.* **4,** 220–231.

JOHNSON, N. F. (1965). Linguistic models and functional units of language behaviour. In Rosenberg, S. (ed.), *Directions in Psycholinguistics,* 29–65. New York: Macmillan.

JOHNSON, N. F. (1966) (a). The influence of associations between elements of structured verbal responses. *J.V.L.V.B.* **5,** 369–374.

JOHNSON, N. F. (1966) (b). On the relationship between sentence structure and the latency in generating the sentence. *J.V.L.V.B.* **5,** 375–380.

LADEFOGED, P., and BROADBENT, D. E. (1960). Perception of sequence in auditory events. *Quart. J. exp. Psychol.* **12,** 162–170.

LENNEBERG, E. H. (1964). A biological perspective of language. In Lenneberg, E. H. (ed.), *New Directions in the Study of Language.* Cambridge, Mass: M.I.T. Press.

MACLAY, H., and OSGOOD, C. E. (1959). Hesitation phenomena in spontaneous English speech. *Word.* **15**, 19–44.

MARKS, L. E., and MILLER, G. A. (1964). The Role of semantic and syntactic constraints in the memorization of English sentences. *J.V.L.V.B.* **3**, 1–5.

MARTIN, E., and ROBERTS, K. H. Grammatical factors in sentence retention. *J.V.L.V.B.* **5**, 211–218.

MCNEILL, D. (1966). Developmental Psycholinguistics. In Smith F., and Miller, G. A. (eds.), *The Genesis of Language.* Cambridge, Mass: M.I.T. Press.

MEHLER, J. (1963). Some effects of grammatical transformations on the recall of English sentences. *J.V.L.V.B.* **2**, 346–351.

MENYUK, P. (1964). Syntactic rules used by children from pre-school through first grade. *Child Developm.* **35**, 533–546.

MILLER, G. A. (1956). The magical number seven, plus or minus two. *Psychol. Review.* **63**, 81–97.

MILLER, G. A. (1962). Some psychological studies of grammar. *Amer. Psychologist.* **17**, 748–762.

MILLER, G. A. (1964). The Psycholinguists. *Encounter.* **23**, 29–37.

MILLER, G. A., GALANTER, E., and PRIBRAM, K. H. (1960). *Plans and the Structure of Behaviour.* New York: Holt, Rinehart and Winston.

MILLER, G. A., and ISARD, S. (1963). Some perceptual consequences of linguistic rules. *J.V.L.V.B.* **2**, 217–228.

SLOBIN, D. I. (1966). Grammatical transformations and sentence comprehension in childhood and adulthood. *J.V.L.V.B.* **5**, 211–218.

SPRADLIN, J. E., and ROSENBERG, S. (1964). Complexity of adult verbal behaviour in dyadic situations with retarded children. *J. Abnorm. Soc. Psychol.* **68**, 694–698.

WASON, P. C. (1965). The contexts of plausible denial. *J.V.L.V.B.* **4**, 7–11.

WERNER, H., and KAPLAN, B. (1963). *Symbol Formation.* New York: Wiley.

YNGVE, V. H. (1961). The Depth Hypothesis. In Jakobson, R. (ed.), *Structure of Language in its Mathematical Aspects,* 130–138. Providence, Rhode Island: American Mathematical Society. (A simpler account is to be found in *Scientific American,* 1962, Vol. 206. No. 6, 68–76).

7

Reading and Learning to Read

G. R. ROBERTS AND E. A. LUNZER

I. INTRODUCTION

EVERY teacher is aware of the controversy between the phonic approach to reading and 'look and say' methods, a controversy which is less acute today than it may have been some years ago, but one which is not wholly resolved. It is interesting to note that a parallel conflict between an earlier alphabetical approach and what was essentially a whole-word or sentence method reaches back at least as far as the sixteenth century (Fries, 1964). Neither position arose by chance.

The divergence between them is based on the dual character of language. Language is representational. It serves the function of communicating 'meaning'. It is a system made up of conventional signs or symbols. It has reference to a content which is extra-linguistic. This is the semantic aspect of language. But language is also itself a form of behaviour, a complex skill. This is its phonic aspect. The difference in approach reflects the two aspects of language. Advocates of the alphabetical, and later the phonic, method based their approaches to the teaching of reading on the assumption that the principal task to be mastered in learning to read is the correspondence between the printed letters and the sounds that they represent. Conversely, advocates of the 'whole word' and sentence methods based their approach to reading on its functional aspect.

However, neither the problem of meaning nor the character of language is exhausted by the representational – phonic dichotomy. Language is not a mere set of symbols but a system of symbols. It comprises units of different sizes – phonemes (corresponding roughly to contrasted letter sounds), morphemes (which would include prefixes and suffixes such as the adverbial ending *-ly* or the negating *un-*, *in-*, as well as recognized words), strings or phrases, sentences and utterances (vocal) or texts (written). The sequential arrangements of these units conform to a system which is the grammar of the language. The child in learning to speak must acquire grammar and syntax just as he needs to learn how to produce the sounds which he intends and to select the words that he requires (see Chapter 6). Linguistic behaviour involves concurrent activity at three levels: representational, grammatical (or sequential), and perceptuo-motor (Osgood, 1957, and Osgood and Sebeok, 1966). The apprehension of meaning in spoken and written language depends in great measure on activity at the intermediate level, and is not limited to mere correspondence between word and 'meaning'.

Recent attempts to develop new methods in the teaching of reading point to a growing recognition that the establishment of skill depends on the acquisition of a high level of automatization at all three levels in relation to the interpretation of the written text.

It should be stated at the outset that such an aim cannot be achieved simply by mixing a little phonics with a lot of look-and-say or vice versa. It depends for its realization on the achievement of a programmed curriculum based on the recognition that the three aspects of language intervene at every stage.

Before attempting to analyse the process of reading from these three aspects, it is instructive to pause and consider the limitations of some of the older methods.

1. *The alphabetic method*

A child learning to read in the nineteenth century would probably begin by learning the names of the letters. He then learned to join two letters by repeating the name of each letter followed by the synthesized sound of the pair, e.g. '/ei/,/bi/ says /æ b/; /ai/,/bi/ says /ib/'. When the child was proficient he progressed to three, four and then five letter combinations. The keynote of the teaching was repetition and a great deal of this was held to be necessary before the child could embark on the reading of text. This led to a considerable amount of pre-reading practice of a narrow kind. Inevitably, when taught by this method, a child's first introduction to text was most successful when the words appearing in the primer were uniformly short. The limitation in vocabulary produced severe deficiencies in the resultant text. Too often this took the form of a stilted prose, although perhaps not always as stilted as the sentence 'If he is as I am, he is in' found in an early nineteenth century book and quoted by Diack (1960).

The alphabetic method, like its successor the phonic method, was based on a recognition of the alphabetical nature of writing in English, i.e. the existence of correspondences between written and spoken language. The correspondence is twofold: between letter (or digraph) and sound, and between the left to right order of the printed symbols and temporal succession in phonation. Both are approximate.

However, the principal objection to the alphabetical method did not arise from the approximate character of such correspondences but from a recognition of the irrelevance of letter names. A child who has progressed to the reading of [*con*] and [*tent*] is well placed to synthesize *content*, because the sounds of the separate syllables are close to the sound of the combination. But the sounding [*si:*],[*ou*],[*en*], is not at all close to that of [kɔn].

It remains to be said that 'nevertheless it [alphabetic method] worked, Shakespeare learned to read by this method; so did Plato, Aristotle and Dante' (Diack, 1960; Stott, 1964, makes the same point). It is a commonplace that the majority of children will learn to read whatever method is employed. A psychologist would say that what is learned by the child does not necessarily reflect what is taught by the teacher. However, the alphabetical method had one strength which is not always recognized: the repetition of the letter names emphasized the correspondence between the spatial order of letters and the temporal order of sounds. And it may perhaps have done that more effectively than the old phonic method, in so far as the child is not called upon at the same time to fuse the letter names.

2. *The phonic method*

The phonic method began to supplant the alphabetic method in the second half of the nineteenth century. As its name implies this method emphasized the phonic aspect of language. But an attempt was made to highlight the correspondence between the temporal order of phonation and the spatial order of letters right from the start. At the same time considerable stress was laid on audio-visual matching. The name assigned to each letter or digraph was its most common sound value (or an approximation to it). By-passing letter naming, the child learnt to match letters and their sounds and then proceeded to join two letters and give them a sound, then three letters and so on. The method was thought to give the child direct knowledge of the basic ingredients of words. By sounding the letters he could approximate more closely to the final synthesized sound of the word.

Advances in the study of linguistics beginning with the work of Bloomfield (1933) lead one to question the underlying assumptions of the method. In particular, when a child, or even a literate adult, is asked to sound the individual phonemes of the word *fun* and then synthesize them, the result approximates more closely to [fə:], [ə:], [nə:], than to [fʌn]. More generally the sound value of a letter depends in large measure on its vocal context (e.g. the *d* in *duck* is not the same *d* as the *d* in *dig*), and the attempt to produce a phoneme in isolation gives rise to a sound which will be different from that of the letter in any context. Both Daniels and Diack (Royal Road Readers) and Stott (Programmed Reading Kit) accept this criticism as their point of departure for a revised phonic approach. The methods that result represent a far more sophisticated version of the phonic approach (see below, Section III).

A second objection parallels the earlier criticism of the alphabetic method. The restriction of vocabulary in phonic texts to regular and short words leads inevitably to a dull set of primers. At the same time, the insistence on phonic build up often involved a great deal of drill leading to boredom and revulsion.

However, the principal strength of the phonic method lay in its recognition of the essential character of an alphabetic writing. When the method is successful it is partly because the child has been taught to heed the correspondences between order of symbols and order of phones. And no one would deny that this recognition is an essential step in learning to read.

Against this, critics of the phonic method have argued that the analysis of printed words into phonemes and syllables and their subsequent synthesis involves a mental process which is too difficult for children with mental ages under six and a half years (see e.g. Schonell, 1945, and compare Doman, 1965, and Lynn, 1963, for statements of a contrary view).

However the isolation and the synthesis of 'phonemes' is in any case suspect, as we have just seen. Failure of younger children to make progress may well have been due to this inherent imperfection in their teaching. The argument that young children cannot synthesize syllables has the status of opinion. There is little research to support or, for that matter, to infirm it.

3. *Look-and-say*

It was as a reaction to the older type of phonic teaching and drill that the word-method, or look-and-say as it is popularly termed, was widely introduced into our schools. Its growing popularity was closely associated with the spread of Froebelian ideas on infant education.

Reviewing the development of reading methods in the eighteenth and nineteenth centuries, Fries (1964) concludes with the comment 'I have not been able to find the evidence to justify the assertion that the published findings of recent educational research [since 1916] have provided the basis of most of the modern reforms in reading instruction'. However the look-and-say method as popularized in America by the work of Gates (1947) and in this country by that of Schonell (1945) owed a great deal to psychological theory, in particular to the work of Thorndike and the demonstrations of Gestalt psychology (see Volume I, Chapter 1).

All learning, for Thorndike, consisted in the formation and strengthening of bonds between stimuli and responses. Stimuli and responses are units. The unit of language was the word. Verbal thinking itself was regarded by Thorndike as primarily a matter of associations between words. The aim of reading, like that of all language, was the communication of meaning. Hence the proper way to approach reading was by beginning with the word, since words were the primary units of meaning. Learning was a matter of strengthening bonds between stimuli and responses by repeated reinforcement. In general, complex skills could be reduced to the component bonds out of which they evolved. Transfer of training existed only in so far as it reflected common elements, i.e. individual S-R bonds.

This emphasis in Thorndike's approach is reflected in the use of the whole word as the starting point for learning, in the emphasis on repetition, and above all in the deliberate restriction of initial reading material by the use of vocabulary controls. In order to maximize formation of associative bonds between spoken and written word the words are repeated (in varying contexts). To minimize interference in learning, words are introduced gradually and old words are consolidated before the introduction of new ones.

A second element in the justification of the method derives from the perceptual experiments of Gestalt psychologists, with whose work Thorndike himself was by no means out of sympathy (Sandiford, 1942). Intuitive reasoning might suggest that the perception of words depended first and foremost on the visual recognition of letters or even of their parts. The demonstrations of Gestalt psychology had apparently shown that perception is a unitary whole. The visual form or appearance of the printed word was such a whole and could therefore provide the stimulus for the response – sounding the word.

It should be added that neither Gates nor Schonell were unaware of the importance of the phonic build up of words, and both provided exercises designed to teach this principle. However, the emphasis on the semantic aspects remained paramount and the introduction of phonics was deliberately postponed to a relatively late stage in learning. Further justification for such postponement could be found in the fact that many of the most frequent words in English are irregular in their spelling, while the rules governing the pronunciation of most of the words occurring in the natural vocabulary of children are far from simple and univocal.

Because of this dual approach the method undoubtedly achieved considerable success in the hands of sensitive and expert teachers. Indeed there is little reason to doubt that the child can achieve a greater fluency in reading text, using this method, rather earlier than he might with any other, albeit with a limited vocabulary. Not any text but text based on careful controls.

However, there is good reason to doubt whether the children who learn by the method of look-and-say are in fact as oblivious of visual-vocal correspondence in order as is sometimes supposed. Rather it appears to be the case that ignorance of this aspect remains a characteristic of those who fail. What is more, it is often apparent that their failure is directly attributable to the character of the teaching thay have received. In her survey of children's reading, Morris (1966) found that 'most of the "poor" readers had an imperfect knowledge of alphabet sounds, and, for nearly half of them, this could be regarded as one of the main causes of their unsatisfactory progress. Many did not clearly understand the difference between letter-names and letter-sounds.'

Even more questionable is the premise that children tend to be ignorant of the letters which constitute printed words. There is no reason to believe that children notice overall composition without reference to the details of *some* of the letters. Furthermore, infant schoolchildren are continually discriminating, in some way, between letters during the very early stages of learning to read. They notice 'snakey shapes' – S, and are intrigued if they learn it says 'ss'. They easily remember 'the curly letter with a stalk' – a, which stands at the beginning of the word 'apple'. These examples were noted with a child exactly 4 years old. We have found 3 year olds recognizing their name by its initial letter and thinking that all words beginning with 'm' and ending with 'y' were like 'monkey'. Similarly, they are interested in the sounds of letters, and love jingles and word play. This is not 'noticing shape alone', it is the start to a careful examination of the letter shapes and sounds within a word.

But the very fact that such distinctions are being made by children probably constitutes one of the most serious limitations of the look-and-say method. For if the pupil could be conveniently shielded from letters while learning words and sentences little harm would be done. He might then be introduced to the fine grain discriminative cues provided by letters at an appropriate stage in his learning (see Volume I, Chapter 1, Section VI, for an introduction to these Skinnerian concepts).

The fact is that since he notices them and uses them at a much earlier stage, he is very apt to use them inappropriately: the right cues become conditioned to the wrong behaviours. There is unwarranted generalization and genuine learning of errors. Both Anderson and Dearborn (1952) and Marchbanks and Levin (1965) found that letters were used more often than word shape as a cue for recognition. In observations with 3- and 4-year-old children, one of the writers found a tendency to confuse the whole word and its initial letters. Even when they could recognize a dozen or more words, they were still not sure whether it was the whole word they should be looking at or merely certain aspects of that word, e.g. the first letter or the first and last letters.

Using the look-and-say method the unwary teacher may even encourage error learning by inviting the pupil to leap at the word on the basis of his recognition of its initial letter (as if all words beginning with an m were '*monkey*', etc.), or to find a word on a previous page (because it was correctly read at the time) regardless of what cues the child might use in finding it and oblivious of the resultant discontinuity in the reading itself.

Perhaps the greatest weakness of look-and-say method is that it reproduces and even accentuates the very faults in motivation which it was designed to correct – if not for the quick learner then assuredly for the slow learner. This is the criticism made eloquently by Daniels and Diack (1960). The aim was to introduce the pupil early to meaningful and interesting text. The result, for the slow learner, was to condemn him to a never-ending repetition of a limited text whose content was so well known that it ceased to carry any meaning whatever. Even the multiplication of supplementary readers based on the same limited vocabulary could hardly offset the resulting apathy. But the cardinal, unpardonable offender is and remains the teacher who insists on perfect reading of a page or even a book before proceeding to the next. For in the end the slow reader does not read at all. He memorizes.

II. THE PROCESS OF READING

1. *Spoken language and reading*

It has been suggested that the relative failure of look-and-say methods to live up to expectation is due to a comparative neglect of the phonic aspect. Early phonic schemes paid insufficient attention to the representational aspect of language and moreover were open to criticism on the grounds of an erroneous interpretation of 'word building'.

However, concentration on the partial failure of these methods should not easily allow one to ignore the fact that, for the most part, they did not result in an illiterate population. Most children learn to read, by whatever method. In the opening paragraphs of this chapter, we described three distinct aspects of language, termed levels by Osgood, the semantic or representational, the grammatical or sequential, and the perceptuo-motor (corresponding to the phonic aspect). Since reading is a linguistic skill, all three are as essential to reading as they are in spoken language. It is difficult to resist the conclusion that such aspects as are inadequately taught by the teacher or realized by the writer of reading primers are none the less supplied by the successful pupil out of his store of linguistic skills. Similar considerations suggest a very general recipe for the development of superior teaching methods. A method should be superior in the measure that it is constructed on the basis of a better understanding of all aspects of language and the way in which they interact or come together in the process of reading. Needless to add, the test of any method will be its success with the slow reader.

Lewis's account in Chapter 5 of the beginnings of speech shows that the development of phonation in the infant consists in a series of progressive differentiations, beginning with the differentiation of the guttural *g* or *k* and the labial *m* and that of the closed vowel [u] and the open vowel [a]. Leaving aside the phonetic analysis of the sounds emitted in crying, neither vowel sounds nor consonant sounds are emitted in isolation. The earliest forms are consonant vowel combinations (cooing and gurgling), to be followed later by reduplications (babbling). Approximation to the sounds of the mother tongue is a matter of schema with correction. Successive differentiations yield a great variety of phones, and it has even been claimed that every infant produces all the variations which figure as significant phonemic contrasts in every spoken language. Be that as it may, the forms of the mother tongue are learnt by trial and error. Forms which approximate to heard language seem to be self-reinforcing, such reinforcement leading to stabilization by means of circular reactions (see also Volume I, Chapter 5, Section II).

The understanding of spoken language develops alongside progress in phonation. The first and in some ways most significant landmark in the development of spoken language occurs when the child utters his first word in a meaningful context (Vygotsky, 1962). It marks the fusion of phonation on the one hand and language as a signalling system on the other. Further progress depends not only on development in vocabulary and in the representational function of language but also on the acquisition of grammar (Chapter 6). The relatively prolonged interval between the utterance of the first single words (*c.* 11 months) and the first word combinations (*c.* 17 months) argues that syntax cannot begin until the phonation of individual words has been automatized. Selection of a desired word can then trigger the vocalic co-ordination required for its utterance without disturbance to the conscious direction of behaviour – this being given over to representational and syntactic controls. There is reason to believe that the acquisition of grammatical rules governing the most common speech patterns follows a similar course; trial and error approximation, substitution of new words in familiar speech patterns, automatization of grammar. Recent research reviewed in Chapter 6 (and see especially Bellugi and Brown, 1964) indicates that the process is largely complete for the more common speech patterns by the age of 3 to 3½ years. The period from 3½ to 5 is marked by further extensions to include more complex speech patterns. This is presumably why length of sentence proves to be one of the most significant indicators of language development in so many research studies (McCarthy, 1954).

This brief reminder of the course of language development has three important implications for the problem of reading. In the first place, the child learning to read is not learning language. As Fries (1964) rightly remarks, he is learning to substitute visuo-spatial cues for audio-temporal cues in an established skill. But the fact that language is a multi-level skill implies that the substitution at the perceptuo-motor level cannot be separated from its context. He is not learning a mere substitution which is what Fries seems to imply. It is a substitution within a schema. In other words although he is not acquiring the representational and grammatical components of the skill, these enter into the process of learning to read at every stage, as will be apparent in Section II. 2.

In the second place, the substitution at the perceptuo-motor level involves an element of regression. Performance at this level is fully automatized when the child is first introduced to reading. To effect the substitution he must begin by monitoring these processes. The fluent speaker does not cognize the words which make up his utterances as separate entities. The beginning reader must. The former never cognizes the constituent phonemes in his words. The beginning reader needs to do this too. Recent studies by Bruce demonstrate that he does not come to this easily. Children below the age of six have difficulty in telling what *clap* would be without the first sound or *road* without the last, etc., the words being given orally and in isolation (Bruce, 1964).

In the third place, there is nothing in the child's acquisition of speech to correspond with word-building, as conceived in the phonic method. The acquisition of spoken words at least at the level of the syllable proceeds entirely by differentiation and substitution within a syllabic whole.

2. *Control of behaviour in skilled reading*

In spite of the voluminous literature which faces anyone who approaches the topic of reading, we have been unable to discover a satisfactory analysis of the process as a whole. Reading is a form of skilled behaviour. It is interesting to recall the following remarks of Bartlett (1947) which he describes as 'fundamental considerations' applicable to any skill: 'The good player of a quick ball game, the surgeon conducting an operation, the physician arriving at a clinical decision – in each case there is a flow from signals interpreted to action carried out, back to further signals and on again to more action, up to the culminating point of the achievement of the task. From beginning to end the signals and actions form a series, not just a succession'.

An attempt was made in Volume I, Chapter 4, to develop a schematic representation of the mechanisms which appear to enter into the regulation of behaviour in general and of skilled behaviour in particular, together with their functional relations with one another. The account draws heavily on the perspectives outlined by Bartlett as modified by his successors in British psychology, notably Craik and Broadbent. It seems to us that this kind of approach enables one to come closer to grips with the analysis of the reading process as a whole, than the mere description of limited aspects taken in isolation. The review outlined in Volume I, Chapter 4, was conceived of quite generally and without specific reference to reading. We believe that the general conception fits the experimental findings in this field surprisingly well, as we will try to show. While this is very far from demonstrative proof it is moderately encouraging.

It is characteristic of Bartlett's approach to the study of skill that one does not proceed by first observing the behaviour of the unskilled performer and then following this stage by stage until the final achievement, but rather by analysing first of all the co-ordinations implied by the behaviour in its final form and then seeking to establish the way in which they are acquired. Let us therefore consider what are the mechanisms which seem to be operative in skilled (adult) reading. It is convenient to set out our hypotheses in a somewhat dogmatic fashion, both as to the general form in which they are cast and in respect of their details. The latter we hope to support by reference to established findings. The justification for the former, such as it is, is set out at some length in the chapter already referred to.

Reading is a skilled behaviour in which one engages to obtain 'information'. The term is intended to be general in its application. Reading a poster or an advertisement provides information about what goods are advertised, what is said about them. Reading a light novel provides information about the persons of the hero, the heroine and the third party, how the plot thickens, how it reaches its climax, and how it is resolved. At every stage in the process, there is uncertainty in the reader; what he reads usually has the effect of reducing the uncertainty in some measure but often at the same time generating new uncertainty. In point of fact reading is often undertaken in the expectation that there will be this cycle of uncertainty – information – new uncertainty, and so on. Indeed, literature, whether serious or light, is written with just this aim in view, although the uncertainties are usually greater and more disturbing in the former than in the latter (Berlyne, 1960). However, the initial object of reading (one may prefer to say with Skinner, the conditions under which reading is undertaken) belongs more properly to the motivation of reading than to its analysis as a skill.

There is a further sense in which the concept of obtaining information (reducing uncertainty) is relevant to our analysis. For, just as the successive paragraphs that one reads provide information, so also do the sentences of which they are composed, the phrases which make up these, their constituent words, the letters in the words, and their salient features. In other words, the concept is applicable at every level in the performance. Moreover, the operation of the process is not confined to those 'molar' segments of behaviour which are conscious (in the sense that the subject can reflect on them and report on them), but extends to its finer details which have usually been so fully automatized that they are unconscious (in the same sense).

Figure 1 is intended as a schematic representation of the various

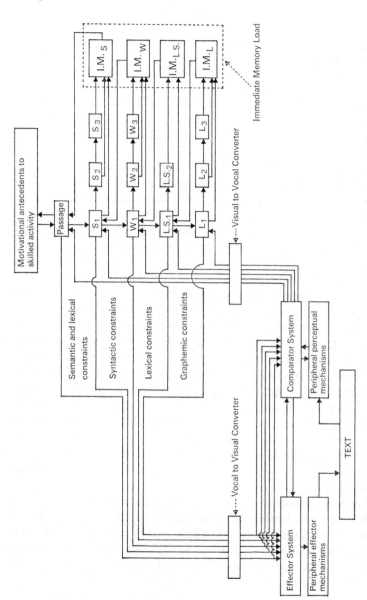

Figure 1. Schematic Representation of the Hierarchical Organization of Reading Behaviour

processes which may be assumed to intervene in the course of reading, with particular regard to their hierarchical and sequential relations. The diagram is essentially a representation of the subject's activity. The input for such activity is of course the printed text which appears at the bottom of the figure. The initiation of the processes is attributed to motivational antecedents (interest in the topic, desire for entertainment, etc.) which are extraneous to the skill itself. The remaining elements represent decision processes or strategies, perceptuo-motor mechanisms and active memory states or processes which enter into the skill itself.

The two lowest levels of regulation are taken to be common to all behavioural organization and not specific to reading. They are, on the effector side, the control of strategic effector co-ordinations (effector system) and, below this the systems of neuro-muscular regulation entering into (here) the control of head and eye movements, pupillary contractions, focussing and so on. On the receptor side, they are the comparator system which is held to determine a heightened sensitivity to a specific range of patterned input and, below this, the peripheral mechanisms involved in perception. A more detailed analysis of the interaction of these elements is given in Volume I, Chapter 4.

Five additional levels are shown as intervening between the processes deemed as extra-skill and the interpretation of text. At all of these levels the mechanisms shown on the left of the figure are to be taken as 'strategies' in the sense of Volume I, Chapter 4: i.e. they regulate perceptuo-motor behaviour by progressive definition of effector behaviour and progressive restrictions of perceptual sensitivity. The levels indicated are: passage or paragraph, phrase or string of words, word, letter string, and letter. Further levels could be shown without affecting the essential structure of the system (e.g. chapter or section, strings of words of various sizes, parts of letters acting as cues to letter recognition).

Reading is a linguistic process, and as such it reflects the constraints of language as a whole, and in particular of spoken language. It is the existence of these constraints which makes reading possible. They mediate the transition from those non-linguistic states of uncertainty to the skill itself and the relevance of the skill behaviour to the reduction of such uncertainty. As Fries correctly insists, the constraints of language are prior to reading and are not a part of what the child must learn when he begins to read. However, these linguistic constraints do form part of the body of schemata entering into the behaviour. They are not separate from reading itself, for the schema is no more than the structure of relations among possible strategies intervening in behaviour. (In the chapter referred to, the schema was likened to the complete wiring diagram of an electrical system and the strategy to any pathway that is activated by throwing appropriate switches, relays, etc.)

For the sake of simplicity we have chosen to represent a single passage, three strings, three words, two syllables, three letters. Also, to avoid a hopeless confusion of lines, we have shown only the input and output to lower levels of the first string in the passage, the first word in the string, and so on. Lateral passage of control, e.g. from the first string to the second, automatically de-activates the former, and the control of subsidiary strategies as well as that of the comparator and effector system is thenceforward determined by the latter. On the other hand, the controlling influence of a higher ranking strategy does not (usually) cease with the activation of a strategy of lower rank, but only when the input conditions determined at its own level have been satisfied, i.e. when uncertainty reduction at that level is adequate. The system is therefore hierarchical and higher ranking strategies operate over longer time intervals than lower.

We do not assume that the behaviour of the skilled reader invariably, or even usually, requires the intervention of all possible strategies at all levels indicated. This would mean the identification of each syllable letter by letter, storing successive syllables in immediate memory, identification of each word syllable by syllable, storing of words, and so on. This is quite obviously not what happens in skilled behaviour. But such delegation can occur at any stage in the process, and may be fairly marked in reading such a sentence as: '*A simplified version of a multiple transmitter mechanism exists in sympathetic ganglia, where acetylcholine affects preganglionic transmission and nor-adrenalin is the postganglionic transmitter.*'

What we have proposed instead is that every level of behavioural regulation has direct access to the effector and especially to the comparator system. Generally speaking, knowledge of the antecedent context is insufficient to allow even the skilled reader to predict what is in the text at a single glance. This seems to be what he does in skimming. Two or three words will tell him by their presence or their absence what he wishes to know. But it is easier to describe what occurs in scanning behaviour after we have considered *verbatim* reading.

It will be useful to consider the course of events in reading a specific passage. The following extract from Gates' *The Improvement of Reading*

H

(1947) will do as well as most for our purpose and has the additional merit that what Gates is saying is very much to the point. He is writing about reversals in children's reading and the wild approximations which may result, e.g. 'new' is seen as 'wen' and read as 'win' because 'wen' is not a word:

> 'Errors of all these types are often criticized as "wild" or "careless" guesses when in fact they are correct or at least ingenious reports of what the pupil actually sees. Far from being careless, they are often the result of almost painfully careful observation. The trouble, of course, is the order or direction of the perceptual attack. It is of utmost importance to realize that such an irregular way of looking over a word is the most natural thing in the world for a pupil to do. It is not at all natural for a pupil to observe a word any more than any other object consistently in the left-to-right direction. Here is a case, then, in which the natural carry-over to the study of words of habits that have worked on every other object will cause great mischief.'
>
> (Gates, 1947, p.187)

Let us confine ourselves for the present to a consideration of how the adult reader reads this passage. If he is reading carefully he is likely to vocalize every word or at least to identify every word so that he could vocalize a string of several words retained in immediate memory if he were stopped at any point and required to do so. If he is reading aloud he must actually vocalize every word.

But the process does not consist in identification of the first word, vocalization, identification of the next, vocalization, and so on. This is abundantly clear from the fact that skilled readers can correctly identify a string of several words at a short tachistoscopic exposure. Therefore the first observation to be made is that the skilled reader reads ahead, i.e. the identification is ahead of the vocalization. But this is not the whole of the picture. Even if complete vocalization is required or occurs (and in scanning it does not occur), the part of perception is limited to the narrowing of possibilities which will be just sufficient to ensure correct reproduction of the text. As the reader's attention shifts along the page the range of possibilities for the words that he encounters varies as a function of the several determinants of language which were noted above.

Semantic and syntactic constraints may be so severe that the probability of a given word in a given position is very high, even approaching unity: the word '*of*' following '*result*' in the fourth line of Gates' text is an example. Semantic constraints in particular are severe for '*types*' and '*careless*' in the first line, '*pupil*' in the third line and so on. They are probably a little less so for '*criticized*', '*wild*', '*guesses*' and '*correct*'. Syntactic constraints are especially prominent in the prediction of the words '*are*', '*as*' and '*or*' in the first line, '*they are*' in the second. The word '*least*' in the second line following '*at*' is rendered more probable than any other by the combination of semantic and syntactic constraints.

The perceptual identification of a word is simply the reduction of whatever uncertainty exists at the moment of perception in respect of what that word is. This means that the word '*of*' following '*result*' need not be perceived at all. Of course the reader can be caught out. This is almost bound to occur when following the rules yields a very high probability of occurrence of a given word or sequence of words and the text does not follow the rules. Several examples of this may be found in Abercrombie (1960), see Figure 2.

Figure 2. The three triangles (read the statement in each triangle). From Abercrombie, 1960, p. 28

The technique of recording eye movements during reading reveals that the skilled reader uses 6–7 fixations in scanning an average line of text (Anderson and Dearborn, 1952). (Even the beginning reader reads 'by successive fixations'. It appears that perception is saccadic, i.e. all visual perception occurs during the intervals between eye movements when the eye is at rest.) Because of the very high speed of skilled reading we have no means of telling whether or not the identification of words in single units of fixation (up to 5 words) is successive. In other words, it is possible that the skilled reader identifies a string of several words at a time. But of this we are not certain. Broadbent (1958) has shown that a listener can correctly identify both lists of words when two separate lists are fed in simultaneously one to each ear. Moreover, it appears that the processing of perceptual input is distinct from the perception itself. What we are certain of is that the existence of constraints greatly reduces the number of cues needed for identification. Moreover since the constraints derive from several levels of linguistic function, the actual perception of words cannot be divorced from the hierarchical structure of language itself. To take an example, the identification of the word *'perceptual'* in the fifth line of Gates' text is identified partly by its probability of occurrence in a text concerned with reading (level of the passage), partly by the syntactic restrictions limiting the range of words which could follow *'direction of the'*, nouns and adjectives being most probable, while many words, e.g. *the, its, my, perceives, perceived* are impossible.

The relevance of semantic and syntactic constraints to the identification of words by the skilled reader is admirably illustrated in an experiment by Tulving and Gold (1963). The subjects, who were students, were required to identify words briefly exposed by a tachistoscope and a measure was taken of the exposure time necessary for recognition. Tachistoscopic presentation of the 'target' word was preceded by continuous exposure of 'contexts' varying in length and in congruity. Thus for maximum length and congruity, the context would be of eight words e.g. *'Far too many people today confuse communism with'* with the target *'socialism'*. The same eight words would appear as an incongruous context for the target *'avalanche'*. A two word context would be *'communism with'*. Zero context was of course the tachistoscopic exposure by itself. It was found that the mean length of exposure for identification with zero context was 70 milliseconds. Increasing the context through lengths of 1, 2, 4 to 8 brought about a steady decrease in identification threshold for relevant contexts and a steady increase for irrelevant.

Morton (1964) varied the degree of approximation to English and measured the frequency of eye-movements following the method of Miller and Selfridge (1950) (see Volume I, p. 173) to test the hypothesis that fast readers would use contextual cues to a greater extent than slow readers. He found that while the speed of reading (as indexed by the lag in syllables between eye and voice in reading aloud) increased with the degree of approximation from zero order to fifth order approximation for the slow readers and remained constant thereafter, the faster readers showed a further improvement with sixth order approximation. However, although the effect of semantic and syntactic constraints on speed of word identification is clearly significant it is not large, i.e. the reduction in time is never greater than fifty per cent and probably usually much less. Preliminary observations carried out by the second writer indicate that the number of words read accurately (aloud), using (*a*) zero approximation, (*b*) syntactic constraints only (e.g. *The head of gentle grown-ups clouds my instep interminably but they often hesitate.*) and (*c*) standard text varied in the ratio 151 : 119 : 100; for silent reading the ratio was 152 : 108 : 100.

Clearly, word identification itself is a skill so highly developed in the adult reader that the facilitation attributable to higher levels of language organization is comparatively small, although greater than marginal. We must therefore consider what are the factors which determine the identification of words below the level of context.

Gates (1947) and others list a number of cues which may be relevant and which appear to be used by children at various stages: at an early stage, length of word and striking characters, e.g. the monkey's tail in *monkey*, the dot over the i in *pig;* at later stages, general configuration (contrasting *hat, pay* and *run*), letter by letter analysis, and various methods of breaking up longer words into constituent parts. However, such observations relate to the strategies used by children taught by look-and-say methods, who have not yet acquired the skill. It seems to us that they reflect the imperfections of the method.

Recent investigations indicate that the principal factor in identification of words is given by the constraints on letter sequences. The method of determining level of approximation was first devised in connexion with frequencies of letter sequences in individual words (Miller and Selfridge, 1950). Thus a random sequence of letters and spaces represents a zero order of approximation; a sequence which reflects letter frequencies in English texts (more e's than x's, etc.) is a first order approximation; second order approximation may be obtained by following each letter with the letter found next in sequence in a random text, using the letter so obtained to supply its successor, and so on. (Second order approximation would allow *xce, xci, xcl, xct* but third order approximation would disallow the last.) An obvious conclusion would seem to be that identification time will be a function of order of approximation. However, Postman and Conger (1954) failed to find any relationship between trigram frequency and speed of recognition. The work of Gibson, Pick, Osser and Hammond (1962), and of Gibson, Osser and Pick (1963) shows the relation to be more complex. Their technique consists essentially in selecting acceptable sequences, viz. a standard beginning, middle and end, e.g. *SPRILK*, or a three letter word, e.g. *AND*, and comparing these with systematic rearrangements e.g. *LKISPR* or *NAD* and *DNA*. It was found that speed of recognition varied as a function of 'pronounceability', as well as, inevitably, length. The authors conclude: 'Among the theoretical implications for psychology, perhaps the most general is this, that while reading is based on the discrimination and identification of visual forms such as letters, it becomes, in the skilled reader, a process of perceiving 'super-forms', and that these tend to be constituted (organized) by their relation to auditory-vocal temporal patterns. Insofar as frequency has a role in the constitution of these units, it is the frequency of grapheme-phoneme coincidence which is crucial, not frequency of exposure to the seen or uttered units alone. The reading of words is thus inseparable from the hearing of words. Since the hearing of words is also inseparable from the speaking of words, reading must be conceived, however, as part of a circular response-process, not simply as a stimulus response process' (Gibson *et al.*, 1962, p. 564). The 1963 article shows the same factors to be operative in the reading of children. In particular, although the frequency of a trigram such as *NSU* far exceeds those of trigrams like *NUS*, the latter are read more accurately by first graders as well as third graders. On the other hand, and this is highly significant, recognition of (five letter) pronounceable pentagrams was not significantly better than that of unpronounceable pentagrams in first graders but highly superior in third graders.

Reverting to Figure 1, it was argued that the process of reading as a whole, together with its constituents at each level, may be regarded as a hierarchical sequence of uncertainty reduction. Assuming not only that the full process involves reading for meaning, but that in the normal course of events (i.e. excluding experiments on reading of syntactic prose, etc.) the lower level strategies are subordinated to this, we may conclude that each cycle is complete only when uncertainty reduction has occurred at the level of the passage. It follows that identification of letter strings, words, and strings of words or phrases must be followed by storage in immediate memory, for the significance of each lower order identification is entirely subordinate to the part that it plays in the uncertainty reduction at the next higher level. It also follows that uncertainty reduction at any level allows the immediate memory store to be cleared at all lower levels, thereby rendering it available for input relevant to the succeeding link in the system. To take an example, we select a text at random from Anderson and Dearborn (1952). (Our partitioning)

'As we have already reported, | Boswell's study of the non-oral method | revealed that lip movement | was almost as common among his experimental cases | as among his controlled cases.'

It seems intuitively reasonable to suppose that the words or at least the most significant words in the first string remain stored in immediate memory until their sense is revealed (arrow from S_1 to S_2 in Figure 1). This in turn is stored in immediate memory at the higher level (or perhaps immediately erased as contributing little by way of uncertainty reduction). The words of the next string are similarly stored up to *method* (it should be recalled that given a speed of silent reading of 300 words per minute, the store will be erased at intervals of the order of one second or less), then their sense is stored, and so on. Completion of the sentence allows the entire store to be cleared up to the level of the passage. The reader is unable to recall the words or the syntax of what he has read a sentence or two back, but, if he is concentrating, and if the sentences concerned are significant to the passage as a whole, he can nevertheless reproduce their sense.

Assuming that this account is at least approximately correct we have two observations of some importance. The first concerns the lowest levels entered by the system in the process of word identification. Given the lexical and syntactic constraints deriving from the uppermost levels, it is altogether probable that recognition of words in the adult reader is immediate. This does not mean that no cues are used or that the cues which are used have nothing to do with letter forms. It means only that patterned combinations corresponding to letter strings of word length are directly available as recognition forms in the comparator system. (Occasionally, as noted earlier the recognition store is inadequate and we have to 'build' an unfamiliar word). The task of learning to read must therefore consist in part of the elaboration of such larger recognition patterns. Also, until that task has been completed the demands of reading on immediate memory will inevitably be far greater.

The second concerns the automatization of the skill. In terms of the model of Figure 1, what this means is simply that behaviour regulated and executed at lower levels does not interfere with decision processes at higher levels, and especially at the level of passage or paragraph.

The reader reads ahead, i.e. he identifies words ahead of the string whose sense he interprets at the same moment. Once again this does not mean that word identification is 'mechanical', for as we stressed earlier, semantic and syntactic constraints are operative in the setting of the comparator itself.

There remains the problem of skimming. On the face of it, this looks like an immediate recognition of content, by-passing all of the levels indicated in Figure 1 below the level of the passage. But what would be the nature of the perceptual cues for such a process? Reading for content may be a highly skilled activity but it is not black magic. A word has specific visual properties (strictly a number of alternative patterned properties depending on the type); a unit such as the general drift of a paragraph has none. The recent work of Neisser (1963, 1964) provides a very strong clue to the nature of skimming. Experiments indicate that subjects (students) can attain very high speeds in scanning a column of letter-groups to identify strings which have a Z or a Q. The rate of scanning far exceeds the rate required to identify all the letters in the list. Moreover, given a certain amount of practice, the subject can scan for any one of up to 10 target letters as rapidly as he can for one single letter. Scanning a list of random words to locate either names of animals or first names is relatively slow: approximately five words per second. But the rate is unaffected by the fact that there are many more first names than names of animals. This experimental task is more difficult than the reading of text in that there are no syntactic or semantic cues from previously processed words. Neisser concludes that identification of a target in visual scanning is a multi-level process: the subject can decide that a string is not what he wants more easily than he can identify what it is, and if it is excluded he can pass on.

Skimming a passage for content is a great deal more rapid than the scanning studied by Neisser. How is this achieved? What probably happens is that the reader identifies words or groups of words at intervals down the page, scanning for certain target words. The semantic and syntactic constraints (which extend to include his knowledge not only of language but of the subject and of the style of writing in the subject, whether scientific or literary) enable him to by-pass more or less extensive sections of text in between identifications: he need not know just what the by-passed section is about; it is enough to know what he is looking for. If this account is correct, then skimming does not by-pass the word level, it simply by-passes many words.

III. LEARNING TO READ

We noted at the end of Section II.1 that the child who starts on reading does so on the basis of an established skill in spoken language. Language is a multi-level skill and written language differs from spoken language only with respect to the lower levels of the hierarchy. However, the new integration necessarily involves the participation of the schema as a whole.

In the last section, we saw that the skilled reader possesses 'engrams' (cue combinations in the comparator system) corresponding to whole words. But the child does not begin with these, nor even with letter engrams. As Gates (1947) rightly remarks the orientation of a shape has no significance as an identifying cue until the child encounters letters. For instance, a cup with its handle to the left is still a cup. A *b* is not a *d*. Similar considerations apply to the order of letters (Vernon, 1957). But we must go further. Differentiation of characters depends first on the selection and combination of cues corresponding to their details (e.g. the curl at the top of the letter *f*, the straight, the cross, and the relations of these parts), and second on the constitution of a recognition 'link' specifically sensitive to the combination of these cues (the famous Gestalt). Gibson (1963) showed that children below the age of seven years are relatively poor at tachistoscopic identification of letter-like shapes as compared with children of nine years.[1]

Thus the recognition of letter shapes is one aspect which children need to learn. Let us consider what other part-learnings are involved in learning to read, taking them in logical order:

(1) That the printed text provides visual cues to a language message (if you look at the page you can get a story).

(2) That the shapes of letters, words and spaces offer differential cues.

(3) That there is a one-one correspondence between the temporal sequence of words as spoken and the left to right spatial sequence of words as printed – with spaces between words corresponding to (possible) minimal pauses in speech.

(4) (5) Differentiation of letter shapes and identification of letter shapes corresponding to their phonic contributions.

---

[1] Indeed there is abundant evidence that the identification of two-dimensional shapes of any kind is a learned skill (some of the best non-verbal intelligence test items are invalid in cross-cultural studies for this very reason). However, children in developed countries are hardly ever deprived of experiences in which two-dimensional recognition is relevant.

(6) That there is an approximate one-one correspondence between the left to right spatial sequence of letters and the temporal sequence of phonemes.

(7) (8) Differentiation and identification of digraphs.

(9) The strategy of forming a temporal synthesis of meaningless vocal syllables obtained by following a left to right sequence to form a meaningful word.

(10) (11) Differentiation and identification of frequent letter strings (-tion, -ing, un-, etc.).

(12) A variety of strategies for scanning words corresponding to 'phonic rules' determining correspondences between spoken and printed word other than those which depend solely on the correspondence of spatial and temporal order, and including rules for syllabification.

(13) Progressive automatization of strategies (1) to (12).

These part-skills have been listed in the approximate order in which they must be acquired. The order of acquisition depends in part on the method of teaching. But there are limitations to the sequencing of the latter also, since many of the later sub-skills depend on the acquisition of earlier ones. These dependencies are shown diagrammatically in Figure 3.

The figure is designed to bring out the close dependence of reading on linguistic skills which exists at every stage. Throughout this chapter we have been at pains to stress that language comprises three distinct aspects. Two of these, the semantic and syntactic, are closely related to one another and operate in similar ways in listening and reading. The third, perceptuo-motor – termed phonic – is also essential to the acquisition and performance of reading, as is abundantly clear from the studies of Gibson *et al.* described in the last section. But it enters, as it were, at one remove, for the primary cues to 'reduction of uncertainty' in text are visual. Therefore, this aspect of language is shown separately in the figure. The principal points at which language constraints play a vital part in the various constituent skills are shown separately for semantico-syntactic aspects and phonic aspect. Because the two do not always operate together and because of the vital part played by each when it does, their contribution is shown separately at every stage in the acquisition of the skill as a whole.

It will be seen that a certain limited facility with reading may be achieved with minimal dependence on the phonic aspect of language. This is the partial skill that receives emphasis in look-and-say methods. It is not wholly divorced from the phonic aspect, since letter form cues

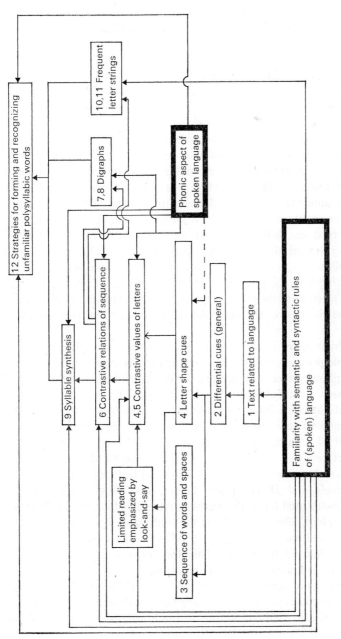

Figure 3. Sequential dependence of constituent reading sub-skills

inevitably play a large part, especially those deriving from the initial letter, and usually the child rapidly learns to associate the initial letter with its phonic value (see the observations of Gates noted on page 206).

It should be obvious that the first steps of reading will be a great deal less perplexing to the extent that the child has some idea of the nature of the task. Such a foundation is represented by the first four component sub-skills. Reid (1966), using structured interviewing techniques with twelve 5-year-old children in their first year at school, noticed a gradual progression towards an understanding of the task. At first they had very little if any notion of what reading involved and they did not realize that written words were made up of letters which stood for sounds. Interviews later in the first year showed a gradual trend towards a better understanding of the elements involved in the task. This was not easily or swiftly accomplished. It seems reasonable to suggest that in the early stages, before and after the child has taken the first steps in learning to read, the adult, when reading to the child, should occasionally follow the print with the forefinger to indicate that the story is emanating from the print in an ordered sequence. The practice of infant school teachers when writing a word or sentence under a child's drawing likewise emphasizes the symbolic nature of text and the relevance of order.

Whereas there is little doubt that children can often make considerable progress with graded-word readers with minimal intervention of the phonic aspect of language, the dangers inherent in this approach have been indicated in Section I.3. A significant advance in teaching method has come from the realization that the sound values of letters (4, 5) and of their position in the word can be approached by the method of 'contrastive discrimination' which appears to correspond fairly closely to a child's earlier acquisition of these same constituents in spoken language itself. This is a method featured in the approaches of Daniels and Diack, Fries, Lefevre and Stott. Unless nonsense syllables are used (as in the methods recently advocated by Bloomfield and Barnhart, 1961), recognizing the contrastive significance of patterns like *mat* and *man*, or *tip* and *pit*, relies on the child's recognition of these as meaningful words. Therefore arrows are shown for both aspects of language terminating on (4, 5).

A four word sentence can be read by a skilled reader following a tachistoscopic exposure of only one hundredth of a second (Anderson and Dearborn, 1952, reporting research carried out by J. McKeen Cattell in 1885). Clearly, the letter and sequence cues are assimilated simultaneously and processed unconsciously (much as the elements in immediate memory are ordered by content in spite of simultaneity of audial input in the studies of Broadbent and, especially Gray and Wedderburn, described in Volume I, Chapter 4, Section I). The processing is automatized in the sense that it does not interfere with the apprehension of meaning and also in the sense that it occurs below the level of consciousness. But the processing of a word obviously occupies longer than one four hundredth of a second, and processing of one word presumably does interfere with that of its successors, which is one of the reasons why reading never attains to the speed of four hundred words per second, as Anderson and Dearborn remark.

That processing of letter sequences ('word building') is essential to skilled reading is evident both from the consideration that English is an alphabetical language and from the research of Gibson *et al.*: pronounceable letter stings are identified with almost the same readiness as real words. Learning to read in the full sense therefore begins with the identification of the sound values of letters (4, 5) and with the recognition of the relation between the written and spoken sequences (6). It is these processes that are automatized, probably within a year of their acquisition. But they are not automatic or even unconscious to begin with. Quite the contrary, we have seen theoretical and experimental evidence of their difficulty, a difficulty which springs not from the complexity of the visual input so much as from the audial analysis which is essential to its interpretation. We refer to Vygotsky's insistence on the automatization of the phonic aspect in the acquisition of language and to Bruce's demonstration that the successive moments which intervene in his articulation are not accessible to the child until he has had adequate practice of the relevant sort. We have already indicated the efficacy of contrastive methods in producing such awareness.

Knowledge of the sound values of letters is of little value without that of sequence. On the face of it there would seem to be theoretical grounds for the expectation that matching a spatial sequence of letters to a (painfully abstracted) temporal sequence of phonemes would be beyond the child's capability below a mental age of 7. For instance, children are unable to copy a linear order (featured by beads of different colours or various articles of dolls' clothing strung out on a line) before the age of 5 or 6 or to reverse the order before the age of about 7. (Piaget and Inhelder, 1956, and see Chapter 8, Section III.) The present task would seem to be as difficult as the reversal since it involves the correspondence of two quite different sequences. However, it looks as if given adequate practice and good teaching, children can acquire this aspect of reading a good deal younger: at least as young as 5 or even 4 (Southgate, 1963; Downing, 1963).

However, even if the majority of children can overcome these difficulties fairly early, there is some evidence that backward readers continue to find them an obstacle, even at the age of 9. Thus Birch and Belmont (1965) found a very gradual development from $5\frac{1}{2}$ to $10\frac{1}{2}$ in the ability to match audial and visual patterns. (The experimenter tapped a pattern of sound e.g. .. .. .. allowing half second intervals between dots close together and second intervals for longer spaces; the child was shown three visual arrangements, e.g. .. .... , ... , ... , and was required to select the correct match.) The test correlated highly with reading age at first and second grade levels, but not beyond. It was also found that retarded readers were significantly less able to make judgements of auditory-visual equivalence than were normal readers. (Birch and Belmont, 1964.) These studies were devised on the hypothesis that progress in reading is dependent on intersensory development (cf. Birch and Lefford, 1963). Blank and Bridger (1966) adapted the technique of Birch and Belmont by substituting a sequence of visual dots for the audial taps, retaining the visual multiple choice; thus the task focussed more clearly on the matching or temporal and spatial sequences, being a visual-visual task. They found a highly significant difference between the performance of good and poor readers at the age of $9\frac{1}{2}$ (I.Q. over a 100 for both groups, and mean R.A. of backward readers 8·4).

Identification of three-letter sequences (4, 5) and (6) is a first and crucial step in the acquisition of the phonic skills essential to adequate reading. Of the remaining component part-skills, recognition of digraphs (7, 8) and of frequently occurring letter strings (10, 11) are self explanatory. The use of the *Initial Teaching Alphabet* enables the pupil to master (7, 8) with the same ease as (4, 5), and that (10, 11) cannot be divorced from (*a*) the phonic value of the strings ('pronounceability', as evidenced by Gibson *et al.*) and (*b*) the position of such strings within the word as a whole (e.g. *-tion* is frequent at the end of a word, *in-* or *inter-* at the beginning, etc.). More generally such frequently occurring patterns tend to correspond with morphemes contributing to regularly contrasted allomorphs in spoken as well as written language (*reach – reached, walk – walked*), or else their etymological and semantic value is tied to their position as prefix or suffix.

But it is important to recognize the complexity of the skills shown as

(9) syllable synthesis and (12) strategies for forming and recognizing unfamiliar polysyllabic words. Here again, the process is rapid and unconscious in the skilled reader, and the rapidity may conceal its structure. Referring back to Figure 1, it is clear that the pupil who has mastered the beginnings of phonic reading is still not in a position to identify words immediately on the basis of comparator facilitations at the level of the word except for short words. Hence there will frequently be occasions where control of behaviour is passed to lower level strategies, notably the level of letter strings. Even assuming that the break-up of longer words is adequate for later synthesis, the product of identification at the letter-string level needs to be stored in immediate memory in vocalized form (i.e. as a vocalization strategy rather than an image of a letter pattern). Moreover such storage is more difficult in the measure that the syllabic unit does not correspond to a known word (in terms of Miller's (1956) analysis of factors affecting short term memory capacity, a known word corresponds to a single 'chunk' where a vocalizable syllable may represent several unreduced 'bits' of information). But the structure of English is often such that the less experienced pupil is often faced with some uncertainty as to how to break up the word. Once a particular split has been decided, he must store the split itself: i.e. having stored the result of the first string and returning to analyse the next, he will have to avoid going over letters which have already been accounted for (e.g. for *reasons*: *re* → /re/; *eas* → /iːz/; *sons* → /sɔnz/); → /reiːzsɔnz/), or omitting strings which have not (as in the familiar error *begging* for *beginning*). The whole sequence of word identification is a multi-level process in which reinforcement, in the sense of feedback contributing to uncertainty reduction, does not occur until control has reverted to the level of the word, when the reader recognizes the satisfactory contribution to meaning of the word he has identified.

Inevitably the process is trial and error at several levels. Various ways of construing letter-strings may be tried until one has been found which yields a satisfactory pronounceable unit. Similarly, various ways of synthesizing such units may be attempted until one yields a satisfactory word. The word itself may not be satisfactory having regard to the semantic and syntactic constraints of higher levels. Failure to resolve the uncertainty at the higher level necessitates repetition of all or part of the process. And so on. Clearly the task is not an easy one and needs to be programmed by the teacher or writer in various ways. These include the gradual introduction of words featuring new phonic rules (as in the *Royal Road* series), the use of contextual aids to by-pass the need for synthesis of all new words (an outstanding feature in the *Oxford Colour Reader* series), and the use of exercises and games as an independent activity additional to reading of text (as in Stott's *Programmed Reading Kit*, Reis' *Fun with Phonics*, Southgate's *Sounds and Words*, etc.).

The wordly-wise teacher will inevitably remark that the pendulum has swung from look-and-say to phonics. It has. But the implication that it must swing back is almost certainly false. For current developments are based not only on the recognition of the essentially 'phonic' elements in the skill of reading but more especially on a psychological analysis of the structure of the skill as a whole and its relation to language behaviour in general. Moreover, there are pitfalls to be avoided in 'new-style phonic' methods as there were in previous methods and these correspond to violations of the restrictions implied by the character of reading as a linguistic and representational process whose primary purpose is the acquisition of information. Typical would be an insistence on the part of the teacher that every new word encountered by the pupil in reading text must be tackled phonically regardless of the resultant burden on short-term memory so that in the process of construing the word the pupil loses track of the passage. Reading then becomes a new kind of 'barking at print' – not in the sense that it is divorced from meaning, for the child still seeks meaning at the level of the word, but in the sense that this is cut off from its hierarchical relation to the text as a whole and thence to the extra-textual interest which alone makes reading a worth-while business.

Indeed, it can be argued that most of the component skills involved in reading can be taught and should be taught independently of the reading of text. The latter serves the function of practice and consolidation as well as providing an end for activities of the former sort (Roberts, 1966).

IV. SUMMARY

This discussion has been based on an analysis of reading as an information processing skill, founded on the possession of language. Reading is seen as a kind of listening with a visual input substituting for an audial input. Since language is a multi-level skill, the higher levels, i.e. the semantic and syntactic determinants, remain unchanged and operate to facilitate the identification of the input. The phonic aspect of language operates in two ways: first, in enabling the reader to make use of cor-respondences between 'graphemes' and 'phonemes', and second, to identify linguistic information and store it in immediate memory.

Skilled reading was seen as a hierarchical process of uncertainty reduction in which the key level was the identification of words. Learn-ing to read is then a matter of the acquisition of a number of part-skills together with their progressive automatization. These did not imply a rigid sequence throughout, but for the most part the more complex part-skills pre-supposed the earlier ones. In the majority of cases both the semantic and the phonic aspects of language were relevant to the part-skill just as they were equally relevant to the skill as a whole.

It is not part of our aim to prescribe a detailed programme of reading instruction. Our aim has been rather to bring out the psychological relevance of various techniques wherever they occur. To this end, several references have been made to the strengths and weaknesses (if any) of older methods as well as of certain more recent innovations. We believe it to be important that a teacher should be aware of what he may expect to achieve by each intervention in the learning process. Given such an understanding he is in a better position to put what 'methods' and texts he is offered to the greatest advantage, whatever their nature, to select among them those that he and his pupils are likely to enjoy, and to devise additional aids of his own.

REFERENCES

ABERCROMBIE, M. L. J. (1960). *The Anatomy of Judgment.* London: Hutchinson.

ANDERSON, I. H., and DEARBORN, W. F. (1952). *The Psychology of Teaching Reading.* New York: Ronald Press.

BARTLETT, F. C. (1947). The measurement of human skill. *Brit. Med. J.* No's. 4510 and 4511.

BELLUGI, U., and BROWN, R. (eds.) (1964). The acquisition of language. *Monogr. Soc. Res. Child Dev.* **29,** No. 1 (Serial No. 92).

BERLYNE, D. E. (1960). *Conflict, Arousal and Curiosity.* New York: McGraw-Hill.

BIRCH, H. G. and BELMONT, L. (1964). Auditory-visual integration in normal and retarded readers. *Amer. J. Orthopsychia.* **34,** 852–861.

BIRCH, H. G. and, BELMONT, L. (1965). Auditory-visual integration, intelligence and reading ability in school children. *Perceptual and Motor Skills.* **20**, 295–305.

BIRCH, H. G., and LEFFORD, A. (1963). Intersensory development in children. *Monogr. Soc. Res. Child Dev.* **28**, No. 5. (Serial No. 89).

BLANK, M., and BRIDGER, W. H. (1966). Deficiencies in verbal labeling in retarded readers. *Amer. J. Orthopsychia.* **36**, 840–847.

BLOOMFIELD, L. (1933). *Language.* New York: Holt, Rinehart and Winston.

BLOOMFIELD L., and BARNHART, C. L. (1961). *Let's Read. A Linguistic Approach.* Detroit: Wayne State U.P.

BROADBENT, D. E. (1958). *Perception and Communication.* Oxford: Pergamon.

BRUCE D. J. (1964). The analysis of word sounds by young children. *Brit. J. Educ. Psychol.* **34**, 158–170.

CARVER, C., and STOWASSER, C. H. (1963). *Oxford Colour Reading Books.* Oxford: University Press.

CATTELL, J. MCK. (1886). The inertia of the eye and brain. *Brain.* **8**, 295–312.

DANIELS, J. C., and DIACK, H. (1960). *The Royal Road Readers Teachers' Book.* London: Chatto and Windus.

DANIELS, J. C., and DIACK, H. (1960). *Royal Road Readers.* London: Chatto and Windus.

DIACK, H. (1960). *Reading and the Psychology of Perception.* Nottingham: Peter Skinner Publishing.

DOMAN, G. (1965). *Teach Your Baby to Read.* London: Jonathan Cape.

DOWNING, J. A. (1963). Is a 'mental age of six' essential for 'reading' readiness? *Educ. Res.* **6**, 16–28.

FRIES, C. C. (1964). *Linguistics and Reading.* New York: Holt, Rinehart and Winston.

GATES, A. I. (1947). *The Improvement of Reading.* New York: Macmillan.

GIBSON, E. J. (1963). In Wright, J. C., and Kagan, J. (eds.) Basic cognitive processes in children. *Monogr. Soc. Res. Child Dev.* Serial No. 86.

GIBSON, E. J., OSSER, H., and PICK, A. D. (1963). A study of the development of grapheme-phoneme correspondences. *J. Verb. Lrng. and Verb. Beh.* **2**, 142–146.

GIBSON, E. J., OSSER, H., and PICK, A. D. (1962). The role of grapheme-phoneme correspondence in the perception of words. *Amer. J. Psychol.* **75**, 554–570.

LEFEVRE, C. A. (1964). *Linguistics and the Teaching of Reading.* New York: McGraw-Hill.

LYNN, R. (1963). Reading readiness II – Reading readiness and the perceptual abilities of young children. *Educ. Res.* **6,** 10–15.

MARCHBANKS, G., and LEVIN, H. (1965). Cues by which children recognize words. *J. Educ. Psychol.* **56,** 57–61.

MCCARTHY, D. A. (1954). Language development in children. In Carmichael, L. (ed.) *Manual of Child Pyschology,* pp. 492–630. New York: Wiley.

MILLER, G. A. (1956). The magical number seven, plus or minus two: some limits on our capacity for processing information. *Psychol. Rev.* **63,** 81–97.

MILLER, G. A., and SELFRIDGE, J. A. (1950). Verbal context and the recall of meaningful material. *Amer. J. Psychol.* **63,** 176–185.

MORRIS, J. M. (1966). *Standards and Progress in Reading.* Slough: N.F.E.R.

MORTON, J. (1964). The effects of context upon speed of reading, eye movements and eye-voice span. *Quart. J. exp. Psychol.* **16,** 340–355.

NEISSER, U. (1963). Decision-time without reaction-time: experiments in visual scanning. *Amer. J. Psychol.* **76,** 376–385.

NEISSER, U. (1964). Visual search. *Scientific American,* June, No. 486.

OSGOOD, C. E. (1957). Motivational dynamics of language behaviour. In Jones, M. R. (ed.) *Nebraksa Symposium on Motivation.* Lincoln: Univ. Nebraska Press.

OSGOOD, C. E., and SEBEOK, T. A. (1966). *Psycholinguistics: A Survey of Theory and Research Problems* with *A Survey of Psycholinguistic Research.* 1954–1964 by Diebold, A. R., Jr. Bloomington: Indiana Univ. Press.

PIAGET, J., and INHELDER, B. (1956). *The Child's Conception of Space.* London: Routledge and Kegan Paul.

POSTMAN, L., and CONGER, B. (1954). Verbal habits and the visual recognition of words. *Science.* **119,** 671–673.

REID, J. F. (1966). Learning to think about reading. *Educ. Res.* **9,** No. 1, 56–62.

REIS, M. (1962). *Fun with Phonics.* Cambridge: Cambridge Art Publishers.

ROBERTS, G. R. (1966). Away from the fun-image of reading. *The Teacher,* January 14th.

SANDIFORD, P. (1942). Connectionism: its origin and major features.

In *The Psychology of Learning. Yearbook of the National Society for the Study of Education.* **41,** Part I I, 97–140.

SAPORTA, S. (1961). *Psycholinguistics: A Book of Readings.* New York: Holt, Rinehart and Winston.

SCHONELL, F. J. (1945). *The Psychology and Teaching of Reading.* Edinburgh: Oliver and Boyd.

SCHONELL, F. J. (1962). *Backwardness in the Basic Subjects.* Edinburgh: Oliver and Boyd.

SOUTHGATE, V. (1963). Augmented Roman alphabet experiment. *Educ. Review.* **16,** 32–41.

SOUTHGATE, V., and HAVENHAND, J. (1961). *Sounds and Words.* London: U.L.P.

STOTT, D. H. (1962). *Programmed Reading Kit.* Glasgow: Holmes.

STOTT, D. H. (1964). *Roads to Literacy.* Glasgow: Holmes.

TULVING, E., and GOLD, C. (1963). Stimulus information and contextual information as determinants of tachistoscopic recognition of words. *J. exp. Psychol.* **63,** 319–327.

VERNON, M. D. (1957). *Backwardness in Reading.* Cambridge: University Press.

VYGOTSKY, L. S. (1962). *Thought and Language.* Cambridge: M.I.T. Press.

8

Systematization of Thought

K. LOVELL

I. INTRODUCTION

MUCH of Piaget's work is concerned with the transformation in the character of children's thinking which extends over the period from the age of 5 or 6 to that of 9 or 10. We may begin by considering two very simple inquiries.

The first is taken from Piaget's earliest book, *The Language and Thought of the Child*, which was first published in English in 1926. A child is told a simple story and then asked to repeat the story to another child. Alternatively, he may be given an explanation of a simple mechanism such as the action of a tap. The second child is asked to repeat the story or the explanation to the adult. What one finds is that the story as repeated by a 6-year-old is disjointed and virtually unintelligible. The same is true of the explanation. In particular, the child is liable to leave out key incidents in the narrative or key features of the apparatus, and to muddle the sequence of those that he preserves, so that the causality of the original is lost, whence the apparent incoherence. This could be a matter of everyday observation. But Piaget took a number of additional steps. He made up a number of leading questions which he directed to the first child as well as the second. This enabled him to establish how much loss of information was due to each stage of the procedure; what the first child had heard but failed to preserve; what he preserved but failed to reproduce, and similarly for the second child. It was found that the first child's answers to the adult's questions were quite adequate: apparently there was little that he could not understand. The loss was attributable mainly to his own spontaneous reproduction and to the way in which it was accepted, 'assimilated', by the other child. However, when the second child was asked whether he was satisfied with the account he had received (incoherent as it was), he invariably declared himself happy: he thought he understood. Piaget's interpretation of these findings was couched in terms of his concept of

225

egocentrism. Both the child's language and his thinking are tied to his own point of view and to the present moment of time in which they occur. Consequently, there is much that he takes for granted. When asked to reproduce what he has heard, he is unable to dissociate that which may be taken for granted and that which cannot: he cannot therefore adopt the point of view of his hearer. But the latter, listening to the account, makes whatever sense he can in terms of his own preconceived notions. Neither child is in a position to impose a coherent framework on the information representing the objective relations of causality and order. How is such a framework achieved? How does the child come to dissociate the things that are needed for objective and therefore logical connectedness from what might be called subjective impressions of good fit?

The second example is taken from Piaget's work on geometry (Piaget, Inhelder and Szeminska, 1960). A child of 5 or 6 is asked to explain a familiar route, say the road which he walks twice a day when he goes to school and returns. He is given a sand tray and suitable bits of apparatus to help in his explanation. Again, one finds his account is incoherent: he goes along there and then he turns and then there's a church and then he's there, and so on. What is more the features which he mentions for the journey in one direction do not coincide with those for the other. And when he is asked whether the two routes are equal in length, he denies this most emphatically. When he dawdles the journey appears longer, and whatever he notices (e.g. a shop where he calls in) is mentioned. Naturally, these elements do not coincide for the two directions. Again one asks how does he eventually come to impose a coherent objective framework of spatial relations on his impressions. What is the mechanism which underlies the substitution of a true 'map' of his surroundings for the moment to moment subjective map which presumably directs his steps as he walks along?

These are the questions with which we will be concerned in this chapter. We shall be dealing more with the how of children's thinking than with the what, more with its form than with its content, more with the logical structure of connectedness of its elements than with the origin of those elements themselves. Yet we will see that some elements depend very much on the evolution of such a logical structure. The distinction closely resembles that between semantics and syntactics. What is the origin of the syntax of thought?

II. THE SYSTEMATIZATION OF THOUGHT

1. *Elementary 'conservations' and the resultant equilibria*

The understanding by the child that certain properties (e.g. quantity or number) are conserved, or remain invariant, in spite of transformations (e.g. changing shape, moving the relative position of objects), is, in Piaget's view, largely responsible for the advance from preoperational thinking to the next stage of thought (Piaget, 1957). To develop this point let us consider a ball of plasticine that is rolled into a 'sausage'; the latter being progressively made longer and thinner. At each step in the elongation of the plasticine the child is questioned as to conservation versus non-conservation of quantity. It is now well known that the 4–7 year-old will affirm that there is more plasticine ('because it is longer') or less plasticine ('because it is thinner') according to whether he centres first on length or width. Or, the child may agree to conservation to a given degree of elongation, and then deny it as the 'sausage' further lengthens. But from 7–8 years of age the conservation of quantity is increasingly in evidence in spite of marked spatial changes.

Piaget believes that the growth of conservation is a process of equilibration of cognitive actions which contains four basic steps, each of these steps being itself a state of temporary equilibrium in a continuous equilibration process. In our illustrative example the steps are assumed to be: (i) the child centres singly on property *A* (e.g. length); (ii) he centres singly on property *B* (e.g. width); (iii) the child oscillates back and forth, wavering between the two; (iv) there is an apprehension of both properties in a single cognitive act (longer but thinner).

During the first of these three phases, the child may be said to be passing judgements about the successive *states* of the object. When he reaches the fourth phase, these states are recognized as *transformations*, i.e. the subject is aware both of the continuity from one phase to the next, and of the characteristic law which governs it: the necessary compensation operating as between length and thickness.

Piaget (1957) offers a probabilistic model to account for this succession. For the first phase he argues that if one rules out previous experience as a factor likely to introduce bias, one can make a good case for a random scanning of the situation. As a result the child's judgement is cued by a property *A* (in this instance, usually length), which is perceptually prepotent. The move to phase 2 is due to the child's subjective dissatisfaction (leading to cognitive conflict) with giving the same response under changing perceptual conditions, especially conditions which involve marked perceptual contrast, as when the 'sausage' becomes long and very thin. There is thus a greatly increased likelihood of the subject centering on the hitherto ignored second property. Phase 3 then follows; for, as the child watches the changing conditions of the situation in front of him, he is likely to centre on properties A and B alternately. This increases the chances that he will sooner or later bring both properties together in a single cognitive act as the switch from A to B and back again becomes increasingly rapid. The child must then move from the comparison of actual $A–B$ (length–width) couples found in any one experiment to their anticipation. In doing so he has moved from a near equilibrium of states to a perfect equilibrium of states and transformations. He has now completed phase 4. The probability of further changes in strategy is nil since the subject has a permanent and parsimonious solution to the problem. The invariance of the property under consideration (in our example, quantity) has been generalized to cover all possible transformations of shape and is now recognized as self evident *a priori*.

Since this account entails no quantitative predictions, it seems doubtful whether one would be justified in regarding it as a probabilistic model in the full sense. However, the description of the first, second and fourth phases corresponds closely with observation. The transition to the fourth appears to be inadequately spelt out. For what one frequently finds (and this includes Piaget's own detailed protocols which the reader will find scattered throughout the various works listed at the end of this chapter) is that the child oscillates between a judgement of conservation and a judgement of difference. To complete the analysis, one needs to take into account a third centering, the determination of judgement by the continuity of an equality which was perceptually apparent before the deformation. This initial situation of apparent equality will hereafter be referred to as $S1$. Such a centering leads to a judgement of conservation, but one which is unstable. When, in the course of everyday life, the child plays about with plasticine and alters its shape, he acts as if he recognizes this identity. But the experimental situation focusses his attention on the perceptual set-up. Hence the determination of judgement first by dimension A and then by dimension B. The intervention of the determinant $S1$ in this situation is therefore delayed until the third phase, where its appearance is facilitated by the mechanism of retro-action (see Section III).

But the determinant $S1$ cannot generate an equilibrium until the child can inhibit the overt successive centerings on A and B, substituting an anticipation of their effects. It is reasonable to assume that the overt centerings (whether these always take the form of oculomotor adjustments as in extreme cases, or whether they simply involve the activity of distinct and mutually inhibitory circuits in the perceptual centres of the brain) are mutually incompatible. By the same token, one may imagine that the anticipations are not. Hence the simultaneity, which is compatible also with the centering on $S1$. But hence, too, the final equilibrium as described by Piaget. From this point on, no overt centering can shift the judgement, for the effects of all three have been anticipated by the schema which mediates the strategy of judgement, i.e. the recognition of successive states as transformations (see above.).

The experiment which demonstrates the gradual acquisition of the conservation of substance (plasticine) is but one example among many.

Piaget has provided a great deal of evidence, which later workers have confirmed, that from $6\frac{1}{2}$ to 8 years onwards the child increasingly conserves over a wide variety of cognitive fields – quantity, number, space, time and so forth. Not all conservations appear simultaneously. For example, number is conserved well before area. Many experiments dealing with conservation are well known and a few will be described later in this chapter. Previous to conservation in any particular instance, judgement is made on a perceptual basis usually involving centration on one aspect only of the situation. The development of the relevant conservation invariably entails a co-ordination of cognitive actions with complete and reversible compensations. There is thus an increase in the systematization of thought in relation to the example. Because the child's thought now conforms to a system, there is a more adequate abstraction of specific aspects from events as a whole. For instance, number is no longer felt as a vague quality associated with size, but as a specific aspect which is precisely defined by the operation of counting. Similarly, the subject elaborates the concept of time so that he can discriminate systematically between events in succession, simultaneous events, and overlapping events. This he does by abstracting and focussing on relations of sequence, and, eventually, by integrating the separate sequences when these overlap. Furthermore with the increasing systematization of thought and the elaboration of a variety of precise concepts, the child slowly builds up, in his mind, a model of external reality. These concepts enable the individual to make sense of, or make significant to himself, external reality, and they often help him to predict within it. Overall the world becomes a more stable place; an environment in which there is law and order despite changes in appearance; a milieu where thinking is a safer guide to action than perception.

2. *Classification*

Systematic and consistent thinking depends on the formation of precise concepts, on clear realization of how they are determined (e.g. by counting, by measuring, by weighing, by timing), and on their resistance to shift. Hence the importance of conservation. But systematic thinking also requires that precise relations be established among these concepts. For, in the final analysis, no concept can exist by itself, and every concept owes its precision, or lack of precision, to its relationship with other concepts, i.e. to its place in a conceptual system. Hence the importance of the elaboration of systematic ways of relating concepts to one another, i.e. of classificatory systems.

Inhelder and Piaget (1964) point out that the logical operations of classification enable the child to reason about discontinuous objects, having regard only to the relations of similarity and dissimilarity, while ignoring relations of spatio-temporal proximity.[1]

We will consider two examples of classification. Both are described by Inhelder and Piaget (1964) and by Lovell *et al.* (1962). In the first the child is given a collection of geometrical figures, letters of the alphabet and so forth, made of differing materials and of differing colours. He is told to 'put together things that go together' or an essential variation of this. In this experiment (as in others of the same type) Piaget finds three stages in the growth of the operation of classification. During the first, which lasts roughly from $2\frac{1}{2}$–5 years of age, the child makes from his materials what Piaget called *graphic collections*.[2] The sorting is done without plan and the subject ends up with a complex visual figure made of various objects (hence the term 'graphic collection'[2]) which may or may not have meaning for him. For example, the child may begin by putting together letters. If the last one was red he may add a red triangle. Or, he may line up rectangles, vertically, and then continue horizontally

---

[1] Piaget draws a distinction between logical operations on the one hand, and infralogical or sublogical operations on the other. The latter are defined as operations that are formally similar to logical ones and which develop at the same time. But they have some attributes which are essentially different from those of logical operations, for their contents are continuous in character and depend on spatio-temporal proximity. Examples of sublogical operations are those involving quantity, measurement, time and space (Piaget and Inhelder, 1941).

[2] French: 'collections figurales'.

with other geometrical figures mixed in respect of colour and shape. Piaget quotes a 5-year-old as putting two rectangles side by side (lengthways) and then adding a blue circle on the right, and a blue square on the left. Part of the collection may be commenced in terms of common attributes and then spoilt by the addition of an object not in the same 'class'. Groupings based on similarity of characteristics are unstable at this age. The child's thoughts do not yet conform to a system; hence in Piaget's view, the subject at this age is unable to differentiate between the criteria which lead him to select the objects in turn and the action of putting them in an appropriate place. Therefore, he cannot co-ordinate:

(*a*) the exact qualities which define the membership of a particular logical class (class intension); and

(*b*) all the objects which possess these qualities (class extension).

The second stage begins around 5 and ends at 7–8 years of age, and is characterized by the construction of *non-graphic collections*. Objects are grouped on the basis of common attributes, and the child can often divide a major group into appropriate subgroups. Piaget quotes the protocol of a child who put the letters on one side and the shapes on the other, and then subdivided the geometrical shapes into rectangles, squares and circles. Nevertheless, Piaget calls this grouping a collection and not a class. The crucial ability necessary for true classification is to keep in mind the relation of inclusion which obtains between a class and a sub-class. In the present experiment, the child's arrangements of his collections provide a clue as to whether he understands this relation or not. During this second stage, children tend to be inconsistent in their mode of arrangement. In classifying squares and rectangles which are large and small, the squares may be subdivided and not the circles, or the actual spatial arrangements do not conform to a clear structure; for instance, what are major subdivisions for one of the two broad collections are minor subdivisions for the other, and vice versa, e.g. rectangles subdivided by colour and each colour further sub-divided into large and small, while the squares are sub-divided by size, each size being further sub-divided by colour, etc. This kind of inconsistency is held by Piaget to argue an inadequate understanding of the inclusion relation, as a result of which the subject deals with the various aspects *seriatim* instead of applying a comprehensive classificatory plan. The third stage is characterized by just such systematic handling of relations and was found to an increasing extent from the age of 7–8 years on.

The three stages, together with the various types of reaction proposed by Piaget within stage I, were all confirmed by Lovell *et al.* (1962).

A second experiment offers a more direct test of the role of class-inclusion in problems of this kind (Piaget and Inhelder, *op. cit.*, ch. 4). The Geneva school used cards showing animals. One set showed 3 or 4 ducks (class A); another showed 3 to 5 birds other than ducks (class A' – cock, sparrow, parrot); and a third set showed 5 animals other than birds (class B' – snake, mouse, fish, horse, dog).[1] Transparent boxes of different sizes were placed inside one another (transparency ensured that the relationships of the boxes to one another could be seen) and the children were asked a number of questions dealing with the placement of the cards in the trays. Assuming the subject has correctly put all the ducks in the innermost tray, the remaining birds in the intermediate tray and the other animals in the outer tray, the two key sorts of questions are (i) 'Would it be all right to transfer one of the ducks to the middle tray?' – to which the correct reply would be yes, because a duck is a bird; and (ii) 'Would it be all right to transfer the parrot and cock to the innermost tray?' – to which the reply should be no, because a bird is not (necessarily) a duck. The protocols derived from the inquiry again revealed three stages:

During stage I children had the greatest difficulty in making the arrangement in the first place and needed help. Once the arrangement is given, they are perfectly willing to alter it in any way to fit in with the experimenter's suggestions.

At stage II, they need little help in making the arrangement, but they cannot answer the test questions correctly. Either their categories are adhered to rigidly, and the answer to the type (i) question is wrong, or they see the possibility of shifting the arrangement while adhering to the classification, but they then confuse the type (i) question with the type (ii), and the reply to the latter is incorrect: if a duck can be put in with the birds, then a bird can be put in with the duck, since ducks are birds. They fail to see that it does not follow that birds are ducks!

Again at stage III, replies are correct.

A systematic attack on classification means that the subject must keep in mind all of the criteria of the classification (e.g. duck, bird,

---

[1] The letters A, B, C are used to designate classes of successive rank, i.e. class C includes B and B includes A; in the example given A = ducks, B = birds, and C = living creatures (animals). The symbol '′' (read *prime*) denotes the *complementary* classes in the hierarchy. In the example, A' = all birds that are not ducks; whence: $A + A' = B$; similarly B' are animals which are not birds; whence: $B + B' = C$.

animal) applying to one and the same item, regardless of changes in spatial arrangement. A classification is a grouping in *extension* (whether actual or mental) deriving from a precise combination of criteria (*intension*). At stage II the child cannot fully co-ordinate these two, so that he still reconstructs the intension as he goes along by drawing on the extension relations which he has made. At stage III he realizes that the inclusion of a sub-class *A* in a larger class *B* does not destroy its identity as a class *A*. Therefore, from the age of 7 or 8 on, he is increasingly able to co-ordinate extension and intension, paving the way to true classification. The actions of classifying now take place in the mind as reversible operations, i.e. as actions which imply the recognition of systematic interrelations, e.g. $A + A' = B$ implies $A = B - A'$.

However, the results also showed how difficult it sometimes is for children under 12 years of age to handle questions relating to the quantification of inclusion where the questions are put in a purely verbal form. Not until that age did two thirds of the subjects answer correctly two questions. These asked if there were more birds or more animals, and if there were more birds or more ducks. Even at 8–9 years of age the proportion of children answering correctly was not greater than about a quarter. On the other hand the task was much easier if the questions were asked in more concrete form; e.g. 'If I take out all the birds are there any animals left?' 'If I take out all the ducks are there any birds left?'

Lovell *et al.* (*op. cit.*) repeated the experiment using toys instead of pictures on cards. Questions of quantification relating to inclusion (e.g. 'Are there more birds or animals?') were found to be as difficult as Piaget found. The subjects appeared to ignore the concrete materials in front of them and attempted to deal with the problem at the abstract verbal level. But once the subjects were encouraged to consider action in relation to the materials, the experimenter asking if there would be any animals left if all the birds were killed, and if there would be any birds left if all the ducks were killed, the number of correct answers rose considerably. The Geneva results were thus generally confirmed.

Overall the experimental evidence suggests that when classes are dealt with at the abstract level, questions of quantification in relation to class inclusion cannot be answered by the majority of children until the stage of formal operations. But so long as the child is encouraged to think of the situation in more concrete terms, his thinking is sufficiently systematized by 8 years of age for him to be able to give correct answers to the questions posed.

3. *Seriation*

Seriation is the third broad aspect of the systematic organization of thought. It concerns the recognition (grading) and above all the ordering of differences.

There is no doubt that an intuitive sort of grading and ordering appears very early in children's development, i.e. about the age of 3 or 4. Many familiar toys make use of this relation: graded rings to be placed on a stick, nesting bricks, Billy and the seven barrels. But here the child's behaviour is intuitive for two reasons. First, because differences in size are gross, so that the child's construction is easily guided by his perceptual anticipation of the finished product; and, second, because quite usually solutions are attained only after much trial and error. In time the child may be able to execute the task quickly, but only because it has become a specific habit. Yet this sort of spontaneous activity ultimately gives rise to the development of systematic concepts involving asymmetrical transitive relations.[1] They are systematic because the transitivity is taken for granted, with the result that there is far less need for intuitive (perceptual) support, and the subject can make deductions based on the transitive relation. An adequate handling of spatial and temporal measurement and of all physical scaling depends on this feature of conceptual development..

Piaget (1952) describes an interesting experiment involving seriation, i.e. the formation of, or putting into, a series. The subjects were shown 10 dolls of differing heights and 10 miniature walking sticks which were also graded in length. The task for each child was to match dolls and sticks, i.e. to seriate both sets of elements and place the matching elements of both sets in one to one correspondence.

Up to about 5 years of age Piaget found that children were unable to construct a series. He interprets this as due to the inability of the child to realize that a given element is longer than the one before it and shorter than the one after it. In other words the child's thoughts do not yet conform to a system so that he can mentally pass through the series in both directions. Often, a child who is asked to construct a 'staircase' with rods will take into account only the tops of the rods and not their bases, with the result that any rod can fill any position. By about 6 years of age the child begins to seriate by trial-and-error, but if one or two sticks are held back at the start, he has difficulty in inserting them

---

[1] A relation, *r*, is transitive if *A r B* and *B r C* implies *A r C*, e.g. longer than, older than, equal to. It is symmetrical if *A r B* implies *B r A*, e.g. equal to, unequal to; otherwise (e.g. longer than) it is asymmetrical.

in the correct position in the completed series. From 7 onwards, however, the child usually takes the shortest stick, then the next shortest and so on, knowing that he can thereby build the series. Moreover, once the child could construct the series he was capable of assigning to each doll the correct walking stick.

These kinds of experiments have been repeated by a number of workers using rather different materials but the results have been found to be much the same, cf. Hyde (1959), Beard (1957). Moreover, Lovell *et al.* (*op. cit.*) have clearly shown (getting the same groups of children to perform various tasks involving the arrangements of materials) that there is a great increase in the ability to perform addition of classes, multiplication of classes, visual seriation, and multiplication of asymmetrical transitive relations,[1] at 7–8 years of age. This is strong evidence, indeed, that by that age thought has become sufficiently systematized in most children for these four operations to be carried out.

There is one aspect of the seriation experiments, however, over which the present writer is in disagreement with the Geneva school. Piaget and Inhelder (1962, 1964) presented a set of 10 differently coloured rods of varying lengths, in disarray, to children between 5 and 10 years of age. The subjects were required: (*a*) to anticipate the seriation of these rods and draw the series with an ordinary pencil; (*b*) to draw the anticipated series with coloured pencils, each coloured pencil corresponding to the colour of one of the rods; and (*c*) to construct the series. The authors claim that drawing the anticipated series with an ordinary pencil was an easier task than using the coloured pencils, for in the latter task there had to be an exact correspondence between the colours used and the colours of the rods. In Piaget's view the latter task is performed only when the child shows evidence of operational thought in his actual construction of the series (*c*).

Work carried out under the writer's direction using similar materials and procedure, suggests that the building of a series using operational thought is easier than drawing the anticipated series even in task (*a*) (black pencils). The two drawing tasks were of equal difficulty. However, we believe this result confirms one of Piaget's principal hypotheses; namely, that if anticipatory imagery is involved in the drawing task, then it occurs at the same time, or follows, the ability to use operational thought. More generally it may be suggested that the systematization of thought either precedes anticipatory imagery or they develop together.

4. *The characteristics of operational thinking*

There is therefore evidence that elementary conservations, systematic classification and seriation all emerge about the same period in the development of the child, i.e. between the ages of 6–8 on average. In each of these spheres the child's behaviour yields evidence that he recognizes implications which link the actions he carries out in a structure which shows a number of important features.

Cognitive actions thus become more divested of their concrete qualities, more schematic of the outside world, and more mobile. They now slowly cohere together to form complex and well integrated systems of actions. Indeed, the system has definite structural properties and only cognitive actions that conform to a system are termed 'operations' by Piaget; for unless thought has certain properties it will show inconsistencies. These properties are:

1. Closure. Any two operations can be combined to form a third operation. e.g. $5 + 3 = 8$. All boys plus all girls equals all children.

2. Reversibility. For any operation there is an opposite operation that cancels it. e.g. All boys plus all girls equals all children, but all children except all boys equals all girls. $2 + 6 = 8$ and $8 - 2 = 6$.

3. Associativity. When three operations are combined it does not matter which two are combined first. e.g. All adults plus all boys and girls equals all boys plus all girls and adults. $(2 + 3) + 1 = 2 + (3 + 1)$.

4. Identity. This is a 'null operation' and is performed when any operation is combined with its opposite. e.g. All boys except all those who are boys equals nobody. $4 - 4 = 0$.

III. ORGANIZATION IN THE MEDIA OF SPACE, TIME AND CAUSALITY

1. *Space*

Piaget and Inhelder (1956) give details of the experiments which they used to study the growth of the child's spatial concepts. From their findings they conclude that the child's first notions of space are topological ones. These later become transformed into projective and Euclidean concepts, both developments occurring over the same period. Projective relations cover perspective, sections, projections and plane rotations; their recognition seems to depend on the co-ordination of viewpoints. Euclidean relations derive from the conservation of straight lines, parallels and angles and from the elaboration of general co-ordinate systems. We will confine ourselves to a brief discussion of the way the individual organizes his spatial environment in terms of a two-dimensional frame of reference.

Piaget denies that children have an innate or psychologically pre-cocious knowledge so that they automatically 'see' objects within a Euclidean grid of horizontal and vertical co-ordinates. This frame of reference, which adults take for granted, is but slowly built up, in spite of the fact that walls, floors, street crossings, tall buildings and the like are in front of the child's eyes virtually all day long, and in spite of the fact that he himself has ample experience of standing up and lying on a bed. The construction of a frame of reference is possible only in the measure that his thinking increasingly conforms to a system. A number of experiments illustrate this growth:

(*a*) An empty bottle is tilted at various angles, and the subject is required to sketch in, on outline drawings of the bottle, or show by gestures, the water level as it would appear if a bottle with water in it had been used.

(*b*) The child has to draw in, on outline drawings of the bottle the position which would be taken by a plumb line if the jar was tilted as shown.

(*c*) The subject is given a model of a mountain and he is asked to put in posts 'nice and straight' at various points. He is also asked to draw such posts, as well as houses, on a prepared outline sketch of the mountain.

To the age of 4 years or so (stage I) Piaget and Inhelder (1956) claim that there is no knowledge of planes at all, the contents of the jar being represented by a scribble which may not even be touching the jar. At stage IIA, the liquid is imagined as simply expanding or contracting, with the water level remaining parallel to the base when the jar is tilted. Posts are placed at right angles to the mountain side without reference to the base of the mountain (i.e. the table top). There is an improvement at stage IIB, for the water level is no longer shown parallel to the base, but there is still failure to co-ordinate prediction with any external fixed reference system. Posts are placed upright on the mountain side, but when drawn they are shown as in stage IIA, while prediction of the position of the plumb line remains poor. Then comes an intermediate phase between stages IIB and IIIA, when the water level is accurately predicted as long as the bottle is horizontal or vertical. During stage IIIA,

I

however, the prediction of horizontal and vertical becomes more generalized but there are some lapses, while at stage IIIB prediction is immediate and accurate.

According to Piaget and Inhelder, stage IIIB is found as early as 7 years of age in a few children but generally it is not in evidence before 9. The discovery of horizontal and vertical stems from the finding that the water level remains level and the plumb line falls true. But these facts can only be noted and applied inductively when they are incorporated in a network of co-ordinating schemata – itself built up out of action and not mere observation – whose organization results in a system of reference. If such a network is not present, no reference frame can be built, for the child's thinking cannot conform to a system in this respect. Smedslund (1963) has shown that *mere observation* of the horizontal level of a water surface when the container is tilted, brings about no learning concerning horizontality in 5–7-year-olds who have no concept of horizontality to begin with, and brings only limited improvements in those who have but initial traces of the notion. Furthermore, Beilin *et al.* (1966) studied the ability of 180 pupils of mean age 7 years and 6 months to represent the water in jars tilted at various angles. 'Unsuccessful' subjects were then trained either by showing them the water levels after their forecast (perceptual training) or by using verbal methods. While training resulted in improved performance there was no transfer to jars of a different form.

All the stages observed by the Geneva school have been confirmed in the course of replication experiments. However, Lovell (1964) found that as many as 15 per cent of the 7- and 8-year-olds had elaborated the concepts of axes of reference (i.e. were at stage IIIB). Dodwell (1963) provides evidence to show that the pattern of development is often irregular, in the sense that a child may be at stage III in the 'water tilting' experiment while still at stage II in the 'mountain' experiment. Dodwell's work suggests that the organization of a frame of reference is not such that it is immediately applicable in all situations. In general, the organization of systematizing schemata during this period appears to be influenced by a variety of factors which are not easily disentangled. This is a topic to which we will return in section IV.

2. Time

The concept of time is also a mental construction. It does not exist in the mind *a priori*, but like other concepts it is slowly elaborated by the child in the measure that his thoughts conform to a system, until in the end he arrives at a concept of time as an abstract set of relations which may be applied to all possible sequences. In one experiment two toy figures are made to move on prepared tracks, as if participating in a race. Both figures move off together and stop together, but they move off at different speeds because the tracks differ in length. Younger subjects deny simultaneity of starting and stopping and even more deny the equality of the duration of movement. For the average 5-year-old, time seems to be mixed up with space, i.e. with the distance run through. Piaget (1946) speaks of it as 'local time', for the 'times' linked with different dolls cannot be co-ordinated in the mind. The child, at that age, fails to construct a 'homogeneous' time, a time universal and 'flowing', a time containing the general and objective event, so that movements that are synchronous or asynchronous, fast or slow, can all be co-ordinated.

In another experiment (Piaget, 1946, Lovell *et al.* 1960) water was siphoned from a beaker, marked at equal intervals, into a tall measuring cylinder also marked at equal intervals. Both beaker and cylinder were of the same capacity, and the volume of water between any two adjacent marks on one container was equal to that between any two adjacent marks on the other. Obviously the marks were further apart on the measuring cylinder than on the beaker, and the water rose more rapidly in the former than it fell in the latter. Younger children found it difficult to put in order a series of diagrams which showed how the water emptied from the beaker and filled the cylinder, matching the appropriate picture of the water in the former with that of the latter. They were also unable to grasp that the time taken for the water to move from one mark to the next on one container was the same as that taken to move between consecutive marks on the other. Again, the younger children invariably thought that the cylinder took longer to fill than the beaker did to empty. These findings all suggest that until thinking is sufficiently systematized, the notions of temporal order, simultaneity and duration are not available to the child.

An experiment relating to age is also very interesting because it reveals that before a child has elaborated the concept of time, age is not separated from size, especially height (Piaget, 1946, Lovell *et al.*, 1960). Children were shown six pictures of an apple tree in various stages of growth which they had to put in order showing how the apple tree grew. They were then given five pictures of a pear tree which they also had to put in order showing its growth. However, they were told that the pear tree was planted one year later than the apple tree, while the fifth picture of the pear tree showed it to be taller than the apple tree as shown in the sixth picture of the latter. The question for each subject was, 'Look at all the trees and tell me which one is the oldest tree this year'. Invariably the 5-year-olds maintained that the pear tree was the oldest because it was tallest.

Piaget's view is that the construct of time is not well elaborated until between 7 and 8 years of age. Lovell *et al.*, working with British school children, confirmed the general trend of Piaget's findings, but found that the age is 8–9 rather than 7–8 years. The child obviously cannot appreciate the equality of synchronous intervals, order of events, age and the like until a concept of time is in process of elaboration. This in turn cannot take place independently of the child's capacity to system- atize his thinking in other fields as well. Thus the logical operations of classification and ordering, and the construction of the concepts of time, space, etc. (i.e. the contents of sub-logical operations),[1] are all dependent on one another. In short, it is the basic fact of a child's thinking conforming to a system that underpins the tendency for developmental unity.

3. *Causality*

Piaget's book *The Child's Conception of Physical Causality* was first published in England in 1930. In this he records his findings in respect of the development of causal reasoning. Children were asked questions about various natural phenomena such as the wind, rivers, the sun, etc., or about actual events observed by the subjects such as the rise in level of a liquid in a vessel when an object was dropped into it, what makes a bicycle or a sailing boat move, etc. In the last chapter Piaget links the growth of the child's logical thought with his increasing ability to understand causality; i.e. he claims that there is a parallel evolution between the logical and the 'ontological' and distinguishes three main steps in each.

The first stage lasts up to 2–3 years of age. In this Piaget claims that we find, from the point of view of logic, a kind of thinking in which the child confuses truth and desire, for that which is desired is deemed to be reality. Reason is impossible; there is only perpetual play, and this tends to distort perceptions while situations are altered so as to accord with the child's pleasure. In the realm of ontology, a primitive *psycho- logical causality* corresponds to this stage of thinking. There is a belief that any desire can influence and control external things; in short a kind of magic holds sway. There is thus confusion between the self

[1] See footnote to p. 230

and the world which produces autism in the realm of logic, and magic in the realm of causality.

Stage two extends from roughly 2–3 to 7–8 years of age. Although the tendency to confuse reality with desire becomes increasingly rare, thought is ego-centric; there is no desire on the part of the child to justify, logically, the statements he makes. Corresponding to this in the ontological domain we find what Piaget calls *pre-causality*. Under this term he includes all those forms of causality originating in a confusion between the psychological activity of a child and the behaviour of the object, often with the result that the child substitutes an imputed psychological activity of the object for the true physical mechanism at work. In the realm of logic the child confuses his own subjective justification with true verification, while in the field of causality he confuses the causal behaviour of things with his own sense of motivation.

In the final stage which begins at 7–8 years of age in normal children we find an increasing ability to think deductively, and an increased capacity to give correct causal explanations. Once again it appears that the child's thoughts begin to conform to a system and he makes progress from the point of view of both logic and ontology.

A thorough study of precausal thinking by Laurendeau and Pinard (1962) has substantiated many, but not all, of Piaget's views. They studied some 500 children aged between 4 years and 12 (50 per age-group). It was found that *realism* (regarding one's own perspective as immediately objective and absolute) was not outgrown until $6\frac{1}{2}$ years; *artificialism* (the child posits the explicit action of a maker at the origin of things) was still in evidence at 9 years; while *animism* (the child attributes life and consciousness to inanimate objects), was frequently found in young children, and traces of it remained even at 12. This lack of synchronism in the disappearance of the different kinds of pre-causal thinking again reflects the absence of a complete systematization of thought in the child of primary school age. Even at the end of this period the child lacks a comprehensive frame of reference, so that his conceptions of the external world are at times highly unscientific.

4. *Increased plasticity of concrete operational structures*

At the stage of concrete operations one is dealing with relations between actions that bear directly on things. Hence the child can elaborate the notions of number, time and other first order constructions, although as we have already seen, these are not available to the child all at once. The present section notes briefly that there is an increased plasticity in the operational manipulation of these first order relations as the child moves through the age range 8–11 or so, and in order to illustrate this, two examples will be taken from Inhelder and Piaget's *The Growth of Logical Thinking* (1958).

In one experiment the subject was presented with a piece of apparatus in which balls could roll down a chute adjusted to make various angles with the horizontal. The balls, of varying weight, rolled down the chute and rebounded from the bottom. A ball could be released from the top of the chute or at any point along its length. The task for the child was to find out which of the possible variables controlled the length of the bound of the ball. He had to discover that the length of the bound from the bottom of the chute depended only on the height of the release point, and has nothing to do with the length of the chute along which the ball rolled, the slope of the chute, or the weight of the ball. At 8 years of age one notices the beginnings of correct formulations of correspondences (e.g. 'where they (balls) go depends on the length of the slide') but the formulations are not systematic and there is no separation of variables. By 9–10 years of age, however, there is the commencement of dissociation of the height of the release point from the slope. At the latter age the subjects are more interested in, and capable of, systematic correspondences.

Another experiment involved a simple balance for weighing. It was shown that the 8-year-old easily discovers, only by trial and error, that equilibrium between a smaller weight at a greater distance and a greater weight at a smaller distance is possible. But by 10 years of age the child begins to understand the qualitative correspondence, 'the heavier it is, the closer you put it to the middle', although he still cannot solve problems involving different weights and different distances by metrical proportion.

In total: as the child moves through the period 8–11 years of age there is an increased plasticity in the operational manipulation of first order concepts, and because of this the child is increasingly able to organize and structure the data of problems using the methods of concrete operational thinking. Further, as he becomes more capable of using these methods, he is better able to recognize their shortcomings, also the gaps and uncertainties brought to light when such methods are used, so that eventually he gropes for new methods for attacking his problems and formal operational thinking comes into being. While it is true to say that concrete operational thought is one clear stage in cognitive growth, it is equally true that within this stage there is an increasing flexibility in the operational manoeuvreability of the first order constructions, eventually leading to the elaboration of relationships between these themselves.

The development of formal reasoning is considered in more detail in the next two chapters. For the present, we may note that when a child is required to solve a practical or theoretical problem by the application of systematic classification and ordering to the causal relations involved, his success is very much dependent on the availability of suitable concepts and on the number of steps demanded in the solution. Thus in section II we were concerned mainly with the type of relation to be established. Here we note that, even when the child is capable of conceiving and understanding a particular type of relation, e.g. serial correspondence, it is not always easy for him to reason without error in the causal field. Factors affecting the availability and facility of logical inferences are so important that we will discuss them more fully in the next section.

IV. THE MECHANISMS OF SYSTEMATIZATION

1. *The role of anticipation and hindsight*

This chapter began with a consideration of the development of conservation, and this section included a discussion of Piaget's 'probabilistic equilibrium model' as set out in his 1957 article. According to Piaget, the elaboration of systematic ways of organizing experience at each successive level and in every domain can only be fully accounted for by assuming a process of equilibration (see Inhelder and Piaget, 1964, Piaget and Inhelder, 1965, and the discussion of Peel in Chapter 10). However, although the concept of equilibration itself is assumed by Piaget to be quite general in its applicability, it is obvious that the succession of phases in section I is relevant only to conservation. Moreover, while our earlier discussion contained some reference to the sources of continuing instability right up to the final completion of the developmental process (conflict arising out of the obvious discrepancies between the different situations involved as well as the influence of the initial situation $S1$), it contained only scant reference to the psychological mechanisms which mediate the transition from one phase to the next. Chapter 7 of Inhelder and Piaget's work on classification (1964) is devoted to a careful analysis of those aspects of children's behaviour that appear to be most relevant to this problem.

We may begin with a brief description of the inquiry. The apparatus consists of an array of cardboard shapes, squares, triangles, rectangles, circles, ovals, differing in several respects: shape, colour, size and edge (which may be straight or saw-toothed). The child may be shown only a portion of these to begin with (for instance, only rectilinear straight-edged figures), so that the introduction of a new dimension later forces him to re-structure his thought. His task is to classify the material, and he may be given boxes or envelopes to help him.

The successive behaviours of children in this situation are discussed in the light of the evidence which they provide for the operation of retro-action and anticipation. The term *retro-action* or *hindsight* refers to the process whereby an individual revises earlier actions in the light of those that follow, i.e. he corrects his errors. *Anticipation* or *foresight* refers to the apparent process whereby the mental representation of actions reverses the sequence of their actual performance, so that, in the resultant behaviour, one finds that actions which occur earlier are modified by those which are to follow. The authors provide evidence that it is the co-ordination of retro-action and anticipation that underpins the child's ability to systematize this thinking.

In describing their experimental findings, Inhelder and Piaget (*op. cit.*) distinguished two modes of classification which they termed *ascending* and *descending* respectively. When using the first method the child starts by making many sub-collections (e.g. green triangles, green circles, red squares, red ovals, etc.), and then combines them step by step until he arrives at one or more broad dichotomies. When using the descending method, children start from a broad dichotomy and later subdivide the classes by making further dichotomies. Those who use the second method usually have less difficulty when they are asked to change the order of their criteria after the first classification has been completed. When the ascending method is used, there may be no conscious selection of properties whereby the classification is made. The grouping of elements (e.g. small red squares, large red squares, small blue squares, large blue squares, small red circles, etc.) into larger collections (e.g. all red versus all blue) is apt to be made on the basis of a property noticed by chance: i.e. there is retro-action but no anticipation. Conversely, the child who begins with the major grouping is more likely to have noticed (and deliberately ignored) the obvious differences between the elements that compose them. However, the authors point out that these are extreme methods and many intermediate approaches are to be found.

A more telling variation was to ask the child to state in advance what classifications he intended to make. His verbal formulations were then compared with his actual classifications and the ability to make subsequent changes of criteria. At the first stage of classification (age usually less than 6), the child fails to foresee any classification. When thinking of a collection he cannot recall what he said a moment before, and because of this he cannot anticipate, for his immediate memory or his 'set' is so fleeting in nature that he cannot retain a consistent idea of what he is seeking. When he actually builds his collection, the results of his previous actions remain in front of him and guide his next move, but this results in a 'graphic collection' (section II). Thus, children under 6 years of age cannot anticipate because they cannot remember or because the 'set' is easily lost. In short, there is no co-ordination between immediate past and immediate future.

At the second stage of classification, which begins at about 6, the subject will, spontaneously, make a partial or complete anticipation of the first classification. More often than not, the verbal anticipation is made in terms of large collections or broad dichotomies (these being favoured by the character of language itself). But when the child actually begins to sort the objects he starts out by making small collections and then slowly moves to the point where he groups these into larger units. Thus his anticipations tend to conform to the descending method, while his actual classifications argue an ascending method. As yet these two processes are not synthesized, so the child cannot, mentally, move to and fro among the collections. In essence there is no reversibility of thought.

The fact that, at this stage, children readily manage to name one or two proposed collections of objects in advance (e.g. circles, squares, roofs, etc.) means that when they construct the actual groups they are no longer dealing with *ad hoc* assimilations. As soon as a child has assimilated a number of, say, 'red 'ones, each to its predecessors, he can go back over his mental moves and 'find', as it were, the assimilatory schemata that he has used; this corresponds, of course, to the common property of the class in question. Moreover, this retro-action is not just a matter of remembering a series of connexions, for the objects have been partly classified in advance by the action of scanning. Although there are a number of ways in which the objects may be sorted, the subject is increasingly able to abstract one of these at a time. Thus constant reappraisal goes on alongside successive assimilations, and the former eventually gives rise to anticipatory schemata. It must be noted, however, that at the second stage, although the child shows some spontaneous retro-action and anticipation, these are largely dependent on the configurations in front of him. He cannot bring these same processes to bear on transformations: i.e. he cannot anticipate the form that the configuration would take if the order of criteria were reversed, so that the criteria of sub-classes became criteria of major classes and vice versa. To be able to do this the subject must be able to pass to and fro between the ascending and descending methods of classification. Retro-action and anticipation will then have reached the level of operational reversibility.

At the third stage of classification, the choice of criteria is based on explicit decision (e.g. the child may ask 'Shall we use same shape or same material?') As soon as one classification is completed he can return to a criterion that he has just laid aside, for the objects can now be re-sorted on the basis of immediate retro-action. Moreover, there is now complete reciprocity between the ascending and descending processes, as is shown by the fact that the child can anticipate transformations as well as con-figurations. In the view of Piaget and Inhelder the growth of operational schemata is closely related to such retro-active and anticipatory pro-cesses. It is the co-ordination of the processes that leads to reversibility of thought and hence to systematic thinking.

Thus, in this account, Piaget ascribes the development of systematiza-tion to the passage from retro-action to anticipation and from antici-pation to the recognition of systematic interdependencies, and hence of *transformation*. For an arrangement of a set of objects which entails that what were sub-classes in another arrangement are now classes and vice versa is a logical transformation with respect to the alternative arrangement. Piaget's treatment here is more general than in his earlier discussion of equilibration, for it would apply equally to seriation and conservation (see Lunzer 1965).

If one compares the situation at stage I, when there is little retro-action and no anticipation, with that at stage III, when transformations are realized, it is apparent that the younger child is limited to single judgements at a time, while the older child can establish relations between (at least two) judgements (cf. Lunzer 1960b). In similar vein, McLaughlin (1963) suggests that limitations of reasoning correspond to limitations in immediate memory or attention. He has proposed that each of Piaget's stages of thought is characterized by the number of items a child can retain at the same time. Thus if we assume that the number of digits that an individual can remember (his digit span) is equivalent to his memory span for concepts, his level of thought may be deduced from this digit span. Thus if a child can retain only two (i.e. 2^1) concepts simultaneously and he compares two objects, they must be either the same or quite different for him since he cannot have a third concept of similarities or differences. At the stage of concrete operations or systematic thought the child must be able to process four (2^2) concepts for he now has the capacity for logical addition and multiplication.

Thus, McLaughlin's thesis puts emphasis on the importance of immediate memory capacity which in turn suggests that maturation of the central nervous system must play a role in the systematization of thought. His paper should be studied for further details of his proposals.

2. *'Horizontal Discrepancies'*

The examples that have been discussed might suggest that the systematization of thought develops smoothly and regularly so that children can solve different problems at the same time, providing the latter have a common operational structure. In fact this is not so as was pointed out earlier in one of Dodwell's studies. Such instances might throw some doubt on Piaget's theoretical formulations, for if he is correct, then there should be a high correlation between performance on different tasks involving the same mental operations.

Earlier, Dodwell (1960) had shown that there was only a moderate relationship between tests which, in Piaget's view, involved the same thinking skills and which all involved integral aspects of the number concept. Likewise Smedslund (1961), also Lovell and Ogilvie (1961), both failed to find close agreement between the acquisition of conservation and transitivity of weight (i.e. the capacity to infer that if *A* is heavier than *B*, and *B* heavier than *C*, then *A* is heavier than *C*). In many other experiments carried out by Lovell, a child was often found to be at a more advanced stage on one task than on another in spite of the fact that the tasks involved the same concepts. For example, Lovell and Slater (1960) found that the equality of synchronous intervals came earlier in the experiment involving the syphoning of water than in the experiment involving the dolls racing on the table. Much the same point is made by Lunzer (1960a) in relation to developments pertaining to one aspect of formal reasoning (see next chapter): the conservation of volume. While Piaget's logical analysis of the systematic relationships entering into the elaboration of the concept of volume suggest that there should be a synchronous development of all behaviours involving volume, Lunzer's experimental data showed that the correlation between them was only moderate.

While some of Piaget's writings (e.g. Piaget, 1950 on the concept of number) make little allowance for such unevenness, many of his more recent works show an awareness of these facts, which is combined with the following explanation. Concrete operations depend on a direct organization or systematization of readily intuitable[1] data. Hence, it is argued, concrete thought cannot be immediately generalized to all physical situations merely on the ground that the logical structure of relations involved may be identical. (Inhelder and Piaget, 1958.) As is well known, thought is systematized in relation to length before it is in relation to weight. In the view of the Geneva school, this is because it is more difficult to serialize, equalize, etc., objects whose properties are less easy to dissociate from one's own actions, e.g. weight, than to apply mental operations to properties that can be rendered more objective, e.g. length. Lovell and Ogilvie (*op. cit.*) also suggest that conservation of quantity comes earlier than that of weight because the former is under immediate visual perception and the latter is not (cf. the size-weight illusion, Chapter 1, Section V. 2). This, in essence, is the basis of the distinction which Piaget draws between what he calls *horizontal* and *vertical age-discrepancies*[2] (Piaget, 1956, Piaget and Inhelder, 1965). Horizontal discrepancies are discrepancies within a given level of structural organization (e.g. conservation of substance and weight); the causes of such discrepancies are held to be contingent on perceptual or intuitable features of the situation, and there may be inter-individual differences in the order of their attainment. Vertical discrepancies correspond to differences in the complexity of the relevant logical structures, as in the age-discrepancy between the conservation of weight and the conservation of volume (especially displacement volume, see Lunzer, 1960a).

Wohlwill (1963) makes much the same point in arguing that responses to tasks deemed equivalent from the point of view of mental structure may develop in sequence rather than simultaneously. Thus some children would pass on a specific task and fail on another, but not vice versa. In support of this he quotes data supplied by Lovell and Ogilvie which showed that 29 per cent of the pupils studied could handle transitivity of weight but not conservation, but only 8 per cent showed the reverse pattern. However, he adds that passing on one task but

[1] = perceptible and/or imageable.
[2] French: 'décalage'

failing on an equivalent task may be due to the unreliability of the measures obtained. Finally, Wohlwill points out that there may be individual differences in intellectual functioning which are not understood and suggests that the 'horizontal differential' of responses must be properly reconciled with, and integrated into, a hierarchical model of mental operations.

A simplified view of Piaget's theory suggests a sharp break between pre-operational and concrete operational thought. But there are many studies at the present time which show that concrete operational thinking is even more task-specific than Piaget would allow.

In the opinion of the present writer, the discrepancies that obtain are so important that they cannot be brushed aside with a simple reference to the intuitable characteristics of the given situation. Among the various factors which merit detailed investigation, we would include lack of specific experience, information and vocabulary. Or again, one sometimes finds that irrelevant information prevents thought from being systematized, as, for example, when Lovell and Ogilvie (1961) point out that many children failed to conserve weight since they believed that as plasticine was cooled and got harder, it also became heavier. In real life, harder materials are usually heavier than softer ones, but such knowledge distorts thought in some situations in which conservation is concerned.

Taking all the evidence into account, the existence of quite sharp 'horizontal discrepancies' does not invalidate Piaget's analysis of the difference in structure between operational thought and pre-operational thought. But it does point to the inadequacy of Piagetian theory as a predictive and explanatory instrument. Our conclusions may be briefly summarized as follows:

Concrete operational thought is a necessary but not a sufficient condition for the elaboration of certain concepts.

The application of the operations to specific problems is always a function of specific learnings.

A study also relevant at this point is that of Zimiles (1966) which dealt with the effect of a number of variables on the conservation of number. For example, he studied, among 5–7-year-olds, the desirability of objects to be conserved (cars *v.* blocks); the actual number of objects presented together with the effect of their shape, size and colour; and the effect of presenting rows of objects on picture cards. His conclusions were that conservation of number is not a unitary trait which functions on an all-or-none basis. Besides necessitating a certain cognitive structure it involves a set of attitudes concerned with the gathering and processing of information. Zimiles found a discontinuity of cognitive functioning in these young subjects, a failure to apply recent experiences in a highly similar situation and to recognize similarity between the events, and a lack of concern to reply consistently. It is not the presence or absence of the concept which distinguished these children from, say, 10-year-olds, but the availability of the concept. It is their mode of organizing and integrating the input of information which seems to distinguish these from older pupils. Studies carried out under the writer's direction among very able children (Terman Merrill I Qs $\geq$ 140) reflect similar differences between average and highly gifted pupils. These findings are entirely consonant with the view that the possibility of elaborating concrete operation structures is a necessary but insufficient condition for the elaboration of certain concepts.

3. *Contributions of information theory*

The chief weakness of the concept of horizontal discrepancies is its vagueness. For while Piaget provides a clear description of the systematic features of logical thinking, together with a plausible account of the way in which these arise, his theory alone is unable to predict those situations which facilitate the systematic ordering of thought and those that impede it. A number of recent studies suggest that concepts derived from information theory can lead to more precise predictions.

Information theory is a branch of applied mathematics concerned primarily with problems of achieving maximum efficiency in communication systems (e.g. telephone systems, radar, etc.). The key concepts include transmitter, receiver, message, signal, coding, information, redundancy and noise. Typically, communication may be said to take place when a message is transmitted from a transmitter to a receiver through a communication channel. The message conveys information to the receiver in the measure that it reduces uncertainty about some state of affairs. For instance, if it is equally probable that it is rainy or fine and the message is 'fine', we say that it conveys one 'bit' of information, uncertainty being reduced by $\log_2 (2)$, i.e. 1. If the message is highly probable, then the amount of information it contains is correspondingly less, for it contributes little to the reduction of uncertainty. A message which describes an unknown situation in detail may contain a great deal of information. One which merely reiterates known information contains zero information. Information may be quantified in terms of a logarithmic scale (number of bits), ranging from zero to infinity. A message containing zero information is redundant.

Generally speaking, a message can only be transmitted by coding the information into signals, physical energy changes which can be passed across the channel. These signals will then be decoded at the opposite end. Even though the message as a whole may not be redundant, it may include redundant signals, i.e. more may be transmitted than is necessary for the reduction of uncertainty to zero. Indeed, this is generally necessary, since if no redundancy were incorporated in the system, adequate communication could only be achieved if communication were perfect. It never is. For what is conveyed by the channel is always distorted by 'noise', i.e. irrelevant physical changes which distort the signal. Noise can only be compensated for by including redundancy in the message. The concepts of information theory have been found useful in relation to a number of psychological problems of cognition, since cognition involves the reduction of uncertainty and the decoding of signals (e.g. visual patterns, language) containing information (for a general introduction see Attneave, 1959).

In an attempt to apply information theory to problems of reasoning, Smedslund (1966a, b, c) studied the frequency of correct and incorrect inferences in simple situations involving the conservation of number. The child is faced with 2 collections of 16 counters. The experimenter executes one or more operations and asks which collection has more (or, a different question, less). 1 step operations involve adding an element to left or right ($+L$, $+R$) or removing one ($-L$, $-R$). Two-step operations may or may not be compensatory ($+L+R$, $+L-L$, etc.). Among his more interesting findings were (1) symmetrical items (e.g. $-L-R$) were easier than reversal items (e.g. $-L+L$): although logically the two are of the same complexity, the second requires an additional transformation; (2) the more steps involved, the harder the problem; (3) items of the type $+L-L+L$ (involving only one 'channel') were easier than items like $+L+R+L$, and items of the type $-L+R+L$ were most difficult of all (involving retention or storage before final processing). It is clear that the factors to be considered include the locus of change (information channel to be attended to), the transformations required, the number of steps and the ease of coding and storage.

Wohlwill (1962) argues that the problem of the move from perception to reasoning can be considered from the standpoint of the decrease in the dependence of behaviour on information from the immediate stimulus field. He indicates that there are three dimensions along which one may consider this move (i.e. from perception to reasoning). These dimensions are:

(a) Redundancy. The amount of redundant information required decreases.

(b) Selectivity. The amount of irrelevant information that can be tolerated without affecting the responses increases.

(c) Contiguity. There is an increase in the spatial and temporal separation over which the total information contained in the stimulus field can be integrated.

According to this viewpoint, the systematization of thought depends upon the growth in autonomy of central brain processes.

Wohlwill undoubtedly considers this approach to be an alternative to the Piagetian analysis. But there are good grounds for considering, with Smedslund, that both types of analysis are necessary. The Piagetian analysis deals primarily with the type of transformations that are evolved and the origin of those mechanisms which determined that particular classes of events shall be deemed equivalent, e.g. in conservation, and hence when information becomes redundant for a given subject. The information theory type of approach seems essential for the closer study of factors determining the availability of such information processing. It is certainly more promising than the concept of décalage[1], which allows Piaget to have his cake and eat it.

A further advantage of accepting the value of both types of analysis is that the second approach suggests ways in which problems can be progressively graded and programmed in such a way as to promote an ever increasing systematic, and hence economical and productive, handling of the environment. It is therefore logical to move from the present discussion to consider the role of experience and learning in the growth of reasoning.

V. THE ROLE OF EXPERIENCE

1. *Specific educational experiences*

In dealing with educational factors relevant to the systematization of experience, we may begin by a consideration of the role of learning in situations that have been deliberately contrived by others. A number of experiments have now been undertaken in which 5–7-year-olds have

[1] p. 248

been subjected to various training programmes, and their performance before training compared with that afterwards. Thus Wohlwill and Lowe (1962) carried out work in connexion with the conservation of number, Smedslund's (1961) work involved the conservation of quantity, while Beilin and Franklin (1962) dealt with the conservation of length and area. In addition, mention has already been made of the work of Smedslund in connexion with the elaboration of a frame of reference in the spatial field. It appears from these experiments that specific experience lasting over a few weeks is not very effective in developing systematic thought unless the child's thinking is nearly ready for it; i.e. until his psychic organization can be restructured by the experience and his thoughts made to conform to a system at least in that specific situation. It is true that Sigel *et al.* (1966) claimed that 4-year-old children, when given training on problems involving multiple classification, multiple relationality, and reversibility, showed improvement on certain conservation tasks compared with control groups. However, it must be appreciated that the mean Stanford Binet IQ of one training group was 149 and of its control group 152, while for another training and its control group the corresponding figures were each 144, so it is very likely that these subjects were at or near a transitional stage in respect of the conservation tasks anyhow. On the other hand, both Churchill (1958) and Phemister (1962) showed that in free play that involved certain contrived situations, conservation of number was helped forward. Thus Phemister indicated that after five months, twelve out of twenty children in the first year of school life who had play experiences of a certain kind conserved number earlier than those in a control group who were taught under more usual activity methods by an able teacher. For her experimental group Phemister provided experiences likely to provoke actions by the child that would help forward the notion of quantity. Thus she provided opportunities for matching, arranging things in order, grouping, sorting and comparing. The child freely chose his own activities, with, of course, the teacher's participation and comment. Such rather structured activities may help the child to grasp, say, that numbers can be divided up and put together again.

The above evidence may be taken to support the thesis put forward by Hunt (1961), that accommodative modifications in central processes of the brain take place only when the child encounters circumstances which so match his assimilatory schemata, that he is motivated by the situation and can cope with it.

2. *The problem-solving method*

Hunt's interpretation of Piagetian theory suggests that if learning is to be non-trivial, then the most effective method of teaching consists in the provision of a succession of graded problem situations.

By the term 'problem', we imply some goal that has to be reached but the way to it is not immediately clear. To understand how the solution of problems may lead to learning it is necessary to consider again the processes of *assimilation* and *accommodation*. Piaget is at pains to point out that these are indissociable from each other. Cognitive adaptation to some new situation (e.g. a problem) involves both, for to assimilate the meaning of the new situation it is necessary to accommodate to it, and to be able to accommodate to it, it must be possible to assimilate it. Thus the child cannot assimilate new objects or events until they have some meaning for him, i.e. until past assimilations have prepared him for the assimilation of the meaning of the new material. The existing assimilatory schemata must be of such a complexity, that when the child attempts to accommodate to the new situation, the meaning can be assimilated to the existing schemata. Clearly there can be no complete break in meaning between the new situation presented and the assimilating schemata already present. Cognitive development is thus a gradual step by step process with the new always building on to the old.

Once the new meaning is assimilated the individual's assimilatory schemata are likely to become more complex, and because of this more complicated accommodations become possible; i.e. existing schemata become restructured. Moreover, assimilatory schemata are not static even when there is no environmental stimulation, for systems of meanings are being re-organized within themselves all the time, and they are being integrated with other such systems as well.

The relation of problem solving to learning can now be made clearer. When the schemata required for the solution of a problem are not too far removed in complexity from those available to the child, then the inadequacy of the existing schemata will force him to accommodate to the conditions of the problem. The result, as has been already seen, will be a modification and restructuring of the child's schemata in the direction of cognitive adaptation. This is true learning, for by increasing the range and complexity of the schemata available to himself, not only does the child solve the question, but he also extends his capacity for further learning. Even in such a case the child may, of course, still have to be given help after he has made some preliminary adjustment to the situations.

But the position may be different if the problems to be solved, or the new ideas to be mastered, are 'given' by the teacher, i.e. they are described and explained in direct fashion. This method is sometimes known as the 'rule and example' technique. In this case learning can only take place if the child's schemata are adequate, or almost adequate, for the teacher's explanations, so they are restructured and made more complex thereby. The teacher who believes in this method will claim that properly graded material does match the child's existing schemata. If, however, the existing assimilatory schemata are quite inadequate for the exposition of the teacher there will be no reorganization of schemata. Indeed, if the teacher attempts to implant a body of knowledge under these circumstances, the content of his teaching may well be assimilated with considerable distortion – as best the pupil can. Not only will this be in evidence when he is questioned or he otherwise tries to reproduce the material, but there will be no transfer of training. Further, there is no useful restructuring of his schemata and hence no growth or increase in the degree of their complexity, and so there is no new 'platform' from which further learning may take place.

A relevant study at this point is that of Smedslund's (1963) relating to the acquisition of the transitivity of weight. He attempted to test two views. (i) Transitivity results from repeated observation that if A weighs more than B, and B weighs more than C, then A weighs more than C (learning theory). It is important to have many occurrences of sequences of the type $A > B - B > C - A > C$, and observations of $A > C$ are necessary on this view. (ii) Transitivity results from an internal reorganization of the schemata. The reorganization is presumably initiated by repeated uncertainties or problems (equilibration theory). Actual observations of $A > C$ are unnecessary on this view. He also studied the effect of *free* practice, in which the child was given three objects and asked to arrange them according to weight by means of the balance scale, and compared the results with *fixed* practice in which the child was first asked to weigh A and B, then B and C, and then to anticipate the relationship between A and C. One might expect the free procedure with its frequent uncertainties as to which to weigh first, to provide more acquisitions of transitivity than the fixed procedure. Smedslund studied five groups of children, comprising 143 pupils aged 7·6 to 9·3 years. One group had free practice with actual observation of $A > C$, and a second group had the same kind of practice but no corresponding observation. Groups three and four both had fixed practice but one group had observation of $A > C$ and the other group did not. The fifth group was a control group without practice of any kind.

Smedslund's results show that the observation of $A > C$ did not affect the frequency of the acquisition of transitivity, but since all four experimental groups improved more than the control group, it seems that the mere frequency of problems is crucial. On the other hand, whereas the younger children seemed to benefit a little more from free practice, the older children profited equally from both free and fixed practice. It seems clear that we need to know much more about the issues involved in a 'free' versus a more 'formal' approach to problem solving.

Russian teachers no less than those in the West, are aware of the snags involved in trying to force new material on children. Kalmykova (1962), dealing with the psychological prerequisites of arithmetic writes, 'Experienced teachers, therefore, organize the explanation of new materials in such a way that the pupils as if by themselves (though, of course, on the basis of the teacher's questions) find the necessary relations between the facts and the questions posed'.

It is, of course, possible that the activation of processes systematically related to some given process will aid the growth of organized thought. For example, the combination of addition and subtraction, with the same numbers in close succession and in practical contexts, might help the growth of elementary numerical relationships in some children. Or, some process may be activated by children seeing one another grappling with it on their own. This at least is the viewpoint of some Soviet workers. The plain fact is that concrete examples of the systematization of thought can be acquired by rote learning, but in these circumstances there will be no generalization for thought is not really systematic. On the other hand, a store of mechanical routines may be the pre-condition for, or may actually accelerate, operational systematization. Only future research can throw more light on this very important issue.

3. *Teaching for transfer*

In the light of what has been said, it would appear reasonable to suggest that meaningful material is better retained than meaningless material; also that when tasks are learned with understanding instead of by rote memorization, new tasks are learnt more readily because of transfer of training. Early students of learning such as Ebbinghaus and Boreas were greatly impressed by the greater retainability of meaningful over nonsense materials. However, later experimental studies have shown the issue to be a complex one.

A great difficulty is that material that is meaningful (i.e. it can easily be accommodated to) is, because of its very meaningfulness, material that has already entered into some learning. Such material can be learned with understanding rather than by rote memorization. What we really need to know is whether meaningful material would be retained better than meaningless material learned to an equal level. Katona (1940) tried to find the answer to this problem. He designed simple but ingenious experiments in which it was possible to commit the same material to memory with or without understanding; also to test the results on new learning. Katona concluded that there is greater retention when learning takes place with understanding. Understanding qualifies the learner to move forward to new learning, whereas rote memorization sometimes tends to narrow the range of problem solving. Although some aspects of this work were criticized by Melton (1941) he agreed that Katona had demonstrated that when learning takes place with understanding new tasks are learnt more readily.

Hilgard *et al.* (1953) repeated, using high school students, the type of experiment that Katona had carried out among College students and obtained the same results. Nevertheless, there were still some questions that Katona had not answered. For example, Hilgard found that although the pupils who learnt with understanding did better on new tasks than those who learnt by memorization, there were still many errors made by the former. Indeed, one third of those who learnt by understanding made errors in the easiest of the transfer tasks and three quarters made errors on the most difficult task. This problem was studied later by Hilgard *et al.* (1954). They point out, amongst other things, that the prevalence of careless errors suggests that when teaching understanding, methods should be devised whereby the student can review and check, through retracing his steps.

Katona maintained that there is a real difference in what happens according to whether memorization or learning with understanding is employed. The subject organizes his task as best he can, and it is only when his attempt at better organization fails that he falls back on rote learning. Thus rote memorization can be looked upon as a kind of organization used by the subject when the material is otherwise quite meaningless for him. Indeed, it seems necessary at this stage and is, perhaps a precondition for later meaningful learning in that area.

It seems that learning by understanding brings about somewhat greater retention and greater transfer of training because operational systematization can be applied to the data in hand and to related data. The role of active verbalization in promoting such understanding forms the subject of a small but interesting study by Tough (1963) designed to teach seriation and ordinal correspondence. This is in keeping with the ideas of P. I. Galperin (1957) who pointed out that in the Russian view, an essential step in the formation of actions carried out in the mind is the mastering of the actions on the plane of speech. Thus, in order to bring about a more adequate handling of numerical concepts in addition, the teaching is broken down into five phases: (*a*) preliminary conception of the task, i.e. finding out what it is about and establishing the nature of the goal; (*b*) direct actions performed on concrete objects; (*c*) description of these actions using audible speech with the aim of developing a link between numerical language and the actions as opposed to a link between language and things only – being the collections which are the result of actions;[1] (*d*) internalization of verbal description and progressive abbreviation resulting in a 'transfer to the mental plane'; (*e*) abbreviation or telescoping or virtualization of the action – termed 'consolidation' by Galperin.[2]

4. *General experience*

The evidence adduced so far indicates that short-term experimental 'training' has little effect on the development of systematization. On the other hand, 'education' can be more effective, especially if the teaching takes full account both of the developmental level of the pupil, and of the necessary phases entering into the learning processes. In the field of 'concrete' learning[3] at any rate, such teaching follows closely on the

---

[1] The reader cannot fail to notice the precise parallel with Piaget's analysis of the transition from judgements relating to states to those bearing on transformations in Section I of this chapter.

[2] cf. Lunzer's analysis of the virtualization of classificatory behaviour in the development of hypothetico-deductive reasoning and the analogy with physical skills in Section I of the next chapter.

[3] It should, however, be added that this remark is restricted to the first-order systematization which is the subject of the present chapter. There is only a little research to date bearing directly on the role of the natural environment in the acquisition of *formal* reasoning: e.g. Peluffo (1964). Both on intrinsic theoretical grounds, and, in the light of studies of intelligence in primitive settings, such as those of Weil (1959), MacArthur (1964), one is led to suspect that formal reasoning rarely develops spontaneously in a primitive cultural background, and only with difficulty in an advanced cultural setting.

pattern which may be observed in the course of education in and by the environment itself – i.e. spontaneous learning. Thus it would appear that most of the cognitive challenge and conflict that causes the child to restructure his thoughts and so eventually systematize his thinking takes place in what one may call natural, rather than contrived situations. There is evidence from underdeveloped societies where children have had no schooling, or schooling of varying quality, that systematization of thought does take place in much the same way as among western children although perhaps a little later. Thus Price Williams (1962) compared the ability of bush (illiterate) with primary school children of the Tiv tribe in Nigeria to classify and sort materials familiar to them. He found no differences over the age range of $6\frac{1}{2}$–11 years. Further, he found the progression of the idea of continuous and discontinuous quantities (earth and nuts respectively) followed that of Western children. Goodnow (1962), working with European and Chinese children of very varying educational and socio-economic backgrounds in Hong Kong, studied the growth of the conservation of weight, area and volume. On the conservation tasks she found that milieu, schooling and socio-economic status had far less effect than had been expected although the groups differed greatly in their performance on Raven's Matrices test. Moreover, Goodnow and Bethon (1966) presented evidence that conservation tasks for weight, volume and surface may be insensitive to schooling whereas performance on combinatorial tasks are greatly affected by school life and work. Similarly Sigel and Mermelstein (1965) claimed that lack of schooling had little effect on the performance of certain conservation tasks by Negro children in Prince Edward County, Virginia. The pity is that we do not really know what kinds of natural experiences or situations best aid cognitive growth. Indeed, these may vary from child to child.

It is not intended, of course, to imply in any way that schooling does nothing to aid the systematization of thought. It is possible that informal primary schools that are in the tradition of Froebel, Susan Isaacs, and the like, may replicate to some extent, learning situations found naturally. In such schools there is broadly what one may call an environmental approach where the greatest use is made of children's interests, and where they are introduced to, and made familiar with, as many ideas as possible that are relevant to them. Yet care has to be exercised in discussing this point. While Gagné (1961) claimed that 'guided discovery' was superior to 'free discovery' and 'rule and example' in a study involving programmed learning, Lovell (1963), in an extensive study, found no difference in reading attainments (including comprehension) among those third and fourth year junior school pupils educated in informal Junior schools when compared with similar children attending formal schools. A similar inquiry by Gardner (1965) showed significant differences in attitude among children whose primary schooling had been based on an 'experimental' or 'progressive' as opposed to a 'traditional' philosophy, but differences in cognitive skills were non-significant, and the control pupils were actually superior in mechanical arithmetic. Again, Pringle and McKenzie (1965) found that progressive, child centred education, did not seem to reduce the degree of rigidity of thinking in problem solving with 11-year-olds although there was some evidence that such an education might be of more value to the children of below average ability in this respect. The plain fact is that the conditions of experiences that best help children to systematize their thinking are not known with any exactitude.

Piaget (1926) argued that social factors play a vital role in helping the child move from cognitive egocentrism to systematic thinking. He did not admit that mere experience of events and objects necessarily brought this about, since the child often distorted his experience of the world to fit his already existing schemata. His argument at the time was that it is the social interaction with peers which forces the child to re-examine his own ideas, so that he can satisfy his need to share the thoughts of others and his need to communicate his own thoughts to other children. Argument with the peer group forces the child to argue with himself, i.e. to reason logically. Thus without interchange of thought and without co-operation with other children, the individual would be retarded in making his thoughts conform to a system. If we turn the clock on thirty-five years we find Inhelder and Piaget (1964) equally insistent that the mental operations of classification are ultimately derived from sensori-motor activities such as bringing together and taking apart. Language contributes to the formation and stabilization of the system of communication constituted by concepts, but it does not appear to be sufficient for the formation of the operations which are the essence of systematic thought. No one can fail to be impressed by the completeness of this shift in emphasis. It can be argued that Piaget is quite justified in not retracting his earlier views (and, indeed, he has not retracted them), to conform with the change in his interest. For the two arguments are not necessarily incompatible: thus, while the earlier formulation deals with the extrinsic motivation which favours the development, the later analysis (which is certainly more fundamental, and also better substantiated) is concerned with the intrinsic mechanisms which make the development possible. However, there are a number of other considerations that affect the systematization of thought and should be mentioned, however briefly. First, there is the degree of familiarity with the materials concerned, and with the definitions by which they are indicated. Second, there is the concreteness of the situation involved. This was clearly shown in the experiment in which children had to consider the class of animals in relation to certain sub-classes, e.g. ducks. Jahoda (1963) has likewise made clear that a good knowledge of geographical terms underpins children's ability to build up a coherent conceptual framework relating to their ideas of country and nationality. Familiarity may at times be a function of attitudes. Thus, Hyde (1963) has shown how concept formation in the realm of religious education (Christian) is dependent upon attitudes to Christian teaching and doctrine. Similarly, few would doubt that emotion can often play a marked role. Presumably when emotion retards the growth of systematic thought it sometimes causes a selection or filtering off of signals, or a damping down of cortical or sub-cortical activity. At other times emotion may bring about the reverse, in the sense that unwanted signals and memories are not excluded or certain notions assume exaggerated importance, resulting in a degree of confusion of thought. Precisely how emotion affects the growth of the systematization of thought and concept formation is unknown; indeed, this is an important research problem of the future. Irrelevant information can also prevent systematic thought in specific situations as was indicated earlier.

REFERENCES

ATTNEAVE, R. (1959). *Applications of Information Theory to Psychology.* New York: Henry Holt.

BEARD, R. (1957). An investigation of concept formation among infant school children. Ph.D. Thesis. University of London Library.

BEILIN, H., and FRANKLIN, I. C. (1962). Logical operations in area and length measurement: age and training effects. *Child Developm.* **33**, 607–618.

BEILIN, H., KAGAN, J., and RABINOWITZ, R. (1966). Effect of verbal and perceptual training on water level representation. *Child Developm.* **37**, 317–329.

262 *Development in Human Learning*

CHURCHILL, E. M. (1958). The number concepts of the young child. *Researches and Studies*. University of Leeds Institute of Education. **17**, 34–49; **18**, 28–46.

DODWELL, P. C. (1960). Children's understanding of number and related concepts. *Canad. J. Psychol*. **14**, 191–205.

DODWELL, P. C. (1963). Children's understanding of spatial concepts. *Canad. J. Psychol*. **17**, 141–161.

GAGNÉ, R. M., and BROWN, L. T. (1961). Some factors in the programming of conceptual learning. *J. exp. Psychol*. **62**, 4, 313–321.

GALPERIN, P. Ia. (1957). Experimental study in the formation of mental operations. In Simon, B. (ed.), *Psychology in the Soviet Union*. London: Routledge and Kegan Paul.

GARDNER, D. E. M. (1966). *Experiment and Tradition in Primary Schools*. London: Methuen.

GOODNOW, J. J. (1962). A test of milieu effects with some of Piaget's tasks. *Psychol. Monogr*. Volume 76, No. 36.

GOODNOW, J. J., and BETHON, G. (1966). Piaget's tasks: the effects of schooling and intelligence. *Child Developm*. **37**, 573–582.

HILGARD, E. R., IRVINE., R. P., and WHIPPLE, J. E. (1953). Rote memorization, understanding and transfer: an extension of Katona's card-trick experiments. *J. exp. Psychol*. **46**, 288–292.

HILGARD, E. R., EDGREN, R. D., and IRVINE, R. P. (1954). Errors in transfer following learning with understanding: further studies with Katona's card trick experiments. *J. exp. Psychol*. **47**, 457–464.

HUNT, J. MCV. (1961). *Intelligence and Experience*. New York: Ronald Press.

HYDE, D. M. (1959). An investigation of Piaget's theories of the development of the concept of number. Ph.D. Thesis, University of London Library.

HYDE, K. E. (1963). Religious concepts and religious attitudes. *Educ. Rev*. **15**, 132–141, 217–227.

INHELDER, B., and PIAGET, J. (1958). *The Growth of Logical Thinking*. London: Routledge and Kegan Paul.

INHELDER, B., and PIAGET, J. (1964). *The Early Growth of Logic in the Child*. London: Routledge and Kegan Paul.

JAHODA, G. (1963). The development of children's ideas about country and nationality. *Brit. J. Educ. Psychol*. **33**, 47–60.

KATONA, G. (1940). *Organizing and Memorizing*. New York: Columbia University Press.

KALMYKOVA, Z. I. (1962). Psychological prerequisites for increasing the effectiveness of learning in problem solving in arithmetic. In Simon, B., and J. (eds.), *Educational Psychology in the U.S.S.R.* London: Routledge and Kegan Paul.

LAURENDEAU, M., and PINARD, A. (1962). *Causal Thinking in the Child.* New York: International Universities Press.

LOVELL, K. (1963). Informal *v.* formal education and reading attainments in the junior school. *Educational Research.* **6,** 71–76.

LOVELL, K. (1964). *The Growth of Basic Mathematical and Scientific Concepts in Children* (third ed.). London: University of London Press.

LOVELL, K., and SLATER, A. (1960). The growth of the concept of time: a comparative study. *J. Child Psychol. and Psychiatr.* **1,** 179–190.

LOVELL, K., and OGILVIE, E. (1961). A study of the conservation of weight in the junior school child. *Brit. J. Educ. Psychol.* **31,** 138–144.

LOVELL, K., MITCHEL, B., and EVERETT, I. R. (1962). An experimental study of the growth of some logical structures. *Brit. J. Psychol.* **53,** 175–188.

LUNZER, E. A. (1960a). Some points of Piagetian theory in the light of experimental criticism. *J. Child. Psychol. and Psychiatr.* **1,** 191–202.

LUNZER, E. A. (1960b). Recent studies in Britain based on the work of Jean Piaget. *Occasional Publications, No. 4.* London: Nat. Foundation Educ. Res.

LUNZER, E. A. (1965). Problems of formal reasoning in test situations. In Mussen, P. H. (ed.) European research in cognitive development. *Mon. Soc. Res. Child. Dev.* **30,** No. 2, Serial No. 100, 19–46.

MACARTHUR, R. S., IRVING, S. H., and BRIMBLE, A. R. (1964). *The Northern Rhodesia Mental Ability Survey.* Lusaka: Rhodes – Livingstone Institue.

MCLAUGHLIN, G. H. (1963). Psycho-logic: a possible alternative to Piaget's formulation. *Brit. J. Educ. Psychol.* **33,** 61–67.

MELTON, A. W. (1941). Review of Katona's *Organising and Memorising. Amer. J. Psychol.* **45,** 455–567.

PELUFFO, N. (1964). La nozione di conservazione del volume e le operazioni di combinazione come indice di sviluppo del pensiero operatorio in soggetti appartenenti ad embienti fisici e socioculturali diversi. *Rivista di Psicologia Sociale.* **2–3,** 99–132.

PHEMISTER, A. (1962). Providing for 'number readiness' in the reception class. *National Froebel Foundation Bulletin.* April 1–10.

PIAGET, J. (1926). *The Language and Thought of the Child.* London: Kegan Paul, Trench, Trüber.

PIAGET, J. (1930). *The Child's Conception of Physical Causality.* London: Kegan Paul, Trench, Trüber.

PIAGET, J. (1946). *Le Développement de la notion de temps chez l'enfant.* Paris: Presses Universitaires de France.

PIAGET, J. (1952). *The Child's Conception of Number.* London: Routledge and Kegan Paul.

PIAGET, J. (1956). Les stades du développement intellectuel de l'enfant et de l'adolescent. In Osterrieth, P. *et al.* (ed.) *Le problème des stades en psychologie de l'enfant.* Paris: Presses Universitaires de France.

PIAGET, J. (1957). Logique et équilibre dans les comportements du sujet. In Apostel, L., Mandelbrot, B., and Piaget, J. Logique et équilibre. *Etudes d'éspistémologie génétique,* Vol. 2. Paris: Presses Universitaires de France.

PIAGET, J., and INHELDER, B. (1941). Le développement des quantites chez l'enfant. Neuchâtel: Delachaux and Niestlé.

PIAGET, J., and INHELDER, B. (1956). *The Child's Conception of Space.* London: Routledge and Kegan Paul.

PIAGET, J., INHELDER, B., and SZEMINSKA, A. (1960). *The Child's Conception of Geometry.* London: Routledge and Kegan Paul.

PIAGET, J., and INHELDER, B. (1962). Le développement des images mentales chez l'enfant. *J. de. Psychol.* 1–2, 75–108.

PIAGET, J., and INHELDER, B. (1965). Les opérations intellectuelles et leur développement. In Fraisse, P., and Piaget, J. (eds.). *Traîté de psychologie expérimentale.* Vol. 7, *L'Intelligence,* 109–155. Paris: P.U.F.

PRINGLE, K. M., and MCKENZIE, I. R. (1965). Teaching method and degree of rigidity in problem solving. *Brit. J. Educ. Psychol.* 35, 50–59.

PRICE-WILLIAMS, D. R. (1962). Abstract and concrete modes of classification in a primitive society. *Brit. J. Educ. Psychol.* 32, 50–61.

RAY, W. E. (1961). Pupil discovery and direct instruction. *J. exp. Educ.* 29, 371–380.

SIGEL, I. E., ROEPER, A., and HOOPER, F. A. (1966). A training procedure for acquisition of Piaget's conservation of quantity: a pilot study and its replication. *Brit. J. Educ. Psychol.* 36, 301–311.

SIGEL, I. E., and MERMELSTEIN, E. (1965). Effects of non-schooling on Piagetian tasks of conservation. Paper read at the annual meeting of the American Pyschological Society.

SMEDSLUND, J. (1961). The acquisition of the conservation of substance and weight in children. *Scand. J. Psychol.* 2, 85–92, 153–155, 155–160, 203–210.

SMEDSLUND, J. (1963a). The effect of observation on children's representation of the spatial orientation of a water surface. *J. Genet. Psychol.* **102**, 195–201.

SMEDSLUND, J. (1963b). Patterns of experience and the acquisition of concrete transitivity of weight in 8-year-old children. *Scand. J. Psychol.* **4**, 251–256.

SMEDSLUND, J. (1966a). Microanalysis of concrete reasoning, I. The difficulty of some combinations of addition and subtraction of one unit. *Scand. J. Psychol.* **7**, 145–156.

SMEDSLUND, J. (1966b). Microanalysis of concrete reasoning, II. The effect of a number of transformations and non-redundant elements and of some variations in procedure. *Scand. J. Psychol.* **7**, 157–163.

SMEDSLUND, J. (1966c). Microanalysis of concrete reasoning, III. Theoretical overview. *Scand. J. Psychol.* **7**, 164–167.

TOUGH, J. (1963). A study of the contributions made by relevant experience and language to the formation of a number concept in 5-year-old children. M. A. Thesis. University of Leeds Library.

WEIL, P. (1959). A educaçao em face da pesquisa nacional sôbre o nivel mental. *Revista Brasilieza de Estudos*. Pedagógicos. **73**, 20–28.

WOHLWILL, J. (1962). From perception to inference: a dimension of cognitive development. In Kessen, W., and Kuhlman, C. (eds.) Thought in the young child. *Monogr. Soc. Res. Child. Dev.* **27**, No. 2. (Serial No. 83), 87–112.

WOHLWILL, J. (1963). Piaget's system as a source of empirical research. *Merrill-Palmer Quarterly.* **9**, 253–262.

WOHLWILL, J., and LOWE, R. C. (1962). Experimental analysis of the development of the concept of number. *Child Developm.* **33**, 153–167.

ZIMILES, H. (1966). Studies in the conservation of number. *Monogr. Soc. Res. Child Dev.* **31**, No. 6 (Serial No. 108).

9

Formal Reasoning

E. A. LUNZER

I. INTRODUCTION

The Growth of Logical Thinking by Inhelder and Piaget constitutes
a landmark in the study of the processes of higher reasoning (Inhelder
and Piaget, 1958, hereafter referred to as G L T). In the course of a
number of brilliantly simple yet highly ingenious inquiries, these writers
showed that the sort of reasoning which includes the formulation and
testing of hypotheses is a very late development, and is not fully achieved
until mid or late adolescence.

Previous to this, one may say that researches into the nature of
reasoning fall into three main groups. The first consists of studies of
the early development of concepts, which were developmental but
largely descriptive, and did not usually extend beyond the age of 7 or 8
(see Chapter 3). The second consists of studies of problem solving in
adults, usually students, and stemming in part from Maier's experiments on insight in the rat (Maier, 1929) and in the human adult
(Maier, 1930). A number of these were largely inspired by the concepts
of Gestalt psychology (see Vol. I, Ch. 1, See III) and were designed to
illustrate the role of structurization in the discovery of insightful solutions, and the value of environmental supporting cues in prompting
such restructurizations (Duncker, 1945, Katona, 1940, Wertheimer,
1945,[1] and cf. Saugstad for a more recent attack on similar problems).
The last group of studies, also using adult subjects, consists of studies of
concept attainment and owes its origin to the work of Hull (1920).
A number of these are referred to in Chapter 3, and some more recent
work in this field is discussed by Peel in the course of the next chapter.
The reader will find a fuller review of the earlier work in Vinacke (1952,
Chapter 7).

---

[1] Wertheimer's work is an exception in that his subjects were schoolchildren.
Nevertheless, it was designed as a study of reasoning in general rather than as a
developmental acquisition, (see Section I V, below).

This chapter is entirely concerned with the Genevan work and a discussion of its implications. There is one characteristic which this work shares with a great deal of the previous literature, and this is a concentration on thinking in situations involving scientific, mathematical or purely logical problems. The next chapter, by Peel, describes the highly original extension of Piaget's work which is being executed in Birmingham under Peel's direction, and has already yielded fruitful results bearing on reasoning in relation to historical, geographical and literary topics, as well as in the field of religious thinking. Because of the uniquely abstract character of mathematical thinking, a third chapter, by Skemp, is devoted to the study of learning in mathematics, based largely but not entirely on Skemp's own work in this field.

The work of Piaget demonstrates that what distinguishes formal reasoning from reasoning in younger children is its hypothetico-deductive character. By this I mean that the subject approaches problems by constructing and testing hypotheses. Rigorous testing of hypotheses entails an awareness of alternative hypotheses and their implications. The subject must be aware not only of the relations between the hypotheses and their consequences, but also of the second-order relations between the various hypotheses. Therefore a first characteristic of formal reasoning is the construction of second-order relations. The construction of hypotheses entails an abstraction from the attributes of reality as experienced and a reconstruction of reality as the manifestation of a lawful system. Both of these processes are considered in detail in the next section. The third section describes an inquiry dealing with conservation at the concrete and formal levels which illustrates the same processes and brings out very sharply the contrast between concrete and formal reasoning. It also introduces what may perhaps be regarded as a third characteristic (although it is probably no more than a derivative from the processes involved in hypothesis construction in general), which is the readiness of the subject to go outside the limits of the situation as presented when constructing and testing his interpretations. The fourth section reviews the same ideas and demonstrates their relevance to the scientific analysis of phenomena. This section also includes a discussion of the difference between explanations at earlier levels and explanations at the level of formal reasoning.

II. THE NATURE OF HYPOTHETICO-DEDUCTIVE REASONING

1. *Hypothesis testing*

The main body of Inhelder and Piaget's work consists in summaries and discussions of fifteen separate experiments. In each of these, children were presented with apparatus which would enable them to deduce some more or less general principle by appropriate experimentation. These situations were introduced to children of various ages ranging from 5 to 16, with instructions directed to set them finding out a general principle for themselves. The method employed was the clinical method described by Piaget in another context (Piaget, 1929): the experimenter records the spontaneous behaviour of the child, feeding him with occasional questions and prompts aimed at establishing exactly what the child is trying to do, encouraging him to do it, and discovering precisely what are the strengths and limitations of the strategies which govern his actions.

We may begin by considering just one of these experiments: the oscillation of the pendulum. The apparatus consists simply in a string which can be shortened or lengthened at will and a set of weights any of which can be suspended from the string. The subject is shown how the pendulum can be constructed and made to oscillate in a regular period. His task is to discover what governs the frequency of oscillation. Within fairly wide limits, the only relevant factor is the length of the string, the period of oscillation being a function of its square root. But to establish this securely, the subject needs to exclude the relevance of the force of release, the height of the point of release and the weight of the bob.

The behaviour of Inhelder's subjects[1] fell into four main groups. Children of 5 or 6 were unable to approach the problem in an objective manner because they could not dissociate their own actions from their effects. Their tendency was to push the apparatus hard to make it go faster without seriously considering the role of length, weight, etc. From about the age of 7, the child is far better able to set up an event and record the result, and he can judge with some accuracy the results of his experimentation. In general, he can discover that shortening the string accelerates the period, but he can not succeed in eliminating all

---

[1] The experiments recorded were devised and executed under the direction of Inhelder, while the interpretation of results in terms of logical models of the child's thought (see Peel, 1961) is due to Piaget.

of the remaining variables (cf. Lovell, 1961, and Jackson, 1963, for detailed findings in more controlled replication studies). Because he is capable of operational seriation (see Chapter 8) he has no difficulty in establishing that the shorter the string the shorter the period. But he can not deliberately set up experiments to prove the adequacy of his hypotheses: characteristically, if he believes that a shorter string and a lighter weight both contribute to the result, he varies both factors at once – to enhance the effect, or he may do so by accident, believing that he is proving the effect of one of these terms, without realizing that the other (or both) might be operative. In other words, he cannot sort out the variables using the method of 'all other things equal'. Even at 11 or 12, children are usually unable spontaneously to devise unambiguous experiments, but now they are better able to realize the inadequacy of ambiguous experimentation when questioned. This is the third phase. Only at the fourth, beginning at 13 or 14, will the adolescent spontaneously adopt the strategy of deliberately varying each of the factors in turn, holding all others constant.

In the present chapter we are particularly concerned to analyse the difference between the second type of reaction, which is characteristic of reasoning at what Piaget terms the concrete level of reasoning, and the fourth, which typifies what he calls formal reasoning. The essential difference is that in order to choose the conclusive combinations in this way, he must at least have an approximate idea of all the rest (GLT, p. 78). The adolescent does not just happen to vary one variable at a time: he does so in order to test a possible law, e.g. increase of weight = decrease of period; at the same time, he does not vary other variables, e.g. length, because he realizes that if he did so, any result could be due to length or weight or both together. At the intermediate third stage, the child can realize the usefulness of isolating the variables when this is pointed out to him, which means that he can appreciate that a given result may be classified according to several causal laws and some are freer from ambiguity than others. But he cannot yet anticipate the possibilities sufficiently to direct his actions in terms of their interplay. At the second of these stages, although he can appreciate logical relationships when these are presented ready-made, as instances of a given law, he cannot yet appreciate how a variety of possible causal factors may lead to mutually interfering, and therefore ambiguous categorizations.

The use of the term 'categorizations' may seem a little surprising since all the child is doing is to set up a variety of events in an attempt

K

to discover a causal connexion. But the categorizations are implied both by the events he sets up and by the laws he deduces. For instance, relative to a given observation, the true hypothesis that rate varies inversely with length yields a set of combinations which are expected to lead to increase in rate, another which should lead to a decrease, and a third which should lead to no change. If we use the letters L for length, W for weight, H for height, and I for impetus, lower case for a variable held constant, capitals for increases, and capitals followed by the symbol ' (prime) for decreases, then the first set includes $L'Whi$, $L'W'hi$, $L'whi$, $L'WHi$, and so on, being all the combinations including L'. The second set will consist of all the combinations including L, and the third all those including l. Similarly, the very reasonable hypothesis that decrease in weight will increase the rate places all combinations including W', e.g. $LW'hi$, $L'W'hi$, and so on in the first category, all those including W in the second, and those including w in the third. The same might be done for height and impetus. Now although it would be tedious to spell all these categories out, one can see at once that any combination including the terms WL, or $W'L'$ will fall into the same category whichever of the two hypotheses is correct.

Now of course no child actually performing the experiment would go through all these categorizations. However, another experiment suggests that adolescents of 12 upwards could have a good stab at doing this if required. Here the subjects are given four flasks containing colourless and apparently identical liquids together with a small bottle of potassium iodide with a dropper and some glasses for mixing. Their task is to find out the part of each of these liquids in producing a yellow colour. In fact three are required, the potassium iodide, one containing an acid medium, and one containing oxygenated water. The other two bottles contain water (which has no effect) and thiosulphate (which bleaches the mixture). It was found that younger children tended to stop short after trying out each of the liquids in turn with a drop from the flask. Those aged 9 to 11 were more inclined to try combinations of two or three liquids with the flask, but they did so in haphazard fashion. Adolescents went through the various combinations systematically enough to solve the problem.

However, to return to the pendulum, although the adolescent does not spell out the categorizations, he shows his awareness of them by deliberately constructing variations which are unambiguous. By using the method of all other things equal, he automatically excludes such variations as $W'L'hi$. To put the matter another way, the subject cannot appreciate the need for keeping invariant the variables which are not specifically being considered, unless, all the while he is testing one hypothesis, he is aware of alternative hypotheses and their consequences. When he becomes aware of these, that is, when he is prepared to regard hypotheses as competing statements of various *possible* relationships, he shows his ability to pass back and forth between statements of causal laws and the categorizations which they imply, first, by recognizing, with respect to a particular event, which of the operative (in our example, three) categories would be predicted for it by two or more relevant laws, and, second, by selecting events which would not be expected to fall into one and the same category by more than one law. Which means that it is not the actual multiple categorizations that underpin the hypothetico-deductive reasoning, but the principle for generating them. There is an analogy here with the short-circuiting involved in skilled performance which is instructive (cf. Chapter 4, Section III). Let us suppose that a reasonably experienced driver notices an elderly person wavering uncertainly on the kerb ahead of him; he will probably move his foot from the throttle and at the same time glance in his mirror as well as at the oncoming traffic. He does not tell himself why he does these things, and, because the pattern has become automatized, he is often unaware that he has done them immediately after they have been executed. Yet the first reflex anticipates the possibility of having to take some action, the second that of braking, and the third that of swerving. But for these behaviours to have become so automatized, two things are necessary: first, that at some stage the various parts shall have been performed with full awareness; and second, that this explicitation be short-circuited so that the necessary behaviour can be performed rapidly and smoothly.

If the analogy is correct, as I believe it is, it carries implications for teaching. It is that the pupil cannot be expected to compass problems which require hypothetico-deductive reasoning unless he has previously had the opportunities to carry out in turn all of the organizations upon which such reasoning is founded. These are (1) simple categorization according to a constant criterion even in the presence of alternative, distracting characteristics of the material to be classified (in the simplest example, classifying cards consistently according to the criterion of colour or size or shape, even though the cards differ along all of these dimensions); (2) passing from a categorization to a causal relation and vice versa (as in the simple spring balance experiment described below); (3) simultaneous categorization according to several criteria (as in cross-classification of the card material just alluded to); (4) anticipation of such cross-classification and its results; (5) passing successively from categorization to the related causal law and back, then to an alternative categorization and the law that would relate to this, then back to the first, and so on; (6) recognizing ambiguity in experimentation (as described for the third stage in the pendulum experiment). Moreover, in many cases (although perhaps not in all), the previous steps will need to have been sufficiently rehearsed to have been fully automatized before the pupil can pass on to the next.

Needless to add, the above remarks do not mean that a particular apparatus such as cards is essential in the development of reasoning (even though it may be fairly useful because easy to construct and concrete). On the contrary, the importance of the development being considered derives from the fact that it is perfectly general. Hence it is exemplified in a wide variety of situations: mathematical, scientific, linguistic, historical, geographical, social and literary (see the discussion in Sections II–IV of the next chapter, by Peel). Again, quite generally, since any categorization involves a system of first-order relations among the objects or events that are classified, the advance to a consideration of the interaction of alternative categories implies the construction of a system of second-order relations.

2. *Abstraction and mental constructs*

The pendulum experiment offers a very clear illustration of one aspect of hypothetico-deductive reasoning: hypothesis testing and what this entails. Let us consider the complementary aspect which may be thought of as hypothesis construction. The pendulum is not a good illustration of the latter, since provided that the subject can compare the effects of several hypotheses at once, hypothesis testing, he has nearly all that he needs to solve the problem. The hypotheses which he may be required to test are intuitively fairly obvious: the role of length, weight, etc. An experiment on flotation brings out more sharply the element of construction which enters into the reasoning which is characteristic of adolescents and adults.

By way of anticipation I would add that the two terms which head this section are not intended to introduce two different elements. Rather, we will be concerned with the psychological processes that appear to enter into what is usually called abstraction and we shall discover that mental construction is an essential feature of these processes.

The apparatus for this experiment consists of several tanks containing water, some larger than others, together with a variety of miscellaneous objects including a toy duck, a toy boat, a large block of wood, stones, a nail, a piece of wax, a metal can, etc. Some of the objects are hollow. The child is first asked to sort out the objects by saying which of them will float in the water and which will sink. He is also asked why he thinks they will do so. Then he is encouraged to try them out to see whether his predictions were correct. If they were wrong, he is asked why, and encouraged to change his ideas, and, if possible, to test them again. The object of the inquiry is to discover what sorts of explanation are offered for the phenomena of flotation by children of various ages and what underlies their mode of explanation.

Once again, Inhelder found that the youngest children tended to interfere with the apparatus and to impose their pre-conceived notions on it (one child actually forced an object down because 'it ought to sink'). Their explanations exemplified their inability to adhere to a consistent criterion when sorting objects: objects floated because they were small or because they were large (and strong) or because they were light, etc.

However, even as young as 7 or 8, children were able to cross-classify the objects up to a point, with the implication that large objects may be light, etc. By the age of 9 they had fully overcome the difficulty of making a clear distinction between absolute weight and relative weight or density, always invoking the latter rather than the former to account for the phenomena. Moreover, Inhelder's 9- and 10-year-old subjects were often willing to try out more general hypotheses to account for the behaviour of hollow vessels and the paradoxical phenomena due to surface tension. Both Inhelder, and, later, Jackson (1963) found that their attempts at explanation usually referred to the idea of air in one form or another: air bubbles in the water, or microscopic pockets of air in the less dense materials. But these attempts at more comprehensive explanations invariably lead the subject into new contradictions.

The idea of relative weight or density does not begin as a sophisticated 'second-order' concept. On the contrary, the notion that some objects and materials may be light or heavy for their size has its origins in the common experiences of lifting (see Vernon's discussion of the size-weight illusion, Chapter 1, Section V). It is this intuitable[1] concept of density which underlies the explanations of children at the level of concrete reasoning. The comparison is always between one type of

[1] intuitable = readily referred to a specific type of perceptual experience.

material and another, e.g. wood and metal, or metal+air and metal+ water. In the present experiment, what distinguishes the reasoning of children as they enter the stage of formal reasoning is the beginning of reference to the weight of the water itself. Children of 11 or 12 are liable to offer some attempt to express the notion that an object floats if it is lighter than an equivalent volume of water, although it is not until considerably later (13 or 14, in the case of Inhelder's subjects, 15 in the studies of Lovell (1961) and Jackson) that the concept is sufficiently established for the subject to realize that it can be verified by using a hollow cube with which he is provided.

Inhelder and Piaget are, of course, well aware that the average child of 11–15 is not an Archimedes, which means that the more adequate explanations which he offers owe a great deal to the schooling which he has received. But in order to understand what he is taught he needs to be in a position to construct the notion of 'an equivalent volume of water'. This is not something which relates to an immediately intuitable experience but rather a deliberate mental construction: '(it) has no visible contours and can be conceptualized only after a preliminary abstraction' (*op. cit.*, p. 41).

The notion of abstraction has three aspects which are equally important from the point of view of psychology if not from the standpoint of logic.

First, there is the obvious factor implicit in the word that the abstract property, in this case volume, is present as one aspect of categorizable events, and that this property is singled out as a unique criterion.

Second, at all levels, i.e. even at the concrete level, the abstraction confirms a method of ordering or organizing the events (using a criterion of classification or seriation), both actual and potential, and it evidently derives from the effort made by the subject to produce such 'closure'. However, the potential ordering of experience is clearly not something which is abstracted from the events themselves but rather from the actions which the subject carries out (i.e. actual classifications and seriations). Therefore the abstraction is at one and the same time an abstraction from the object (the events), and abstraction from the actions of the subject, and the active construction of an order which is imposed on reality.

Finally, at the level of formal reasoning, but not at the previous levels, the ordering which is imposed induces the subject to re-construct mentally the events or objects out of the interaction of the abstract notions at which he arrives. Deliberate construction of events is evident in the pendulum experiment where the subject deliberately selects weight, length, height of drop, etc., in order to test a given hypothesis. It is even more apparent in the present experiment in the mental construction of an equivalent volume of water. The scientist will have no difficulty in seeing that what we are concerned with here is the origin of the transition which needs to be made from the notion of a systematic arrangement of reality to that of conceiving certain of its manifestations as constituting a *closed system* which is fully explicable in terms of precise laws.

3. *Contrast with the concrete level*

Taking together the results of the two experiments which we have examined in detail, the twin characteristics of hypothetico-deductive reasoning emerge as: (1) the fact that the subject needs to entertain several hypotheses at once; and (2) the part played by abstraction and systematization in inducing him to reconstruct the events out of their notional constitutents. However, these are not necessary features of all a child's experimental activity, nor even of all hypothesis-testing, as is very apparent from a consideration of an experiment described by Inhelder and Piaget (1964).

Children of 4 to 9 were shown a letter balance together with a collection of boxes. The balance is largely concealed in a frame (so that only the pan is visible) and the apparatus is so rigged that when a certain weight is put on the pan, the pointer on the dial protrudes through a slot at the side of the frame, this effect being heightened by a ball on the end of the pointer. The boxes used as weights are of two weights and two sizes and two colours, so that there may be eight kinds of boxes altogether. The problem is to find out which boxes will make the ball appear. In this experiment it was found that even as early as 6, a majority of the children tested could not only find out for themselves that the heavy boxes were the ones they needed, but could also *prove* that not all the large (or red, or blue, etc.) boxes were heavy by correctly pointing to those of the required size which happened to be light.

On the face of it, this is a result which flatly contradicts the thesis that hypothetico-deductive reasoning, in the sense of framing and testing hypotheses, is a form of thinking which is not achieved until the period of adolescence. For not only do young children discover how to work the apparatus, but they can also disprove what amount to incorrect hypotheses.

However, if he refers to the two criteria just stated, one finds that neither is satisfied. In the first place, the fact that the material is ready-made means that when the subject tests the hypothesis that 'all the blue boxes are heavy', etc., this is the only hypothesis that he need bear in mind; in the second place, because all the boxes are present and ready-made for the experiment, the subject has no need to abstract the properties of weight, colour, etc., and deliberately construct an event or an object out of its relations or its attributes. He has only to classify the material that is in front of him.

Finally, the fact that there are two weights, two sizes and two colours tends to favour an early solution of the problem. The symmetries and dichotomous arrangements make the classification itself easier, which is why successful solutions are found right at the beginning of the phase of development at which children evolve (first-order) operational co-ordinations. (cf. Lunzer, 1964.)

4. *Summary*

In the first sub-section, starting from the pendulum experiment, we saw that the process of hypothesis-testing implies the simultaneous consideration of several hypotheses. At the same time, we noted that whereas such formal reasoning was closely dependent on classificatory behaviour – inasmuch as any causal hypothesis implies a categorization of potential phenomena, the multiple classifications are virtual rather than actual, so that the determinant factor in the reasoning was less the categorization itself than the mechanism for generating it. Finally, we noted a striking analogy between this developmental process and the acquisition of skilled behaviour; the short-circuiting which allows a principle or generating mechanism to stand for a complex behavioural chain in the determination of a higher ranking strategy seems to arise in the course of repeated practice of the several components which must be automatized.

In the second sub-section, starting from the flotation experiment, we noted a second feature of formal reasoning (already implicit in the foregoing), that the reasoning of the subject is not confined to the carrying out of actions (e.g. groupings or seriations) on the objects and events as he finds them. (Nor does the essential difference consist in the interiorization of such actions – presumably by inhibition of the effector connexions in the brain. For although such interiorization is essential in formal reasoning, it is not criterial, since it is equally essential in concrete reasoning.) Instead we found that the solution of the problem entailed the construction or the reconstruction of the objects and events out of their abstracted constituents. The notion of 'an equivalent volume of water' was taken as a paradigm for such reconstruction.

We saw also that this reconstruction of the object is inseparably bound up with the mechanisms of abstraction. But the recognition of the role of abstraction in this sort of mental construction requires a more penetrating analysis of the concept of abstraction. Regarding this as a description for certain psychological processes (rather than as a formal criterion of logical 'types'), we saw that it entailed three such processes: the abstraction of criterial features from the objects or events such as would serve both for potential categorizations and for potential constructions of hypothetical events and test-situations; abstraction of the structural relations inherent in the subject's own actions of grouping and ordering, which alone will enable him to elaborate the structural relations that are necessary to the construction; and, finally the reconstruction of objects and events in such a way that certain of their essential aspects may be apprehended by the subject as constituting a closed system, completely determined by the operation of necessary laws.

III. TWO EXPERIMENTS ON CONSERVATION

ALL OF the characteristics of formal reasoning described in the last section were very clearly brought out, in the course of two experiments carried out by the present writer in Geneva (Lunzer, 1965a). They provide a striking confirmation of the contrast between concrete and formal reasoning, the more so as the results, although predictable, were in many ways paradoxical.

1. *The false conservation inquiry*

Both experiments involve the phenomenon of false conservation. If one begins with a square and transforms this into a series of successive rectangles, holding the perimeter constant, the area decreases progressively, being asymptotic to a limit of zero area where the two longer sides of the rectangle coincide. Similarly, if one cuts a triangular section from one corner of a square and transfers it along one of its axes until it is superposed on the original figure, the area of the new figure is conserved but its perimeter is increased. The two situations are illustrated in Figures 1 and 2.

For the first experiment the apparatus consisted of a board fitted

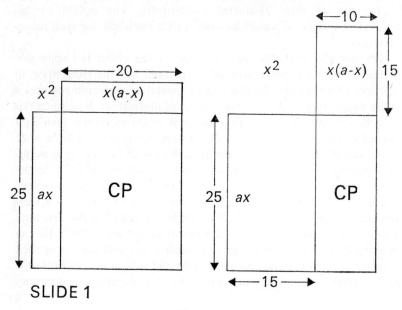

SLIDE 1

Figure 1. Deformation of area

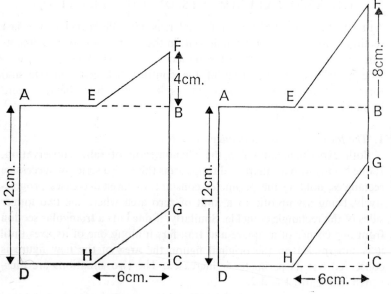

Figure 2. Deformation of perimeter

with sets of nails which would form the corners of a series of rectangular figures: I 25 cm.; II 30 cm. × 20 cm.; III 35 cm. × 15 cm.; IV 40 cm. × 10 cm; V 45 cm. × 5 cm. and VI 50 cm. (line). The square is marked out with a heavy black line, and the subject is first shown the figure with a closed length of string round the square. As the inquiry proceeds, so the string is moved from the square to each of the rectangles in turn. The subject is asked to compare first the perimeter of the rectangle and then its area with those of the original square. He is also asked to verify his judgements by measuring the various parts of the figure, using previously prepared cards of appropriate dimensions.

The mode of experimentation for the second experiment was very similar. Here the apparatus consisted of a square of green card measuring 12 cm., and five further squares cut as in Figure 2, but with the triangular section increasing progressively in height from 2 cm. to 10 cm. Once again, after the child has offered his judgements about area and perimeter for all of the figures compared to the square, he is given the opportunity to measure the perimeter of one of these, the last but one in the series (height of triangle = 8 cm.), using a small board in which he can fit first the original square and then the transformation. The board has nails marking the corners of the two figures and two lengths of string attached to the bottom left nail. One of the strings is red and just long enough to go round the nails at the corners of the square; the other, black, is longer and stretches round the other figure.

In both experiments the child is told a little story to clarify what is intended by area and perimeter. The figures are supposed to represent fields belonging to a farmer and the transformations are alterations which he makes to the shape of his field. The farmer is shown walking all round each of these fields (perimeter) and his cow is shown eating all the grass inside them (area). Also, in both cases, the subject is asked to correct his judgements for each of the figures in turn if he so desires after he has done the measuring.

It was expected:

(a) that children at the concrete level of reasoning would judge both perimeter and area to remain constant for all figures. Realizing that something was preserved, and at the same time appreciating that added height in figure is compensated by diminished width (and that the triangle is simply displaced in Figure 2), they would regard the conservation of both area and perimeter as logically necessary for both figures (see Lunzer, *op. cit.*).

(*b*) that these children would resist the evidence of perception, particularly in the case of the first situation, in spite of its compelling nature (see Chapter 8, Section I).

(*c*) that children at the formal level would appreciate the generality of what they saw: if the perimeter (or area) is shown to have changed when the transformation is marked, then it must also change when the transformation is less marked, even if the other measure remains constant.

The original investigation was carried out in Geneva. The subjects for the first experiment were eighty children whose ages ranged from 5 to 15, sixty-four of these also served as subjects for the second experiment. Both experiments were subsequently repeated in Manchester with certain added controls. The Manchester subjects consisted of three groups of twenty children, representing the following three age-groups: 9;6–10;6, 10;6–11;6, 14–15. All of these underwent both experiments, half in one order and half in the other.

For both experiments, the characteristic behaviour of these subjects fell into one of five main groups, albeit with minor variations. These were as follows. For the first experiment (conservation of perimeter with decreasing area):

Level I. There is no conservation; judgements are one-dimensional, having regard only to the increase in height. Both perimeter and area are seen as increasing throughout the series.

Level II. No conservation. Perimeter is seen as increasing throughout the series. Area is judged as first increasing then decreasing.

Level III. Conservation of perimeter and false conservation of area. The subject maintains both principles in the teeth of perceptual evidence to the contrary. Some of the more mature subjects may be able to deduce from measuring that the area has decreased for the figure they have measured, but they revert to the judgement of conservation for all other figures.

Level IV. The initial judgements are identical with those of the previous level. But the subject is more prepared to accept the evidence of measurement. Looking at figures other than that which he has measured (square and 15 × 35 cm. rectangle), he analyses them carefully, and admits that the area of the rectangle is less, although the perimeter is conserved. But the admissions are grudging and each figure must be examined individually. If these subjects are asked to compare a square with a rectangle which is nearly but not quite square, they revert to the judgement of conservation of area.

Level V. Subjects at this level, unless they have previously performed the second of our experiments, usually begin by judging both perimeter and area to remain constant. But when they are faced with the marked perceptual difference in area between the taller and narrower rectangles and the square, they promptly analyse the figure to account for the discrepancy and deduce that their original judgements were in error for all *transformations.* This generalization is always spontaneous and complete.

The relation between age and level, and especially the comparative maturity required by *level V* will be immediately apparent from the results shown in Tables 1 and 2.

The responses made to the second inquiry also fell into five levels, with some correspondence in content:

Level I. No conservation. Area and perimeter are seen as increasing steadily.

Level II. The subject oscillates between judgements of conservation of area and perimeter and judgements of increase. This is clearly a transitional phase.

Level III. As in the previous experiment, there is conjoint conservation. Area is conserved, and so is perimeter. Towards the end of this level, subjects may begin to dissociate area and perimeter after the experience of measuring. But the more common response is highly enlightening.Having established that the string which reaches round the square is not long enough to reach round the transformation, the subject accepts this evidence, for all figures (and not only for the one he had measured). But he introduces an artifical dissociation between the string and the distance round the figure. He states that the distance round the square and the transformation is identical, that if the farmer were to walk round the two fields he would take as long round the square as the other, but if he had a wire fence surrounding the square field it would not suffice for the other.

Level IV. Area is conserved while at the same time the subject recognizes the increase in perimeter. Often but not always, the dissociation is immediate. These responses differ from those of level V in that the child cannot account for the increase in perimeter except by some such statement as 'He (the farmer) has to go all the way round'.

Level V. The subject analyses the figure and points out that the hypotenuse of the triangle is longer than its base. The children tested at

Development in Human Learning

TABLE 1. *Level of response to deformation of area (Geneva)*

Age	N	I	II	III	IV	V
				Level		
5	9	8	1	—	—	—
6	4	2	2	—	—	—
7	8	—	7	1	—	—
8	6	1	2	3	—	—
9	7	1	—	6	—	—
10	6	—	1	4	1	—
11	7	—	—	3	4	—
12	5	—	—	—	5	—
13	6	—	—	—	5	1
14	14	—	—	—	4	10
15	8	—	—	—	3	5
Total	80	12	13	17	22	16

TABLE 2. *Level of response to deformation of area (Manchester)*

	Deformation of Area (Manchester)			
	II	III	IV	V
9;6 – 10;6	I	15	4	—
10;6 – 11;6	—	7	13	—
14+	—	—	3	17

age 12 knew nothing of Pythagoras, not did they use these terms, but their meaning was clear.

It will be apparent from Tables 3 and 4 that, apart from cases of young

TABLE 3. *Level of response of deformation of perimeter* (*Geneva*)

Age	N	I	II	Level III	IV	V
5	5	4	—	—	1	—
6	4	—	3	1	—	—
7	8	1	2	3	2	—
8	7	—	2	2	3	—
9	6	—	—	5	1	—
10	6	—	—	4	2	—
12	2	—	—	—	1	1
13	6	—	—	—	2	4
14	12	—	—	—	2	10
15	8	—	—	—	1	7
Total	64	5	7	15	15	22

TABLE 4. *Level of response to deformation of perimeter* (*Manchester*)

	Deformation of Perimeter (Manchester)		
	III	IV	V
9;6 – 10;6	10	9	1
10 – 11	3	12	5
14+	—	—	20

children at level IV, there is a clear progression in these levels. But it is equally clear that corresponding levels are reached appreciably earlier than in the first experiment.

The general trend of these results is clear. All of the initial hypotheses are confirmed. There is false conservation at the concrete level of reasoning, and it is remarkably resistant, as may be seen from the resistance to perceptual infirmation in the first experiment and in the artificial distinction drawn between the fence and the perimeter in the second (in subjects who clearly had an operational understanding of length, and who, before actually performing the measurement, had been very certain that the perimeters would prove equal). Also, area and perimeter are clearly dissociated at the formal level, and both are assumed from the start to vary according to some necessary law, whether or not the same law.

However, if one considers more closely the reasons underlying the false conservation at level III and its resistance at level IV in the first experiment, the inquiry brings out very clearly the principal differences between concrete and formal reasoning.

2. *Simultaneous hypotheses and second-order relations*

The first feature noted above was the ability to entertain several hypotheses simultaneously. In the present investigation the phase of concrete reasoning is represented by level III. Here the subject's reasoning takes the following form: either there is conservation or there is not; there is compensation (of height by width or of triangle by displacement) and the object (the string – and, with it, by an erroneous assimilation, the figure – or, in experiment II, the cards) is virtually unchanged; therefore there is conservation.

It should be added in parentheses that, in the control inquiry carried out in Manchester, half the subjects in each group were examined somewhat differently: the most pronounced transformation was shown first, and the remaining transformations in a descending series; also, the subject was asked first to compare the figures in respect of the variable which had altered (area in experiment I, perimeter in experiment II), and only then about the other (conserved) variable. The results for these subjects were no different from those for the remainder – in spite of the fact that this technique was designed to reinforce the (perceptual) factors tending to judgements of non-conservation.

By contrast, subjects reasoning at the formal level (here represented by level V) are prepared to consider the two hypotheses of conservation and non-conservation simultaneously. Conservation with respect to the dimension which is in fact conserved is taken for granted (the relevant analysis having been fully automatized); but without abandoning this judgement, the subject is prepared to entertain the opposite judgement as a hypothesis in respect of the other dimension, and to confirm it (which he does by infirming the conservation hypothesis, demonstrating that the compensation is not adequate).

3. *Reconstruction of the object*

The second feature, noted in the flotation experiment, was the ability to construct, or reconstruct objects and events, whether real or virtual, out of their constituents. By contrast, the subject reasoning at the concrete level simply accepts the objects and events as he finds them and imposes a logical order on them where he can. In the present inquiry, the latter reasons about the figures as objects in both experiments. The actions which he (or the experimenter) performs – cutting up and displacing, or rearranging the boundary – are regarded as actions performed on the object, and the only question is whether it is 'really' changed (by addition or subtraction) or whether it remains substantially the same, although altered in appearance. Area and perimeter are both seen as essential characteristics of the object (because of the compensations involved), and, since the object is taken to be the same (again by reason of the continuity and the compensations) the subject is convinced that the two must go together. As one subject protested in the course of repeated attempts to make her 'see' what was happening: 'If it's the same for the cow it's the same for the farmer', and, soon after, 'if it's more for the farmer it's more for the cow'. Or, as a student remarked: 'There is a remarkably strong bond of attachment between the farmer and his cow'.

There are four aspects of the inquiry which illustrate the object-bound character of concrete reasoning:

(*a*) The pronounced time lag between the eventual dissociation in the two experiments. In experiment II, the dissociation is complete (generalized) at level IV, and all levels are achieved some two years earlier. What has to be dissociated from the transmutation of the apparently invariant object is the perimeter, and the perimeter is less obviously part of the object.

(*b*) A number of children dissociate the perimeter and area in experiment II although aged only 7. Their response is indistinguishable from level I V, but it is a pseudo-level I V response. The conservation of length is a comparatively late acquisition (Piaget, Inhelder and Szeminska, 1960 and cf. a series of experiments carried out by the present writer and described in the same article as the present inquiry). Because length is often not conserved at 7, it is not regarded as a necessary property of the invariant object. At the true level I V it is dissociated in spite of the conservation of length in situations where it applies.

(*c*) The paradoxical argument given by many subjects at level I I I in experiment I I after the experience of measuring: the perimeter of the figure is conserved as indicated by the distance round and the time taken, but the length of fence needed to bound it is not – the fence is another object! (It should be borne in mind that the anticipation of these subjects was that the measurement would show invariance, and the paradoxical reply is no more than a last-ditch stand to resolve a 'cognitive dissonance' (Festinger, 1957, Brown 1965).)

(*d*) In the case of experiment I, nearly all children at level I I I recognized immediately that the area is zero for the limiting transformation (line) while still holding that it equalled that of the square for all others. This is not an isolated finding, for it was shown again and again in a series of brilliant experiments devised by Bang (1965), all featuring false conservation, and reported in the same monograph. The child's reasoning seems to be: the limiting case is a different object, so the conservation no longer applies; there is still the string but the field has been removed.

By contrast, at level V (experiment I) and to some extent at level I V (experiment I I) the subject is prepared to examine the variation of area and perimeter as thought-objects in their own right. At level V in both experiments, he uses the figure to aid him in his mental construction of what equalities and compensations would be inherent in a figure where area (or perimeter) would be conserved. In other words, the object is seen as something which may be constructed to the desired specifications.

4. *Going outside the figure*

There is another feature of formal reasoning which appears most obviously in geometrical situations, where it takes the form of a willingness to go outside the figure, and which is apparent in the measuring at level V.

In the case of experiment I (which is where this behaviour is manifest), the subject is first given cards which may be superposed on the part

ax in Figure 1 and transferred to the top of the figure where they will inevitably project over the portion x^2. Only if he fails to carry out the required measurement is he offered another card, equal to $x(a - x)$. In nearly all cases, subjects at levels III and IV were at a loss after superposing the first card on the part marked ax, not knowing how this would help in measuring the rectangle. When given the smaller card, those at level IV and a few at level III were well able to superpose this on the part of the figure to which it corresponded, and to deduce from the fact that it was smaller than ax that the area of the rectangle was less: i.e. $CP + x(a - x) < CP + ax$. Conversely, nearly all subjects at level V immediately transferred the card $= ax$ to the portion of the figure $x(a–x)$, allowing it to project over x^2, reasoning: if the two were equal in area these should correspond, but they do not; therefore the rectangle is less by the amount x^2.

Willingness to go outside the limits of the figure was noted in several of the experiments described by Piaget, Inhelder and Szeminska (1960) as a characteristic of formal reasoning. Figure 3 illustrates one of these: the subject is asked to reproduce the triangle A B C exactly, being provided with rulers, but no protractor. A number of children

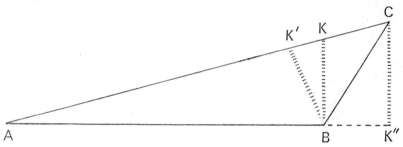

Figure 3. Copying a triangle (From Piaget, *et al*, 1960 p. 185)

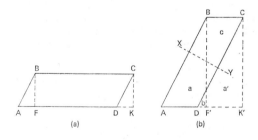

Figure 4. Calculating the area of a parallelogram (based on Wertheimer, 1945 p. 48).

towards the end of the concrete level of reasoning discover that this can be done without trial-and-error by putting in and measuring the perpendicular B K. Children at the former level frequently, though not invariably, drew and measured the perpendicular C K″ on the projection of A B.

The well-known experiment by Wertheimer (1945) is in reality based on the same requirement: a conventional solution of the problem can only be achieved by going outside the figure.

Since the pupils have been shown how to draw the line C K outside the figure in situation 4(a), they are willing enough in some cases to take the process a little further and draw in BF′ and C K′ in situation 4(b). But to use these constructions they need to argue:

$$a + b = a' + b \text{ (congruent triangles)}$$
$$\text{therefore } a = a'$$
$$\text{therefore } a + c = a' + c \text{ (QED)}$$

But the first step in this reasoning involves a mental union first of a part of the parallelogram, and then of a (different) part of the rectangle with one and the same triangular region which falls *outside both.*

The step is taken hypothetically so that the unwanted region can be discarded at step 2.[1]

Wertheimer's 'insightful solutions', which consist either in rotating

---

[1] In this instance, and perhaps in all, the going-outside-the-limits is mediated by the strategy of arriving at proof by beginning at the opposite end: try to imagine some condition, which if it were fulfilled, would permit of the desired conclusion to be deduced; if one finds such a condition, then try to see how that can be deduced from the original premises, either directly, or by repeating the process; in the event of failure, try an alternative starting again from the conclusion. This principle is at least as old as Descartes (*Règles pour la direction de l'esprit*, Règle XVII), and its usefulness has been beautifully drawn out by Polya (1962). In the course of a brilliant and much publicized study, Newall, Shaw and Simon (1958) were able to construct a programme for a computer which enabled the machine to arrive rapidly and economically at the solutions of problems in logic, partly by incorporating this heuristic principle in the programme. However, their splendid mathematico-scientific feat is not simply a by-pass whereby the problems of developmental psychology may be circumvented – even though it may well provide a suitably resistant vehicle for negotiating some of the pitfalls along the route. For the essence of the present discussion is that, so far as the human brain is concerned, the method is not built-in from birth but elaborated gradually in the course of ontogenesis. The same method is evident in Bartlett's highly original inquiries into what he calls 'gap-filling', 'reasoning in closed circuits' (Bartlett, 1958), and his methods have been somewhat extended in a developmental study by Donaldson, 1963, the findings of which are consonant with those of Inhelder and Piaget.

the figure 4(b) so that it resembles figure 4(a), or in cutting it along a line XY perpendicular to AC and BD and reassembling the resultant segments in a rectangle, are really strategems which enable the subject to solve the problem without going outside the figure. The fact that they are far less general than the hypothetic-deductive method brings out the essential limitation of Gestalt psychology: structure is seen solely in terms of the relations inherent in the object – which are assumed to be 'there' for the discovery, given enough 'intelligence' or sufficient cues to structurization. What I have tried to show, following Piaget, is that the 'structure' is derived as much from the subject as it is from the object, that it reaches back to the co-ordination of his potential and real actions. Often the structure which cannot be accommodated directly to the situation as found, but requires that the situation be first extended or transformed by inclusion of the possible, alongside the given. It is more a structure of reasoning than a structure of the object itself, and, as such, it is a feature of formal reasoning, and is rarely seen even in the 12-year-old.

5. *Summary*

The experiments on false conservation illustrate once more the use of second-order relations to reconstruct the object (the figure is eventually seen as a construct made to certain specifications both with respect to its linear dimensions and to the resultant area). At the same time formal reasoning appears in sharp contrast with concrete reasoning (where the figure is seen not as a construct but as an object, which is then taken to be substantially the same or radically different but not both at once – i.e. conjoint conservation or conjoint variation). The type of measuring used at the formal level also illustrated a third feature of formal reasoning, one which Piaget had already noted in his work on geometrical reasoning; willingness to go outside the figure. More generally, the subject's willingness to go outside the figure in geometrical problems should be seen as the specific form taken by more advanced reasoning in this context: it is the geometrical expression of reasoning structures which cannot be imposed directly on events in the form in which they occur but require a prior excursion into the realm of the possible.

IV. SECOND ORDER RELATIONS AND THEIR ROLE IN EXPLANATION

The 16th chapter of GLT is devoted to a discussion of the most general attributes of formal reasoning. Piaget begins by considering two attributes which seem relevant and which he himself had previously entertained; verbal mediation and the use of second-order concepts, he rejects the former as inadequate, and then shows how formal reasoning entails an inversion of the relations between the real and the possible. The presentation is somewhat complicated by being stated in terms of Piaget's theory of equilibration. In the opinion of the present writer, the theory is as yet too ill-defined to warrant acceptance (cf. Bruner, 1959), while the delineation of the structural and functional characteristics of formal reasoning is one of Piaget's lasting contributions. Therefore I propose to deal with the latter rather than the former.

1. *Formal reasoning and the use of language*

It is altogether probable that the type of reasoning with which we are concerned cannot occur in the absence of language. This is because it consists in the application of a precise system of relations to a set of terms which are already abstract in the first of the senses already referred to, terms which represent selective aspects of a complex perceptual reality. A language[1] referent would therefore appear to be necessary for the identification of these terms themselves, and especially for their short-term storage and recovery (as in following through the arguments of a syllogism).

By the same token, there is no doubt that some reasoning can occur in the absence of language. Obvious examples are the reasoning of animals (see Volume I, Chapter 5) and of infants (see Chapter 3 and the clear statement of Vigotsky, 1962).

Therefore it is tempting to conclude that formal reasoning simply expresses a particular use of language. And indeed there are verbal problems which, in spite of the simplicity of their referent, are not easily solved by children of 8 or 9, as in the problem of Burt: 'Edith is fairer than Susan; Edith is darker than Lily; which is the darkest of the three?' But the difficulty is accidental rather than essential. Because the two relations expressed are the inverse of one another, the subject

---

[1] The term 'language' is being used in a general sense – as a set of symbols relating more or less (depending on the language and its user) unambiguously, but not necessarily in one–one correspondence with the elements of an extra-linguistic referent (which may be thought of as 'reality'). It is in this sense that one may speak of the language of mathematics or logic or of computers, as well as of, say, the English language.

cannot solve the problem without inverting one of them to realize the transitivity: Lilly – *fairer than* – Edith – *fairer than* – Susan.

The inversion argues a degree of flexibility of thought, but it does not entail a higher-order structure.[1] For instance, in an experiment where the subject is set to discover what he can about Galileo's law of motion by experimenting with balls of various weights and sizes to be rolled along a horizontal slide, even 9- and 10-year-olds were apt to reverse the original problem by arguing about what makes the balls stop instead of what makes them carry on (GLT, Chapter 8).

However, the fact that the evolution of formal reasoning cannot be put down simply to its verbal expression is abundantly clear from the fact that problems of an elementary nature, involving only the potential but direct grouping and ordering of objects and events, can be performed nearly as easily when given as verbal problems as they can when presented as concrete material: – as in the simpler form of the above problem. E. is darker than L. and L. is darker than S., etc. Thus as Piaget rightly remarks: 'All verbal thought is not formal and it is possible to get correct reasoning about simple propositions as early as the 7–8 year level, provided that the propositions correspond to sufficiently concrete representations.' (GLT. p. 252). The reader who has little experience of young children need only refer to some of the examples of verbal reasoning recorded in Susan Isaacs' observation of 3–7-year-olds at Malting House (Isaacs, 1930), to be convinced that even the restriction to 7 or 8 is unwarranted.

The use of the term 'concrete' to describe the direct application of Piaget's logic to reality is apt to mislead some into thinking that children of 7 or 8 can only reason logically with the material in front of them. This is certainly a misunderstanding of Piaget, and even more certainly, it does not correspond to the facts. Whether in its broader and more technical sense or in its narrower conventional sense, it is highly probable that language does enter into formal reasoning. But it is equally liable to enter into reasoning at earlier levels. However, this is not to deny that studies of the ways in which children understand language, such as those reported by Peel in the next chapter, may be extremely

---

[1] A recent study by N. B. Coventry throws considerable doubt on the validity of Piaget's inquiry in 1923. While Piaget's clinical method led to considerable confusion in a group of 37 subjects aged 12 and over, Coventry obtained a majority of correct answers in a paper-and-pencil test, even at the age of 8 (300 subjects).

relevant to the development of reasoning. Similarly, there is good reason to believe that the analysis of the structure of children's spoken and written language reflects their cognitive development (see Chapter 5).

2. *Formal reasoning and second-order operations*

Although one may not define formal reasoning purely in terms of its use of language, it is much more reasonable to think of it as reasoning in terms of second-order relations, i.e. of relations between relations. (Piaget's term second-order 'operations' differs only in that it implies a reference to the virtual actions of the subject in establishing such relations.)

For instance, when the subject in the pendulum problem selects a particular pair of events for comparison using the method of 'all other things equal', he is clearly invoking a relation of incompatibility between the categorization of the events entailed by the hypothesis to be tested and the categorizations entailed by alternative hypotheses. The entailment of a categorization by any one hypothesis is itself a set of relations 'of the first order', so that the comparison is indeed a second order relation.

In the course of an inquiry into formal reasoning characteristics using a simple group test, the present writer confirmed (somewhat to his surprise) that simple problems of verbal analogy – e.g. LEATHER is to SHOE as WOOL is to . . . (multiple choice including the correct term CARDIGAN and strong distractors such as LAMB) – are not usually tackled with any degree of success by children below the age of 10 (Lunzer, 1965b and cf. Watts, 1944). Where no strong distractor is given, the problem may well be solved by simple association, but where the subject must choose the correct term in the light of a careful analysis of the precise relation between the first two terms, such problems argue a second-order relation (of identity) between the two relations constituting the analogy. However, perhaps because of the practice given to British children in such tasks, or especially because here the subject is asked only to establish the relation and does not need to use it in problem solution, this sort of achievement is probably best seen as transitional to formal reasoning rather than as an instance of formal reasoning proper.

The interaction of operations and the relations which they engender is apparent in all of the inquiries dealing with the later development of reasoning that one finds scattered throughout Piaget's works. To take an example from his study of the concept of movement (Piaget, 1946) one asks a child to move his pencil along a groove which is cut in a board made of plywood so as to draw a line on the paper beneath, but while he does this, the board itself is made to slide in a different direction. The subject is required to anticipate the direction of the line. For instance if the groove is vertical and the board moves in a horizontal direction, the line will be oblique, etc. This anticipation is not made in general before the age of 11 or 12. There are several analogous instances in Piaget, Inhelder and Szeminska, 1960, Chapter 10. Or again, to take a verbal (but somewhat contrived) example, one may consider an extension to the familiar problem of comparing classes and sub-classes (see Chapter 8, Section I). Towards the age of 8 or 9 (the development is relatively late), most children can tell you when asked that there are more birds than there are ducks, or more animals (living creatures) than birds; but they cannot tease out the relations involved in the problem *Are there more creatures that are not ducks or more that are not birds?* until they reach the level of formal reasoning. (Inhelder and Piaget, 1964.)

However, the richest collection of experiments illustrating formal reasoning is undoubtedly GLT itself. We have already noted that the combination of hypotheses involved in such situations as the pendulum experiment is a clear instance of the formation of second-order relations. But the combination of hypotheses is probably itself only a sub-class of the combination of relations in general. The scientific analysis of phenomena in terms of the (usually) reciprocal interaction of precisely defined variables is a second, and major, sub-class. We will consider just one of these.

The experiment concerns the processes involved in the discovery of the relationship among the forces governing the distribution of pressure in communicating vessels. Two situations are reported but I will describe only one of them. The apparatus consists of two tubes connected by a rubber hose at the bottom. Both are open at the top, but one is tall and narrow, while the other, which is shorter and wider, is provided with a piston which exerts pressure on the liquid. Weights can be added to the piston to increase this pressure, and the situation is varied by substituting alchohol or glycerine for the water in the system. The problem for the child is to discover what affects the height of the liquid in the narrow tube, and how the various effects may be compensated.

Considering only the responses of children at the concrete and formal levels of reasoning: the former are well aware that the piston exerts pressure on the liquid, causing it to rise in the narrow vessel; and they also understand that the density of the liquid, as well as its amount, enters as a factor in the system; but they are unable to appreciate exactly how these forces interact: some therefore argue that the heavier liquid causes the greater rise in the narrow vessel – thinking only of the downward pressure exerted by the liquid in the other vessel, which they add to that exerted by the piston; others realize that the greater rise occurs in the case of liquids having a lesser density, but they explain this by a vague reference to movement of the liquid in the narrow tube (ignoring once again the upward pressure exerted by the liquid on the piston). Older children, however, appreciate clearly that, to the downward pressure exerted by the liquid in the tube there corresponds an upward pressure which operates in the other vessel in a direction opposite to that of the piston and weights. And, towards the end of the stage, i.e. at 14 or 15, a number show an awareness of the action of the system as a whole: i.e. that an equilibrium is reached when the pressures in all directions are uniform and compensate one another.

It is not difficult to see that, quite apart from the abstraction involved in the concept of pressure as a system of forces acting uniformly in all directions and tending towards an equilibrium in which there is perfect compensation of all forces at all points, the initial problem is to combine the relational system implied by the piston and liquid in the first vessel with that implied by the liquid in the second.

There is some analogy between the second order relations involved in qualitative compensations of this sort and the quantitative compensations which figure in the determination of an equilibrium based on the proportional interaction of two or more forces. The classic experiment here is one in which the child is required to find out how to compensate differences in distance from the fulcrum on one arm of a balance by varying the weight which is suspended from the other arm, and vice versa (GLT, Chapter 11, and cf. Lovell, 1961). In general, one finds that problems requiring for their solution a recognition of the equality of ratios are not solved until the level of formal reasoning. Moreover, younger children invariably try to solve the problem by adding or subtracting the quantities involved. I have tried to show elsewhere that the resistance to multiplication may be partly due to its one-sided presentation in schools. Children are led to understand numerical multiplication as cumulative addition ($3 \times 4 = 4 + 4 + 4$) only, and not simultaneously as a functional one-way correspondence ($3 \times 4 =$ *for each unit in 4, take 3*, or $3 \times 4 = 3 + 3 + 3 + 3$). The latter formulation is the more usual inverse to division and is more relevant in scientific analysis (Lunzer, 1965b, Lunzer and Pumfrey, 1966). However, once again it is not difficult to see that the equality of two ratios always constitutes a second order relation, and even a system of such relations: $a/b = c/d$ implies $ad = bc$ and $a/c = b/d$.[1]

Reverting to the central issue, which is the role of second-order relations, we may consider once more the false-conservation experiment. Because the subject at level V treats the variations in perimeter and area as thought-objects in their own right, he arrives at a re-appraisal of the situation which he now sees for what it is, viz. a series of transformations which approaches a fixed limit by the laws linking area and perimeter, e.g. that for a given perimeter to bound the largest area, the figure must be circular, or, if a rectangular quadrilateral, square (see Bang, 1965b). Since this conception is based on the relations between area and perimeter, and each of these are well-defined relations existing in the figures, one is correct in speaking of the construction of second-order relations as a distinctive characteristic of formal reasoning in this type of situation as in others.

However, it seems to me dangerous to think of the figures or even of the set of transformations as a second-order concept, suggesting that the child can have no intuition of it until he has reached the level of formal reasoning. If, for instance, we use some such technique as an animated film cartoon to show the transformations, it is apparent that much younger children will 'form the concept' in the sense that we and they will be talking about the same kinds of things. But because they have not arrived at the concept by a construction out of first-order relations, they will still be unable to use the concept in the same way as the adolescent.

In general, one finds that the distinction between formal reasoning

---

[1] The reader who is familiar with G L T may wonder why I have omitted all reference to the I N R C group, which figures so largely in Piaget's treatment of this material, just as I have not referred to the sixteen ways in which two propositions may be combined in discussing the pendulum and related experiments. The omission is quite deliberate. I believe that Piaget could not have arrived at his penetrating analysis of the development of thinking without using a logical notation to tease out the inferences which the child is capable of making at successive phases. But in attempting to construct a semi-axiomatic and comprehensive presentation of the 'logics' which correspond to such phases, one is apt to be side-tracked into avenues which are not only difficult for the mere psychologist, but also sometimes misleading (*see* Lunzer, 1965b, but see also Apostel *et al.*, 1963, for a more complete, and a more sympathetic discussion.)

and other kinds of reasoning does not define particular content-areas but rather the ways in which the subject reasons and behaves in relation to such areas. For instance, the concept of density is an intuitive one, but the concept of specific gravity as a relation between displacement and mass is a product of formal reasoning. The same is true of pressure, which is first experienced either as effort exerted by the subject or as resistance to such effort arising from the object. There is even an intuitive understanding of the relation between pressure and area, as anyone will know if a woman wearing stiletto heels treads on his sandalled toe. Nevertheless, the concept of pressure as force per unit area is very clearly a product of formal reasoning, as we have just seen.

In other words, what defines the level of conceptualization is not the situational content covered by a concept, but the method by which the concept is defined and generated. A concept exists only in relation to other related concepts and it is the set of relations among the concepts which is critical.

In summary, the concept of formal reasoning as arguing the construction and application of second-order relations corresponds to the first feature that we noted in Section II: the simultaneous consideration of hypotheses. But it is also a more general way of specifying the development concerned, for it appears in a slightly different guise in a wide variety of situations: verbal analogies, composite movements, the interaction of forces, proportional functions relating variables in systems of equilibria.

3. *Inversion of the relation between the real and the possible*

If we return for a moment to the 'hydraulic press' experiment described in the previous sub-section, we find that it exhibits abstraction and systematization as well as the interaction of relations. Indeed these various aspects are inseparable from one another, for we saw that each of them was manifest in all of the experiments that we considered in detail: the pendulum, flotation, false conservation.

Thus, in order to disentangle the relations operating between the various forces exerted in the system, the subject must begin by separating out, or abstracting, the factors and re-combining them in terms of a system to be imposed on the phenomena. Most obviously, he does this by considering the force exerted by the column of liquid together with the piston and weights in the first limb which must be compared with the column of liquid in the second. But neither the column of liquid in the second arm nor the composite in the first is an immediate datum in the apparatus. For there is no obvious boundary between the two. What the subject does is to deliberately create such a boundary by considering the lowest point in the apparatus and then construct a mental model of the opposing forces. Moreover, in order to give this model precision, he has to consider what is the effect in each column of the force exerted by the other column *taken by itself*, for only then can he arrive at the notion that the force exerted within the column must compensate this other if there is to be equilibrium.

Thus, once again, one sees that the solution of the problem in terms of formal reasoning depends on the analysis and reconstruction of the situation as perceived, in such a way as to permit its consideration as a determinate system. And, once again, the process entails abstraction of the relevant portions of the situation itself, abstraction from the subject's potential actions to bring out the order which is conceived, and the construction on this basis of a mental model of the events conceived as a closed system.

However, although this analysis adequately expresses what the subject does, i.e. what is entailed by the successive moments of his behaviour, it does not fully bring out the change in the character of his approach to the situation. For in reality it is the conception of the possibility of a system which must generate the abstraction and the construction. Now the system is essentially a conceptual model made up of (necessarily) abstract elements (e.g. the forces exerted by this or that factor at a specified point), and the relations among them. The system does not describe the observed phenomena. It is a more or less general model which is designed to *explain* the phenomena as the necessary consequence of the particular values which obtain at any given moment in the set of all possible phenomena which it embraces.

This is what Piaget means by the subordination of reality to possibility (GLT, p. 255), which he takes to be the most general characterization of formal reasoning.

The notion of explanation, like so many others on the boundary between logic and psychology, is a loose one. In its broadest sense, explanation is not something which occurs only about the period of adolescence. Even very young children are capable of giving perfectly valid explanations of phenomena: they know that the wind causes the movement of trees, or that rain comes from clouds, and so on. Because they cannot refer events unambiguously to one another by imposing a precise order on them, and because the categories which they use to describe events are lacking in exact definition, their explanations are apt to be contradictory (little things sink because they are too weak to swim; little things float because they are light; etc.). But they are not *always* inadequate, and they are more often realistic than magical, as Oakes (1947) pointed out in the course of an inquiry prompted by Piaget's early inquiries on children's causality (Piaget, 1930). However, Oakes had missed the point of Piaget's thesis, which was not that young children's reasoning was always, or mostly, couched in terms of magic, but rather that they had no means of distinguishing between magical explanations and causal ones, nor could they avoid contradictions, so that in the course of more extended inquiry, their replies tend to drift in the direction of magic (Laurendeau and Pinard, 1962).

Explanation in the same wider sense is far more adequate at the level of concrete reasoning, when contradictions are avoided, and the events under consideration are more precisely defined and ordered. But what is this wider sense of the term? *It is the subsumption of phenomena under the category of a general class of events subject to a necessary law.*[1] For instance: objects which are heavy for their size tend to sink; the greater the distance from the fulcrum on one arm of a balance the greater the weight necessary as a counterbalance on the other arm; whenever nothing is added to or removed from a collection, the number remains invariant; and so on. This sort of explanation undoubtedly entails a conception of possibility, since the child anticipates what will happen in a whole class of eventualities. It also entails a recognition of *necessity*. For the laws (of conservation, etc.) which the child deduces are accepted by him as necessary. Nowhere is this more evident than in the example of false conservation, where his certainty of invariance and of the necessary concomitance of area and perimeter lead him to the denial of the perceptually evident.

By contrast, the explanations which characterize the level of formal reasoning (in the sense that these do not occur before, not that the others do not persist, for they undoubtedly do) consist in the *interpretation of the phenomena in terms of the interplay of necessary laws which depend, for their enunciation, on the complete analysis of the events and the abstraction of their determinants*. Since the determinants are not given they must first be discovered, and the impetus for their discovery can only arise out of the challenge of explanation itself.

Thus, one way of pointing the contrast between the two kinds of

---

[1] The same definition could be applied to the earliest level, but omitting the word 'necessary' and substituting 'loose category' for 'class'.

explanation is to say that the child at the level of concrete reasoning is prepared to recognize a necessity in the regularities appearing in the course of his experience, while the individual at the formal level is prepared (sometimes) to *demand* such a necessity, which demand forces him to a re-analysis and reconstruction of experience. Thus, at level V, in the false conservation inquiry, the subject notes the contraction in the area of the figure in a more extreme transformation and immediately deduces that the contraction must be general (he then seeks to find out why), while even at level IV, he was quite prepared to admit this as an exception to an apparently self-evident rule.

In effect, what this means is that where the former is inclined to think of the possible as an extension of what is real, the latter is apt to view what is real as but one instance of a more general necessity governing the set of all possibilities (and excluding the set of all impossibilities).

Which explains not only why he comes to construct systems which may be imposed on reality, but also, and very obviously, why in the course of doing this, he is often apt to 'go outside the limits of the figure', i.e. to extrapolate from the evidence (see next chapter).

4. *Formal reasoning and the regulation of behaviour*

From the point of view of the organization of behaviour, it follows from all this that the subject's approach to the situation is determined by his available schemata, i.e. by the kinds of connexions which he is capable of effecting between its several aspects, as well as between the given situations and others which he is led to relate to it. In other words, while it is convenient for the experimenter to define the situation as an objective 'stimulus complex', it is the subject's schemata which determine what will function as a stimulus for him, i.e. what he will attend to in the perceptible set-up, and what he will retrieve from his 'memory store' to aid in the interpretation of these data. Similarly, while it is essential for objective experimentation to fix on aspects of the subject's behaviour which will be taken as criterial 'responses', the actual response of the subject consists first in the assimilation of the situation to a schema, and this in turn permits the activation of a strategy to guide his behaviour in the direction of solution. As we noted in the second section, it is more than likely that much that goes into the construction of the schema – being the inferences that he would be apt to take for granted as and when the need should arise – is in fact highly telescoped or short-circuited in the strategy, i.e. in the actual sequence of behaviour in which he engages. It is the aim of Piaget's clinical method to reveal not only the strategy but also the schema from which it derives. The use of the term 'strategy' implies an awareness on the part of the subject of the end to be reached and also of the routes which it would be fruitful to follow. No doubt at much more primitive levels of behaviour one may speak of strategies which do not entail awareness as such, but only the intervention of processes to which such awareness might later correspond. But it is silly to deny awareness at this level. What I am saying is that the schema precedes the strategy and the strategy precedes the response.

The same problems are dealt with by some psychologists (e.g. Osgood, Kendler) by invoking the intervention of 'mediating responses' between the stimulus and the observed response. If by this one intends that non-observable events occur in the subject's brain, all would concur. But the point is that even if these events were observable, as in fact they may well be in a few years' time, their recording would not accomplish the psychologist's purpose (although they would help to guide his efforts more surely). For one is concerned not with the events as such but rather with the connexions that they imply. To use an analogy, one is not concerned with the flashing bulbs (in the sci.fi. computer) but with the circuitry itself. (See Vol I, Chapter 3.)

From the point of view of learning and education, the central questions are, of course, how are schemata and strategies acquired, what are the reinforcing situations which facilitate their elaboration, and so on. This is a field which will doubtless continue to repay investigation. Its discussion forms an important section of the next chapter.

5. *Summary*

The use of language is relevant to formal reasoning but it is not its distinctive feature. The systematic reconstruction of reality on the basis of second-order relations permits a higher level of conceptualization. But it does not necessarily imply the intervention of new concepts in the sense of new groupings of events. What is criterial is how the events are grouped, i.e. their systematic interrelations. The systematization of formal reasoning also determines a new and more genuine kind of explanation. The real is seen as a consequence of the necessary intervention of fixed and necessary laws governing the determination of the possible. In other words, the possible is just as important in explanation as the real, where previously the possible was seen only as an extension of the real. Finally, the actual behaviour of the subject in situations requiring formal reasoning is seen as the outcome of strategies which in turn are determined by the activation of a formal schema.

REFERENCES

APOSTEL, L., GRIZE, J. B., PAPERT, S., et PIAGET, J. (1963). La filiation des structures. *Etudes d'épistémologie génétique*. **15**, Paris: P.U.F.

BANG, V. (1965a). Intuition géometrique et déduction opératoire. Chapter I in Bang, V., et Lunzer, E., Conservations spatiales. *Etudes d'épistémologie génétique*. **19**, Paris: P.U.F.

BANG, V. (1965b). De l'intuition géométrique. Chapter 2 in Bang, V. et Lunzer, E., Conservations spatiales. *Etudes d'épistémologie génétique*. **19**, Paris: P.U.F.

BARTLETT, SIR F. C. (1958). *Thinking: an Experimental and Social Study*. London: Allen and Unwin.

BROWN, R. (1965). *Social Psychology*. London: Collier-Macmillan.

BRUNER, J. S. (1959). Inhelder and Piaget's *The Growth of Logical Thinking*. I, A psychologist's viewpoint. *Brit. J. Psychol.* **50**, 363–370.

COVENTRY, N. B. (1968). Some aspects of the thinking of 8, 9 and 10-year-old children. M. Ed. Thesis, Birmingham University.

DONALDSON, M. (1963). *A Study of Children's Thinking*. London: Tavistock Publications.

DUNCKER, K. (1945). On problem-solving. *Psychol. Monogr.* **58**, No. 5. (Whole No. 270.)

FESTINGER, L. (1957). *A Theory of Cognitive Dissonance*. New York: Row Peterson.

HULL, C. L. (1920). Quantitative aspects of the evolution of concepts. *Psychol. Monogr.* **28**. (Whole No. 123.)

ISAACS, S. (1930). *Intellectual Growth in Young Children*. London: Routledge.

INHELDER, B., and PIAGET, J. (1958). *The Growth of Logical Thinking from Childhood to Adolescence*. London: Routledge.

INHELDER, B., and PIAGET, J. (1964). *The Early Growth of Logic in the Child*. London: Routledge.

JACKSON, S. (1963). The growth of logical thinking in normal and subnormal children. M. Ed. Thesis, Manchester University. (Abstract in *Brit. J. Educ. Psychol.* **35**, (1965), 255–258.)

KATONA, G. (1940). *Organising and Memorising*. New York: Columbia U.P.

LAURENDEAU, M., and PINARD, A. (1962). *Causal Thinking in the Child.* New York: International Universities Press.

LOVELL, K. (1961). A follow-up study of Inhelder and Piaget's *The Growth of Logical Thinking. Brit. J. Psychol.* **52,** 143–153.

LUNZER, E. A. (1964). Translator's introduction. (See Inhelder and Piaget, 1964.)

LUNZER, E. A. (1965a). Co-ordinations et conservations dans le domaine de la géométrie. Chapter 3 in Bang, V. et Lunzer, E. Conservations spatiales. *Etudes d'épistémologie génétique.* **19,** Paris: P.U.F.

LUNZER, E. A. (1965b). Problems of formal reasoning in test situations. pp. 19–46. in Mussen, P. H. (ed.) European research in cognitive development. *Mon. Soc. Res. Child Dev.* **30,** No. 2. (Whole No. 100.)

LUNZER, E. A., and PUMFREY, P. D. (1966). Understanding proportionality. *Mathematics Teaching.* **34,**

MAIER, N. R. F. (1929). Reasoning in white rats. *Comp. Psychol. Monogr.* **6,** No. 29.

MAIER, N. R. F. (1930). Reasoning in humans I. On direction. *J. Comp. Psychol.* **10,** 115–143.

MAIER, N. R. F. (1931). Reasoning in humans II. The solution of a problem and its appearance in consciousness. *J. Comp. Psychol.* **12,** 184–194.

MAIER, N. R. F. (1945). Reasoning in humans III. The mechanisms of equivalent stimuli and of reasoning. *J. exp. Psychol.* **35,** 349–360.

NEWELL, A., SHAW, J. C., and SIMON, H. A. (1958). Elements of a theory of human problem solving. *Psychol. Rev.* **65,** 151–166.

OAKES, M. E. (1947). *Children's Explanations of Natural Phenomena.* Teacher's College, Columbia University. Contributions to Education, No. 926. New York.

PEEL, E. A. (1960). *The Pupil's Thinking.* London: Oldbourne.

PIAGET, J. (1923). Une forme verbale de la comparaison chez l'enfant. *Arch. de Psychol.* **18,** 141–172.

PIAGET, J. (1929). *The Child's Conception of the World.* London: Routledge.

PIAGET, J. (1930). *The Child's Conception of Physical Causality.* London: Routledge.

PIAGET, J. (1946). *Les notions de mouvement et de vitesse chez l'enfant.* Paris: P.U.F.

PIAGET, J., INHELDER, B., and SZEMINSKA, A. (1960). *The Child's Conception of Geometry.* London: Routledge.

POLYA, G. (1962). *Mathematical Discovery.* New York: John Wiley.

SAUGSTAD, P. (1960). Problem-solving, past experience and availability of functions. *Brit. J. Psychol.* **51**, 97–104.

VINACKE, W. E. (1952). *The Psychology of Thinking.* New York: McGraw-Hill.

VYGOTSKY, L. S. (1962). *Thought and Language.* New York and London: John Wiley.

WATTS, A. F. (1944). *The Language and Mental Development of Children.* London: George Harrap.

WERTHEIMER, M. (1945). *Productive Thinking.* New York: Harper.

10

Conceptual Learning and Explainer Thinking

E. A. PEEL

I. A NEGLECTED FIELD OF ADOLESCENT THINKING

BEFORE the appearance of Inhelder's and Piaget's monograph on the growth of thinking (1958) there had been almost no single comprehensive study of the growth of adolescent thinking. Practically all the work of Wertheimer (1945), Duncker (1945), Maier (1930) and Szekely (1950) had been with university students and, like the study of Inhelder and Piaget, was concerned with thinking in science and mathematics situations.

Much of school work is concerned with operations, material and situations less well defined than those in science and mathematics, as in history, geography, literature and contemporary affairs. Here language plays a bigger part and the concepts evoked in thinking may be less clear. But it is of interest to know how far the generalizations reached after studying the pupil's scientific and mathematical thinking extend to the non-science subjects and whether there is anything peculiar to non-science thinking. It is important in learning science since even here language plays an important part (Peel, 1960).

A suggestive pointer was made by Lodwick (1958; Peel, 1959) when he studied the interpretations of 7- to 15-year-old pupils to short passages of popular history. He found an unmistakable development in the power of the children's thinking clearly marked by three phases: the first of fragmented and inconsistent judgements, the second of relevant but partial judgements, and the third, found generally in older children, of more circumspect and comprehensive judgements. The technique was refined and extended by using contrived passages demanding general comprehension (Peel, 1965 and 1966).

The purpose of this chapter is to discuss these findings and others and to link them with views about concept formation and usage and to see how far they provide the basis for understanding the development of thought during adolescence.[1]

II. CONCEPT FORMATION AND LEARNING

Early stages in the formation of concepts have been treated more fully in Chapters 3 and 8. For the purposes of our study of adolescents, we need only to remind ourselves that when a person classifies material, as say in the Vygotsky block test, he has to find a basis for the classification. Thus the successful learner of this test forms four criteria of action by which he groups the different blocks, and eventually divides them up according to whether they are: (i) large and tall, (ii) large and flat, (iii) small and tall, or, (iv) small and flat.

A familiar instance of a similar classifying process is seen in elementary chemistry when the pupil learns to classify oxides into basic, acidic, neutral, etc., as a result of carrying out simple element burning experiments and testing the products with water and litmus. In this case a further mental operation is carried out when the basic oxides are related to metals and the acidic oxides to non-metals.

There is another aspect of classification which is concerned with the logic of classification. The young learner can only form actual classes successfully when at the same time he is capable logically of including subordinate within superordinate classes, when he is capable of manipulating the classes, including the complementary class.

To every act of classification or relating there seems to correspond a logical structure which must be a part of the pupil's mental equipment. Piaget considers that the growth of mental structure is largely a consequence of experience allied with the child's urge to search and come to intellectual terms with his environment (Piaget, 1964).

At first the child cannot classify and he cannot discriminate according to criteria which appear obvious to older people (Inhelder and Piaget, 1964). He forms half objects – whimsical collections (to adult eyes), collections with changing bases, incomplete groups with residuals left which cannot be incorporated into the groups made. This is because the two-sided power to group the material according to certain actions and to comprehend the properties of these actions has not been developed. Evidence of this lack is shown also when the child responds

---

[1] The fuller and more searching analysis of this attempt to provide a comprehensive account of adolescent and adult thinking is given in *Learning, Understanding and Thinking* (Peel, 1968).

indiscriminatively and more generally than the instructions require.

Once he has formed criteria of action, then we get the type of classification we require in all human activity and the capacity to classify in any particular way ceases to be one of formation and becomes instead one of attainment. This is the case in the work by Bruner and his colleagues (1956) and in the monograph by Shepard, Hovland and Jenkins (1961). In both researches adults are asked to make classifications on the basis of concepts which they have already formed, colour, shape, size, etc., and for which they already possess the required rules of action and thinking structures.

But much of adolescent and adult thinking involves more than concept attainment. Very often the thinker is in the position where he lacks criteria of action for classifying and he has to construct them. Nearly all original scientific discovery involves an element of formation in addition to attainment. Induction of the nature of heat, of dominant and recessive traits in biology, of the nature of electricity and of linguistic categories and other categories based on mediated responses are all instances. Good examples from the frontier of scientific knowledge are the forces suggested by nuclear physicists in connexion with sub-atomic phenomena.

A concept is based on a classification, but it is different in that the rule of action for making the classification can be stated and communicated to others. The three parts of a concept all play an important part in education.

(i) The extension of objects or attributes which have to be classified.

(ii) The rule which leads one to so group them – the intensive property of the concept.

(iii) The class or rule may be given a name.

Any two of these three parts may be utilized in research on concept learning and formation.

Bruner *et al.* (1956) presented an array of instances and non-instances of the concept (i) and asked for the rule (ii). Vygotsky (1962) presented the name (iii) on the back of each block, that is each instance (i) and called first for the correct arrays for each name (i) and then the rules defining the concepts (ii). The Geneva studies (Inhelder and Piaget, 1964) present an array of material in different colours and shapes and a general rule such as: find those which are alike (ii) and the child has to group the material correctly (i). Werner and Kaplan (1950) present six sentences embodying the concept (i) under an invented name (iii)

and ask for the meaning, that is the rule, of the exemplified and concealed concept (iii).

III. THE CONCEPTUAL BASIS OF HYPOTHESIS AND SPECULATION

1. *Explainer thinking*

We have one further assertion to make before we pass on to the sub-
stantive part of this study of adolescent thinking. Whenever we are in
a problem situation where we are compelled to look for explanations,
whether in school or outside, our search for possible causes entails
guesses, speculations, or hypotheses. Thus we have such propositions
as:

Perhaps it's because it's too long. Is it a case of symbiosis? Is the
engine too cold? Does he lack foresight? It is an example of expansion
under heat. There should be universal franchise.

We almost invariably openly invoke a concept or analogy and always
imply the use of one.

Since also such speculations lead to further action if and when it is
required, we may say that concepts once formed tend to shape our
behaviour even if at the same time they are also extended and even
changed by it. It is for this reason that concepts have so often been
referred to as organizers of human action.

Thinking which involves relating new stimuli, phenomena or experiences to established concepts may be called explainer thinking (Peel,
1965, p. 171) since in such cases we invoke the concepts to place the
novel phenomena. If the thinker only describes the parts of the stimulating situations in relation to each other – without invoking external
ideas or attempting to interpret the phenomena – we may say he is
indulging in describer thinking (Peel, 1965, p. 171).

2. *Testing hypotheses*

We may also note that the concepts available to the young thinker
are used by a process of setting them up as possible explanations or
hypotheses and then testing them against the features of the problem
being investigated. This process of monitoring is not always so explicit
that it finds expression in words, but it always reveals itself in the actions
of the experimenter. The result of the monitoring leads, of course, to
acceptance, modification or rejection of the explanation. But it is not
only in science that these processes reveal themselves. Elsewhere

(Peel, 1960 p. 103) I have shown how they are present in solving a code, and in general comprehension in the preceding sub-section.

The process involves the elimination of alternative hypotheses and this often proves to be the most difficult part of the operation. In secondary school science, particularly in chemistry, where the products of reactions are involved and only qualitative methods are used, it is often difficult and time consuming to eliminate all possible alternatives. Possibly the teacher too readily infers a particular product from evidence which would also support another, e.g. as in testing CO solely by burning (H_2 would also satisfy this test) and failing to weigh the products.

The failure to eliminate alternative hypotheses remains a feature of thinking in mature years. Wason (1960) set adult subjects to find the concept '*three numbers in increasing order of magnitude*' by first giving them an instance: 2, 4, 6, and then asking them to give another instance – with their reasons, to which he replied whether it conformed to the concept or not, Wason was able to determine to what extent the examples chosen were eliminative (of alternative concepts) or enumerative (of the concept) and to obtain the frequency of negative instances deliberately used to confirm the concept.

Only a minority made extensive use of the eliminations of possibilities and generated negative instances and Wason concluded (*op. cit.* p. 139) that 'very few intelligent young adults spontaneously test their beliefs in a situation which does not appear to be of a "scientific" nature'.

This problem was thoroughly investigated by Inhelder and Piaget (1958) with regard to the pupil's interpretation of simple science experiments and their work has been more fully discussed in the last chapter.

Mealings (1961, 1963), prompted by Inhelder's and Piaget's experiments, carried out a careful statistical inquiry in order to examine how secondary school pupils interpret simple experiments in physics and chemistry. He also confirmed with dismal certainty that, in spontaneous problem situations in science, the capacity to think operationally, to set up hypotheses and test them, and to work systematically eliminating disproven possibilities is lacking in 13- to 15-year-olds unless they have mental ages of 17 upwards.

Thus one problem demanded the investigation of a white powder (actually consisting of a mixture of salt and chalk), given water and hydrochloric acid, to find out if it was one substance or two. The necessary apparatus for dissolving, filtering and evaporating was also supplied. Each of fifty-seven pupils carried out the experiment individually and Mealings personally recorded all that was done and said. Here two hypotheses are possible: a *one-salt* or a *two-salt* substance.

Over half of the pupils tested were unable to proceed much beyond trial and error methods. They reported observations correctly but gave no evidence that their actions were directed by the two possibilities stated in the problem. This group had a median age of 14+. Only three pupils were able to reach a correct solution, involving the elimination of the *one-salt* hypothesis. These three all had mental ages of 18+. There was a group of nine pupils, median mental age 17+, who effectively separated the salts by shaking up with water, filtering and evaporating but who failed to eliminate the *one-salt* possibility by using the hydrochloric acid available.

It seems that in general *spontaneous* elimination of alternatives is not obtained in a wide range of topics until late adolescence. Probably direction in the form of teaching and discussion of the results of experiments and the possible causes of phenomena would do much to promote eliminative thinking in adolescents and young adults.

IV. COMPREHENSION, IMAGINATION AND HYPOTHESIS FORMATION

The research mentioned earlier in this chapter (Peel, 1960; Lodwick, 1958; Peel, 1959) suggests that there is little evidence of a well developed capacity in children to set up possibilities to account for events in stories, as opposed to mere describing, before the age of 13+. Nor is there much evidence of their capacity to examine such possible explanations in terms of the data in the stories. Up to this age they appear in general to seize upon what content is available in the story and base their decisions solely upon this evidence even though, to the mature thinker, it is manifestly limited and insufficient.

In order to investigate this possibility further the main task was then to construct material and questions which would enable one to concentrate upon the quality of children's judgements and the changes taking place in them over the critical years between 9 and 15.

It was hoped not only to demonstrate clear-cut differences between the thinking of the 10-year-old and the 14-year-old pupil, but also to reveal what finer changes may take place between the gross extremes.

The main problem concerned the upper ranges and it was proposed to look into the lower levels of pre-logical thinking. However, the passages and questions have been so devised that irrelevant, inconsistent and tautological responses can be evoked.

The material consisted of two short anecdotes (Peel, 1966), each followed by an open question about some feature of the passage and a second question asking for the reasons for the answer given to the first question. The two passages consist of *logically* similar material.

Here is one passage and its questions.

Only brave pilots are allowed to fly over high mountains. This summer a fighter pilot flying over the Alps collided with an aerial cable railway, and cut a main cable causing some cars to fall to the glacier below. Several people were killed and many others had to spend the night suspended above the glacier.

(1) *Was the pilot a careful airman?*

. . . .

(2) *Why do you think so?*

. . . .

The passage contains a leading statement which is irrelevant to the judgement required in answering the question put to the pupil, *Only brave pilots are allowed* . . . Then follows a short section in which a happening takes place, *crashing the cable*, which is related to the question, but which is not by itself adequate or sufficient to form the basis of a judgement. A limitation is also imposed by other implied circumstances, e.g. the hazards of flying over the Alps.

Thus the passage could evoke responses at least at three points in the scale of maturity of judgement.

(a) Where irrelevancy, tautology and inconsistency may dominate.

(b) Where the content (cutting the cable) solely may decide.

(c) Where extenuating possibilities are invoked to account for the crash.

Also information might be available about the intermediate sequence on the scale of maturity between points (*b*) and (*c*). (The age range of the population tested restricts the demonstration of any extensive evidence of changes between points (*a*) and (*b*).) Our interest is in what happened between (*b*) and (*c*).

Four grades of answer were detectable.

(Category c). Yes, No, Maybe, invoking or imagining extenuating possibilities, vision, weather, state of the plane.

(Category b_2). No, because if he was careful, he would not have cut the cable.

(Category b_1). No, because he hit the cable, etc.

(Category a). Yes or No, with irrelevant comment or denial of the premiss. e.g. Yes, he was brave; Yes, the cable shouldn't be there.

The reliability of this categorization was measured by comparing the five grade groupings produced independently by two judges. The results were as follows where r is a product moment correlation coefficient: $r = 0.89$, S.E. $= 0.005$.

The results of the analysis of the answers are given in Table I.

TABLE 1. *Was the pilot a careful airman?*

Category		n	C.A.		M.A.	
			m	σ	m	σ
c	Suggests extenuating possibilities	24	161·2	15·5	176·2	28·8
b_2	No, if he was careful, he would........	34	149·0	21·0	164·3	31·9
b_1	No, because he crashed	10	145·5	21·2	140·5	21·1
a	Tautologies, irrelevances, denial of premiss	10	124·5	17·9	134·5	23·7

Ages given in months

There is a clear progression as the pupils become older, particularly by chronological age.

Omitting category *a* with its pre-logical answers we may start with the lower *b* category (b_1) where one piece of content, or circumstantial evidence, namely the crash, is seized upon to support the simple unqualified inference that the pilot is not careful. It is judgement in terms of content which is correlated with the statement implied in the question. However, there is one difference between this judgement by content and a concrete judgement in the usual sense of the term. Even though it is limited, this judgement by circumstance consists of a proposition. It is understandable that verbal material should give rise to propositional statements and, as we shall see, the significant changes in quality of thinking as we pass up to higher categories are marked by increased transformation, imagination and co-ordination of propositions.

When we turn to the higher category *b* answers (b_2) we notice there is no difference in the substance of the judgement, but that there is a significant change in its form. Instead of the stock answer

> *No, because he crashed . . . etc.*

we have the transformed judgement;

> *No, if he was careful he would not have crashed . . .*

Such transformations characterize early adolescent thinking and language usage from that stage on. Newton's law of motion: a body continues in its state of uniform motion except in so far as it is acted upon by external forces, embodies the same transformation. The law describes what would happen to the body if certain forces were not there. In the actual physical world they are always there and the body stops.

Such transformations may appear because the *trait* of carefulness dominates in (b_2) and the crash is seen as an exception to it, whereas in (b_1) the thinker is dominated by the circumstance described.

Category (c) answers bring out the quality of invoking or imagining possible causes of the crash other than lack of care and provide one of the real defining qualities of mature thinking. Such imagined hypotheses are checked against the data of the problem. In the case of the above anecdote, which is very simple, the hypothesis has to be plausible, that is connected with weather, plane, pilot or mountains.

Summing up we see that the major features of the genesis of the pupils' thinking comprehension seem to consist generally of:

(1) The capacity to think propositionally by pupils at least as young as 11–12. A proposition is produced by linking that implied in the question with the salient feature of the story related circumstantially to the question. Other possibilities do not enter. To this extent the judgement is partial and circumstantial;

followed next by

(2) a transformation of this judgement by forming its complement with the addition of no new inferences from the material. This phase appears at ages from a half year older than that associated with the Category (b_1) answers,

followed finally by

(3) recognition that there might have been other elements outside the pilot's control which made it not possible for him to see the cable, etc. The answers at this stage shift to invoked explanations and suggestions to account for the incident. Their plausibility reveals that they have been related to the data of the problem. Chronological ages of $13+$ and mental ages of $14+$ years seem to be associated with this phase.

In brief, first we get a circumstantial judgement that fails to take account of the incompatible competing element, then a partly formal transformation of this judgement by inversion, and lastly the shift of emphasis in the answer to possible explanations.

It is possible to analyse the growth of thinking-comprehension by using school material, both to bring out the changes suggested above and to demonstrate other qualities. Thus Rhys (1966) worked with secondary school geography. One of his test situations described what happened when a South American farmer cut down the trees in an Andes valley to clear the land for farming, and planted corn year after year. Eventually soil erosion took place with alternating flooding and drought.

One question put by Rhys on the passage was:

What could the farmer have done to prevent the destruction of his farmland?

and is calculated to stimulate the thinker to imagine a course of action and to relate it to the essentials of the situation. Five recognizable phases seemed to make up the development of the pupil's thinking. First there were pre-logical eccentric answers showing a failure to grasp the problem. Then there were those offering a single imagined suggestion which took no cognizance of the actualities of the situation, namely that the land had to be farmed under the conditions prevailing. Thus there was the answer.

He could have left the big trees up because they would have kept his soil fertile.

In the next phase it is recognized that the land has to be farmed in spite of the difficulties and one or two suggestions are made.

(1) *He could have left some of the trees in the ground.*
(2) *Build a dam and have less water running down.*

In the fourth phase we see the first explicit awareness of the crux of the situation in the disturbance of the balance of nature by the action of the farmer and the possible action open to him to re-establish the balance and farm successfully.

If he had cut down some of his trees and then left a border all the way round, the wind and rain would not have blown or washed soil away. By this he would have been able to go on farming.

Finally at the highest level the answers consisted of a more positive and integrated statement of possible remedies.

The brook could have been boarded at either side to stop the floods covering the land and taking pieces of earth with them. A barrier of trees could have been left at the top of his land to protect it from winds and rain, and he could have left the dead leaves down to act as a manure.

The mean ages in months associated with these five recognizable phases beginning with the least mature were as follows:

TABLE 2. *Problem of soil erosion*

Phase	n	CA	MA (Raven)	Notion
1st	9	135·8	133·6	pre-logical
2nd	21	133·5	141·0	not reality orientated
3rd	35	150·8	159·5	single proposal; reality orientated
4th	21	167·0	177·4	recognition of the need to re-establish balance
5th	34	183·0	195·9	comprehensive proposals

It is noteworthy that only at $12\frac{1}{2}$ years of age are proposals linked with the realities of the situation and only at 14+ is there clear recognition that the problem involves the disturbance of a natural environment. Rhys points out that this is the essential for understanding man's relation to his geographical environment.

In general the imagination only becomes harnessed to reality after the second phase.

The comprehension test about the Pilot showed the influence of the circumstantial element in the comprehension of verbal material by younger adolescents. Another test, now to be described, is concerned with the problem of (a) how far the children's judgements are tied literally to the direct evidence supplied in a short passage in relation to a question asked about it, (b) how far the thinking is more adventuresome, based on probabilistic[1] inferences invoking assumptions about evidence not presented and under what conditions such a judgement is likely to be more mature than (a), and (c) how far the passage evokes a mature response in which the inference is set against the direct evidence.

There is no *direct* evidence given in the test passage to support the assumption raised by the question. The material takes the test a little further from the point of limited evidence to no direct evidence at all, but the circumstances support the questions much more plausibly.

The test was as follows:

I've seen Mary standing at the edge of the skating rink with skates on her feet. I often see her walking and running to school and standing about. I've seen her watching the skating at the rink and she is always talking about skating.

(1) *Can Mary skate?*

. . . .

(2) *Why do you think so?*

. . . .

Skating is regarded as a conjunction of wearing skates (s) and moving (m). The binary conjunctions of ($\bar{s}m$ v $s\bar{m}$ v $\bar{s}\bar{m}$) are given but not the defining conjunction sm. In addition the passage contains a logically irrelevant but circumstantially suggestive element:

I've seen her watching at the rink and she is always talking about skating.

In the analysis of the results, first the answers are grouped into three classes according to the main response: *No, Yes, Not sure.* Then the answers under the main categories *No* and *Yes* are subdivided into

---

[1] By probabilistic I have in mind inferences based on material not actually given. (See also last chapter, pp. 286 ff.).

(a) irrelevant, tautological or premises rejecting responses,
(b) simple judgements on the basis of the facts given,
(c) elaborated judgements in which the propositions such as *she was standing on skates* are explained or justified, as for example by the remark, *she doesn't like to try in front of people.*

The frequency of responses are set out below under the categories listed. The mean mental and chronological ages of the group of pupils under each category are also given with the corresponding standard deviations.

TABLE 3. *Can Mary skate?*

Category of Response		n	CA m	CA σ	MA m	MA σ
Not sure		6	166	18·4	185	31·1
Yes	Elaborated Judgement	8	148	18·2	155	26·5
	Simple Judgement	23	142	23·1	161	29·4
	Irrelevance	1	156	0	126	0
No	Elaborated Judgement	23	164	14·2	181	27·0
	Simple Judgement	38	146	23·1	159	29·1
	Irrelevance	4	120	9·2	117	4·9

Ages given in months

The differences between the mean 'Not sure' and 'No' chronological and mental ages are least significant and generally the differences in the former ages are more significant than those in the latter.

We may infer that growth of maturity of judgement in this problem is slightly more a function of age than intellectual maturity.

Instances of the categories in Table 3 are as follows:

Not sure: Maybe or maybe not. She might be able to skate but maybe she isn't in the mood. Maybe she can't skate so she goes there to watch the others and while she's watching she's learning at the same time.

Yes, elaborated judgement: Yes, but not very well. I think she likes to skate but can't do it very well.

Yes, direct judgement: I think Mary can skate because she's always talking about skating.

No, elaborated judgement: No, Mary probably talked about skating because she had to be noticed – so as not to be left out.

No, direct: Because it says she just watches the skaters and it says nothing about her skating ability.

On the basis of these results it would seem that the few 'Not sure' judgements were made by the older and intellectually more mature pupils.

The three basic groupings of responses into: Not sure, Yes and No may be compared by pooling the Yes and No subgroupings of Table 3 (excluding irrelevant responses). When this is done we obtain the following results:

TABLE 4. *Can Mary skate? Pooled categories*

	n	CA		MA	
		m	σ	m	σ
Not sure	6	166	18·4	185	31·1
No	61	153	20·3	167	28·7
Yes	31	144	22·0	159	28·7

Looking first at Table 4 we see that the 'No' answers seemed on the whole to be made at the next lower level of maturity followed by the 'Yes' answers at the lowest level. Which takes precedence appears to depend on the general plausibility of the proposition implied in the question. In another parallel passage where the activity is painting, the 'Yes' answers are given by the maturer pupils. As one of them put it, it is highly unlikely that a person cannot paint something (as painting is judged these days) whereas it is more likely that a person cannot skate.

Apart from these differences the most interesting thing about Table 3 is the generally greater maturity of the pupils who made the elaborated judgements. This suggests that the quality of the judgement, 'Yes' or 'No' is important. It is the supporting thinking which makes for superiority, this being marked by elaboration in the form of imagined possibilities not actually provided in the text. So the adventuresome thinker is the more mature. The results support the point made earlier that in verbal thinking and comprehension the capacity to imagine and invoke explanations is most indicative of maturity.

V. ASPECTS OF THE DEVELOPMENT OF THOUGHT

So far the problem of thinking has been presented as a developmental phenomenon without any attempt to set out the factors that might influence its growth. For example no speculation has been offered about the results put before the reader in Tables 1, 2, 3 and 4. Are they wholly a consequence of maturation? What part does schooling play in them? I cannot yet give an answer to these questions, but I can speculate as to possible causes. It is proposed to use a schema which was proposed by Piaget in a symposium held in Berkeley in 1964. He listed four essential factors in development: maturation, experience, social transmission, equilibration.

Taking maturation first, if this is seen as a psychological 'reflection of an inner maturation of the nervous system', most claims made for it after the first few years of life in the child must be considered as largely speculative, since we know so little about neurological maturation in older children. It is also a hypothesis which is not easily falsifiable by experimental probes. In fact, what evidence we have from cross cultural studies of young children's thinking suggests that it is far from being the sole factor, even in very young children. Research carried out in Martinique showed the same sequence of development in children's thinking that is almost invariably found elsewhere – but the children of Martinique were four years behind those of Paris in their development, common language and school system notwithstanding.

Maturation, therefore, is a factor we must keep in mind particularly with younger children, but it is not all there is to development and its role in adolescent thinking may be much smaller. Negative evidence to support the idea of it as the psychological mirror of the neurological is, of course, widespread and clear in the reverse process of degeneration of thinking with old age.

Thinking and knowledge involve action by the person on his environment and clearly any account of thought is meaningless without reference to the role of experience. Piaget (*op. cit.* p. 11) cites the appearance of conservation of substance prior to that of weight or volume as something that could not have arisen by experience. His argument is that weight is something a child perceives whereas an amount of substance cannot be perceived. I have never been convinced about the weighing of objects on a balance as the means to convince children of the equality or inequality of the pieces of plasticine weighed. The balance involves concepts which, according to other work of Piaget, do not appear until later. Furthermore, we all believe that the earlier responses of children are global and undifferentiated – one could argue that the idea of substance is the more primitive and reached by a global perception and that out of it weight appears later as a differentiated development.

On the positive side there appear to be two aspects of experience which count for much in the child's development. These have been touched upon in Section II on concept formation. Firstly there is physical experience which 'consists of acting upon objects and drawing some knowledge about the objects by abstraction from the objects'. This is the usual kind of experience that everyone recognizes and uses to shape his behaviour. But there is also another kind of experience mentioned on page 305 called 'logico-mathematical experience' where knowledge is drawn from the *actions* effected by the persons. This knowledge consists of the discovery of the properties of the set of actions used by the person in abstracting from and ordering the physical phenomena of his environment. The laws of associativity and commutativity

$$a(bc) = (ab)c$$
and
$$ab = ba$$

of ordinary algebra are examples, as are those of the logical structure of classes and relations as outlined in Chapter 8, Section II, and further discussed in Section II of this chapter.

We have then two fundamental kinds of experience leading to recognition of the properties (*a*) of objects and material, and (*b*) of the actions carried out on the objects.

One of the most fundamental findings of the Geneva School is that the two experiences develop hand in hand and that attempts to teach a child to carry out certain abstractions about his environment will be fruitless unless he possesses also the related 'structure of action'. The growth of thinking, in fact, consists of the movement from structures of prior and lower order to those at a higher plane.

These observations take us naturally to the third element in the growth of thinking – social transmission. By this Piaget means formal and informal teaching by the use of language. It is fundamental and necessary but like the other elements not by itself sufficient. As will be appreciated from the comments of the previous paragraphs the child can receive real information by such means 'only if he is in a state where he can understand this information'. The state requires that the new information is presented in a form demanding not more than the structure of action which the child has already formed. The child will make of the information what he can by virtue of his particular level of development – but this may not be what the adult intends. Hence the so-called discrepancy between language and thought. There is much evidence on this topic and my own work with F. Davies investigates the problem with respect to the young child's ideas of implication, incompatibility and disjunction (see Peel, 1967b).

The last element of the growth of thinking is so fundamental that its self-evidence comes as a revelation when it is described.

In the act of knowing the person is faced with a *need* to resolve a discrepancy basically between him and his environment which constitutes to him an external disturbance. Consequently he seeks equilibrium by active resolution and compensation. The most obvious and general action of this kind in adolescence is the need for and process of explanation. When a person explains a phenomenon he effects an equilibrium. Such an equilibrium is not stable in that better explanations may be forthcoming with more knowledge, etc., but explanation is far more stable than description, which is a relatively unstable form of equilibrium. Description, as I have defined it, does not relate an event or phenomenon to the wider context of knowledge. The equilibrium of description will always lead to that of explanation.

The above refers to equilibrium between person and environment, but the process of finding equilibrium also refers to parts within the phenomenon. All natural and contrived situations involve the idea of equilibrium – disequilibrium. Behind this interaction there are the ideas of cancelling an operation or a state and compensating for such a change to re-establish equilibria. This was well illustrated in the short geographical anecdote about the Andean farmer on page 14. The geographical environment is a continuously changing state of dynamic equilibrium where the forces of climate, terrain and organic life are constantly operating on each other. When man intervenes by agriculture, mining, building and the like he disturbs the equilibrium much more rapidly. As Rhys showed, only older adolescents appear to realize the full equilibria of the geographical environment. When, in connexion with the erosion, floods and drought, he asked the question

> *Why had this not happened before when there were trees in the ground?*

he received such answers as:

When the trees were on the valley sides they prevented the soil from moving in many ways. Firstly, the trees were in vast numbers and so their roots were intertwined in all directions, which hold the top soil together quite efficiently. Secondly, the tree branches sheltered the surface soil when there was a rain storm, and finally the trees sheltered the land from excess wind. When the farmer removed the trees he had signed the land's death warrant.

from 15-year-olds.

The behaviour of men towards each other, as seen in history, provides another clear instance of the equilibrium of cancellation and compensation. The state of affairs immediately prior to the two world wars reveals this position of balance very clearly. In 1914, Germany might or might not have invaded Belgium; if she did, England would take compensatory action by declaring war. In 1939 we had a similar position regarding the possible invasion of Poland. The understanding of history involves a sensitivity to such balances of political and human forces which does not seem to be fully revealed until mid-adolescence (Peel, 1960). I discuss this problem more fully elsewhere in relation to history (Peel, 1967a).

As to contrived phenomena, Inhelder and Piaget (1958) first revealed the growth of understanding of the equilibria of physics in their set of experiments on liquid pressure and the lever (see last chapter).

VI. LEARNING TO THINK

What we hope ensues from learning mathematics, physics or history, or any other subject is not merely data collections but the power to think in the way inherent in these disciplines, so that years later, although particular theorems, laws or changes are half or wholly forgotten, they can be resuscitated and used in the proper manner and circumstance. Furthermore, fresh information and problems can be dealt with appropriately. This is learning to think and we now comment briefly on three aspects of the process: 1. the role of mental development and structure, 2. formation of learning sets to facilitate concept usage in shaping future behaviour, 3. general and specific methods of thought.

1. *The role of mental development and structure*

The point has been made (p. 320) that a person responds to learning situations according to the level of his mental development. The barest formulation of learning as

$$\text{stimulus} \longrightarrow \text{response}$$

is quite inadequate to account for any but the simplest and educationally most trivial of learnings. Piaget (1964) calls such responses 'copy responses' and he points out that a much more important class of responses is produced by transformation of these simple responses and that this change is effected by operations of thought and by the processes of assimilation and accommodation which enable the learner to come to terms with his environment. Many other writers have touched on the need for such mechanisms to account for the richness of human learning. These have been variously described as structure (Piaget), cognitive structure, as the organization, stability and clarity of knowledge (Ausubel), learning sets (Harlow), organization, orientation, schema, conceptual pattern, aptitude (Cronbach). (See Vol. I for a detailed critique and an integrative approach.)

Piaget stated most clearly the limitations imposed by the child's operational structure on what he can take from furthur instruction, and Smedslund demonstrated that any attempts to accelerate the child's cognitive development will only be temporary unless the method of learning is based on structures available to the child at the time of learning.

Learning to think entails both the learner's experience of his environment and the sets of logical operations he has already built up. In the passages on the Pilot and the Andes farmer these two components in fact determine together the level of response we obtain to the questions asked about the passages.

Whilst the influence of the concepts formed by the learner about his environment is widely recognized in research on learning and methods of teaching, the role of the second, of the structured sets of logical operations available, has not been studied widely. Exceptions to this generalization are, of course, the work at Geneva and that of Smedslund in Norway, and incidentally the researches of Ausubel (1963) and Suchman (1964). The reader is also recommended to refer to Hunt's monograph on this topic (1961).

In any kind of teaching, and in particular in programmed learning, the use of prompts, on-going behaviour, established repertories of responses, analogy and models are all instances of the first component.

The second component operates most obviously in the case of mathematics, but it is present in more descriptive subjects, as seen in the cancellation-compensation equilibria of science, history, geography and human affairs.

2. *The formation of learning sets*

When a person has to perform many similar tasks like discriminating between shapes, it has been discovered that he learns more than proficiency in the particular tasks. There develops also a learning set which predisposes him to learn related tasks more readily. He becomes aware of general features and in this respect a learning set resembles a concept. A learning set facilitates concept usage and bears on the method of future learning.

The question most often posed about learning sets is how far the learning should be broad or deep. Thus Leith and Clarke (1965) wished to prepare pupils to add and subtract in the 6-base number system by building up a learning set on the basis of other non-10 bases. They had three groups of learners and four programmes of 99 frames on addition and subtraction in each of the 4 systems in 5, 7, 8 and 9 bases.

Group A took each programme once.

Group B took each of the 7 and 8 bases twice.

Group C took 8-base four times.

The test included 6-base number operations. Group B was the best, being slightly better than A. C was significantly lower than these. The research demonstrates that a combination (b) of breadth (as in A) with depth (as in C) is better than either alone, but that if this is not possible, breadth of learning will best promote an effective set. These results relate to the findings of Morrisett and Hovland (1959), who studied the solving of samples with geometrical figures and had three groups of learners:

I 192 trials × 1 problem
II 24 trials × 8 problems
III 64 trials × 3 problems

In terms of errors made the three groups came out as follows:

III < I < II

They also support the findings of Callantine and Warren (1955) that breadth is more effective than depth.

Starting with the assumption that knowledge is productive learning, which itself implies the mastery of a class of tasks Gagné and his co-workers (1961 and 1962) have extended the idea of learning sets to that of the hierarchy of learning sets required to build up to a particular class of problem solving, say solving simple algebraic equations. They achieve these learning sets by starting from the finally solved problem and working back in stages by asking at each stage what information would be required immediately prior to it, to the very fundamentals which they equate with basic mental abilities. As the learner proceeds through the programmes devised for each of these ascending learning sets, Gagné was able to demonstrate transfer and the extent of the sufficiency and necessity of each step for the next. The findings are convincing and could link with the idea of ascending cognitive structures.

The problem of acquiring a learning set can also be seen in terms of the relative efficiency of guided and unguided learning. This approach is seen in the Minnesota arithmetic study by Swenson (1949). In her study of the learning of the first hundred addition facts, Swenson compared a meaningful method with a drill method and a drill plus method that made use of the single arithmetical meaning of equal 'Size of Sum', that is, for example, of the fact that 2 + 7, 8 + 1, 6 + 3, 7 + 2 are all '9' sizes. In her meaningful method the pupils related the different number facts by active direct 'figuring out' and composition in terms of the number system. Drill in the facts followed this generalization in terms of the number system. The drill method presented each fact as a discrete bond or association to be learned and the order of presentation was based on 'difficulty studies' (2). When measured against a criterion including immunity from retroactive inhibition and transfer of the learning to untaught material, the meaningful method was found to be superior to the other two.

Gagné and Brown (1961) examined how newly acquired concepts

enter into the activity of solving problems. They devised three types of learning programme;

(i) where the concept rule was stated first and then a linear programme brought about identification and application of the rule,

(ii) a discovery programme where the rule had to be found by the learner,

(iii) a guided discovery programme where instances are worked with guidance for particular cases and the learner extends the rule to other cases.

The order of efficiency was found to be

Guided Discovery > Discovery > Rule and Example

Wittrock (1963) analysed guidance and discovery into explicit terms of giving or not giving the rule and giving or not giving the answer. He found that for transfer to new tasks the intermediate combination was the best: Rule given, answer not given > Rule given, answer given > Rule not given, answer not given.

The picture is not wholly clear but it seems that guided discovery in some form is better than the extreme possibilities of no-discovery or all-discovery.

3. *General and specific methods of thought*

The extent to which thinking can be taught in terms of a few general precepts is much debated and far from clear. Certain basic general skills seem to be involved in recognizing the validity of generalizations and inferences, in carefully checking hypotheses and the like, but just as different subjects, like the sciences, mathematics, history and foreign languages emphasize and use different aspects of concept formation and usage, so these disciplines entail different methods of thinking.

Crutchfield and Covington (1963) devised a training programme which they claim trains 'for a *generalized* problem-solving skill'. Using programmed learning techniques they presented thirteen lessons in which aspects of thinking, problem solving and detection were involved. In their own words.

'Inasmuch as our aim was to train for a *generalized* problem-solving skill, the problems did not pertain to specific curricular content, but dealt rather with a variety of mysteries and puzzling occurrences, such as the theft of a statue from a museum, and a case of strange goings-on in a deserted house.

Each lesson posed a single mystery problem which the child was to solve. The lesson was constructed so that each child, by being given successively more clues and information, was finally led to discover the solution for himself. At various points in the story the child was required to restate the problem in his own words, formulate his own questions, and generate ideas to explain the mystery. Immediate feedback was given to his responses in the form of examples of other ideas or questions that he might have thought of in the given situation. These examples were primarily ones which fifth-graders would find novel and uncommon, and which would open new lines of investigation or new ways of viewing the problem. It was assumed that presenting numerous examples of this type would tend to broaden the child's limits of acceptance as to what constitute important questions and fruitful ideas.'

Each lesson was part of a continuous theme and required forty-five minutes. The children were then given the Duncker X-ray problem together with other problems, and it was found that of ninety-eight children taking the auto-instructional programme, 35 per cent solved the X-ray problem, whereas, among a matched control of ninety-seven children not so instructed, only 13 per cent were able to solve the problem.

Among the general properties of thinking worked into the programme by Crutchfield and Covington were the following:

1. the necessity of identifying and defining the problem appropriately;

2. the importance of asking questions and of taking time for reflection rather than leaping to conclusions;

3. looking closely at details, looking for discrepancies;

4. the necessity of generating many ideas;

5. the necessity of looking everywhere for clues;

6. not being afraid to come up with silly ideas.

Others, however, are not so convinced by this possibility, (Berlak, 1963).

Berlak represents the other point of view and maintains that it is much more useful to carry out an analysis of the output of a piece of successful thought in a particular field, say scientific, historical, social, etc., list the intellectual processes involved, attempt to re-create the project from this relatively meagre information and repeat the whole process until better prediction is obtained.

Probably the best account of the methods of thinking would be one that included a reference both to general qualities of thinking and the more specific features which characterize separate school subjects.

REFERENCES

AUSUBEL, D. (1963). *The Psychology of Meaningful Verbal Learning.* New York: Grune and Stratton.

BERLAK, H. (1963). The construct validity of a content analysis system for the evaluation of critical thinking in political controversy. Unpub. doctoral diss. Cambridge: Harvard Grad. Sch. of Educ.

BRUNER, J. S., GOODNOW, J., and AUSTIN, G. A. (1956). *A Study of Thinking.* New York: Wiley.

CALLANTINE, M. F., and WARREN, J. M. (1955). Learning sets in concept formation. *Psychol. Rep.* **1,** 363.

CRUTCHFIELD, R. S., and COVINGTON, M. V. (1963). Facilitation of creative thinking and problem solving in school children. Paper presented in symposium on learning research pertinent to educational improvement. Cleveland: Amer. Assoc. Adv. Sci.

DUNCKER, K. (1945). On problem-solving. *Psychol. Monogr.* **58,** No. 5. (Whole No. 270.)

GAGNÉ, R. M., and BROWN, L. T. (1961). Some factors in the programming of conceptual learning. *J. exp. Psychol.* **62,** 4, 431.

GAGNÉ,, R. M., MAYOR, J. R., GARSTENS, H. L., and PARADISE, N. E. (1962). Factors in acquiring knowledge of a mathematical task. *Psychol. Monogr.* **76,** 7. (Whole. No. 526.)

GAGNÉ, R. M., and PARADISE, N. E. (1961). Abilities and learning sets in knowledge acquisition. *Psychol. Monogr.* **75,** 4. (Whole No. 518.)

HUNT, J. McV. (1961). *Intelligence and Experience.* New York: Ronald.

INHELDER, B., and PIAGET, J. (1964). *The Early Growth of Logic in the Child.* London: Routledge and Kegan Paul.

INHELDER, B., and PIAGET, J. (1958). *The Growth of Logical Thinking.* London: Routledge and Kegan Paul.

LEITH, G. O. M., and CLARKE, W. D. (1965). Unpublished research on arithmetic learning sets. Univ. Birmingham School of Education.

LODWICK, A. R. (1958). An investigation into the question whether the inferences that children draw on learning history correspond with the stages of mental development that Piaget postulates. Unpub. Dip. Ed. diss., Univ. of Birmingham.

MAIER, N. R. F. (1930). Reasoning in humans I. On direction. *J. Comp. Psychol.* **10,** 115–143.

MAIER, N. R. F. (1931). Reasoning in humans II. The solution of a problem and its appearance in consciousness. *J. Comp. Psychol.* **12,** 184–194.

MEALINGS, R. J. (1961). Some aspects of problem solving in science at the secondary school stage. Unpub. M. A. Thesis, Univ. of Birmingham.

MEALINGS, R. J. (1963). Problem solving and science teaching. *Educ. Rev.* **15,** 194–207.

MORRISETT, E., and HOVLAND, C. I. (1959). Three methods of training in human problem solving. *J. exp. Psychol.* **58,** 52–55.

PEEL, E. A. (1959). Experimental examination of some of Piaget's schemata. *Brit. J. Educ. Psychol.* **29,** 89–103.

PEEL, E. A. (1960). *The Pupil's Thinking.* London: Oldbourne.

PEEL, E. A. (1962). The growth of high school pupils' judgements. Unpub. research memo., Univ. of Birmingham.

PEEL, E. A. (1965). Intellectual growth during adolescence. *Educ. Rev.* **17,** 3, 169–180.

PEEL, E. A. (1966). A study of differences in the judgements of adolescent pupils. *Brit. J. Educ. Psychol.,* 77–86.

PEEL, E. A. (1967). Some problems in the psychology of history teaching. 2 chapters in: Burton, W. H., and Thompson, D. (eds.) *Studies in the Nature and Teaching of History.* London: Routledge and Kegan Paul.

PEEL, E. A. (1967). A method for investigating children's understanding of certain logical connectives used in binary propositional thinking. *Brit. J. Math. and Stat. Psychol.* **20,** 81–92.

PEEL, E. A. (1968). Learning, understanding and thinking. Unpublished manuscript.

PEEL, E. A., and DAVIES, F. (1965). Young children's logical thinking. Unpub. research, Univ. of Birmingham.

PIAGET, J. (1964). Development and learning. In Piaget Re-discovered. *J. Res. Sci. Teaching.* **2.**

RHYS, W. T. (1966). The development of logical thought in the adolescent with reference to the teaching of geography in the secondary school. Unpub. M.Ed. Thesis, Univ. of Birmingham.

SHEPARD, R. N., HOVLAND, C. I., and JENKINS, H. M. (1961). Learning and memorization of classifications. *Psychol. Monogr.* **73,** 13. (Whole No. 517.)

SWENSON, E. J. (1949). Organization and generalization as factors in learning transfer and retroactive inhibition. *Learning Studies in School Situations. Studies in Education*, No. **3**, 9–39. Minneapolis: Univ. Minnesota Press.

SZEKELY, L. (1950). Productive process in learning and thinking. *Acta Psychologica*, **7**, 388–407.

VYGOTSKY, L. S. (1962). *Thought and Language*. Cambridge, Mass: M.I.T. Press.

WASON, P. C. (1960). On the failure to eliminate hypotheses in a conceptual task. *Q. J. exp. Psychol.* **12**, 129–140.

WERNER, H., and KAPLAN, E. (1950). The acquisition of word meaning: a developmental study. *Monogr. Soc. Res. Ch. Dev.* **15**. (Whole No. 51.)

WERTHEIMER, M. (1945). *Productive Thinking*. New York: Harper.

WITTROCK, M. C. (1963). Verbal stimuli in concept formation: learning by discovery. *J. Educ. Psychol.* **54**, 4, 183–190.

11

Social Learning and Perspectives in Adolescence

J. F. MORRIS

I. INTRODUCTION

BROADLY speaking, there seem to be three ways of handling the material in a discussion of social learning. First, it can be presented as a story. Second, it can be expressed as a series of viewpoints, or perspectives. Third, it can take the form of a set of problems, with possible answers. A good example of the first approach is provided by psychoanalytic theory. Critics of psychoanalysis have often commented caustically on the dramatic interplay between Id, Ego and Super-Ego in the Freudian account of personality development, and complained that the theory has closer affinities with Sophocles and Shakespeare than with Newton and Darwin.

Yet there are many advantages in presenting social learning as a story. One is continually reminded, for example, of the personal implications of learning to take part in social life, and the dramatic nature of some of the encounters producing learning. But there are also disadvantages. The most important of these, from our point of view, is that not enough is known about social learning for one coherent story to be told. There seem to be many stories, intertwining with one another in a most confusing way. Furthermore, some of the processes involved in social learning seem to be quietly continuous, like the small increments in one's vocabulary after the giant leaps of early childhood, the slow pace of physical growth before the 'adolescent growth spurt' and the increased power in discriminating new social roles in later childhood. These are not in themselves the stuff of a very exciting story. Psychoanalysis, it will be remembered, began with some very dramatic materials – the symptoms of neurosis and psychosis, and their possible origin in the fantasies of early childhood.

The second way of handling the materials concerned with social learning is to present a series of pictures. These, if carefully selected, will give a clear impression of the key stages in development. Each will be static, but the sequence will suggest movement. The literature of human development is replete with 'views', 'perspectives' and 'portraits'. An excellent recent example, discussed later, is the study of American adolescents by Douvan and Adelson (1966). This is described by the publishers thus, 'The authors argue that an accurate view of the American adolescent has been hard to obtain . . . [They] have carefully pieced together . . . a composite picture from a mass of information . . .' The attraction of such a picture is that one can experience a sense of unity and coherence that is difficult to achieve in any other way. The weakness in such pictures follows from their attraction. They all too easily give a misleading impression of finality, sacrifice much contradictory and confusing detail to sharpen the portrait, and encourage the viewer to forget the selection that went into the composition.

In short, the first two ways of presenting social learning have serious inadequacies, despite their obvious attractiveness. Our ignorance of the subject forces us to adopt another approach. As Paul Mussen has put the matter in a recent survey of early socialization, 'The number of questions still unanswered increases geometrically as one thinks about the lacunae in our knowledge . . . The areas about which there is reliable knowledge seem miniscule in comparison with the vast terrain of ignorance.' (Mussen, 1967, p. 104.) But he immediately adds, 'This would be a very discouraging state of affairs if it were not for several obvious facts. First of all, there have recently been some tremendous advances in our understanding of basic processes. Theoretical analyses are continually becoming more penetrating and more sophisticated. And most importantly, relevant research is increasing in quantity and gaining immeasurably in quality.'

The best way of representing both our ignorance and the very heartening increase in knowledge is to use the third approach (with occasional bows to the other approaches, as in the 'perspectives' attributed to adolescents). What, then, are the problems of social learning, especially in later childhood and adolescence? One of the key problems is undoubtedly that of role-learning. In social life, a reasonable measure of order depends on the accurate discrimination of the appropriate role to play in each type of social situation, in the family, at school, and with friends in one's leisure. Later, the occupational roles of working life become vitally important for most of the waking day. Not only must the appropriate role be recognized, it must also be 'performed' (or enacted, or played; the different terms have implications which will be briefly considered later). This requires skills that are motor as well as perceptual and cognitive. How does all this happen? Is there one process of role-learning, such as imitation, or several? Attempting to answer the problem of role-learning is difficult, but the problems of socialization hardly end with role-learning. Men and women are not wholly bounded by their roles, however varied these may be. They experience themselves as persons, and a characteristic of such experience is the sense of selfhood or personal identity. Are the identities which persons experience in any way influenced by social learning? If so, in what ways? The position taken here is that social learning plays a large part in the development of personal identity, and a paradox of socialization is that a sense of individual uniqueness, of a separate identity, only becomes possible in a social milieu.

The study of role-learning and the development of personal identity raise further problems. Morality constitutes a vital link between social conventions and personal standards of conduct. Social conventions – the *mores* from which the term 'moral' was originally derived – are concerned with the world of social roles. Personal standards, on the other hand, seem to be closely linked with a sense of personal identity, shading into individual responsibility or autonomy. How is the development of morality related to social learning? It is a commonplace that personal standards can bring a person into conflict with social convention. Can this kind of conflict be linked with social learning?

A further problem emerges from the study of adolescence as an important stage in physical development. At first sight, sexual development, the most striking feature of adolescence, is a physical 'fact of life' which owes nothing to social learning, even though society must take account of it. On closer inspection, however, it appears that sexual attitudes and conduct may be closely related to social expectations and values, varying from one time and place to another in a most accommodating way, often with quite bewildering speed. This raises an extremely interesting and important problem: how far is sexual development a matter of social learning? It has become customary in studies of socialization to talk of sex-role typing and sex-role identity. What do these terms imply? If social influences play a large part in sexual development, to what extent can educational policy and methods control such learning? What problems does this involve, for pupils, teachers and the public?

Finally, returning to the topic of personal identity, to what extent does the experience of adolescence create characteristic strains for young people? Do these strains, where they exist, threaten the maintenance and development of personal identity, leading to an adolescent 'search for identity'? It has been suggested by Erikson, Fromm and others that the crisis of identity in adolescence is associated with the pathological state of 'self-alienation'. What are the implications of this assertion?

Here, then, are a substantial number of problems of social learning. The rest of this chapter consists in a series of attempts to throw light on them, using a wide and varied range of materials. To begin with, it is necessary to consider some of the problems of social learning in childhood, taking up the themes so ably discussed by Dr Schaffer in Chapter 2.

II. ASPECTS OF SOCIAL LEARNING IN CHILDHOOD

1. *Behaviour systems, social roles and the self-concept*

The study of infra-human and human behaviour clearly reveals a number of behaviour systems related to physical or social requirements. Examples of these are the clusters of activities focussing on eating, excretory functions, sexual expression, social dependence and independence, the expression of affection and aggression, the achievement of competence and social success, the expression of fear and anxiety, the activities of work and play, and the activities of rest and sleep. All of these behaviour systems, whether obviously 'social' or not, are of social concern, since they involve scarce resources on which others may have a claim or, if not, they may affect in other ways the interests of others.

Several of these systems show striking similarities of pattern between the human species and some of the more highly developed infra-human species, and extremely interesting work has been done on pointing the parallels (although the similarity can sometimes be somewhat dramatically over-stated, as in the recent books by Lorenz on aggression and Ardrey on territoriality). A possible procedure for the study of human social learning would be to take each of these behaviour systems and show how it is developed through infancy, childhood, adolescence and adulthood, with a consideration of the major influences on the processes of development.

Another procedure, and the one adopted here, would be to look at the way in which some of the more central social roles develop, and the

M

social implications of the fact that human beings develop an awareness of certain aspects of their own activity, a fact which leads to self-control of their activity, and particularly their social activity. These two themes – the development of role-learning and the influence of the self-concept – tend to cut across the behaviour systems just mentioned. Admittedly, some of the systems, such as that centred on sexual expression and that centred on work, become the organizing focus of an important social role (the sex-role and the occupational role). Roles are so fluid, and readily focussed on any issue of social moment, that it would not be difficult to give extensive lists of social roles that, at least ostensibly, are focussed directly on each of the specific behaviour systems so far mentioned; such as the roles of diner, friend, lover, enemy, soldier, competitor, hero, coward, worker, player and sleeper. Recent studies in educational psychology delineate roles of 'under-achievers' and 'over-achievers'. But when this has been said, the point remains that many important roles, and above all the self-concept, bring together these specific behaviour-systems in comprehensive groupings, as the role of son or daughter includes aspects of eating, dependence and independence, affection and aggression, and so on. Even somewhat more specific roles, such as that of school pupil, typically include many behaviour systems, grouped together into a schedule that enables them to be expressed at appropriate times in appropriate places. Those behaviour systems that are marked by frequently arising cycles of activity (eating, sleeping) have to be allowed for, though often in very diverse ways, in all those roles which are performed over periods of time of more than a few hours. Thus, family roles, working roles, educational roles, military roles and religious roles, must all make provision for these behaviour systems, though they often attempt to modify them into a form that is congruent with the remainder of the role.

Returning briefly to the self-concept; this too cuts across separate behaviour systems by its very nature. It is true that these systems may prove intractable, and may even fail to be recognized, or accurately perceived, by a person involved in activities that are related to them. This provides material for a good deal of clinical psychology, as in studies of repression, rationalization, and symptomatic distortion of behaviour. These difficulties in achieving effective integration only serve, though, to point to the fact that some measure of integration is both typical and useful to the person.

The approach here, then, is to look at both the learning of social roles and the learning of a self-concept. Unexpectedly, perhaps, the two types of learning prove to be very closely related; though the relative stability of the self-concept, as compared with the ease with which roles can be learned, and unlearned, brings out that they are not to be too closely identified with one another. We begin with a consideration of the learning of social roles.

2. The learning of social roles

How are social roles learned? It seems sensible to assume that the child first develops a clear sense of self, just by virtue of being a human being, and then learns to play the various roles allocated to him in a complex social system. And indeed it is true that self-awareness precedes any sense of one's self or other people in a role. But the self is learned in a social context and knowledge of 'the other' as a social object is acquired before knowledge of oneself. So it is useful to start our discussion with the learning of roles, not only because it is more obviously the business of a chapter in social learning to look at roles than at learning about one's self, but because the social conditions of social learning *imply* the importance of roles right from the beginning of life.

This is because social roles are small systems of attitudes and behaviour which may be inferred from social relationships, and which do not need to be recognized as roles in order to be influential. As Mead and Wolfenstein (1955), and other students of childhood in different cultures have shown, social expectations about the appropriate behaviour of children can vary strikingly from one country to another. While the social psychologist or sociologist is concerned with showing that these expectations cohere into roles, the parents and children 'in' the roles typically regard their behaviour and their expectations as 'natural' rather than socially-conditioned. Our initial question, then, becomes on closer inspection at least two questions. First there is the question of how the individual components of social roles are learned, without necessarily leading to any understanding on the part of the learner that he is involved in a complex process of 'role-learning'. Second, there is the question of the way in which the person becomes aware that there is a logic to his behaviour and attitudes – that they form systems that can be seen as such; that is, as social roles.

Our main concern here is with the first question, but it is in the nature of human intelligence that the categories used in making discriminations tend to become explicit at a later stage of development, especially if they come into conflict and thus create a state of uncertainty in the person's range of knowledge. Thus, in answering the first question adequately, a possible answer to the second question is found.

The acquisition of language is relevant to both questions. Language enables different aspects of the social environment to be classified explicitly, and it then provides a set of expectations about the categories into which these aspects have been classified. An important distinction is made between personal names and role-labels. By learning to make this distinction, the child takes with it an implication – that those with personal names are non-equivalent to others in many significant respects, while those with the same role-label are in many respects equivalent to one another.

This early social learning is not a once-for-all matter, but a continuous process of building up appropriate expectations of individual people and sets of expectations of role-incumbents. At first, the child has a tendency to regard both persons and social roles, himself included, concretely rather than reciprocally. That is, he finds it difficult to recognize the ways in which the behaviour of one person influences that of another. In this lack of perspective, the child is not alone. Even adults find it difficult to give due weight to the effects of their behaviour on that of others. There is a tendency, particularly with those that they are not well acquainted with, to see the behaviour of others as the almost inevitable outcome of well established attitudes and abilities.

One of the most important aspects of social learning, then, is a gradual improvement in the ability to recognize social interdependence and to make allowances for it in the anticipation and explanation of behaviour. This broadly matches the recognition by the child of interdependence in the physical world (as considered in Chapters 8–10) but the social world tends to be associated with stronger emotional involvement, has complex, shifting (and often apparently arbitrary) rules, and does not lend itself to experiment in quite the same way as do physical objects.

The work of Bernstein (1965) on language and social class is very relevant here. Bernstein distinguishes between different types of linguistic 'code' – an *elaborated* code, which is highly differentiated, works accordingly to fairly explicit rules, and is relatively objective in its relations to its subject matter, and a *restricted* code, which takes a good deal of shared experience between the users for granted, is highly expressive, and allows for idiosyncratic shifts in the rules.

His suggestion is that all social groups tend to use a restricted code with their close associates, but that the middle and upper classes have greater skill in the use of the elaborated code. This is of great social significance, because it enables members of these classes to move more confidently and effectively in a world of strangers. It seems reasonable to draw an analogy between the wide range of flexibility and control that a firm grasp of an abstract scientific and technical language (i.e. code) gives to its possessors in their dealings with the physical world, especially those aspects that go beyond 'common sense', and the enhanced understanding and control that are given by skill in using an elaborated code for the description, analysis, and even the construction of a social world.

Bernstein's work has been developed within a single, highly complex type of society. Other work (e.g. Whorf, 1956) has shown some of the differences in social attitudes and values reflected within the language systems of societies of varied sizes and degrees of complexity. Brown (1958) in an admirable survey and critique of much of this work, suggests that modern societies are so complex that there is room within them for every kind of linguistic variability. 'When we know the psychology of children, of psychotics, of bureaucrats, of creative artists I shall be very much surprised if there will not be some segment of our society to match whatever strange cognitive modes the ethnolinguist may turn up.' (Brown, 1958, p. 258.) Certainly Bernstein's work quite explicitly disavows an exclusive preoccupation with linguistic differences of the main social classes.

Studies of this kind bring out the enormous influence of social learning on every aspect of human behaviour. Even such fundamental forms of human behaviour as sexual behaviour are influenced by social learning, and this is briefly discussed in a later section. But at this point it seems worth quoting the following comments from a contributor to a recent symposium (Beach, 1965). 'Every human society has found it expedient to employ a combination of repression and encouragement in regulating the sexual behaviour of its constituent members, and we know that human beings are remarkably modifiable in this regard. Only cultural rather than physiological factors can explain some of the vast differences in sexual behaviour. . . . Our society includes a number of subcultures consisting of different socioeconomic levels and ethnic groups with differing sexual mores which strongly influence the behaviour of the constituent members' (*op. cit.*, pp. 487–488).

Although it seems appropriate to emphasize variability in a discussion of role-learning from the social-psychological perspective, it must be remembered that personality systems and role systems *are* systems, even though they are open, variable and in some respects unstable. They are not random aggregates of activity. Clearly the child does not learn every form of behaviour that he observes or hears about. What, then, are the determinants of the learning that actually occurs? Here one enters a most confusing and rapidly developing area of controversy in the study of social learning. Putting the issue at its simplest, there are those theorists, mainly clinicians, who see social learning from the standpoint of the very young, highly dependent, emotionally unstable child seeking satisfaction of urgent physical needs and a reduction of terrifying uncertainty. The major concept used by these theorists is *identification*, which they see as a very complex set of processes by which the child becomes a person, guided by internal standards, with a personal identity that can be clearly recognized. Identification, they believe, is typically with the parents.

Contrasting with this approach, there are those theorists, associated with an emphasis on overt, observed behaviour, who see social learning from the standpoint of detached scientific observers, interested in the whole range of social behaviour and the observable conditions which influence it. They are inclined to use the concept of *imitation*, believing that this is more flexible and neutral, since it indicates only the matching of the behaviour of others, either through direct observation or through some form of mediation (such as verbal description). Two of the most productive workers using this approach are Bandura and Walters (e.g. Bandura and Walters, 1963). The strength of this second approach lies in its experimental method, which enables the relative strength of carefully controlled variables to be assessed, and for vague, global concepts to be sharpened into analytical tools. But there is a danger that, just as the clinician generalizes from his collection of cases to the whole world (possibly implied in Freud's famous remark, 'The whole world is my patient'), the experimentalist, having gone to great pains to control small sources of disturbance in his experiments, tacitly takes these experiments as a paradigm of complex human behaviour in the real world.

It would be convenient if we could make a sharp distinction between two forms of social learning – identification and imitation – and splendid if it then turned out that identification is the process by which the self-concept is learned and imitation is the process by which roles are learned. Identification would then be a 'central' process of learning and imitation a 'peripheral' process. This may not be wholly inaccurate, but it does not match the clinical and experimental evidence very well.

In writing of the attempts to make clear conceptual distinctions in the field of observational learning (that is, learning from the behaviour of others) Bandura and Walters (1963) write, 'Observational learning is generally labelled "imitation" in experimental psychology and "identification" in theories of personality. Both concepts, however, encompass the same behavioural phenomenon, namely, the tendency for a person to reproduce the actions, attitudes, or emotional responses exhibited by real-life or symbolic models' (*op. cit.*, p. 89). After looking at some of the further distinctions made by other theorists between imitation and identification, the authors trenchantly state, 'It is possible to draw distinctions between these and other related terms – for example, introjection and incorporation – based on certain stimulus, mediating, or terminal-response variables. However, one might question whether it is meaningful to do so, since essentially the same learning process is involved regardless of the content of what is learned, or the stimulus situations in which the relevant behaviour is emitted. Therefore, it is in the interest of clarity, precision, and parsimony to employ the single term, imitation, to refer to the occurrence of matching responses' (p. 90).

This seems a cogent argument against making a sharp distinction between imitation and identification. Undoubtedly, some theorists have over-stressed the differences between the concepts, relating all the most important aspects of learning to identification and viewing imitation almost as an insignificant hangover from earlier evolutionary stages of development.

But, nevertheless, it might better serve the interests of precision to be less parsimonious, and we shall here use the term, imitation, when the emphasis is on the matching of observable behaviour (especially relatively discrete items of behaviour). The term, identification, then becomes appropriate for the matching of attitudes and emotions, that is, the more central cognitive/dispositional states inferred from behaviour.

Piaget's work on the successive phases of imitation in early childhood (discussed in Volume I, Chapter 5) effectively brings out the systematic and developmental nature of the process. He traces six distinguishable phases in the first two years of life, through which the child becomes able to match more and more complex activities, with closer fidelity, with more subtle attention to cues, and, most important for later development, longer periods of delay between the matched activity and its reproduction. Finally, with the development of higher-order, symbolic processes, the child is able to 'take off' into a world of more complex social learning. At this later stage, the child is able to make analogies between his own behaviour and experience and that (perceived, heard of, or imagined) of others. It is this process that leads to the development of the self-concept.

The earliest roles that the child learns are in many ways the most important, and serve as important organizing elements in all his later, more differentiated roles. The sex-role is, of course, of crucial significance in all social organization, even in our own highly 'instrumental' society, which tends to see people in terms of economic roles rather than their domestic or expressive activities. This role, because it is so important, tends to become a vital constituent of the self-concept. If all role-learning were of this fundamental kind, there would be no point in making a conceptual distinction between role-learning and the learning of a self-concept. A person would *be* his roles, and his self-concept would be his awareness of himself enacting his roles. It is, one supposes, a possibility that there could be social organizations in which the attitudes of the members were so completely satisfied by their role-requirements that there would be no sense of one's self beyond the role, but this is unlikely (cf. Brim and Wheeler, 1966).

It is always possible to identify the self-concept and one's roles by sleight of definition. For example, if everything that a person does, thinks and feels in a social context is his role, there would be little point in making distinctions of the kind that we are making here. If one started with the role we would end with the person (though we would, of course, recognize that the person has more than one role). If we started with the person we would, as we observed his behaviour and made inferences about his attitudes, be discovering his roles.

Social life, however, is not usually so resonant to the ways in which people actually act, think and feel in a social context. In addition to attitudes, there are group norms, and the two are, despite the processes of social learning, seldom two sides of the same coin. Roles, in other words, are parts of social structure and functioning. In actual life, they allow for a good deal of diversity in performance. They are often defined in terms of conforming behaviour, and make few demands on central dispositions, as long as appropriate behaviour is made available. The experience of role-learning, then, is an experience of selecting roles which are personally congenial, if this is possible, and modifying those roles which are involuntary as far as sanctions will permit.

This suggests that an important dimension in role-learning is the degree of importance of the role to the person learning it. If role-behaviour is rewarding, it will tend to be strengthened and to lead to further learning. In this sense, a role could be shaped in a Skinnerian sense by external agencies, and held in place by continued external reinforcements. But the person seems to find satisfaction in shaping as well as being shaped, and once the child has become an agent in social interaction, he will be able to reinforce and inhibit his own conduct by reference to a representation of himself in action. The importance of a role lies not only in the external reinforcements which it offers the person enacting it, but in the relation of the role to his own conception of the kind of person that he is and wishes to become. This 'self-concept' is profoundly influenced by social learning, but, once formed, becomes a source of rewards and punishments in its own right. In the next section, some aspects of the self-concept in childhood will be briefly considered.

3. *The self-concept in childhood*

All of the available studies of the child's development of a sense of himself show the great complexity of the process (see Wylie, 1961 for a good summary of a wide variety of studies, concluding 'there are enough positive trends to be tantalizing . . . but there is a good deal of ambiguity in the results, considerable apparent contradiction among the findings of various studies, and a tendency for different methods to produce different results'.) But despite this complexity, it seems clear that with increasing age, the child becomes able to distinguish descriptive from evaluative aspects of himself with greater precision, to set goals for his own performance, to select and reject behaviour in accordance with personal standards, to show greater ability to explain and justify his conduct, and to communicate personal experience and intentions more effectively. This should not be taken to suggest that the self-concept is the same as the whole structure of personality, the self in action. (See Vol. I, Chapter 6, Section V.) It is a representation of the personality: a map of personal reality rather than the reality itself. Like a map, it does not reproduce its whole subject matter. Like a map, it can be judged in terms of several criteria: accuracy, inclusiveness, explicitness, usefulness. And like a map, its very existence can have a profound effect on the reality that it represents.

As Harry Stack Sullivan (1953) suggests, the self-concept is closely linked with situations involving important and uncertain issues. By providing changing representations of the appearance, performance and potentialities of the person of which it is a part, it offers the possibility of more adequate adaptation to changing circumstances. To the extent to which it is a well-integrated system, it can provide this adaptive service more swiftly and easily. But to what extent the self-concept is a system is difficult to assess. There seem to be marked individual differences in the degree of systematization, and the age-trends are by no means clear.

One age-trend, which raises difficulties for effective integration, is towards differentiation of the self-concept. This is the result of the wider participation of the adolescent and adult in diverse social groupings, often internally and externally in conflict. This differentiation is seen, among other things, in the much larger repertoire of terms used by the older person in describing and evaluating his own personality.

Kelman (1958, 1961) has suggested that there are three distinguishable modes of attitude formation and change. They are *compliance, identification* and *internalization*. The first is related primarily to external rewards and punishments, and tends to change as these change. The second is related to the perceived attitudes of a valued person, and is dependent on the continuance of the social relationship with this person. The third mode, internalization, refers to the integration of the attitude into a central system which is self-reinforcing. This is clearly linked with the self-concept, since a central system of values is not likely to go unrepresented in the self-concept.

Not many theorists have followed Kelman in distinguishing between identification and internalization, partly because the behaviourally inclined theorists have not wished to make distinctions between degrees of internalization, but only in degrees of persistence and generality. The psychoanalytically inclined theorists, on the other hand, have been accustomed to using the concept of identification as a deeply central process. This is because they have focussed on the early identifications with the parents, rather than with later and more transient identifications.

Psychoanalytic theory, in its original Freudian formulation, distinguished between primary and defensive forms of identification. Both of these are with the parents. Primary identification (also known as anaclitic identification – a 'looking-back' to the original identity with the mother) refers to the child taking the mother as the model of appropriate behaviour. She is the source of need satisfaction and identification with her is an indication of the total dependency of the child on her. The nature of this form of learning is difficult to study reasonably objectively insofar as it involves the formation of a self-concept. The child's ability to report on his relationship to the mother is very limited, and one can only speculate on the content of the very early self-concept.

Defensive identification – or, as Anna Freud termed it, identification with the aggressor – refers to the conflict between the male child and his parents at the age of four or five. Freud believed that the boy entered into rivalry with his father for the love of the mother, that this rivalry had a distinctively sexual tone, and that the father either openly or covertly threatened to resolve the conflict by castrating his son. The son typically resolved the conflict by identifying with the father. Later investigators have been distinctly sceptical about the need to postulate a distinct castration anxiety as the lever to bring about acceptance of the father as a model for the son's behaviour. Blum (1952) shows the presence of castration anxiety in a set of college students responding to an ingenious projective test (the Blacky test), but the links with defensive identification are by no means clear. Since Freud (1949) suggests that the extreme painfulness of castration anxiety leads to its total repression, it is clearly not easy for investigation to take place at all.

The intensive study of the conditions determining selection of a model for social learning of a significant kind has suggested many modes of influence. Secord and Backman (1964), for example, distinguish not two but seven determinants of identification. They are (i) *secondary reinforcement* – the learner is frequently rewarded by a person who then becomes a model; (ii) *vicarious reinforcement* – a person is chosen as a model because he receives rewards which are experienced vicariously by the learner; (iii) *withholding of love* – a person is chosen as a model because the learner fears that otherwise the person will withhold his love; (iv) *avoidance of punishment* – a person is chosen as a model because the learner fears the person will otherwise injure him; (v) *status envy* – a person is chosen as a model because he is envied as a recipient of rewards from others; (vi) *social power* – a person is chosen as a model because he has the power to reward (but does not necessarily reward) the learner; (vii) *similarity to the learner* – a person is chosen as a model because the learner perceives that he has a trait similar to one of his own.

These determining factors do not seem to be of equal importance, especially during early childhood. The most important at this period of development are probably the first and third, namely those seen by psychoanalytic theory as primary identification, with a smaller part being played in boys by the fourth (see Sears, Rau and Alpert, 1965).

Several of these factors often act together, and experimental work is beginning to throw light on the relative significance of these modes in different circumstances (e.g. Bandura, Ross and Ross, 1963). It will be noted that a number of the above determinants, such as vicarious reinforcement, clearly imply the process of social comparison, which involves the self-concept. It is characteristic of the operation of the self-concept that it enables forms of learning to take place which then serve to modify it.

Kelman's distinction between identification and internalization draws our attention to the difference between attitudes which are taken over from others, and not fully assimilated, and those which are systematized and centralized. In a later section, the adolescent preoccupation with consistency is emphasized by using the concept of 'ego-identity' rather than self-concept. The latter term tends to smack of the processes of identification with others which give it birth. The former implies a core of independent selfhood.

A person who is a differentiated self – a person in his own right – is able to act intentionally in ways that interfere with the needs of others. By what means is his behaviour to be controlled? External rewards and punishments are of considerable relevance. But we have stressed the growth of central attitudes that guide conduct. Some of these are of special interest in that they evaluate behaviour as desirable or appropriate.

These attitudes are the concern of the next section, which discusses the growth of morality in childhood and adolescence, beginning with an examination of the work of Piaget.

III. THE GROWTH OF MORALITY IN CHILDHOOD AND ADOLESCENCE

1. *The work of Jean Piaget*

Piaget's classic pioneering study (1932) emphasizes moral judgement rather than moral feelings or observed conduct. This is entirely in line with his lifelong interest in the development of knowledge and the ways in which knowledge becomes, through the person's growing experience, more objective and coherent.

The first line of approach adopted by Piaget is the examination of rules as exemplified in children's games. 'All morality consists in a system of rules,' writes Piaget at the beginning of *The Moral Judgment of the Child*, 'and the essence of all morality is to be sought for in the respect which the individual acquires for these rules' (p. 1). The great advantage of taking children's games is that their rules are elaborated by children and not by adults. By playing the game of marbles himself, and by questioning children about it, Piaget noted four phases in the application of rules: (i) a purely individual, motor relationship to the materials of the game: the child may develop characteristic habits or rituals in using these materials, but does not regulate his behaviour by reference to general prescriptions; (ii) between the ages of 2 and 5, the child imitates the behaviour of older players, following the rules that they adopt, but in an individual way; (iii) this is followed by a more co-operative relationship with others in playing, but an unclear formulation of the rules (this is between the ages of 7 and 8 at the beginning of the stage and 11 to 12 at the end); (iv) in the final stage noted by Piaget (who was, it will be remembered, studying fairly young children) the child is able to codify the rules. 'Not only is every detail of procedure in the game fixed, but the actual code of rules to be observed is known to the whole society. There is remarkable concordance in the information given by children of 10–12 belonging to the same class at school, when they are questioned on the rules of the game and their possible variations' (p. 17). By 'society', in this context, Piaget means the age-group.

These stages refer to the application of rules. What of the consciousness of rules? Piaget here distinguishes three very roughly delineated stages which are broadly correlated with the practice of rules. It is around these stages that much of the later research has centred. First, the rules are either not perceived, or are even seen as facts without binding force. Second, 'rules are regarded as sacred and untouchable, emanating from adults and lasting forever. Every suggested alteration strikes the child as a transgression' (p. 18). Finally in the third stage, a rule is seen as co-operatively maintained for the general advantage, and capable of being changed if general opinion is in favour of doing so.

Piaget notes, in the course of studying the rules of games, an interesting sex difference which has not, so far as I am aware, been specifically taken up in the many post-Piagetian studies of moral judgement. This is based on the observation of the games which are preferred by girls, such as hopscotch. These games typically had simpler rules, and the girls preferred to invent new contents for the games, rather than new rules.

The boys appeared to have a strong interest in a legalistic approach, taking an interest in rules for their own sake. In both sexes, however, the same broad trend could be observed, from a complete absence of concern for rules to a flexible use of rules to aid the process of social adaptation. How is one to account for this trend? Partly, it seems, by the development of intelligence. As the child builds up more complex and flexible schemata, he is able to move freely from the consideration of facts to the making of judgements, and then relate these back to the facts. He is able to distinguish between the consequences of an action and the intentions of the actor. This growth of ability to make relevant distinctions is well documented by an ingenious but simple method of investigation used by Piaget with great skill. This consists in devising simple stories, involving children in a familiar setting, engaged in activities on which moral judgements can be made. The children are then asked for their comments on the stories, one at a time.

One set of stories, for example, contrasted children who were disobeying a rule with others who were trying to be helpful. In each case, by accident, the children broke something of value. The helpful children were involved in breakages of more things than the children disobeying rules. In the comments made by children on these stories, it appeared that younger children found difficulty in separating the intentions of the children in the stories from the consequences of their actions. Thus, not only were the helpful children blamed for accidental damage, but they were often seen as deserving more serious punishment than the other children, since the number of objects broken had been greater! Older children interpreted the breakages as accidental, and allocated blame to the children disobeying rules for the breach of rules rather than the accidental breakage.

Piaget obviously feels, in his analysis of the children's replies to his questions, that the development of intelligence is not enough to account for the change towards greater reciprocity and equity in the children's judgements. He finds a simple and striking explanation in the contrasting attitudes of parents and other adults in positions of authority, on the one hand, and groups of children on the other. In their relationships with children, adults are inclined to use simple, somewhat absolute rules, which they back with their very considerable authority. Children, in their relationships with adults, have little choice but to accept the rules, and either obey them or run the risk of being punished.

But in their relationships with one another, children are able to engage in mutual discussion and discovery. The rules can be tested, and their limits modified if the group wishes. This diagnosis of the situation leads Piaget to postulate two major stages of moral development, which he terms 'the morality of constraint' and 'the morality of co-operation'. It may seem that he has committed himself to a rather dogmatic, over-simplified position, but the very close analysis that he gives to his data, from the varied sources of observation, experiment and careful questioning, belies this.

In fact, Piaget has been attempting a most difficult feat – a combination of detailed developmental analysis, derived from a small group of children in Geneva, and broad sociological theory, based on Durkheim's contrast between highly specialized and relatively unspecialized societies. Not surprisingly, the interconnexions creak rather loudly. Nevertheless, a number of interesting trends are revealed. The youngest children are barely able to guide their conduct in the small social world of the family, directed by adult rules which they interpret over-literally. The adolescent, on the other hand, is able to take a variety of points of view, and adapt his judgements accordingly. (Piaget's study stops short of full adolescence, but he takes us up to the threshold, a year or two beyond the first decade of life, and we are left to assume that the progress continues.) The older children, then, are aware of discrepancies and even conflicts in rules and in the applications of rules. They recognize that others may not share one's point of view, because they have a moral perspective of their own. They realize that punishment, though it may be deserved, is not the sole response to a breach of rules.

We begin to see, in the responses of these young people, the implications of a larger society, which they are beginning to understand in part. But as Piaget sharply moves the focus of attention to this society in his last chapter, the reader feels a sense of strain. After the knotty complexity of the actual judgements, it is difficult to move to a wide-ranging contemplation of social evolution and its implications for the development of morality. We find some difficulty in keeping a sense of scale.

It may be for this reason that Piaget's successors have all followed him in close observation and limited experiment with children and adolescents, while some have linked development with socio-economic variables, but few have followed him in his broad sociological speculation and the links between social structure and moral judgement are still seriously under-emphasized. Before we go on to look at some of the later work, it may be useful to recall the two distinguishable themes of Piaget's study. First, he suggests that there are trends in the use of, and understanding of, moral rules. These trends are (i) greater ability to distinguish between the relevant factors involved in moral judgement, for example between intentions of the actor and the consequences of his action; (ii) less emphasis on expiation of misconduct; (iii) greater ability to judge from the standpoints of others involved in the situation. Second, Piaget believed that these trends in moral judgement are influenced by the authority of the adult and the solidarity of the 'peer group'. Adult authority sets constraints on the free understanding of rules, an understanding which must come from participation in setting and modifying rules. The co-operative activity of one's peers enables a reciprocity to develop. Although the transition from one morality to another is gradual, Piaget treats them as being qualitatively different.

2. *Other studies of moral judgement and related topics*

The purpose of this section is to discuss a number of studies of moral judgement and moral conduct. No attempt will be made to give a comprehensive review of the complex literature on moral development, for this has already been done (see, for example, Morris, 1958; Havighurst and Peck, 1960; Kohlberg, 1964; Eppel, 1966; Pease, 1966). Our concern here is with the two questions arising from the work of Piaget: is there a clear line of development in moral judgement, from a rigid and concrete 'morality of constraint' to a flexible and conceptual 'morality of co-operation'? And is there evidence that this trend is largely influenced by a shift from the influence of adults to the influence of one's peers?

The first question is not easy to answer. As Piaget noted, many of the trends found in his study were part of general intellectual growth. These have been corroborated by other investigators. For example, the later studies all document an increase, with age, in the ability to understand more complex moral rules, to allow for individual differences in moral judgement, and to reckon with situational differences. Young children can cope with one set of factors at a time. For example, they can distinguish a category of intention in behaviour, and they can distinguish differences in the consequences flowing from behaviour. But they find difficulty in combining the two categories and establishing varying relationships between them. In short, the development of moral judgement as part of the development of intelligence is well established. (See Vol. I, Chapter 6, Section V.2 for a critical examination of the relation between moral judgement and moral feeling.) It is easy to forget that Piaget's study came relatively early in his formidable list of works and that his own later research throws a good deal of light on the difficulties of moral judgement. We can now see more clearly that Piaget's subjects were experiencing, in their attempts to handle the concepts of moral reciprocity, the kind of difficulty that they encounter in building up conceptions of reciprocal influence in the physical world. Aside from the intellectual problem, there is, of course, the complicating problem of guilt and anxiety associated with parental attitudes to the intentions and consequences in morally relevant situations. But this is another matter.

Piaget's later studies remind us that intellectual development provides the person with a set of abilities that are not wholly integrated and which are sometimes in conflict. Psychoanalytic theories stress even more strongly the ever-present tendency to regression under stress. Morally relevant situations, since they are concerned with the self-concept, and with reward and punishment from 'significant others', are particularly liable to produce regressive tendencies, and the result is that a person who is able to reason formally on a topic of less emotional importance, produces responses that are characteristics of an earlier phase of development.

It is probably this fact about moral judgement that accounts for the extraordinary amount of diversity in the post-Piagetian studies. MacRae, for example, is typical of many of these studies (MacRae, 1954). He found that statistical analysis of data derived from Piaget-type problems yielded three relatively independent groups of responses. Their inter-correlation was extremely low, when age was controlled (varying from 0·10 to − 0·09). These groupings were (i) responses to questions concerned with the evaluation of acts in terms of either intentions or consequences; (ii) responses to questions concerned with attitudes to punishment, contrasting the view that punishment is the inevitable consequence of wrongdoing with the view that punishment is a socially contingent response; (iii) responses to questions concerned with breadth of perspective – that is, ability to take the role of other persons in a situation. This third group of responses was derived from some questions used by Lerner (1937) in his investigation. MacRae added some questions of his own, on what Parsons would call moral universalism (the tendency to maintain general principles in situations in which friendship is involved). This, when age development had been allowed for, also showed very little relationship with the other groups of responses.

It is worth noting that the group studied by MacRae ranged in age from 5 to 14, and that Havighurst and Taba (1949) in an intensive study of moral judgements of young people in a small town in the American Midwest, conclude, 'The ability to apply moral beliefs to an increasing range of conflicting life situations is quite undeveloped at the age of sixteen' (*op. cit.*, p. 95). The picture emerging from these studies is of a gradually developing set of abilities to disentangle morally relevant aspects of complex situations. But at any given age, these abilities do not form a coherent unity; they remain specific to particular situations.

It is perhaps not surprising that the post-Piagetian studies bring out the theme of differentiation in development rather than that of integration. Almost by definition, morally relevant situations involve matters about which it is easy to disagree: principles are to be weighed against inclination, one principle against another, intentions against consequences, and so on. The challenge of moral maturity is to integrate a highly differentiated moral perspective. If signs of differentiation rather than integration are to be found in development up to middle adolescence, this seems no reason for surprise. In later sections, this theme will reappear in the form of the adolescent search for identity.

Perhaps the most substantial work on the development of moral judgement, following on that of Piaget, has been Kohlberg's. In a series of studies, he has tested a six-stage conception of moral development. His six stages, with their leading characteristics, are:

1. Orientation to obedience and possibility of punishment. Egocentric deference to superior power or prestige. Tendency to avoid trouble. 'Objective' responsibility (akin to Piaget's heteronomy).

2. Naïvely egoistic orientation. Right action is that which instrumentally satisfies one's own needs, and occasionally those of others. Awareness of relativism of value to each actor's needs and perspective. Naïve egalitarianism and orientation to exchange and reciprocity.

3. 'Good boy' orientation: that is, orientation to approval and to pleasing and helping others. Conformity to stereotypical images of majority or natural role behaviour, and judgement by intentions.

4. Orientation to authority and maintenance of social order. Orientation to 'doing duty' and to showing respect for authority and maintaining the social order for its own sake. Regard for the earned expectations of others.

5. Contractual legalistic orientation. Recognition of an arbitrary element or starting point in rules or expectations for the sake of agreement. Duty defined in terms of contract, general avoidance of violation of the will or rights of others, and majority will and welfare. Conscience or principle orientation.

6. Orientation not only to actually ordained social rules but to

principles of choice involving appeal to logical universality and consistency. Orientation to conscience as a directing agent and to mutual respect and trust.

In a complex social system, it would seem that only the last stage of moral development is strongly integrative. But there are elements of integration in stages 4 and 5 as well. It remains for further work to see just how clearly these integrative aspects can be delineated.

In commenting on the first question arising from Piaget's work, that of the trends in moral development, we have commented in passing on the second. Some early studies seem to bear out Piaget's view that social influences can facilitate or inhibit development. But they are inclined to look at patterns of authority and equality, rather than at the particular source of these patterns in adults or children. For example, Harrower (1934) compared middle-class children attending a private school with working-class children at a London elementary school. She found that the middle-class children showed very few signs of moral heteronomy, but that these were clearly indicated in the responses of working-class children. She suggested that private-school teachers and middle-class parents are much more inclined to give reasons for their moral judgements than working-class parents or the teachers at elementary schools. Similarly, a study in the United States by Lerner (1937) focussed on the parents' attitudes to their children's moral conduct. Those parents who used physical punishment, and who do not give grounds for the moral rules which they are supporting, are more likely to have children showing heteronomous responses to the Piaget stories. That is, less authoritarian parents tended to rear children who used more autonomous moral judgements.

Many other studies have explored the influence of parents on the attitudes and conduct of their children. The main finding of these, it seems, is that the relationships between parents and their children are extraordinarily complex, and are profoundly influenced by situational factors. The relationships between parents and children tend to be both emotionally intense and free to vary according to the discretion of the individuals concerned. This combination produced a great deal of strongly marked individual differences, and we can add to Tolstoi's dictum that 'all happy families are alike, but each unhappy family is unhappy in its own way', the comment, 'All happy families, too, are happy in their own way'. Recent studies of child-rearing practices (e.g. Sears, Rau, and Alpert, 1965) have used complex scales of attitude and behaviour for studying moral development, and bear out the point made earlier, that moral development is not a unitary concept, but is a loosely knit cluster of attitudes, many of which are not even loose knit, though they may become so at later ages, which have not yet been adequately studied. If this variability characterizes the relationships between parents and children, which are usually described as 'formal' in some sense, then what may we hope to say of the relationships between peers from the point of view of moral development? We certainly cannot say that the studies of peer-group pressures support Piaget's ideas of co-operation as the main form of peer group relationships. Many studies of the operation of group norms in groups of young people (from the classic experiments of Sherif and Asch, described and discussed in Volume III, Chapter 6 to the observational studies described in the section on 'Adolescent Social Groupings') show that intense pressures for uncritical conformity are often generated, so that it is by no means unusual to find cases where parents encourage their children to maintain an autonomous position in the face of peer-group pressures for conformity (in fact, this is probably one of the characteristic child-rearing factors making for a high achievement need). We must, I believe, sum up as follows: Social influences are of great importance in moral development. They provide the 'content' of moral judgements, and also provide a structure within which moral judgements and conduct take place. But the model provided by Piaget is oversimple. It omits the variation in patterns of parental behaviour which can include the encouragement of autonomy as well as the setting of constraints. Nor, as MacRae shows, is there a clear trend in parental attitudes with the increases in the child's age. Authority can be curvilinear in form, and not 'monotone' (for example, an adolescent girl's activities may be in some respects more circumscribed than they were in childhood). The peer-group is not only a source of co-operation, but also of pressure for uncritical conformity. Although Piaget's work remains as a classic introduction to the systematic study of moral judgement in sociological and psychological terms, we are in many ways as uncertain as ever about the nature of moral growth, in so far as it is not just an aspect of intellectual growth in generalization, discrimination and objectivity.

It is, perhaps, of interest that the lack of 'content' in our discussion on moral development has led to a strangely bloodless consideration of trends without much substance or feeling. And yet moral experience is strong in feeling, though the form of development is to get the feeling increasingly under control. The area of moral control that is most striking is that of the sexual and aggressive forms of behaviour. We shall not give much space to aggression in this discussion, but will look carefully at sexual growth and development, which is one important aspect of physical growth in adolescence. In the next section, the focus will be on the main changes that take place, and their relationship to development in social learning.

IV. PHYSICAL GROWTH IN ADOLESCENCE AND ASPECTS OF SOCIAL LEARNING

One of the main difficulties in studying learning and development in adolescence is the bewildering diversity of the individual differences in the age range. As Gesell (1956) observes, 'By the time of adolescence the differences which have become apparent stagger description' (p. 25).

Yet as he goes on to remark, there are discernible patterns in these individual differences. One of the most obvious places to look for such patterns is in the relatively stable processes of physical growth. Although many studies have shown the powerful effects of inadequate nutrition and other deficiencies on physical growth, and it is known that these are socially influenced, it is still true to say that distinctively social influences can do little to alter, except by way of handicapping, the limits of physical growth. Individual differences in physical growth are considerable. If we take the most clear-cut signs of adolescence – the onset of puberty in boys, with the concomitant appearance of pubic and facial hair, the beginning of seminal emissions, the deepening of the voice, and the onset of the menses in girls – we will find typical, non-pathological, variations in age of between 11 and 17 years in boys, and 10 years and 15 years in girls. These physical changes form the basis of all other changes. Although they do not normally disrupt psychological continuity (ego-identity) they provide strikingly different contexts for psychological development.

It is important, though, not to over-stress the rate at which these changes occur. To the student of human development, a godlike perspective is possible in which a year seems like a day. But to the boy or girl growing up, days are much the same length as they are to other people. To some adolescents, in fact, change can seem all too slow, rather than unmanageably fast. Many studies of delinquency report a desperate boredom, which welcomes law-breaking as a diversion.

The most balanced picture is drawn by the small number of

longitudinal studies of child and adolescent development (Kagan and Moss, 1962). These show continuity of development with a 'growth spurt' in early adolescence. Tanner (1961), summarizing some of these studies, writes, 'Perhaps the increments of growth at the cellular level are discontinuous, and proceed by starts and stops; but at the level of bodily measurement, even of single bones measured by X-rays, one can discern complete continuity, with a velocity that gradually varies from one age to another. The adolescent spurt is a constant phenomenon, and occurs in all children, though it varies in intensity and duration from one child to another. In boys it takes place, on the average, from $12\frac{1}{2}$ to 15, and in girls about two years earlier, from $10\frac{1}{2}$ to approximately 13. The peak height velocity reached averages about 4 inches per year in boys and a little less in girls; this is the rate at which the child was growing at about two years old ... The earlier occurrence of the spurt in girls is the reason why girls are bigger than boys from about $10\frac{1}{2}$ to 13 years. Boys are larger than girls by only 1–3 per cent in most body measurements before puberty, so that the girls' adolescent growth spurt soon carries them ahead of the boys. The boys catch up and pass the girls when their greater and probably more sustained adolescent spurt begins to take effect, and they finish some 10 per cent larger in most dimensions' (pp. 17–19).

The term 'spurt' is, of course, to be taken in the context of the twenty-year-long development cycle that brings an infant to early adulthood. But even on the day-to-day scale of experience, the 'growth spurt' can be a challenge to the growing child, partly because it constantly shifts the body image (one of the most fundamental sources of personal security; Schilder, 1951) and partly because of the individual differences in the phasing and rate of growth. The problem of differential times and rates of growth is particularly great with the learning of adolescent sex-roles. For example, consider three different boys entering on puberty. If they are acquaintances, they are likely to find that they do this at widely different times. They are also likely to respond with different attitudes, stemming from different models and early emotional experiences. One boy may experience the bodily changes of puberty as deeply shameful, and try to conceal what has happened even from those closest to him. Another may relieve the tensions of sexual development by frequent masturbation, related to a mixture of homosexual and heterosexual fantasy. A third boy may immediately increase the intensity and variety of the heterosexual relationships that he has already established, and soon begin to engage in sexual intercourse

(Schofield, 1965, gives interesting indications of the range of variation).

All of these differences in attitudes and values are within the normal range of early adolescent behaviour in sex roles. It is because of these very varied responses to the 'same stage of physical growth' that programmes of sex education have been difficult to establish in schools, which traditionally divide their pupils into 'year groups'. Tanner, in the work already cited, criticizes these age-groupings as being too narrow for many educational purposes. The criticism seems especially apt in the case of sexual development, because it occupies such a salient position in the interests of adolescents. The combination of extreme heterogeneity of sexual growth and attitudes and high social importance placed on maturity of development produces strong and even explosive tensions in groups of young people, and it is not surprising that many traditional teachers have refused to become involved in the process of educating young people to understand the nature and significance of sexual growth.

What kinds of relationships are there between fundamental species-wide processes of development (of the 'critical period' variety discussed in Volume I, and in Chapters 2 and 4 of this volume) and social learning, so far as sexual development is concerned? After all, we have referred to the learning of sex roles and the possible relevance of educational programmes, assuming that individual differences can arise both from social learning and what is commonly called maturation.

It is difficult, if not impossible, to tease out the processes of maturation from learning in the growth of sexual attitudes and behaviour. Confronted with the formidable complexity of sexual behaviour, and its tendency to link up with many other forms of human behaviour (the variety of human activities termed 'sexual' by psychoanalytic writers is a good indication of this), students of sexual development have tended to form contrasting and often conflicting schools. One very influential school, now somewhat weakening in the face of ethological evidence, is that which sees many of the most important aspects of sexual attitudes and activities as being the result of cultural differences.

The most well-known exponent of this view has undoubtedly been Margaret Mead (1935, 1949). In a comparative study of three New Guinea tribes – the Arapesh, Tchambuli, and Mundugumor – Mead argued that a whole range of possibilities of sexual temperament was expressed. The Arapesh showed a pattern of gentle nurturance, and did not expect women to have a different sexual temperament from men.

The Mundugumor, a tribe with a tradition of cannibalism, also expected much the same attitudes from men and women, but these were aggressive and suspicious. The Tchambuli showed a more complex pattern. They too had been cannibals in the recent past, and the pattern had then been one of male dominance. But with the suppression of cannibalism by a Western colonial power, and the consequent weakening in the position of men in tribal life, the women had become more dominant. Thus, the traditional Western pattern of male activity and female passivity had originally been expressed by the Tchambuli, but had latterly been reversed.

Mead has attempted to relate these findings to the sexual problems of Western industrial society (and particularly the United States). Her view is that beliefs in certain sexual attitudes and activities as 'natural' must be given up, and replaced by a recognition that these are matters of cultural standards, influenced by historical changes.

In more recent work (e.g. Tanner and Inhelder, 1960), Mead has placed greater emphasis on maturational stages, and has attempted to integrate three levels of analysis – the rather conservative processes of maturation linking human beings with the infra-human, the more variable elements of salient zones on which attention focusses at different phases of growth (her views on this middle level are much influenced by psychoanalytic reconstructions of human development), and the level of attitude and behaviour that lends itself to modification by social learning.

This seems a promising approach, and the emphasis on differing levels, with varying 'degrees of freedom' for the impact of learning, is one that has been used throughout this work. A related, rather simpler approach is that of Robert Havighurst (1953) who uses the concept of 'developmental task'. This implies a set of required skills, forms of knowledge and attitudes, related to healthy human development.

The nine tasks for the adolescent period (12 to 18 years) include four that seem clearly linked with sexual growth. They are (i) accepting one's physique and a masculine or feminine role; (ii) establishing new relations with age-mates of both sexes; (iii) gaining emotional independence of parents and other adults; and (iv) preparing for marriage and family life.

The educational system seems to have placed far more weight on the other five tasks: achieving assurance of economic independence, selecting and preparing for an occupation, developing intellectual skills and concepts necessary for civic competence, desiring and achieving socially responsible behaviour, and building conscious values in harmony with an adequate scientific world-picture. If this is in fact true, it would be understandable that large, relatively impersonal social organizations with problems of maintaining national standards of effectiveness should place greater emphasis on the knowledge and skills that fit their members for participation in the wider society, rather than those which are relevant to the family. There are, of course, other reasons why schools and colleges have found it difficult to engage in sex education, and these will be discussed in a later section. The educational implications of sexual development have to be placed in the context of development of the person as a whole. This is the topic to which we now turn.

V. THE ADOLESCENT SEARCH FOR IDENTITY

So far, we have been examining the impact of rapid physical growth on the developing personalities of adolescents, with special emphasis on the challenge of sexual development and learning. The sex-role, one of the most important social roles, is strongly influenced by social learning, and is mediated by a number of different persons, including parents, brothers, sisters, friends and others. Between these persons, who serve as 'models' for learning, there may well be contrast or conflict, since cultural diversity is the norm rather than the exception. This raises important questions: How do young people cope with these differences? What implications do these contrasts and conflicts have for healthy individual development?

In the second section of this chapter, pre-adolescent social learning was discussed in terms of two themes: the learning of social roles, which enable a person to play an acceptable part with others in a social situation, and the acquisition of a self-concept, serving as an emotionally-charged central point of reference in social behaviour. The self-concept was seen as a person's ability to reflect on his own attributes and performance in relation to those of others. The spontaneous tendency to relate one's own activities to those of others, and to seek to bring the two into balance when subjectively unacceptable discrepancies are noted, is one of the more important, but often unrecognized, conditions of social learning. In Charles Madge's term, used in a different context, it is part of 'society in the mind' (Madge, 1964). By the stage of adolescence, it is often a centre of personal and social conflict – with the desire for social conformity on the one side and an aspiration after individuality on the other. This section attempts to document and clarify the conflict by looking at empirical studies of adolescent attitudes and behaviour, but even more by paying attention to the concepts used by behavioural scientists to study adolescents. Our first problem is with the concepts that have to do with central functioning. The most influential among these have been self, self-concept, and ego-identity. Psychologists have been divided over the need to use concepts of this kind, and many of those who are experimentally inclined have done their best to avoid concepts that cannot be unequivocally linked with observable behaviour. In our discussion here, we do not go this far, though it must be granted that the 'anchoring' of central concepts to observable behaviour provides a useful discipline, for it can seldom be sustained for long.

Once we fully accept the implications of social learning, and realize that socially-related schemata and strategies are built up from social perception and interaction (often using the 'short cut' of observational learning from social models), we see that the self is inextricably linked with social relationships in its origins, and only extricates itself partially in reflective thought in later years. This being so, one's self is a social object (person) to the reflective schemata, and any terms coined to encompass the range of activities of this reflective activity are likely to be difficult to keep separate. As Lynd puts it, in her perceptive study of shame and its connexion with the search for identity, 'The self goes by many names, and the word self has many meanings. Almost every psychologist has certain terms referring to the self he defines elaborately, others which he slips in as if everyone knew what they meant' (1958, p. 166). And later, 'Self and ego are still more slippery in usage. The terms slide around like the shiny balls under glass in a child's puzzle, which no matter how the board is tilted refuse to stay lodged in any particular hollows' (p. 167). It would be pleasant if one could guarantee that this slipperiness will be avoided here, but all that can be offered is a reason for this confusing state of affairs. This is that the strategies and schemata that we infer from the observed behaviour (including verbal reports) of others are mediated by our own strategies and schemata. When we try to form a logic from the behaviour of others (which psychologists, among other students of human behaviour are trying to achieve), we do so by virtue of our own reasoning abilities, into which we fit the data obtained from observation. The tendency to attribute our own processes of reasoning to others, and especially to impute to others the reflective operations that we are ourselves using, has been called the psychologist's fallacy.

But to return to the concept of identity. It is perhaps not surprising that the psychologists who have devoted most attention to this are the clinical psychologists, like Erikson (1963), who are particularly sensitive to the problems of achieving independence in the face of the anxieties provoked by insecurity. Erikson tends to move readily from identity as a state of integration of the higher-level schemata representing the self (in other words, the 'ego' of psychoanalytic writers) to a *sense* of identity as a person's awareness of his own degree of integration or otherwise.

The following passage, from *Childhood and Society* (1963) gives both senses. In discussing the developmental stage of early adolescence, Erikson writes, 'The integration now taking place in the form of ego-identity is . . . more than the sum of childhood identifications. It is the accrued experience of the ego's ability to integrate all identifications with the vicissitudes of the libido, with the aptitudes developed out of endowment, and with the opportunities offered in social roles. The sense of ego-identity, then, is the accrued confidence that the inner sameness and continuity prepared in the past are matched by the sameness and continuity of one's meaning for others, as evidenced in the tangible promise of a "career" ' (pp. 261–262).

It might be thought that the 'ability to integrate all identifications' is itself no mean feat, but to have a three-stage integration between basic needs (libido), identifications with others, and the opportunities of social roles seems a major achievement. It is with this kind of achievement that David Riesman (1951) has been particularly concerned, in his work on autonomy. In a strict sense, autonomy is indefinable, because it essentially takes the form of personal uniqueness. But Riesman goes far towards giving us some sense of its meaning, by detailed illustrations of the difference between autonomous activity and attitudes, and the much more common patterns of social adjustment. Riesman's main point is that autonomous activity is of great social importance, and is deeply satisfying for the person (though he is not in any way sentimental about the joys of a form of activity that is often deeply disturbing and painful). Since autonomy requires unremitting intelligence and vigilance, people settle for some form of social adjustment. Riesman describes three types of adjustment: 'tradition-direction', 'inner direction' and 'other-direction'. These are learned patterns of adaptation to social requirements expressed in on-going roles. (Riesman stresses, by the way, that no actual individual will be purely 'tradition-directed' or 'other-directed', even less is he likely to be wholly autonomous. He is using a first approximation to the complex trends that exist among the millions of diverse individuals in social life. In short, he is concerned primarily with a set of broad patterns that constitute different types of 'social character'. Each individual shows idiosyncratic variations from th's set of characters.)

The tradition-directed character is one who is unreflectively guided by specific rituals and customs acquired by social learning from elders (whether parents, other adult relatives, tutors or older peers). These traditional forms of behaviour are not incompatible with deviance, but this will characteristically be followed by shame or guilt, and not by questioning the grounds for the tradition.

The inner-directed character has more flexibility, but is 'gyroscopically' kept in balance by broad values acquired in the early years of life, in the family. These values are not critically examined, but form the ends, to which varied means can be adapted.

The other-directed character is particularly sensitive to the current behaviour and attitudes of selected reference groups (these groups are, typically, peers with whom the person is in daily contact). Since these forms of behaviour will vary as a function of changes in the social environment (though the source of change can clearly not itself be 'other-directed'), the other-directed character is extremely volatile.

To return to autonomy after this brief survey of the three main forms of social adjustment, the autonomous person, as Riesman describes him, has been influenced by all these factors – tradition, family origins, and the views of contemporaries – but has been able to transcend and integrate them.

The arguments used by Fromm, Riesman and Erikson have one important point in common. They see the achievement of ego-identity as of great importance to healthy personal development. The 'crisis of identity' (to use Erikson's striking phrase) brought about in adolescence by the processes of rapid and diverse change is considered by these theorists to be of the first importance in the study of social learning and development. One of the criticisms that they have made of social development in modern industrial society is that the adolescent may well fall between two stools. He is not able to move imperceptibly from childhood to adulthood, as in the Samoan society of a past generation described so memorably by Mead (1928). Neither is he given the security of a clear-cut and dramatic transition from one age-group to another. Fyvel (1963), for example, has analysed the changes in social structure, and in particular the changing role of the family, in these terms. He concludes that while some of the more stable and intelligent young people may gain from the fluidity of modern society, and enjoy more independent and exciting lives, many others are bewildered and confused, and likely to become (to use his own key phrase) 'insecure offenders'.

Zweig (1963), in a study of a rather older and more privileged group – the university students of Oxford and Manchester – suggests that many students are under greater inner pressure to live up to complex and demanding standards. He concludes, after examining the varied conceptions of the 'ideal student', that students do attempt to live up to this conception, which is very personal in its emphasis on qualities of character (self-confident, acceptably dominant, carefree, sociable, altruistic, able to control himself in the interests of his commitments). The difficulty of developing integration around such a high standard may indicate (Zweig considers) that the aims are too severe, too laden with cares and responsibility.

While Zweig does not go so far as to suggest that students are experiencing a crisis of identity, he certainly gives the impression that continued healthy development would take the form of a well balanced and integrated personality. In this sense, he is at one with some of the other students of development. One of his 'tentative suggestions' for improvement of the universities is 'an obligatory course of practical psychology, including training in relieving tension, and practical hints on uniting thought and feeling in integration of the personality' (p. 211).

What happens, then, we are inclined to ask, if ego-identity is not achieved? Riesman sets his concept of autonomy against the three forms of social adjustment. Thus, if one has not achieved autonomy, one is either an adjusted person or an anomic one (in Durkheim's sense of being unable to fit in to a socially acceptable niche, but not autonomous). Erikson sets his concept against role confusion, or diffusion. This takes several forms: an escape into deviant roles (delinquent, beatnik, hipster), an over-identification with celebrities, a loss of personal identity in a strong group of contemporaries, an anxious moving from group to group. Some of these expressions of confusion seem closely akin to the self-alienation extensively documented by Fromm in a number of influential studies (e.g. Fromm, 1955). In these studies, self-alienation is classified as a pathological state of uncertainty about the authenticity of one's experience. Unlike schizophrenia, which is the extreme of rejection of social experience in favour of isolation, self-alienation is characterized by a flight to compulsive sociability. Without others, the person feels empty, meaningless, and anxious. The alienated person is often a strong 'conformist', because the approval of his group is the only source of 'reality' for him.

It is not surprising that these interrelated 'identity' theories have been influential with laymen, to a greater degree than with professional psychologists. The contrasts are easily recognized in everyday experience, and are dramatic in their simplicity – autonomy versus adjustment, identity versus role diffusion, maturity versus self-alienation. And since all of these theories allow ample scope for social learning and re-learning, they are meliorist. This is least true of Erikson, who is essentially a developmentalist, seeing the role of social factors as constituting either obstacles or opportunities for a deep-rooted process, but this still gives much room for improvement. As he writes in *Growth and Crises of the Healthy Personality* (1953), 'We have learned not to stunt a child's growing body with child labour; we must now learn not to break his growing spirit by making him the victim of our anxieties. If we will only learn to let live, the plan for growth is all there.'

But is it? The evidence for a developmental drive towards integration, or identity, is by no means clear. The current emphasis in many scientific fields is on systems of forces – and most of the psychological theories that are currently influential are inclined to stress the unity of personality. There is no doubt whatever that many part-functions of the person have the properties of self-maintaining systems (e.g. Cannon's studies of homeostatic mechanisms). But the tight inter-connexions of these part-systems are by no means clearly discernible on the level of, say, attitude formation and change, even though the various balance theories of Heider, Osgood, and Festinger have marshalled interesting evidence to show tendencies towards equilibrium among these structures. It seems that there are striking individual differences in the strength of the tendency towards equilibrium. In some people, the integration is achieved at the expense of accommodation to the environment (e.g. in paranoid states, and, to some extent, in the 'authoritarian personalities' studied by Adorno *et al.*, 1950). An important dimension in the assessment of persons is flexibility-rigidity (Cattell, 1957 and 1965, discussed by Warburton in Volume III, Chapter 3). The ego-identity described by Erikson is one that is compatible with adequate reality-testing. But the problem of combining the necessary flexibility to cope with the characteristically high rate of change in modern social life with the achievement of identity is one that must not be underestimated.

A relatively recent topic of study in social psychology has been the linking of identity with effective performance within a role. It will be recalled that this is one of the three levels of effective ego-identity mentioned by Erikson, the other two being the integration of identifications, and the relating of identity to basic personality needs. A pioneering examination of role identity is provided by Foote and Cottrell (1955) in *Identity and Interpersonal Competence*. This work takes a strongly interactionist line, and sees identity as the motivational aspect of role-performance. Interpersonal competence – or social skills as we term them here – is acquired, as Foote and Cottrell see the matter, by practice in role interaction, learning from the 'feedback' that is an established feature of social interaction generally. Both Foote and Cottrell have become distinguished practitioners of role-playing as an educational method for improving interpersonal competence.

The most recent systematic study of role-identity is McCall and Simmons' book *Identities and Interactions* (1966). This concept is defined as 'the character and the role that an individual devises for himself as an occupant of a particular social position' (*op. cit.*, p. 67). The authors believe that a concept of this kind can be helpful in several ways: it can account for the 'fine texture' of actual role performance and throw light on the varying criteria that people use for assessing their performances. 'In fact, they give the very *meaning* to our daily routine, for they largely determine our interpretations of the situations, events, and other people we encounter. By providing us with plans of action and systems of classification, our role-identities go far to determine the objects of our environment, their identity and meaning. This is particularly true of persons as objects, both ourselves and others' (pp. 69–70).

As this extract suggests, one of the functions of role-identities is to enable discriminations to be made, and not only to enable positions to be taken. This is a point made earlier in the discussion of role-learning. A person is not completely free to maintain any role-identity that he chooses, because it may not be acceptable to others who are holding certain expectations of his identity within the role. Where a person's role-identity is accepted by others, we can speak (with McCall and Simmons) of *role-support*. Adolescence can be seen in these terms as a particularly important phase of social learning, in which new role-identities, including the role-identity of 'adolescent', are being established and claims to role-support are being made. During this period, the nature and range of the roles open to a person become increasingly evident, and the subtle interaction of personal qualities (abilities and attitudes) and social factors becomes a matter for discussion and reflexion.

It is an ever-present possibility that role-identities are woven together into a well-integrated ego-identity. But the possibility may not always be translated into actuality. This may not interfere with the continued development of high-level social skills within the separate roles taken on by a person. But the links between identity of the person and the skills available to him may well be closer than one thinks. For example, social situations are often precariously balanced between routine and high drama. As Goffman has so unforgettably shown, in a diverse series of examples (Goffman, 1959) the impressions on which social encounters are based are as open to disruption as the more elaborate convention of the theatre. People can forget their lines, or respond to the wrong cues, or fail to appear at the right time. The skill to deal with such eventualities may be developed within single roles, but frequently seems to be the fruit of a social perceptiveness that transcends individual roles and expresses the complete person. The ideal of the Christian gentleman, as one looks back on it, was very much concerned with the discovery of a self-forgetful, altruistic, but integrated person, well able to deal with the unexpected, because he had grown beyond the limits of particular roles to become a person. It is, of course, a familiar irony that the subtle and difficult procedures for helping the gentleman to grow, lost their sensitivity with time and hardened into a series of training routines for producing insensitivity and complacency, so that the word 'gentleman' is now irremediably tarnished.

In closing this section, it is perhaps worth commenting on the relationship that seems to exist between ego-identity, role-identities, and social skills. A person could have a strongly developed sense of ego-identity with only a modest development of social skills. The intellectual skills needed for bringing the diverse facets of one's behaviour and experience into a unity are not of the same order as social skills. This seems to be the reason for the powerful image, in Western culture, of the fool, who is derided by his fellows, and lacks the most elementary ability to accept established social conventions, but has a deep insight into the human condition, his own and that of others.

It may be that we are touching on aspects of introversion and extraversion here. In Jung's original treatment of these terms, they referred to a flow of energy to the inner world, on the one hand, and the outer world, on the other. Eysenck, in a variety of recent studies (e.g. 1967) suggests that introversion–extraversion is a psychological continuum, or dimension, linked with neurophysiological conditions of sensitivity and persistence. If, as Eysenck believes, the person at the introverted end of the dimension is characterized by high and persistent states of activation, highly sensitive to stimuli, it seems entirely possible that he would develop a number of defensive procedures to protect him from excessive irritation and uncertainty. One of these might well be the systematic development of awareness, especially awareness of one's own personality. This, of course, would be ego-identity.

Role-identity, as we have seen, is a more specialized concept than ego-identity, and points to the coherence of a person's involvement in a single role. Social skills can relate either to a person's whole range of social relationships, focussing on his abilities in maintaining and developing these, or can refer, more narrowly, to competence in the social relationships required in the performance of a particular role. In the next section, the development of social skills in adolescence will be further discussed.

VI. THE DEVELOPMENT OF SOCIAL SKILLS IN ADOLESCENCE

It may be useful to begin with some comments on some unfortunate associations of the word, skill, which may lead to misunderstandings of the nature and implications of social skills. Technical skills, of the kind involved in handling instruments, tools and physical materials, are very appropriately manipulative. The skilled operator selects his materials to serve the ends that he chooses, or is committed to achieving. He extends his perceptions with instruments, and his limbs with tools. Every craft, from the humblest to the highest, has its own code of conduct. Tools should be handled with care, instruments should be kept accurate, and materials selected and processed according to the job in hand. This code does not, however, concern itself with the interests or welfare of the materials, because they are inanimate. The sole concern is with the competence of the performance, and extreme competence has a grace and beauty of its own, reflected in the outcome (see Chapter 4).

Social skills immediately raise the question: are they manipulative? Is the skilled person *really* friendly and concerned, or is he assuming the outward behaviour in order to achieve his own purposes? The inanimate materials of the craftsman or the operator are not able to ask these questions. But they loom very large in social life, especially in those social relationships that are 'diffuse' or 'discretionary', that is, personal.

These questions are not so often asked in 'task-centred' social activities, where people are working together to a common goal. In

N

these activities, people are not looking at one another, but at the ways in which they hope to achieve a mutually satisfying outcome. People, including children and adolescents, will recognize and value an effective organizer, a person who knows how to start things off, to keep them going along the right lines, to deal effectively but acceptably with people who deviate or delay, and, not least, how to stop.

These skills have been extensively studied, especially by the socio-metric school, deriving from Moreno (Moreno, 1953; related succinctly to education in a British study by Evans, 1961). It is clear that they are closely related to opportunities for observing and practising them in a congenial but critical setting. 'Leadership training' has become an established feature of management and administrative education (e.g. Rice, 1966) and appears to have a definite, if limited, effectiveness.

Social skills, then, are properly named, and when the ways in which they are learned are more fully and widely understood, it is less likely that their systematic study and cultivation will be seen as the encourage-ment of a manipulative, Machiavellian approach. It is useful to make a rough distinction between social knowledge, or breadth of perspective, and effectiveness in social relationships. This is analogous to the dis-tinction between input and output, between perception and motor activity, or 'knowing about' and 'knowing how'. The growth of social knowledge, or perspective, will be considered first.

The main change here in the period of adolescence is a great step forward in gaining a conceptual understanding of a social system, with different types of strata, including social classes, and vertical divisions into functional groupings, such as occupations. This is typically the achievement of middle to late adolescence, and studies of occupational choice (e.g. Veness, 1962) and knowledge of social classes (Himmelweit *et al.*, 1952) show that this understanding of the structure and function-ing of society still has far to go.

A corollary of the increased understanding of social organization is an interest in and growing knowledge of other societies, and the ways in which these compare with one's own society. These not only include contemporary societies, but societies as they have functioned at different times. There is a growing knowledge of trends in social relationships in one's own society, and some of their possible implications.

This widening of perspective encounters formidable difficulties in achieving a reasonable sense of proportion and level of accuracy. This is because the social reality of modern society is enormously complex and volatile. This makes understanding extremely difficult, even for an objective professional observer (see, for example, the comments of Sampson in the revised edition of his *Anatomy of Britain Today*, 1965). The adolescent, by comparison, is a somewhat prejudiced amateur.

On the other hand, of course, these rapid changes in the social system of modern societies have focussed public attention on social structure and function, and the behavioural sciences are themselves the beneficiaries of this greater attention. Slowly, as these sciences grow, and confidence is established in their contribution to our collective knowledge, material is drawn from them to feed in to the educational system. From formal lectures on civics, based on somewhat unreal assumptions about the amount of participation in public affairs required of the citizen, the schools have moved briskly to vigorous discussion, project work, and reading in social studies. The process of systematic self-scrutiny (to use Foote and Cottrell's phrase, 1955) is still in its early days in Britain. But it is already clear that the appetite for learning about social life, in documentary and fictional form, is almost insatiable.

This growth of social perspectives supplements the earlier learning of the fine texture of roles in the immediate social groupings to which the child belongs. There are probably few adolescents, even the most informed and intelligent, who are completely at ease in relating their own social groups systematically to the surrounding neighbourhood, the region of which this is a part, one's own country, and finally the international society, in so far as it exists. But the ability to integrate these social structures into a rough but coherent system seems to grow sharply (see references to Jahoda's work in Chapter 14).

Three limiting factors on the continued growth of perspective in adolescence seem to be (i) difficulty in co-ordinating the rather large number of elements needed to handle information about a large, complex and changing social system. This is an information-processing problem, and only slow progress has been made in developing school subjects that will contribute significantly to its solution. The lack of adequate methods of gathering and disseminating information means that most people ignore or seriously distort extremely important information about social change. (ii) Part of the reason for this may be anxiety about confronting change, rather than the sheer inadequacy of our knowledge and systems of communication. Fromm, in particular (1942, 1955) has drawn attention to the 'fear of freedom' found in many large societies. He sees this fear as being linked with the growth of authoritarian régimes, of simple political ideologies, and the forcible suppression of social differences. All of these have one thing in common: they promise to make life very much easier to understand. This need for 'cognitive simplicity' is by no means characteristic of all members of modern society, young or old, but is particularly often found in the type of personality that has been dubbed 'the authoritarian personality' (Adorno *et al.*, 1950; summarized and discussed in both Brown, 1965 and Madge, 1963). The work associated with the study of this personality type draws attention to the close dependence of knowledge and behaviour. (iii) This leads to the third factor limiting the growth of social perspective, namely, the problem in modern societies of gaining balanced participation of their members in decision and implementation of policy. Where the person is not required, or encouraged, to exercise some form of responsibility in social, economic or political affairs, he has no incentive to develop a more complex perspective. This does not mean that he may not develop the perspective first, and then demand the enlarged range of responsibility that he can now envisage. But the relationship is two-way.

We have not as yet considered the development of the 'output' skills of social conduct. These can be summarized quite briefly. First, the adolescent becomes more adept than the child at dealing with complex social situations: for example, switching rapidly in a large group from one role-relationship to another without severe disturbance. Second, he is less easily thrown off balance by unexpected changes in a social situation, because he has more flexible expectations and a wider behavioural repertoire within each social role, and greater ease in anticipating breakdowns in social arrangements. Third, he can deal effectively with a larger number of situations, including situations involving 'strangers'. Fourthly, these skills enable him, usually in concert with a small group of friends, to initiate changes in social arrangements, often in the light of cogent criticisms of inadequacies in the existing arrangements. Fifth, he is able to sustain social interaction for a longer time without 'dropping out of role'.

Because of these developments in social skill, which are very evident to those adults who work closely with adolescents, the adolescent is permitted to enter groupings of adults on more or less equal terms. The effectiveness of adolescent social skills, especially at the present time, commonly leads those adults who are not able to see the 'fine texture' of the behaviour of young people to make two mistakes. First, they are inclined to exaggerate the degree of skill actually possessed by adolescents, and to expose them to situations that are so unpredictable and demanding that the skills break down, and produce embarrassment and later difficulty. This is most obviously seen in the area of personal relationships between the sexes. Second, they are often over-defensive in the face of adolescent criticisms of existing social arrangements and adolescent social initiative. It seems important for adults to remember that young people are to a considerable extent self-trained in some of the more complex social skills. They are by no means fully aware of the advantages of adult rituals and ceremonials, and often make ill-informed and superficial judgements about them. Again, initiatives taken by the relatively unskilled are likely to be somewhat unbalanced, and this is certainly true of many adolescent social initiatives, as any parent and teacher can testify.

These considerations serve as a reminder that the development of adolescent social skills is by no means systematic, and that often it is found that enlarged and critical social perspectives are not matched by equal achievements in social conduct (this is still true of adults, of course). The formal aspects of education have not shown much recognition of the need for systematic development of these skills, and it is only very recently that social education has received some measure of official acceptance. One of the major difficulties has been the problem of analysing, assessing and teaching social skills. Progress has been slow, but there are very recent and encouraging indications of activity in the behavioural sciences, focussing particularly on analysis and measurement (e.g. Lunzer, 1967; Kellmer Pringle, 1966; and, for a most interesting analysis of social skills in terms of complex motor skills, see Argyle, 1967).

While the formal recognition of social skills and their development has been inadequate, their recognition by informal groupings of young people has been sustained and appreciative. Have these groupings in fact grown into a relatively integrated 'adolescent culture', providing social education?

VII. ADOLESCENT SOCIAL GROUPINGS

The contrast between young and old is one of the most ancient social distinctions. Non-literate societies commonly group their young men and women into a clearly demarcated section of tribal society. So the idea of a 'sub-culture' of adolescents is not in any sense an invention of twentieth-century industrial society. If anything, it might be argued that the fragmentation of modern society is so great, owing to the specialization of work for industrial and commercial purposes, that age-grades are *less* noticeable than in traditional societies.

This is worth keeping in mind, because some of the comments on 'youth culture' are distinctly lacking in historical or sociological perspective. Frequently the contrast is drawn between two or at most three generations and their experiences in growing to adulthood. As if this were not restrictive enough, there is an additional tendency to idealize the past at the expense of the present.

The problem is, then, to get behind the welter of opinions to some reasonably well-established facts about social groupings of young people. Unfortunately there has, until recently, been a paucity of fact, and such studies as we have available are often cross-sections of a rapidly moving process, and include limited or unusual groupings (for example, the studies of delinquent sub-cultures and the surveys of one particular age-group, such as that of Douvan and Adelson). An interesting example of a small-scale study that may have wide implications is Coleman's recent study of ten high schools in the Chicago region (Coleman, 1961).

Although Coleman calls his book *The Adolescent Society* it must not be supposed that modern society has produced a rigidly homogeneous sub-culture to which most of its young people belong. Coleman's study has been purely exploratory, and concerned with the leadership roles among informal groupings of students in the ten high schools studied. He has shown that although the schools vary quite markedly, with some of the student groups placing more weight on standards of scholarship than others, there is a tendency for the 'peer groups' in each school to produce a set of values and associated activities that are characteristic of the students rather than the school. In other words, the picture that emerges from his study is akin in many respects to that drawn by industrial sociologists (e.g. Lupton, 1963) of the informal groupings of workers in modern factories and offices.

Coleman did not set out to test the hypothesis that there is a coherent adolescent society, with a certain amount of 'pluralism' in its values and activities, and his study leaves the matter rather open. It is likely that broadly similar circumstances within different schools produce broadly similar responses from the students. The contrast between the weight placed by the school on educational achievement and the weight placed by the students on pleasant appearance, friendly personality, and 'not working too hard' is a fairly familiar one (see the chapter in Volume III by Hargreaves which examines such value-contrasts in detail within one English school). In some respects, the question of whether a series of peer groups can in some sense be regarded as a peer *culture* is rather like the question of the 'reality' of social classes in modern industrial society. Both questions remain substantially unanswered.

The reason for this is partly a matter of definition. As Gross showed (Gross, 1953) in an ingenious study of people's perceptions of social stratification in Minneapolis, the form of the question often suggests a particular kind of answer, when the materials to which the question relates are rather complex and poorly integrated. Thus, what appeared to be substantially similar questions about social stratification elicited very varied responses which were not at all amenable to reduction to a single overall scheme. But although one is impressed by such evidence, it seems likely that underneath this wide range of contextual reference (which we have called 'the fine-textured response') there are broad themes of a more integral kind. The problem is essentially one of showing the precise links between the broad integrative themes and the varied and sometimes contradictory responses.

In this task, the mass media play an interesting role in suggesting integrative themes of great specificity. That is, their message is often of the most stereotyped nature, but they present their materials in very specific form. This is most obviously so when the materials are sharply controversial or dramatic. The Mod and Rocker disturbances of recent years, for example, were typically presented as characteristic of a whole age-group, and not only of small and often deviant groupings.

This tendency of the media to 'homogenize' an otherwise rather diffuse and fragmented grouping is very striking, and we must not forget that the media are not merely a response to perceived needs of the consumers and to the technical requirements of the media themselves (well discussed by Boorstin, 1963, and McLuhan, 1964). They are also, within limits, establishing norms and characteristic patterns of behaviour.

The limits are, it seems, rather narrow, since the influence of direct reference groups, such as families, school groups, and the peer groups themselves are strong. This is brought out in a variety of studies, and particularly in the extensive survey of American adolescents conducted by Douvan and Adelson. Here, the rootedness of these young people in a solid culture of family and neighbourhood was very evident, and there was a clear-cut sex difference of quite a traditional form. That is, the boys emphasized autonomy – the achieving of personal independence – while the girls emphasized the achievement of success in personal relationships. This survey showed that adolescents in a nation-wide sample showed broadly the same aspirations and attitudes. What, then, are we to make of all this? Are adolescents gaining a relatively unified perspective in a youth culture, which is given up as they grow older and move into more fragmented groups of young adults? The answer is by no means clear. It seems likely that the factors producing similarity between young people are not interactive in nature, or the result of common social norms imposed on young people by outside social agents, such as parents, or teachers. The probable answer lies in the common social situation of young people. They are not so much responding to one another, as to the developmental tasks described in an earlier section.

It would be unwise to sharpen this discussion overmuch, by claiming that an influence such as peer group norms is completely unimportant, or that developmental tasks are really nothing but group roles taken on by adolescents as aspiring members of a 'youth culture'. These factors are all of some importance, and the research studies so far have done little more than show the diversity of the factors operating in adolescent social learning. Not much can be said as yet about the relative strength of these factors. The only doubt that we have been trying to cast is on the conception of a cohesive 'society' of several million adolescents, actively shaping a set of social institutions which in some sense stand outside or against the institutions of the larger society..

And by stressing the 'common situation' of adolescents, one does not wish to deny the extraordinary diversity of attitudes and behaviour found among young people. Obviously such comparative terms as 'similar' and 'different'imply a point of reference and a scale of measurement. One of our main difficulties in looking at adolescents is that we lack a generally agreed set of reference points and scaling units. In this respect, as observers of adolescents, we are like adolescents themselves. The reference points are most easily found in the immediate groupings of crowds, gangs and smaller friendship groups (well documented in a recent book on adolescent reference groups by the Sherifs; Sherif and Sherif, 1964).

VIII. EDUCATIONAL IMPLICATIONS

What are the educational implications of the foregoing discussion? Perhaps the most important implication is that the teacher is reminded, in some detail, that he is dealing with a complex, developing individual

– a person whose development is capable of systematic study because it is in part a deep-seated process of maturation. But linked with this process of maturation is a set of processes of learning which also display discernible regularities. We have focussed here on social learning, showing some of its bewildering complexities but continually attempting to delineate patterns in the processes. At a high level of abstraction, it is possible to talk of being 'moulded' by 'Society'. But at the grass-roots level on which the child and the adolescent actually live, 'Society' is a diverse, often contradictory set of pressures and opportunities. Part of it has been learned, in the form of knowledge and skills clustering around social roles. That most central, warm and private part of the person – his self-concept – has been profoundly influenced by his social experience and in turn shapes his attitudes to his experience.

All of this occurs whether the school puts 'social education' into its curriculum or not. But if teachers are lacking in understanding of social learning in adolescence, they may find two disturbing things occurring. First, they may find that the familiar supports that have enabled the curriculum of the school to be taught reasonably effectively are undermined by changes in the attitudes and values acquired by pupils from other parts of the social system. By failing to recognize that these changes are part of social learning, the teacher may be reduced to condemning the process without having any influence on it. Second, many adolescents are bewildered by their own physical and psychological development, and by the social changes that they see taking place around them. They often seek advice from those that they see as having more knowledge and skill than themselves. And if the school makes no provision for such needs, other agencies may find it profitable to offer some kind of provision. Thus, Hemming (1960) shows the vast amount of informal social education that is being provided by comics and magazines, often by people who have no claim to be qualified to deal with the problems in which they become involved. This is particularly noticeable with sex education. Schofield (1965), in his recent and extensive survey of adolescent sexual attitudes and behaviour, to which we have already briefly referred, notes, 'In view of all the discussion about sex education in recent years, it was surprising to find so many teenagers who said they were never taught about sex at school. A possible explanation is that the teachers think they are giving sex education but the adolescents do not recognize it as such. . . . Sex education, when it occurred, seemed to concentrate on biological and physiological matters and seemed to be unrelated to human affairs. . . . Nearly half the boys

(47 per cent) and girls (43 per cent) felt they should have been told more about sex at school' (p. 249).

Although we have been rather sceptical of the view that adolescents are in imminent danger of 'alienation' and almost wholly immersed in an adolescent society, there is evidence that schools are often found deeply unsatisfying by older pupils. In infant and junior schools, a great deal has been done to encourage individual and group participation in school activities. But the secondary school, and particularly the grammar school, seem to have found it extremely difficult to involve pupils in these ways. The key to this problem is, in our view, the provision of facilities for increasing competence. A study of the leisure activities of young people shows that they seem to be heavily committed to self-definition, self-expression and self-extension. The emphasis placed on self in this context is by no means incompatible with group participation. When schools are seen as places where one can grow, places which are open to challenge while offering some measure of security, teachers will be astonished at the energies and skills that are released.

Having said this, it must be granted that there are formidable obstacles to offering these challenges to growth, unless they take forms which are well established, and which have been readily granted to the school by the surrounding society. An example of this latter is provided by the Duke of Edinburgh's Award scheme, which encourages the development of physical skills with moral implications. That is, the difficulties that the young person encounters in developing the skills of boating, rock-climbing, or pot-holing present more than technical challenges. They also confront a person with his own fears and insufficiencies. In Britain, more than most other countries, perhaps, the school has been seen as a place that can justifiably set opportunities of this kind before the boy or girl. But even the most enthusiastic advocate of these activities would not claim that they are a complete social and moral education.

Returning to the need for sex education, it is clear that there are a number of cogent reasons why schools should find it difficult to teach the knowledge and skills relevant to sexual development. Many teachers are not sure about the nature of their 'mandate' from parents on these emotionally charged matters. The education and training of teachers, and the rather formal nature of their role, together with the tendency to organize the curriculum into examinable 'subjects', create difficulties for sex education.

The difficulty has been met in a number of ways. One is to make a clear distinction between topics which the school can appropriately teach, and those which should be left to other agencies, particularly the parents. Another is to select a number of aspects of sex education which can be linked with established subjects and to teach these aspects in the usual way. Human reproduction, for example, can be taught as a part of biology, and becomes either an aspect of human anatomy and physiology, or an aspect of mammalian reproductive processes. Another way is to broaden the whole theme of sex education, and to talk of 'education in personal relationships'. Sexual learning then becomes an integral part of social learning, with particular emphasis on the implications of sexual attitudes and behaviour for family life, and friendship.

The exploration of personal relationships requires considerable delicacy on the part of the teaching staff. One effective procedure has been to distinguish between relatively straightforward matters of fact, which can be presented in books or formal teaching sessions of the traditional kind, and matters of belief and opinion, where personal experience must be respected. The educational methods that can be used in this latter area include informal discussion groups (well described in Abercrombie, 1960; and Miles, 1959) and role-playing (described in Klein, 1961). On a more personal level, individual counselling can be provided by schools, in the way that it has been provided on a modest scale in the school psychological service. Some of the more forward-looking education authorities are already appointing teacher/counsellors, and universities and colleges of education are beginning to offer special courses for this new teaching role. Perhaps the best title for this is social education.

Although sexual education in adolescence has often been considered as the vital centre of these developments in social education, a wider view shows us that schools and colleges must re-think a good deal of their current activities, and not merely see social education as a euphemism for sexual education. As this chapter has attempted to show, social learning is broader than sexual development, and any attempt to reduce one to the other would be disturbing and distorting. But, as so often in discussing these matters, one discerns a note of exhortation creeping in. This is a warning to us to round off the discussion and to attempt a summary and concluding comments.

IX. SUMMARY

The approach taken in this chapter has been to state a number of problems and to attempt to throw light on them. This has been difficult for several reasons. The problems of how young people learn to cope with the society of which they are members are innumerable, and selection of key problems is itself a problem. Having selected some problems for study, it is found that our knowledge is slight, and not the least difficulty is to find ways of studying the complex processes of role-learning and forming a self-concept. The appropriate terms for describing these processes have proved a source of some confusion, and particularly the concept of 'identification', which has been discussed at some length.

The two themes of the chapter have already been stated – the role of the self-concept in guiding and reinforcing social attitudes and activities and the function of social roles, and social skills, in enabling the growing person to participate in social situations with appropriate effectiveness (including the ability to keep an appropriate 'role distance', a point effectively discussed by Goffman, 1961). Each of these themes has shown certain patterns and possibilities.

In the first, there is the possibility of acquiring some measure of autonomy. The development of autonomy, as the concept itself implies, is essentially one of becoming a particular kind of person, rather than a mere social functionary, once of the less recognizable 'faces in the crowd' (Riesman, 1952). As Fromm, Riesman and others have been at pains to point out, autonomy is not easily achieved. By far the commoner human condition is that of social adjustment to the currently prevailing norms and customs. Some persons are neither adjusted nor autonomous. They are, in Durkheim's striking term, anomic – unable either to transcend their social condition or to accept it with effectiveness and good grace. Social adjustment, although it may be dismissed on the common-sense level as 'conformity', has many diverse modes, since the established patterns of social behaviour vary even in relatively stable and traditional society. In a volatile and highly differentiated society such as our own, adjustment must always be related to the social models to which the adjustment has taken place.

This diversity is characteristic of the human condition. Even in times of social stability and strong tradition, there are patterns of deviance. One of the factors accounting for these wide individual differences is the human ability to represent one's experience – one's reactions to objects and events and not only the objects and events themselves. This incorporation of a world within the person, a world which is 'personal' but to which one can have attitudes just as one does to the other world, makes possible the enormous degree of individuality that, if not freely revealed in the dramas and rituals of everyday life, lurks beneath the enforced routines.

It would be impossible to have a self-concept without the roles that one performs in social relationships with others. This was the great insight of Cooley and G. H. Mead, among others: the realization of the extraordinary extent to which one's personal behaviour and self-concept are built from public materials, and especially from language.

Once formed, the self-concept performs a two-fold function. It not only serves to bring the person into relation with others by processes of social comparison. It also enables the person to become aware of his individuality and of the possibility of modifying others by persuasion or calculated coercion. These contacts with others are expressed through social roles. The other side of social learning, then, is the acquisition of role behaviour, which starts in a humble way with imitations, immediate and then deferred, and then moves to the more complex level of identi-fication with the experience of significant others. Role behaviour and the self-concept are closely linked, as we have shown. But since one stresses the actual pattern of activity or interaction into which a person enters in a particular type of social situation, and the other refers to his immediate conception of himself in relation to others, the contrast is made, and worth maintaining in the organization of the discussion in this chapter.

Role-behaviour is related to guiding social norms. The self-concept is linked with personal values. How are the two linked? This is the story of the growth of morality. The treatment of this very complex topic (perhaps the most difficult in the whole realm of developmental psychol-ogy, because of the status of the concepts involved in the study) was focussed on the work of Piaget. In the two-part section, Piaget's attempt to show that personal norms are at first the child's literal interpretations of the standards of the adults in authority over him (typically, his parents) and that they then became mellowed into equitable stand-ards as a result of co-operative interaction with his peers was first dis-cussed, and then set in relation to later work.

The importance of morality for social development is that the person is able, through a personal morality, to make judgements in his own right which are, nevertheless, social in implication. This is not only obviously true of the ethic of the socially adjusted, which is clearly taken over from other members of the society, but also true, though much less obviously, of the ethic of autonomy. This is based on a conception of 'right relationships' which may go directly counter to the established social morality (as with the ethic of Jesus or of Socrates). It would, therefore, be unreasonable to say that such an ethic is in some way derived from 'Society as it would be at its best'. These novel ethics are genuine human achievements of the highest order. But they are, as we have remarked, social in implication. They reach forward to a state of social order that has not yet been attained. Just as an understanding of physical relationships must be learned before even the most original and radical inventions are possible, and the invention then implies the understanding of physical relationships, so an understanding of social relationships is necessary for the development of social and moral innovations.

To say this is not to try to force a Pyrrhic victory for social learning in the face of achievements which seem at first sight to be uniquely individual. It is, rather, an attempt to show the ubiquity of social, as of physical learning. The one is concerned with ways in which objects can be conceived and manipulated, and not only with the set currently observable. The other sees the ways in which persons and roles can be conceived and formed into viable relationships.

The Freudian position, which we briefly discussed, is that moral development is focussed on certain human needs of a socially challenging nature. These are sex and aggression. Every social order, however simple, has to make arrangements for dealing with these potentially anarchic forms of human behaviour. Part of the defence against these impulses, Freud argues, is in the structure of society, in the taboos which regulate sex and aggression. A more interesting part lies below the surface of the individual consciousness, in the form of 'complexes' of inhibition, learned in the very early years of life. The specific forms of control postulated by Freud, and the nature of the sanctions reinforcing the controls (and particularly the threat of castration) were regarded somewhat sceptically in our discussion, but the strategic importance of sex and aggression in social, especially moral, learning was readily accepted.

Physical development in adolescence brings with it the possibility of more effective physical aggression, through enhanced size and strength. This has been traditionally obvious in the development of boys, and penal codes have set adolescence as the point at which physical aggression begins to be sanctioned severely. In recent years, with the relative emancipation of women, not only politically but also socially and educationally, the size and strength of girls has been notably increasing, and new patterns of female delinquency are slowly emerging.

In the discussion of these matters in this chapter, aggression was given relatively little attention, and the available space was spent on looking in some detail at the vicissitudes of sexual development.

The extraordinary individuality of sexual development was noted and discussed. There seem to be two reasons for this: in the first place, the complexity of the whole process, and its delicate interrelationships with other biological sub-systems, requires a good deal of individuality. In a species as individual and complex as the human species, it is usually seen that every aspect of physical development is individual, though broad species-wide patterns of development can be discerned.

In the second place, the degree of privacy accorded to sexual development, even in the twentieth century, is high. Where communication between individuals is relatively inhibited, there is a good deal of room for divergence in practice, even when persons are motivated to conform to what they believe to be the current practice and belief.

This latter point is of considerable importance. Although sexual behaviour and attitudes are surrounded by inhibitions, this by no means indicates a lack of social concern with these areas of human behaviour. Quite the opposite. To a great extent, the tendency to regard sexual matters as private is one way of keeping them out of the important areas of public behaviour.

One of the main themes of psychoanalytic theory has been the disruptive effect of sexual development on the sense of personal integration or identity. The two-fold approach of the first part of the chapter was resumed in the last part, and a number of viewpoints on the 'identity' crisis of adolescence were described and discussed. Although the issue was considered real and important, some doubt was expressed as to the desirable degree of integration in the individual personality. While it seems undeniable that an integrated personality is one with less conflict, a greater likelihood of achieving a balanced output of activities, and greater stability, it is possible to set the advantages of diversity, dialectic, and specialized effectiveness against it. The problem is, of course, that integration and differentiation cannot be simultaneously maximized, so that one must consider, at any given level of performance, the advantages of development along one line rather than another. It is persuasive to argue, as many critics of modern society have done, that the technological systems of industrial and commercial organizations have forced an unremitting differentiation on people in their working hours, and that some measure of integration is a crying need of our unbalanced social system. But, looking at such evidence as is available on the problem of identity, it is by no means clear that specialization must be halted, so that a strong sense of ego-identity can be more commonly experienced.

While this point is intensely controversial, the acquisition of effective social skills is not. It is generally agreed that the ability to engage in effective relationships with others is of great personal and social value. But the relationship between social skills and a sense of ego-identity is a close one, and there are implications for identity in social skills.

For example, it might be argued that one of the most valuable forms of social skill is the ability to cope effectively with unexpected situations: the occasion when a vital member of a group is inexplicably absent, or delayed, the serious and embarrassing breach of social convention, the invasion of a group's privacy by noise or an offensive odour. It may well be that such skill is built up within well-established social roles by experiencing the inevitable vicissitudes of social life. But it may prove to be the man who can transcend his role, who is a 'person in his own right', who can cope, while the social specialist cannot. If this is so, it would account for the emphasis being placed on identity at the present time, when social situations are tending to be fluid, and the complexity of our social life throws up frequent accidents.

At this point, the discussion turned to social skills and their relationship with adolescent groupings, most of which are spontaneous and informal. It was agreed that these groups meet a number of needs which more formal and enduring institutions are not particularly well-fitted to meet at the present time. These include the provision of a sense of solidarity, protection in an unfamiliar social environment, the provision of guidelines which are continually revised to meet changing circumstances, and the opportunity to experiment at moderate risk.

This said, it was felt that the 'adolescent society' has been over-emphasized by some writers. There has been a tendency for 'social impressionists', writing about the young people of modern industrial society, to piece together sundry fragments of evidence to produce a sharply drawn picture of an alienated, intensely conformist adolescent society – almost a complete foreign country in the middle of that ruled by the older generation. Recent surveys, and other reasonably systematic and comprehensive studies, show the strong influence of established social forms.

Finally, the educational implications of social learning in childhood and adolescence were discussed. The main need was seen to be the lack of systematic help to pupils and students in the development of social skills and self-insight. The traditional themes of formal education have been the uses of language and number, and the development of basic technical skills. Social skills and self-insight, and particularly the full understanding of sexual needs, have been left to parents, siblings or informal sources of information, such as friends, books and papers.

By the end of adolescence, even in the most favourable circumstances, a good deal of uncertainty, frustration and concern about one's competence remain, to provide some of the dramas of adulthood. But the main shape of the person as a social being has been clearly delineated, and the characteristic preferences for social roles and for personal styles of playing them are established. If the child is father to the man, perhaps the adolescent has come close enough to his own adult state to be his brother. But the richness and variety of our society are so great that brothers do not always recognize one another.

REFERENCES

ABERCROMBIE, M. L. J. (1960). *The Anatomy of Judgment*. London: Hutchinson.

ADORNO, T. W., FRENKEL-BRUNSWIK, E., LEVINSON, D. J., and NEVITT SANFORD, R. (1950). *The Authoritarian Personality*. New York: Harper.

ARDREY, R. (1967). *The Territorial Imperative*. London: Collins.

ARGYLE, M. (1967). *The Psychology of Interpersonal Behaviour*. Harmondsworth: Penguin Books.

BANDURA, A., ROSS, O., and ROSS, S. A. (1963). A comparative test of the status envy, social power and secondary reinforcement theories of indentificatory learning. *J. Abnorm. Soc. Psychol.* **67**, 527–534.

BANDURA, A., and WALTERS, R. H. (1963). *Social Learning and Personality Development*. New York: Holt, Rinehart & Winston.

BEACH, F. A. (ed.) (1965). *Sex and Behaviour*. New York: Wiley.

BERNSTEIN, B. (1965). A socio-linguistic approach to social learning. In Gould, J. (ed.) *Penguin Survey of Social Sciences*. Harmondsworth: Penguin Books.

BLUM, G. S. (1952). *Psycho-analytic Theories of Personality*. New York: McGraw-Hill.

BOORSTIN, D. (1963). *The Image*. Harmondsworth: Penguin Books.

BRIM, O. G., and WHEELER, S. (1966). *Socialization after Childhood: Two Essays*. New York: Wiley.

BROWN, R. W. (1965). *Social Psychology*. New York: The Free Press.

BROWN, R. W. (1958). *Words and Things*. New York: The Free Press.

CARTER, M. P. (1962). *Home, School and Work*. Oxford: Pergamon Press.

CATTELL, R. B. (1957). *Personality and Motivation. Structure and Measurement*. New York: World Books.

CATTELL, R. B. (1965). *The Scientific Analysis of Personality*. Harmondsworth: Penguin Books.

COLEMAN, J. S. (1961). *The Adolescent Society*. Glencoe, Illinois: The Free Press.

DOUVAN, E., and ADELSON, J. (1966). *The Adolescent Experience*. New York: Wiley.

DOWNES, D. (1965). *The Delinquent Solution*. London: Routledge and Kegan Paul.

EPPEL, E. M., and M. (1966). *Adolescents and Morality*. London: Routledge and Kegan Paul.

ERIKSON, E. H. (1953). Growth and crises of the 'Healthy Personality'. In Kluckhohn, C., and Murray, H. A. (eds.) (1963). *Personality in Nature, Society and Culture*, second edn. London: Cape. (pp. 185–225).

ERIKSON, E. H. (1963). *Childhood and Society* (2nd revised edition). New York: Norton.

EVANS, K. M. (1961). *Sociometry and Education*. London: Routledge and Kegan Paul.

EYSENCK, H. L. (1967). *The Biological Basis of Personality*. New York: C. C. Thomas.

FESTINGER, L. (1957). *A Theory of Cognitive Dissonance*. Evanston, Illinois: Row and Peterson.

FLUGEL, J. C. (1945). *Man, Morals and Society*. London: Duckworth.

FOOTE, N. N., and COTTRELL, L. S. (1955). *Identity and Interpersonal Competence*. Chicago: University of Chicago Press.

FREUD, S. (1949). *An Outline of Psycho-analysis*. London: Hogarth.

FRIEDENBERG, E. Z. (1959). *The Vanishing Adolescent*. Boston: Beacon Press.

FROMM, E. (1942). *The Fear of Freedom*. London: Routledge and Kegan Paul.

FROMM, E. (1955). *The Sane Society*. London: Routledge and Kegan Paul.

FYVEL, T. R. (1953). *The Insecure Offenders*. Harmondsworth: Penguin Books.

GESELL, A., ILG, F. L., and AMES, L. B. (1956). *Youth: the Years from 10 to 16.* London: Hamish Hamilton.

GOFFMAN, E. (1959). *The Presentation of Self in Everyday Life.* New York: Doubleday & Co.

GOFFMAN, E. (1961). *Encounters.* Indianapolis: Bobs-Merrill.

GROSS, N. (1953). Social class identification in the urban community. *Amer. Soc. Rev.* **18,** 398–404.

HARROWER, M. R. (1934). Social status and moral development. *Brit. J. Educ. Psychol.* **4,** 75–95.

HAVIGHURST, R. J. (1953). *Human Development and Education.* New York: Longmans Green.

HAVIGHURST, R. J., and TABA, H. (1949). *Adolescent Character & Personality.* New York: Wiley.

HAVIGHURST, R. J., and PECK, R. F. (1960). *The Psychology of Character Development.* New York: Wiley.

HEMMING, J. (1960). *Problems of the Adolescent Girl.* London: Heinemann.

HIMMELWEIT, H. T., *et al.* (1952). The views of adolescents on some aspects of the social class structure. *Brit. J. Sociol.* **3,** 148–172.

KAGAN, J., and MOSS, H. A. (1962). *Birth to Maturity.* New York: Wiley.

KATZ, E., and LAZARSFELD, P. (1956). *Personal Influence.* New York: Free Press.

KELLMER PRINGLE, M. L. (1966). *Social Learning and its Measurement.* London: Longmans.

KELMAN, H. C. (1958). Compliance, identification and internalization: three processes of attitude change. *J. Confl. Resolut.* **2,** 51–60.

KELMAN, H. C. (1961). Processes of opinion change. *Publ. Opin. Quart.* **25,** 57–78.

KLEIN, J. (1961). *Working in groups.* London: Hutchinson.

KOHLBERG, L. (1964). Development of moral character and moral Ideology. In Hoffman, M. L., and L. W. (eds.) *Review of Child Development Research.* Vol. I. New York: Russell Sage Foundation.

LERNER, E. (1937). *Constraint Areas and the Moral Judgment of Children.* Menasha, Wisconsin: George Banta Publishing Co.

LERNER, E. (1937). Perspectives in moral reasoning. *Amer. Sociol.* **43,** 249–269.

LORENZ, K. (1966). *On Aggression.* London: Methuen.

LUPTON, T. (1963). *On the Shop Floor.* Oxford: Pergamon Press.

LUNZER, E. A. (1967). *The Manchester Scales of Social Adaptation.* London: National Foundation for Educational Research.

LYND, H. M. (1958). *On Shame and the Search for Identity*. London: Routledge and Kegan Paul.

MCCALL, G. J., and SIMMONS, J. L. (1966). *Identities and Interactions*. New York: The Free Press.

MCLUHAN, M. (1964). *Understanding Media*. London: Routledge and Kegan Paul.

MACRAE, D. Jr. (1954). A test of Piaget's theories of moral development. *J. Abnorm. Soc. Psychol.* **49,** 14–18.

MADGE, J. (1963). *The Origins of Scientific Sociology*. London: Tavistock Publications.

MADGE, C. (1964). *Society in the Mind*. London: Faber & Faber.

MEAD, G. H. (1956). The Social Psychology of G. H. Mead (ed. A. Strauss), Chicago, Illinois: Phoenix Books, University of Chicago Press.

MEAD, M. (1928) *Coming of Age in Samoa*. New York: William Morrow.

MEAD, M. (1935). *Sex and Temperament in Three Primitive Societies*. New York: William Morrow.

MEAD, M. (1949). *Male and Female*. London: Gollancz.

MEAD, M., and WOLFENSTEIN, M. (eds.) (1955). *Childhood in Contemporary Culture*. Chicago: University of Chicago Press.

MILES, B. M. (1959). *Learning to Work in Groups*. New York: Columbia University, Teachers' College Press.

MORENO, J. L. (1953). *Who Shall Survive?* (Second edn.) New York: Beacon House.

MORRIS, J. F. (1958). The development of adolescent value – judgments, *Brit. J. Educ. Psychol.* **28,** 1–14.

MUSSEN, P. (1967). Early socialization: Learning and identification. *New Directions in Psychology* **III**. New York: Wiley, 51–110.

PEASE, K. G. (1966). A study of the development of moral ideas and judgments in children aged 11–16 years. Unpub. M.A. Thesis, University of Manchester.

PIAGET, J. (1932). *The Moral Judgment of the Child*. London: Routledge and Kegan Paul.

PIAGET, J. (1954). *The Construction of Reality in the Child*. London: Routledge and Kegan Paul.

RICE, A. K. (1966). *Learning for Leadership*. London: Tavistock Publications.

RIESMAN, D. (1951). *The Lonely Crowd*. New Haven: Yale University Press.

RIESMAN, D. (1952). *Faces in the Crowd*. New Haven: Yale University Press.

ROGERS, C. (1959). A theory of therapy, personality and interpersonal relationships, as developed in the client – centred framework. In Koch, S. (ed.) *Psychology: A Study of a Science.* Vol. III. New York: McGraw-Hill, 184–256.

SAMPSON, A. (1956). *Anatomy of Britain Today.* London: Hodder & Stoughton.

SCHILDER, P. (1951). *The Image and Appearance of the Human Body.* New York: International Universities Press.

SCHOFIELD, M. (1965). *The Sexual Behaviour of Young People.* London: Longmans.

SEARS, R. R., RAU, L., and ALPERT, R. (1965). *Identification and Child Rearing.* Stanford, California: Stanford U.P.

SECORD, P. F., and BACKMAN, C. W. (1964). *Social Psychology.* New York: McGraw-Hill.

SHERIF, M., and SHERIF, C. W. (1964). *Reference Groups.* New York: Harper & Row.

STRAUSS, A. (ed.) (1956). *The Social Psychology of G. H. Mead.* Chicago, Illinois: Phoenix Books, University of Chicago Press.

SULLIVAN, H. S. (1953). *The Interpersonal Theory of Psychiatry.* New York: Norton.

TANNER, J. M. (1961). *Education and Physical Growth.* Oxford: Blackwell Scientific Publications.

TANNER, J. M., and INHELDER, B. (eds.). (1960). *Discussions on Child Development, Volume 4.* London: Tavistock Publications.

VENESS, THELMA (1962). *School Leavers: Their Aspirations and Expectations.* London: Methuen.

WHORF, B. L. (1956). *Language, Thought and Reality.* Cambridge, Mass: Technology Press.

WYLIE, RUTH, C. (1961). *The Self Concept.* New York: University of Nebraska Press.

ZWEIG, F. (1963). *The Student in the Age of Anxiety.* London: Heinemann.

12

Programmed Instruction

H. KAY

I. INTRODUCTION

THIS chapter is primarily about a communication system. The air passenger in the lounge of the jet aircraft or the housewife in her own lounge watching television are everyday examples of how we use communication systems today. The school child sitting in his class of forty watching his teacher write on the blackboard is another example – but it may seem closer to the nineteenth than the twentieth century. Why should so much teaching have this old-fashioned look? Interest in all forms of communication has so dominated our century that it is surprising we have not many new ways of instructing. It would seem as if new instruments – the projector, the television programme, the tape recorder – were so attractive in themselves that we have been satisfied to use them in the same way as the standard chalk and talk method. Their use was almost an end in itself, not a means to some goal.

It is one of the achievements of programmed instruction that it reverses this trend, and places the emphasis upon what is received rather than upon what is transmitted. The criterion for programmed instruction is whether a student has understood and learned, not how wittily he was instructed. It is worth considering briefly how this accords with general ideas of communication.

One of man's most obvious achievements is the flexibility of his communication systems. Nearly all animals can communicate in some form with other members of their species but this is usually over a limited range of events. When man invented an abstract form of symbols he widened both the range of subjects he could discuss and the means that could be used to send and receive information. It was some time before the implications were appreciated and, for example, printing developed. More recently we have had a spate of developments in radio, television, and artificial satellite transmissions where the receiver of the message is often unknown to the sender. These are all examples of an increasing tendency to use what the communication engineer cites as open-ended systems – where messages from one source reach an unspecified number of receivers, who in their turn need communicate nothing back to the sender. This is not, of course, a teaching system and may be contrasted with the early tutorial or Socratic method which has held pride of place in educational theories. But as the number of students in the world has increased teachers have found themselves accepting responsibility for larger and larger classes, and educational theory in its turn has accepted that students are being taught in these situations. It is not always easy to demonstrate this point convincingly, for it is not enough to show that students have learned. Much learning occurs in everyday life that is accidental or incidental, and certainly not taught. The efficiency of classroom teaching, particularly where it is closest to the open-ended communication system, may be much less than is imagined. One psychologist who looked at it in the 1950s was clear in his own mind that it was less, for it failed to meet the elementary criteria that he had found essential in his own laboratory experiments. He therefore set out to design a method that would meet these criteria – the linear programme of Professor Skinner was the result (Skinner, 1954).

II. DIFFERENT FORMS OF PROGRAMMES

1. *Linear programmes*

Skinner's was not the first teaching machine and programme but it is useful to consider it first because it was designed as a complete system. To rectify the deficiencies he saw in the classroom Skinner proposed that a text should be prepared with the following characteristics:

1. Material is divided into a series of small but related steps (named *frames*).

2. Each frame gives information to a student and requires him to make an overt, usually a written response. (Skinner calls this a *constructed response*.)

3. As soon as a student has responded he is given the correct answer.

4. Because the steps are small the material can be written so that students have every opportunity of making correct responses. Skinner contends that giving the correct answer reinforces a student's correct response. (Only correct responses can be reinforced in this way.)

5. A student works through the text at his own pace.

The heart of Skinner's method is that a student understands the material sufficiently well to respond correctly to each frame, and that he has the response immediately rewarded (reinforced). The theoretical issue of how far this is a reinforcement procedure strictly comparable with the food reinforcement given to a hungry animal in an operant conditioning experiment is debated by some psychologists (Lumsdaine, 1962: Kay, 1964); nevertheless, it would be agreed by nearly all that irrespective of the niceties of the theoretical argument, the method is a good one and has every chance of success. Indeed, some teachers might well claim to try to do much the same with their present classes. Skinner, however, is laying stress upon individual instruction within the classroom and to this end would use teaching machines to assist in controlling student behaviour. With a machine a response has to be made before receiving the correct answer and advancing to the next frame. We should be clear that a teaching machine for use with a linear programme is the simplest of devices for presenting frames and recording a response. It consists of little more than a plastic box, transparent cover and foam rubber rollers and usually requires no electrical power.

The question arises whether a machine is necessary with a linear programme since it is obvious that the heart of this system lies in the programme. Many linear programmes have been published in book form, with several frames printed on each page and the answer generally on the following page. Programmes in this form have demonstrably taught efficiently, as did Hartley's on logarithms (Hartley, 1964). When this was being evaluated it was presented in simple booklets to seconddary modern school children in their ordinary classrooms. The children made relatively few errors and showed a high degree of learning on both immediate and later retention tests. The administrative convenience of handling, say, thirty books against thirty machines in a classroom is obvious enough.

But booklets have limitations. Hartley noted that some of his children had 'cheated' when working with them, that is, they had looked up some answers and written them in as their own responses. The consensus of evidence indicates that this behaviour handicaps learning, and seems to be largely a carry over from a test situation where a pupil takes it as read that *he* is on trial, not the programme. The machine not only prevents deliberate 'cheating', it prevents self-deception where a student indulges in a look ahead on the pretext of confirming a response that he is convinced he was going to make once he has seen the answer. Such behaviour, only too easy with a book, is controlled by a machine.

Again, children of all ages find a machine has a novelty value, and it gives the impression of being designed for a student's individual use.

A linear programme of the Skinner type is written then to conform to certain principles derived from the laboratory. It does raise certain theoretical issues for the psychologist. The procedure of telling a student that he is correct as soon as he has made a response is an acceptable principle to nearly all learning theories, but for psychologists who regard such confirmation as a form of knowledge of results it is not necessary, as it is for Skinner, that all responses should be correct to be beneficial. From Skinner's point of view a wrong response cannot be reinforced, but from the standpoint of knowledge of results a student can derive information by being informed that his response is wrong, and to this extent he may learn. It was the desire to make more use of error responses that created the branching type of programme.

2. *Branching programmes*

Learning from programmes is intended to be a full-time activity, designed to function with the maximum participation from a student. He cannot go to sleep or the whole operation immediately stops. It may seem an obvious question to ask whether more use could not be made of students' responses. Where they are correct it is assumed a student has understood, but where a mistake has been made might it not give some indication of that individual student's difficulty. This is the reasoning behind branching programmes, where the particular sequence of frames is not fixed as in linear sequences but is partly determined by a student's responses. More material is presented on each frame than in the linear programme and at the end a direct question is asked. Responses are often restricted by making a student select one of several possible responses, each of which is associated with a different frame. The student selects the frame, and, if he is correct he will be told so, and further information will then be presented. In Figure 1(*b*) this would correspond to choosing Frame 6 from Frame 3. But if a student chooses a wrong response, as illustrated by Frames 4 or 5, he finds there an explanation why his response is wrong and the preceding information in the main frame is reviewed to clarify the problem. He is then told to return to the main frame and make another attempt.

It was objected that giving a student multiple-choice answers from which he had to choose would confuse him, in so far as he would be exposed to both right and wrong responses. Results have not supported the objection, for students have learned efficiently with this method. It should be pointed out that the alternative responses are carefully chosen to diagnose possible difficulties of students, and to provide further explanation why these responses are not satisfactory. On the debit side it will be appreciated that a student has to select his response from a limited number of choices – generally two or three. It may happen that different students who choose the same answer do so for different reasons but receive the same explanation. Or they may have been forced into selecting one particular answer because it seemed the least objectionable for them. It is not therefore strictly accurate to speak as if this choice necessarily represents the particular difficulty of an individual student, though it usually does.

3. *Skip-branching programmes*

It should be mentioned that constructed responses may be used with branching programmes, just as multi-choice questions may be used with linear programmes. Indeed Pressey, who first used teaching machines in the 1920s based his machines on multi-choice questions but made each student continue responding to each question until correct, and only then did the machine advance to the next frame. All students with Pressey's machine saw the same material in a linear sequence.

When constructed responses are used with a branching sequence a slightly different system known as skip-branching is followed. Here, after a student has made his response, he is shown the correct answer, and he acts as his own comparator. If he is right he continues in the main sequence of frames – the 'A' frames in Figure 1(c) – but if he is wrong he is branched into a sub-sequence, the 'B' frames. This sub-sequence does not attempt to deal with the specific difficulty of any one student; it assumes that the main sequence frame has failed to communicate satisfactorily and it attempts to explain the material more simply and in greater detail. In one respect it is very much like using a linear programme within a branching programme.

This skip technique is now becoming much more widespread with both branching and linear programmes. A student is presented with a frame that is primarily for diagnostic purposes. If he shows that he already has the necessary knowledge he is directed to a frame much further on in the programme; if he has not, he is presented with the intervening frames to ensure that when he does reach that critical point in the programme he will understand the material.

(a) Linear Programme

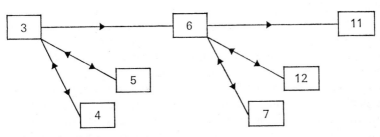

(b) Branching Programme

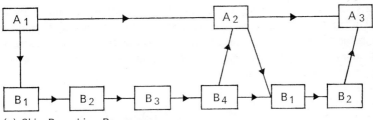

(c) Skip-Branching Programme

Figure 1. Three types of programmes.

4. *Machines and books presenting branching programmes*

There are now several standard machines for presenting branching programmes and these are fairly complex devices. Machines such as the AutoTutor or GrundyTutor use a back projection system with a 35 mm. film on a screen size of about 7 in. × 9 in. At the end of a frame, a student is asked a direct question and each possible answer is identified with a particular key. The student presses the key whose letter corresponds with the response he thinks is correct, and the machine automatically advances the programme to that frame; there is a return key for taking the programme back to the preceding frame when the student has made a wrong choice. Most students enjoy working with these machines for they are easy to operate, they are quick in action and there is a very definite feeling of exploration as a student finds out whether he has selected correctly. They are a little noisy, especially if several are operating in one room, and alas, by educational standards, they are expensive, being over £200.

Branching programmes can also be presented in book forms – the so-called scrambled books. In these books the pages are numbered sequentially but the branching is achieved by giving page numbers to the alternative answers to questions. Thus a student finds himself having to select one answer from, say pages 42, 48, 53. He selects his response, turns to the page to find out whether he is right or wrong, and is there given further information relevant to his particular answer. The system does control behaviour in so far as it ensures that students follow the material in the prescribed order, but it is an awkward method of reading a book. There is too the objection that applies to all multi-choice branching: a student may select one of the alternative frames but as soon as he sees that he is wrong, he merely returns to the master frame to make another choice instead of reading the explanation. This can be partly overcome by writing frames in such a way that it is not immediately obvious the wrong choice has been made; for example, by explaining the mental steps that have led to this choice before pointing out the error. On the whole scrambled books seem an ingenious attempt to control the presentation of a programme, but they may not be a permanent contribution.

III.   PRINCIPLES OF PROGRAMME CONSTRUCTION

1. *Programming not tied to one specific psychological theory*
In the early days of programming much was made of the differences between linear and branching systems, mainly because they were derived from different psychological schools of thought. Today many programmers, particularly in Britain, would stress the similarities more than the differences and indeed some programmes are being written containing both linear and branching sequences.

We will consider, briefly, what is common to all types of programming, and how the emphasis in programming has changed in the light of recent experiences.

Both linear and branching programmes require a student to behave in a certain way and aim to teach by controlling that behaviour. The size of step may vary but both systems ensure that the instruction has been received and understood. The programme is designed to be administered to an individual student, it caters for his response and provides him with an answer. He may proceed at his own pace, and spend just as long as he wishes on a frame. (Experience has shown that students are, in fact, influenced by the speed of other students when they are in the same classroom, even when they are working on different programmes.) Above all programmes are written so that students may understand the material. The aim here is not to baffle a student with a display of erudition, but to climb the stairs of knowledge step by step. Where students fail to make a particular step then the programme has failed and must be rewritten (see later 'Evaluation').

2. *Conditioning*

Different systems may have been devised to accord with different laboratory procedures or theoretical ideas but there are relatively few instances where it would be possible to predict that learning would take place according to one system and would not according to the other. Indeed the closer one examines the different formulations the more they appear alike. Conditioning procedures, both classical and operant, are established primarily by manipulating spatial and temporal continuities, that is to say they take the two most important dimensions of our physical world and demonstrate that they have a pronounced effect upon a biological organism. It is hardly surprising. A biological evolutionary mechanism is an adaptive system, and is therefore naturally sensitive to the physical space that surrounds it and the sequence of events that happen to it. But of course there is no reason why it should learn from reacting to these events. Conditioning experiments demonstrate that organisms do learn but of course they do not tell us why they learn. They are descriptive studies. In Skinner's studies (operant conditioning) an animal presses a lever, it receives food at once and it subsequently demonstrates that it has learned to do this by pressing the lever immediately it is put in the same situation. Similarly with the classical studies of conditioning where no response is demanded of the animal at the beginning of training. The bell rings and food is produced before the animal responds. Nevertheless, the temporal contiguity of the conditioned stimulus (the bell) and the unconditioned stimulus (the food) will eventually produce the conditioned response (salivation).

In neither instances have we an explanation why the nervous system of the animal which records and initiates the responses in the conditioning studies should be influenced in its retention and learning of them by the giving of food. What is the tie up between the stomach and the brain? Theories have tried to find it in the postulation of drive

(Hull, 1943), or in the hunger motivation of the animal that is satisfied by food and therefore terminates its goal seeking behaviour (Deutsch, 1960). These are attempts to understand the evidence as we have it today and we have to accept the limitations of this kind of explanation. We cannot say at present what particular role the actual eating or digesting of food plays in this complex activity of the central nervous system, and on the other hand there are examples where organisms will learn in situations where no food is eaten.

3. *Feedback and communication systems*

In the main, then, conditioning studies give the exact situation under which learning will take place but are essentially descriptive of what happens. The same may be said of Thorndike's Law of Effect (Thorndike, 1911) together with his subsequent invocation of knowledge of results (see review by Annett, 1961). Thorndike's law which states that responses 'which are accompanied or closely followed by satisfaction' to an organism will be strengthened and repeated on later occasions anticipates Skinner's practical demonstrations of operant conditioning and its application in programmed learning.

One difficulty here is that knowledge of results has two (at least) quite different functions. On the one hand it may be motivating, as when we encourage a student by telling him his response is successful. But the other role of knowledge of results is informational and ties up closely with communication concepts. It indicates to a performer both how he has responded and how he should modify his actions. The skilled performer and the trainee need to rely upon such information to monitor responses. In a teaching system we are trying to use knowledge of a student's results as a guide to presenting material. We wish to modify our subject matter on this basis of how far he is, or is not, understanding our presentation. An appropriate functional model is shown in Figure 2. Material is drawn from a subject matter store, and displayed in frames to a student, who then has to respond. The student's response is an essential link in the system, for it not only ensures that the material has been received and understood but, where it has not, it allows appropriate action to be taken. It is important that we appreciate that the basic functional system is much the same in both simple and sophisticated teaching systems. When we try to evaluate a student's response we need to place it in relation to the rest of his performance and have a set of decision rules to determine our next choice of subject matter. In the normal teacher-class situation all this has to be done on the spur of the moment and is based largely on the teacher's experience, knowledge of his class, and awareness of the complexity of his material. With simple linear programmes this is achieved in the early stages of preparation – the evaluative stage – by analysing students' responses and modifying the size of individual frames, order of presentation, type of explanation, and so on. With more sophisticated adaptive systems, which range at present from branching programmes to computer-assisted methods, modification to the programme is taking place throughout an individual student's learning. Indeed with a fully adaptive system a student is rewriting the programme to meet his own requirements. Here the system depends upon the student's responses, to determine both when and what it will present.

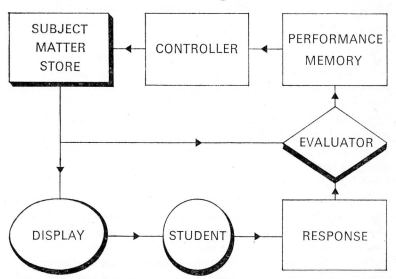

Figure 2. Closed-loop system of teaching. This attempts to control teaching by ensuring that the information transmitted to the student has been received and understood. The material to be taught is adapted on the basis of the student's responses. From *Teaching Machines and their Use in Industry*, by H. Kay, J. Annett and M. E. Sime

It is in this sense that the teaching machine system operates as a closed-loop system, and as we saw in the introduction, is in marked contrast to so many trends in present communication methods that rely upon open-loop systems. Radio, television, large-scale lecture halls allow one speaker or source to address vast audiences, often with little or no indication how far the information has been received. Sometimes efforts are made to close the loop by follow-up studies on sample audiences but in general the larger and wider the audience the more difficult it is to record the feedback. The teaching machine system has reversed this trend and made feedback an essential feature in the system. But we should note that whilst the communication model is excellent at describing a situation where information is received and understood, it may be objected that it has nothing to say about learning. It was not designed to do so, nor does it. As with the conditioning studies it describes the situation under which learning will take place and it is unambiguous in setting forward its criteria for efficient teaching. But as with the other formulations it cannot say why learning has taken place, only that these conditions are advantageous for its occurrence.

4. *Parallel lines of thinking in different systems*

This is one reason why many workers, such as the writer, do not feel it is necessary in programming to identify with any one school of thought, for there is substantial agreement between them about ideal conditions for learning. When we examine the different theories it is apparent that each would predict, for its own reasons, that programming would be favourable for efficient learning. This is brought out in Table 1. S–R Theory stresses the significance of immediate reinforcement, Thorndike would have emphasized immediate knowledge of results, information theory would view programmes as a controlled feedback system, whilst pedagogy has its model of presentation – answer – confirmation. It is not our purpose here to examine in detail these parallel lines of thought. Phenomena may, of course, be described from several different standpoints which, at this level, are not mutually exclusive. But programming systems have presented the theoretically minded psychologist with a controlled and delineated situation, within which it is possible to examine these various formulations. The obvious question is under which conditions will the different theories predict different results. It is our contention that these are not so numerous as we might think. One example would be in the case of an error response, which would not be reinforced from the standpoint of operant conditioning. To this extent Skinner would predict no learning, whereas a communication model or knowledge of results would argue that information had been received and that some learning would occur. Here the theories would predict differently but even so it is recognized that learning is more efficient with positive than with negative instances.

TABLE 1.

Parallel lines of thought in the various teaching systems.

Type of Theory	Display	Action	Effect
	Programme frame	Select key or write answer	Answer and further information on next frame
S-R Theory	Stimulus	Response	Reinforcement
Thorndike	Problem	Action	Knowledge of Results (KR)
Information Theory	Information (input)	Output	Feedback
Pedagogy	Presentation or question	Answer	Confirmation

5. *Accent upon programme preparation*

In the early programmes the accent seemed to be upon frame writing, as this was the new feature. The most marked change in programming has been a shift in emphasis to the initial preparation of programmes. Today the stress is upon analysing what exactly the programme is to teach, and ascertaining what are the initial abilities and knowledge of the students. These are exact exercises. It is not enough to put forward some general description of what the students are supposed to know at the end of the course. This has to be considered in detail; for example, what will a student be expected to do when he has finished a programme? what questions should he be able to answer? what tasks will he have to carry out? This anticipated final behaviour has to be rigorously defined.

Programming is now seen as a carefully prepared exercise in which subject matter is scrutinized to ensure that it is relevant and sufficient for the task in hand. It is then arranged into a logical teaching sequence, and here again various techniques are used to verify that the best sequence of material has been set out. An early suggestion was the RULEG system of Evans, Homme, and Glaser (1960). The name – rule and example – is derived from the practice of putting forward a rule, or principle, with a full technical definition, followed by an example of it. Thomas *et al.* (1963) have proposed a useful extension of this procedure in which the arrangement of rules into a programme sequence is achieved by means of a matrix system. It is worth considering their procedure as a useful suggestion in itself and as a striking example of the detailed care that has to go into the preparation of programmes.

The authors distinguish between concepts and rules. They accept the dictionary definition of concepts – 'an idea of a class of objects, a general notion' – and they point out that this is taught by defining the relevant characteristics and relationships. These are called rules. As an illustration the authors consider the concept of expansion and the various rules making up this concept such as: most materials expand when heated; most materials contract when cooled; expansion is a function of temperature variation, and so on. Concepts may be subtle and complicated and often several rules will be required to embrace them. A programmer has to ensure that he has identified all the necessary rules, and that he has broken down each one into the simplest form. This is not easy.

The rules are then arranged into a programme sequence and their relationship to each other is examined by means of a matrix. The rules are numbered consecutively so that they may be easily identified. A sheet of squared paper is used with as many squares on each side of the paper as there are rules. In Figure 3, for the sake of simplicity, only ten rules are considered, and their numbers are written in serial order along the diagonal line of squares. The relationship between the rules is then examined. If there is a relationship between say rule 1 and 2 it is indicated in square (*a*) according to a predetermined key. It is worthwhile distinguishing between an association and a discrimination and this can be indicated by using different codes. If there is no relationship between rules 1 and 2 square (*a*) is left blank. The relationship between the other rules is then examined; a relationship between rules 1 and 3 would be marked in square (*b*); and between 1 and 4 in square (*c*), and so on. All the rules are considered in turn: (*d*) indicates a relationship between rules 3 and 5; (*e*) between 5 and 9. In the completed matrix the two halves are mirror images of one another, the lower providing a check on each relationship.

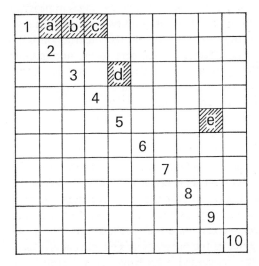

Figure 3. Construction of matrix. After Thomas *et al.*, 1963

It will be noticed that if each rule is related to the next then all the squares adjacent to the diagonal will be marked. This would be ideal, but in practice other relationships between different rules will also exist. Where we have a set of relationships a number of adjacent squares will be marked and this gives a pictorial representation of this 'concept area'. The matrix has many such uses in indicating where an inadequate sequence of rules has been attempted and can be rectified, where different orders may be examined, and where gaps occur because some rules have been omitted.

Thomas and his co-workers suggest that the use of a flow diagram may assist in the detailed planning of frames. The rules are plotted into actual frames and the programmer has to decide how many will be needed to teach each rule. It is recommended that the programmer should first try to express the rule in a general statement and then illustrate it in subsequent frames. The programmer allows for frames where he may have to assist a student by prompts or cues, and he also records in a flow diagram the location of revision frames.

We have discussed the matrix and flow diagram system in some detail because it is an example of one of the more elaborate programming methods, which aims to assist the initial writing of frames by a more careful analysis of the material that should be put into them. In practice, it has been found useful at many stages in programme preparation, for it provides a framework – in two senses. Like a set of plans for a building it is not only the guide to its construction but a most useful check that the final result does adhere to the original concept. This is relevant, for programmes have a tendency to stretch into longer and longer versions, particularly as a result of evaluation tests. The matrix and flow diagrams are a guide to the shape and size of what was envisaged against what has been achieved.[1]

6. *Evaluation*

Programmes are claiming to be able to teach without the intervention of a human teacher. This is challenging and therefore there should be good evidence that a programme can meet such a criterion. It is here that the evaluation stage is essential, for where a programme has been fully evaluated one can state the specifications that it meets. Evaluation is a guarantee of the programme's effectiveness (Hartley, 1963).

We are here concerned with what is sometimes called internal evaluation: that is, the testing and subsequent revising of a programme in an attempt to improve its teaching efficiency. This is contrasted with external evaluation where a programme is compared with other recognized teaching methods whose efficiency may or may not be known – generally not. Internal evaluation is an attempt to make maximum

---

[1] Alternative principles to RULEG include 'Discovery',' Guided Discovery', etc. See discussion by Peel in Chapter 10, Section VI.

use of feedback information. A first draft of a programme is adminis-tered to a few students and obvious difficulties are corrected. These are frames which have been written cumbersomely, where the intention is ambiguous, where questions may be misinterpreted and where one frame may cause subsequent errors to later frames. The amended pro-gramme is then given to a number of students, often in a classroom situation, and afterwards a test of what has been learned is adminis-tered. The analysis of responses is more than a matter of adding up how many errors have been made. Such a total may give some indication of how suitable the programme is for the standard of student (to take the extreme case, a programme where every student had got every frame right or every frame wrong would indicate that it was hopelessly out of keeping with the student's initial abilities). But the analysis attempts to see whether particular frames are causing difficulties, what is their nature and whether they lead to future errors. Often a mistake on one frame can only be removed by rewriting earlier frames.

Where linear programmes are being used the feedback at the evalua-tion stage is the only means of adapting the programme to student needs. It becomes extremely important that the programme should match the abilities of the students and for this reason it is often advo-cated that a pre-test of the student's knowledge should be given before the evaluation study. The pre-test is particularly useful where students have had widely different experience in a subject. Without it, teaching might be wrongly attributed to the programme, and it is often difficult to understand a student's performance without this background information. Where the time between the beginning and end of a pro-gramme is a matter of weeks or more, it is simplest and most informa-tive to use the same examination for the pre- and post-test.

When evaluation has been carried out the following details may be given in the introduction to the programme and they serve admirably to identify it. They are a specification for the programme (cf. Hartley, 1963; Rothkopf, 1963).

1. The characteristics of the population for whom the programme is intended. This should give the scholastic background: if school-children, their age, their IQ range, or where relevant their attain-ment levels, say in reading or mathematical ability.

2. The initial knowledge required by the students.

3. A statement of what the programme aims to teach together with a final performance test for students.

4. The scores obtained in the evaluation studies by similar populations of students. These scores are sometimes summarized in the form of, say, 85/80, meaning that there were 85 per cent or more correct responses to all the frames in the programme and 80 per cent was the average score on the final test.

5. Further characteristics of the programme – how long it takes to give, how it may best be administered, etc.

It need hardly be added that the proportion of programmes giving these particulars is, so far, very limited.

IV. RESEARCH RESULTS

A great deal of research has been done over a comparatively short time and this in itself is one of the successes of programmed instruction. It has focussed interest upon teaching, upon what is achieved and by what methods. The results are varied and the following points are only a selection from them.

1. *Influence of social factors upon research*

It has to be remembered that research studies with programmed instruction, particularly when conducted with schoolchildren, take place against a continuing background of standard educational methods. The research findings are therefore influenced by numerous social factors that cannot always be controlled by the experimenter. For example, the majority of studies involve relatively short programmes, extending to only a few lessons. Students appreciate that these are novel situations and respond to the novelty. It is significant that their attitudes towards working with programmes are more favourable with the shorter than with the longer sequences. As yet it must be admitted there are insufficient studies with longer programmes. Popham (see Schramm, 1962) noted that his group of sixth-grade children regarded the continuous use of machines as monotonous, while Hartley (1965) mentions that as his logarithm programme was revised and increased in length there was a 'decline in popularity'. Dick (1963) after using continuously a 3,512 frame programme reports neutral attitudes from his students, though Klaus and Deterline (Deterline, 1962) with a 1,600 frame programme, and Deterline (1962), found favourable opinions. By contrast, it is fair to say that with shorter studies some 70 to 90 per cent of subjects have responded favourably towards programmed instruction (e.g. Jones and Sawyer, 1949; Skinner and Holland, 1958; Crowder and Zachert, 1960; Feldhusen, 1961; Smith, 1962; Hughes, 1962).

2. *The effectiveness of programmes*

A substantial majority of results show that programmed instruction does teach successfully; that is to say, a variety of findings indicate that programmes have taught what they aimed to teach, or that they have taught the material in shorter time or to a higher level of efficiency than more conventional methods. There was an early tendency for research to concentrate upon comparing programmed instruction with human teachers, but this is not a particularly profitable form of study. There is no 'standard human teacher' for the comparison and the whole approach may be queried on the grounds that either the programmed instruction itself or the teacher are atypical – we might expect a good programme to beat a bad teacher and vice versa. But for what it is worth programmed instruction came out well enough in these studies, indeed so well that experienced research workers were surprised at such clear-cut results (see Kay *et al.*, 1963; Hartley, 1963).

More basic research examined specific issues such as whether programmes had met their criteria, the kind of difficulties students had run into, how well the material was retained, how far students who had completed programmes did in fact understand the subject matter, and so on. On these counts programmed instruction was successful.

One of the most useful attributes of programmed instruction is that student responses are numerous enough to provide a wealth of data for analysis. For example, research is examining such variables as the size of frames, the mode of responding, the transfer from programmed learning to future work, and the relationship between error rate in responding to the programme and subsequent retention and understanding. Early programmes attempted to reduce error rate to a minimum but it has not always followed that students have learned best from programmes where they made the least number of errors. And to date we have no experiments where students have tried to learn from a programme in which they have made a very large number of errors, say 50 per cent or more.

One obvious method of reducing error rate is to keep the size of step as small as possible. There are many definitions of step size such as the number of words in a frame, number of steps to cover a body of material, number of different responses in a programme and number of errors per section of programme. There is general agreement that the smaller the step size the longer time a student will take over the programme, but results are not clear-cut that learning will be more effective.

Again early programmes emphasized the importance of students making overt responses, and intuitively many of us felt this emphasis upon the active participation of a student was desirable. Yet when comparisons have been made between overt and covert (not observable) responding to programmes there have been no clear trends in results, except that covert responses took a shorter time (Evans *et al.*, 1959; Eigen *et al.*, 1962). It should also be noted that in some cases where overt responding did achieve significantly better test results (Poppleton and Austwick, 1964; Krumboltz and Weisman, 1962) the time taken on the programme was longer, making it difficult to compare directly the two response modes.

Similar problems arose between constructed and multi-choice response modes. Again there seemed *a priori* grounds for favouring a constructed response and it was pointed out that confronting students with wrong answers might confuse them. But comparison studies have not favoured either mode. This seems another instance where firmly held opinions, when put to the test, have not been substantiated.

3. *The use of programmes with normal classroom instruction*

There is a tendency to contrast the results of programmed instruction with those of human teachers as if they were necessarily opposed. This is not so and though programmes may have to function in situations where no human teachers are available, an important issue is how far programmed instruction can contribute to more effective teaching when used in conjunction with human teachers. Results are encouraging. In a well controlled study by the Navy (Wallis, 1964) the theoretical work for a four-week electronics course was taught by three different systems: standard teaching machines, human instructors, and 'integrated programmed instruction' where tutorials and active guidance from an instructor officer supplemented programmed instruction. In this third group twice as many students were under the control of one teacher as in the standard teaching group. The proportion of tuition time allocated to the integrated programmed instruction group was 42 per cent to programmed instruction, 30 per cent to laboratory and 28 per cent to class tutorials. (The authors suggest optimal times could be 40 per cent, 40 per cent and 20 per cent respectively.) The results were most significantly in favour of the integrated programmed instruction group, and in spite of teaching twice as many students the method was favoured by the instructor. This integration of old and new methods is most encouraging and should be further explored.

4. *Linear and branching programmes*

Much early research was devoted to comparing the effectiveness of these two kinds of programme, in the expectation that one form would be shown to be better than the other, or to be more suitable for some subjects or students. Again it is not the most profitable of comparisons for whilst it is obvious that a poor example of, say, a linear programme should not be classed against a good example of a branching programme, it is not clear how we ascertain that each example is of equal merit within its own class. On the whole nothing startling resulted from these studies: both systems were found to teach successfully, neither showing an overall superiority over the other. Linear programmes were favoured for teaching students of similar abilities who were beginning a subject, and, conversely, branching programmes saved time where student abilities in a particular subject differed widely. The simpler the material the more the tendency to use linear programmes. This is one reason why linear programmes have been more widely used with younger children, though this tendency has been further influenced by the actual difficulty of teaching a young child to use a branching system. The linear programme can be presented very simply in book form when one page is given to each frame, and it has been used in this way with mentally retarded children. At present there are many more linear than branching programmes, though it should be stressed that the trend is now to minimize the distinction between the two systems and even to include both within the same programme.

5. *Subject matter*

A glance at a volume such as 'Programmes '63' (Hanson, 1963) would seem to reveal that an enormous range of educational subjects has been programmed. There is every kind of title both in the arts, sciences and technology. But first impressions of these data may be misleading. When we see a programme listed it rarely means that a whole syllabus in that subject has been programmed, rather that there are available a limited number of programmed lessons. There are notable exceptions to this, and they are increasing, but there are many short sequences because in the first stages programmers were often trying to examine whether it was possible to write a programme in a particular subject. The answer has nearly always been positive and indeed the interest now is mainly in trying to write programmes which differ not so much in their content as in their presentation and teaching aims. It was a popular belief at first that programmes would be ideal for teaching factual material with a mass of details requiring rote learning. They do teach this material efficiently but their success has been greater with subjects requiring understanding. This is leading workers to attempt more ambitious programmes such as the teaching of formal logic or the improvement of art appreciation by increasing a student's ability to make subtle discriminations (Hanson, 1963). In these programmes the accent is upon creativity, and the aim is for a student to be able to generalize and transfer the teaching to widely different situations (Cartier, 1964). It will be appreciated that if programmes are successful in this aim then they are meeting some of the most rigorous criteria of teaching.

V. IMPLICATIONS FOR THE FUTURE

1. *Per ardua ad alta?*

Programmes are not testing students but trying to facilitate their learning. The question is often asked whether this will teach anything beyond the immediate material. For many years education has supported the idea that there is something virtuous in overcoming a difficulty: *per ardua* can become a maxim no matter what the goal. But anything can be made difficult. Teachers are not complimented for making a subject difficult for their students. Today there is so much knowledge to be gained, so many new ideas to be understood that every student needs to progress as far as possible along the road of knowledge. The query arises whether he will go further if he is taught in such a way that he understands each step and has confidence in his ability to respond correctly, or whether he should be brought face to face with the 'uncut' problem and left to solve it for himself. A wealth of issues lies here. On the one hand, if the student never faces a problem in his tuition will he inevitably fail when on his own? On the other if a student is not being guided in the kind of problems he tackles, how far is he being taught? No teacher throws problems indiscriminately to his student.

Programmed instruction has something positive to offer. It can compare the effects of different methods of teaching without the intervention of that incalculable variable, the personality of the teacher. And because it has such a complete record of a student's progress different procedures can be accurately compared. The implications of this are not always fully realized. For example, it is sometimes said that the good teacher will break down material into digestible units of information, ensure participation of students through questioning, reward correct responses by approval and concentrate on the slower learners (an extract from a recent governmental committee report). This is true. Provided his class is not an impossible size, a 'good teacher' will teach by these means; but any average programme will do this as a matter of course, even to ensuring that the slower learners are able to respond. And programmed instruction will provide much more information for future guidance, for responses are available for every frame in the programme. The difficulty of a later lesson can be compared with that of an earlier, and the progress of students of different abilities can be accurately assessed. The mean or medium score may not give a true indication of what is happening. Hartley (1964, 1965) in his analysis of percentage errors for his branching and linear programmes compared the scores for the 1st and 3rd quartile ranges. He found that as students worked through a programme the error rate for both quartiles decreased with his branching programme, but increased for the linear programme. This increase was attributable largely to the scores in the 3rd quartile. This kind of interesting finding may be expected when we make a detailed analysis of errors. Here the explanation may be that fewer errors were made in the later lessons of the branching programme because the material was getting easier, but in view of the fact that this did not happen in the parallel linear programme it is more probable that all subjects had adjusted to the branching programme and were performing more efficiently in the later lessons. This result also raises the question that it may be possible with some programmes to produce a proportionately greater improvement in the response scores of the poorer students than in those of the better students. We will consider this point further for it could be a significant contribution to teaching.

2. *A teaching aim*

We accept that learning is highly correlated with IQ scores, and indeed whatever is or is not implied by IQ it is in several respects synonymous with learning ability. But teaching is directed learning, that is, directed in terms of who shall learn and what shall be learned. Above all it is directed in the sense that it is something more than accidental or incidental learning. For this reason teaching should not be prepared to accept the high correlation between IQ and learning as inevitable. If no teaching occurs it will remain. It has to be seen as a challenge in which the teacher is trying to enable all students to learn and where many weaker students will be guided to reach a higher level of performance than they would otherwise achieve. It would seem that it is here that programmed instruction could excel, for it can both diagnose its progress and accurately examine all difficulties. Doubts have been expressed that programmed instruction is learning made easy and that it provides no training for a student to meet the difficulties that will inevitably confront him. But this view fails to take in the whole scene. Programmed instruction should be used to take students as far as they are capable of progressing, and the hope is that they will journey beyond the limits that are set at present. It may be that eventually the good students also will go beyond their present limits and that the correlation between IQ and learning ability will remain; this would be acceptable provided both weak and good students have been taught to a higher level than they would have achieved unaided.

An example of teaching improvement was demonstrated to the writer in a local school for ESN children. The headmaster with untiring devotion had written and produced reading programmes for his classes. It was impressive to see his children in action. They were obviously interested in their repeated successes and were keen to get on with their 'reading'. Records are now being kept over several years to examine how far the reading age of the pupils does change as a result of programmed methods.

3. *Group machines*

These are early days for programmed instruction and it would be misleading to regard our present examples as representing some permanent form. Programming is an empirical exercise and one of its contributions has been to make us take a hard look at how we are teaching. Many fundamental questions are being asked about teaching machines that might well have been asked earlier about standard teaching procedures; for example, programming has forced upon us the distinction between having a store of information and an efficient means of communicating, and has put the stress upon the students' reception and not upon the teacher. It would seem to the writer to be too early yet to make general statements, forecasting that programmed instruction will enjoy greater success with retarded learners than with gifted students, or even with scientific and technical subjects rather than with the arts. Future systems may differ very much from the present. For example, programmes at present are designed for individual use and students proceed at their own pace. But if control over teaching is effective it may well be possible to present the programme to a whole group and allow individual members facilities for responding. This requires a form of mechanized classroom, and experiments are already being undertaken with this system, as in the Psychology Department at Sheffield University. Several features of standard programmes are changed, notably that in the group situation some form of pacing is introduced; that is, each frame is exposed for a certain length of time and students have to make their responses within that time. Experiments to date suggest that control is maintained, students have learned successfully and it is possible for even a casual observer to detect at once where a programme is proving difficult or where an individual student cannot cope (Moore, 1967).

Again another form of group study is where pairs of students are working together upon one programme. Children discuss problems and explain points about the programme to each other. Early results have been encouraging (Dick, 1963). Several workers in Britain such as Leith (1964) have examined the effects upon learning of pairing students who are of markedly different abilities and have found beneficial results. Hartley (personal communication) is currently comparing the progress of students who have been paired together because of their different abilities with pairs of similar abilities. Early results indicate differences in the rate of progress of these groups. This is the kind of learning situation that can be effectively examined by programmed instruction.

4. *Computer-assisted instruction*

Turning to more lavish equipment, there have been several experiments, mostly American, using computers to teach a class of students. The best known are PLATO (Programmed Logic for Automatic Teaching Operations) and CLASS (Computer-based Laboratory for Automated School Systems). The central computer operating at high speed and with a large capacity has the time to handle the responses of each individual student (Coulson, 1962). This is still an extravagant way of employing computers, but with the introduction of smaller computers this line of development is likely to increase.

The writer believes that the small-scale computer offers the most exciting and practical possibility of controlling teaching. Whereas present systems have to rely upon the student's response to a particular question to determine whether teaching has been successful, the computer can base its assessment upon a succession of responses. One of the best-known of these adaptive machines is S A K I. (Self-organizing Automatic Keyboard Instructor) devised by Pask (1960) for the training of card punch operators.

A trainee is given cue information (an indicator light) so that he learns to press an appropriate key for a particular problem. When he presses his key the problem light and cue light extinguish and the next pair are illuminated. A prescribed time is allowed for each problem and if the trainee fails to press the correct key an error is recorded and the machine moves on to the next problem. Items are presented slowly at the beginning of practice but gradually the exercise is speeded up and the cue light diminishes in intensity.

M. E. Sime in our Department has built his own adaptive device which teaches a similar keyboard coding skill by selecting those responses where a trainee is least adept. At the beginning of a teaching session the machine presents a random set of problems but as a subject learns it biases selection in favour of the items where he is experiencing difficulty. Sime's adaptive machine is of particular interest because he can vary the interval between presenting and re-presenting the same problem. As we might expect, the shorter the interval the quicker the performance, but it does not follow that learning is also quicker with the minimum interval. Indeed one plausible hypothesis that is being examined at present is that learning will be optimum with the maximum delay that is compatible with the student remembering the response. In other words we are trying to re-present the problem just before the student forgets the solution. Of course this would be impossible in a situation which did not cater for the needs of an individual but this is precisely the strength of the adaptive machine. It will be appreciated that the machine is in fact writing a different programme for each student, based on his individual learning results. A striking feature of learning under these conditions is the manner in which the variance between students has been reduced. A whole group has been brought up to the standard of the best students who were learning under normal conditions with randomly presented material.

Of course these are simple keyboard coding skills where the material – letters of the alphabet – has no hierarchical structure that demands one letter combination be taught before any other. With these independent items we can now improve our teaching schedule only by improving the decision rules upon which the machine's choices are based. This pin-points our future need. We may well know the best decision rules for our simple teaching situation but we appreciate that we do not know them for complex materials. Already computer assisted instruction can make significant contributions to teaching, but the limitations are not in the computer but in our knowledge of teaching. Once we do know the decision rules that we wish to build into such teaching systems we can make significant advances. Fortunately the computer-assisted method does provide us with a first-class tool for examining the efficiency of different decision rules and from which we should be able to increase our understanding of teaching strategies.

A final point that has emerged from our studies with adaptive machines is the remarkable way in which students respond to a programme that is being individually prepared for them. It is apparent that motivation is exceptionally high. In part this arises from the sheer interest of working at a task that is tailored for a particular person. It fits. But it is also extremely economical. A student does not waste his energy going over something he already knows or lose time waiting for a new item. He is directed all the time to the parts of the task that he needs to learn. We often find that students working with an adaptive machine are loath to give up at the end of the teaching session.

VI. CONCLUSION

Programmed instruction has created a world-wide interest. It is particularly active in the States and is now extensively studied in Britain. In the 1963 circular of the Research and Intelligence Branch of the Ministry of Education many Local Education Authorities reported work in programmed learning in primary and secondary schools, grammar schools and colleges of further education. The work ranged from remedial reading and spelling programmes to chemistry classes at University level.

At present the main effort is being directed to producing programmes. The gay stage of inventing machines or simple presentation devices has passed. It begins to look as if programmes will be presented either in book form or fairly elaborate machines which have a number of special facilities to offer such as branching and audio and visual presentation, etc. The plastic box type of machine that serves mainly to prevent cheating (deliberate or unintentional) hardly seems to be worth the increased effort. Meantime, research is concentrating more upon how programmes might be written and how computer controlled machines might change the programmes that need to be written.

In this chapter no attention has been given to the kind of arguments that have arisen about programmed instruction and the purpose of education. This has been deliberate for so far little has been said that is worthwhile. It is our contention that such discussions have been based upon a misunderstanding of the role of programmed instruction. It is for educators to decide what they want to be taught; but they should appreciate that a powerful new instrument is being offered to them to help in that teaching. And we would go further. Teaching machines should not be seen as something competing with human teachers for they may well find their most useful role when used in conjunction with teachers. Inevitably with the world-wide shortage of teachers we must turn to machines to redress the balance between students and staff.

REFERENCES

ANNETT, J. (1961). The role of knowledge of results in learning: a survey. Nautradevcen 342–343. Fort Washington, New York.

CARTIER, F. A. (1964). Programming thinking. In Ofiesh, G. D., and Meierhenry, W. C. (eds.), *Trends in Programmed Instruction*. Washington, D. C.: NEA.

COULSON, J. E. (1962). *Programmed Learning and Computer-Based Instruction*. New York: Wiley.

CROWDER, N. A., and ZACHERT, V. (1961). Use of the Autotutor at Keesler Air Force to train in fundamentals of electronics. Memo. Report No. 1. Contract No. AF 33 (616) – 6983 CPEE.

DETERLINE, W. A. (1962). *An Introduction to Programmed Learning*. Englewood Cliffs, N.J.: Prentice-Hall.

DEUTSCH, J. A. (1960). *The Structural Basis of Behaviour*. Cambridge: Cambridge University Press.

DICK, W. (1963). Retention as a function of paired and individual use of programmed instruction. *Journal of Programmed Instruction III*, **3**, 17–23.

EIGEN, L. D. *et al.* (1962). A comparison of modes of presenting a programmed instruction sequence. *Journal of Programmed Instruction*. **1**, 2–5.

EVANS, J. L., GLASER, R., and HOMME, L. E. (1959). A preliminary investigation of variation in the properties of verbal learning sequences of the 'Teaching Machine' type. In Lumsdaine, A. A., and Glaser, R. (1960).

EVANS, J. L., HOMME, L. E., and GLASER, R. (1960). The Ruleg (rule example) system for the construction of learning programmes in Lumsdaine, A. A., and Glaser, R. (1960), 619–20.

FELDHUSEN, J. F. (1961). Reactions of college students to self-instructional teaching devices and programmed instruction. AID No. 4.

HANSON, L. P. (ed.) (1963). *Programmes '63.* New York: Center for Programmed Instruction.

HARTLEY, J. (1963). *Some Guides for Evaluating Programmes.* London: Assoc. Programmed Learning.

HARTLEY, J. (1964). *Logarithms.* London: Methuen.

HARTLEY, J. (1964). A study in programmed learning. Unpub. Ph.D. Thesis. University of Sheffield.

HARTLEY, J. (1965). Linear and skip-branching programmes: a comparison study. *Brit. J. Educ. Psychol.* **35,** 320–328.

HUGHES, J. L. (1962). The effectiveness of programmed instruction: experimental findings. In Margulies, S., and Eigen, L. D. *Applied Programmed Instruction.* New York: Wiley.

HULL, C. L. (1943). *Principles of Behaviour: An Introduction to Behaviour Theory.* New York: Appleton-Century-Crofts.

JONES, H. L., and SAWYER, M. O. (1949). A new evaluation instrument. In Lumsdaine, A. A., and Glaser, R. (1960), 644.

KAY, H. (1964). General introduction to teaching machine procedures. In Austwick, K. (ed.), *Teaching Machines and Programming.* Oxford: Pergamon.

KAY, H., ANNETT, J., and SIME, M. E. (1963). *Teaching Machines and their use in industry.* London: H.M.S.O.

KRUMBOLTZ, J. D., and WEISMAN, R. G. (1962). The effect of overt *vs* covert responding to programmed instruction on immediate and delayed retention. *J. Educ. Psychol.* **53,** 250–253.

LEITH, G. O. M. (1964). *A handbook of Programmed Learning.* Birmingham: University of Birmingham.

LUMSDAINE, A. A. (1962). Instructional materials and devices. In Glaser, R. (ed.), *Training Research and Education.* Pittsburgh: Univ. of Pittsburgh Press.

LUMSDAINE, A. A., and GLASER, R. (ed.) (1960). *Teaching Machines and Programmed Learning: a Source Book.* Washington, D.C.: NEA.

MOORE, D. (1967). Group teaching by programmed methods. Unpub. Ph.D. Thesis, University of Sheffield.

PASK, G. (1960). The teaching machine as a control mechanism. *Transactions of the Society of Instrument Technology.* **12,** 72–89.

PRESSEY, S. L. (1926). A simple device for teaching, testing and research in learning. *School and Soc.* **13**, 373–376.

ROTHKOPF, E. Z. (1963). Criteria for the acceptance of self-instructional programmes. In Lysaught, J. P., and William, C. (ed.), *A Guide to Programmed Instruction.* New York: Wiley.

POPPLETON, P. K., and AUSTWICK, K. (1964). A comparison of programmed learning and note making at two age levels. *Brit. J. Educ. Psychol.* **34**, 43–50.

SCHRAMM, W. (1962). *The Research on Programmed Instruction: An Annotated Bibliography.* Institute for Communication Research, Stanford University.

SKINNER, B. F. (1954). The science of learning and the art of teaching. In Lumsdaine, A. A., and Glaser, R. (1960), 99–113.

SKINNER, B. F., and HOLLAND, J. G. (1958). The use of teaching machines in college instruction. In Lumsdaine, A. A., and Glaser, R. (1960), 159–172.

SMITH, N. H. (1962). The teaching of elementary statistics by the conventional classroom method versus the method of programmed instruction. *J. Educ. Res.* **55**, 417–420.

THOMAS, C. A., DAVIES, I. K., OPENSHAW, D., and BIRD, J. B. (1963). *Programmed Learning in Perspective.* London: City Publicity Services.

THORNDIKE, E. L. (1911). *Animal Intelligence.* New York: Macmillan.

WALLIS, D. (1964). Experiments on the use of programmed instruction to increase the productivity of training. *Occup. Psychol.* **38**, 141–160.

Since the writing of this chapter there has appeared the important compilation of papers edited by R. Glaser.

GLASER, R. (ed.) (1965). *Teaching Machines and Programmed Learning, II.* Data and Directions. Washington, D.C.: NEA.

13

Schematic Learning in Mathematics

R. R. SKEMP

I. INTRODUCTORY IDEAS

THE devotion of a chapter to the learning of a single subject, mathematics, needs perhaps some explanation. The reason is that mathematics shows a particular kind of learning, namely abstract schematic learning, in its purest form. Other subjects involve this process to varying degrees – probably all do, to some extent. Since in mathematics it can be seen most clearly at work, an understanding of the process can best be reached by studying it in this context. When we know what we are looking for, we can then more easily find it in other areas of learning where it is combined with other factors.

A further justification is that mathematics covers a much wider field than is usually thought by the non-mathematician. In his *Prelude to Mathematics*, W. W. Sawyer says: 'Mathematics is the classification and study of all possible patterns.' This is a far cry from the dreary mechanical computations of long divisions, multiplications of fractions, and the like, which is unfortunately the image of mathematics for so many. (To these, Sawyer's book is strongly recommended for getting the feel of what mathematics is really about.) So in studying the learning of mathematics, we may hope also to discover a little more about the nature of mathematics itself. Some readers may even reach the conclusion that what they so disliked at school was not, in fact, mathematics at all!

I will begin by trying to convey, in general terms, what is meant by 'schema'. The word was taken over by Bartlett from a neurologist, Head, and later used by Piaget in his difficult though important book *The Psychology of Intelligence*. It is used to include all mental structures which integrate existing knowledge and behaviour.

The emphasis here is on 'structure', as distinct from 'habit'. And though it would be reasonable enough to insist that a habit is but a particularly simple kind of schema, there are differences which are

415

important enough to need marking by the use of different words. (A cat's mew or purr could be described as a 'language': but if we want to emphasize the *difference* between these and human language, with a view to investigating what the latter can do that the former cannot, it would be better to use a different name for the sounds made by a cat.)

For example, I sometimes walk from the Advisory Centre in Leicester (a town which I do not know well) to the station. I regularly follow the same route, and each corner or cross-road is the cue to turn right, go straight on, or turn left as the case may be. From the Advisory Centre (A) I also sometimes walk for lunch either to a Chinese Restaurant (C) or a public house (P). So I soon knew these three routes A S, A C, and A P quite well. But these were initially isolated habits.

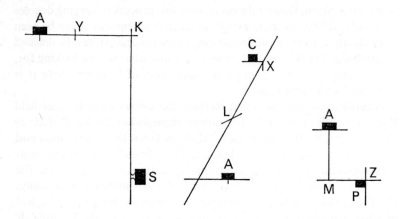

These habits had been learnt separately. Not knowing the relationship between A, S, C and P, I could not go from P to C without first returning to A, nor plan the shortest journey taking in several of these places. It was not until I had formed in my mind an idea of the general structure of this part of Leicester that I was able to walk at will from any one point in it to any other.

This difference is well shown by comparing an A A route with a road map. The route represents a particular journey; the map gives the structure of a whole area, from which we can (and must) select the information we need for a particular purpose. The structure takes longer to learn, but is much more flexible in the uses to which it can be put.

The rigidity of a simple habit is shown in extreme form by the path-habits of the shrew. Lorenz (1952) describes how they will always follow their accustomed path to their nest-box, even though this may cross and recross itself as in the diagram. Partly no doubt because of their very poor sight, they are unable to relate together the different parts of their route sufficiently to take either of the possible shorter

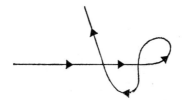

paths if once the longer one has been learnt.

What is lacking in the shrew is the ability to see (literally) that two particular points on its path, though encountered at different times, are in fact the same point. And it is the ability to see (literally or metaphorically) that two objects, actions, relationships, or other experiences are in certain ways the same which is most characteristic of intelligence. Much of the time we take this ability for granted. When the awareness comes suddenly, we call it 'insight', and the pleasure which we then experience derives from the contrast of this state with our previous one of 'being in the dark'. The pleasures enjoyed by mathematicians are largely derived from the experience of a succession of insights; and the unpleasure of those who try but fail at mathematics, from their perpetual state of darkness. It is therefore the function of teachers to arrange, if they can, for the former.

An awareness of something in common between two or more experiences is what we mean by a concept: so the formation of concepts is fundamental to schematic learning.

In our Leicester example, it is only by recognizing that X, Y and Z are different parts of the same road that the two separate routes can be integrated into a mental map like that which appears on p. 418

Similarly in geometry, it is only by seeing what is common to the two figures lower down on p. 418 that a pupil can integrate what he knows about parallel lines and a transversal with what he knows about triangles, to derive new knowledge about equiangular triangles. Concepts are the connecting links joining the elements of a schema.

Concepts are also the elements themselves. Consider again these two

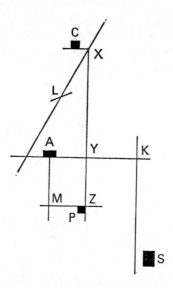

examples. In the former, the fusion takes place between 'the route A B' and 'the route C D', meaning what is essential to making these journeys, and ignoring whatever else may have been experienced at the time such as a cold wind or a sunny day, which pavement we walked on, or who may have been with us at the time. We take such abstraction for granted, but it is only by their aid that we can pre-form new actions by mental combinations – not of past events, but of concepts derived from past events.

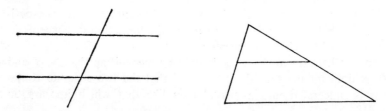

Similarly in mathematics, at the root of the whole process is the ability to class together *all* pairs of parallel lines (ignoring their length, distance apart, position on the paper), and likewise *all* triangles (ignoring size, shape, orientation), in both cases ignoring the day of the week, whether the figure was seen in chalk, or pencil, or printer's ink, etc., etc.

If mathematics is simply the formation and use of conceptual schemata, and if the latter is something we are continually doing in our everyday life, what is the difference between these? Or have we (like Molière's 'Bourgeois Gentilhomme' who found that he had been speaking prose all his life) been doing mathematics all our lives without knowing it?

II. WHAT IS MATHEMATICS?

The answer is: to some extent, yes, we have. Every time we put on a pair of shoes (as opposed to two odd ones) or buy a dinner set, we are using the mathematical idea of a set: that is, of a specified collection of objects. If when we lay the table we make sure that there is a place for everyone, with no place left empty, we are using the idea of one-to-one correspondence between two sets – the set of places, and the set of diners. These two concepts are fundamental in mathematics.

When we look at a Tube map, we find that it does not show distances or directions: it abstracts just two properties of the underground railway system, betweenness and connectedness. These, together with the names of the stations, are all we need to choose the particular route we need from the network. Such a representation is said to be *topologically equivalent* to the network. (Similarly, a triangle and a circle are topologically equivalent to each other, but a figure eight is not topologically equivalent to either.) Topology is apt to be regarded as quite an advanced branch of mathematics: yet here is an application of it which many non-mathematical Londoners use daily.

The truth is that many of the basic ideas of mathematics are used daily by most of us without knowing it. Compared with an animal or a primitive man, we are all mathematicians. We do not notice it because everyone else is doing it too, so that we take for granted what may be quite sophisticated ideas. It is only when we encounter ideas beyond those which we are used to, and have mastered intuitively and almost unconsciously, that we start calling them mathematics.

It would, however, be stretching the point too far to insist that using a Tube map is just as much a mathematical activity as solving a differential equation. Of the same kind, yes: but not of the same degree. The chief differences between 'everyday mathematics' and what is practised under the specific name of mathematics are three in number: the order of the concepts, the degree of abstraction, and the extent of the structure. These three differences can best be made clear by examples from mathematics itself.

(i) A conceptual hierarchy

Let us begin from two ideas which have already been mentioned: set, and one-to-one correspondence.

A set is any well-defined collection of objects. 'Well-defined' simply means that given any object, we can say whether it belongs to the set or not. So 'All good people' does not define a set (are you good?), nor does 'All boys' (at what instant does a boy become a man?). But 'All living human males' defines a set, and so do 'The set of all roses', 'The set of road wheels of my car', 'The set of present members of Parliament'.

From these examples, a naïve reader would no doubt have formed the concept of a set. In so doing, he has taken a step from the concrete to the abstract: several, in fact. We can point to a rose, but not to the set of all roses: and our ability to say, given some particular flower, whether it is a rose or not depends on our already having formed the class-concept 'rose' from a number of particular (and visible) examples of the concept. I call 'rose' a *primary concept,*[1] since it derived from sensory or motor experiences in the outside world. When we talk about 'the set of all roses' we are using the class-concept as the *characteristic property* of a set: that is, to define a set by saying what property (or properties) our object must have to be in the set. All the sets mentioned earlier were defined in this way. It is equally legitimate to define a set by listing its elements (e.g. the set consisting of my house, your nose, Nelson's column, and the Mona Lisa) but usually less profitable.

The concept of a set is found from examples of various particular sets; which is to say that it is formed from other concepts, not from experiences in the outside world. To mark this difference, I call it *a secondary concept.* We shall find that all the concepts of mathematics are secondary concepts, which means that they are dependent for their formation on the pre-existence of the other concepts from which they are derived. The latter may be primary concepts, or secondary concepts of lower order.

Given two sets, we can choose for each object in the first set a corresponding object in the second set. For example, given any set of words, and the set of letters of the alphabet, we can match each word with a letter by choosing the initial letter (or by any other system we like). In this example, we may get several words having the same initial letter, and some letters with no corresponding word. Sometimes, however, we

---

[1] This and related ideas have been discussed at greater length elsewhere: e.g. Skemp (1962b, 1965). But a brief account is also essential here.

have just one object in each set corresponding to just one object in the other set, with none over in either. This kind of matching is called a one-to-one correspondence, and is common in everyday life. When we dress, we arrange a one-to-one correspondence between our shoes and our feet, also between our socks and our feet. Laying the table was given earlier as an example of one-to-one correspondence. For physically normal people, the following sets can all be put in one-to-one correspondence: their eyes, their ears, their feet, their thumbs . . .

Suppose that we now collect together all the sets mentioned in the last sentence, together with all other sets which can be put in one-to-one correspondence with any (and therefore all) of them. We now have a new set. The objects in it are all themselves sets, but there is nothing to forbid this. What is the characteristic property of this new set? It is *the number two*. Given any set at random, we can check whether it has this property by matching it against any of the existing sets in the collection. If it matches one-to-one, with none over on either side, then the number of the given set is also two. If it does not, there are two possibilities. The given set may have a number other than two; or it may not have a number at all. (Sets of the second kind are called non-denumerable.)

Confining our attention to sets of the first kind, we see that these can all be collected together into sets of sets which have the characteristic property of being in one-to-one correspondence. Each of these characteristic properties is a number; and conversely, each and every number is a class-concept derived from a particular collection of (one-to-one corresponding) sets.

To each number (which is a concept) we give a name (one, two, three . . .). The name of a number is called a *numeral*.

Numeration is a system for naming all possible numbers, however large, with as few different names as convenient. In the decimal system of numeration we use ten basic names, in the binary system two. The invention of a really good system of numeration, in conjunction with suitable digits (such as 1, 2, 3 . . .) was crucial to the further development of mathematics. It was for lack of this that the Romans made no real progress in mathematics, while that of the Greeks was confined mainly to geometry.

Given a suitable set of numerals, *counting* uses these in a brilliantly simple device for finding the number of a given set of objects in a systematic way. It involves two further preceding steps, which the reader may care to try to work out for himself.

A detailed discussion of the last few concepts might well warrant a separate treatise of its own. What I hope has become clear is that the most basic ideas of mathematics – numbers, numerals, and counting – are themselves second order concepts of considerable subtlety. (A number is the characteristic property of a set of sets; 'numeral' is the name of a name.) And these are but the merest beginning. Addition is a concept derived from repeated actions of combining sets of objects, so it is a new kind of concept: an operation. Multiplication comes from repeated addition, subtraction is the inverse of addition, division the inverse of multiplication. Fractions, negative numbers, ratios . . . , algebra, calculus, wave mechanics . . .; each new stage consists of new concepts of yet higher order, a necessary (but not sufficient) condition being the existence in the mind of the learner of a sufficient number of contributory concepts at each preceding level. Even by elementary algebra, the order of the concepts involved (being the number of successively higher order concepts which have to be formed) is probably far higher than that of any other concepts either in everyday use or in other school subjects.

The account which has been given of the concepts leading to that of number may arouse several possible responses. One is that of pleasurable discovery: 'So that is where it all comes from!' Another, opposite in kind, might be that the reader has managed to count, add, multiply . . . for many years without all this fuss about what a number really is. There is some justification for this attitude, provided that this is all that he wants to do. True, he is using techniques which have taken some of the most progressive of human minds many thousands of years to develop: but he may be content to 'stand on the shoulders of giants', yet see only half as far as they did. It is also true that for some purposes, understanding is not necessary, and can be replaced by the mechanical use of rote-learnt habits. What is more, concepts can be well formed and successfully used at an intuitive level without the kind of conscious analysis which has here been made.

This attitude can, however, never be justified in anyone connected with teaching – for at least three reasons.

First: we teach what we are at least as much as what we say. So we cannot expect to raise inquiring minds if our own are not also, throughout our lives, still seeking further understanding.

Second: since the higher structure of mathematics is entirely dependent on the fundamental concepts of which a few have been mentioned, the aim must be for pupils to form these in the clearest and best-integrated way possible. A concept is not either present or absent:

it can be present in a woolly, inaccurate form or a well crystallized, accurate form, with all degrees in between. Later progress is likely to depend largely on how well the early concepts have been formed: so the teacher's own concepts must continually be sharpened and improved.

Third: the earlier concepts can only be communicated by carefully chosen examples, not by verbal definitions, and still less by any form of rote memorization. (See particularly Skemp, 1965.) The correct choice of examples will depend on the teacher[1] having an explicit and conscious awareness of the concept which he is trying to arrange for his pupils to form. Intuitive knowledge is not enough for this purpose.

The first characteristic of mathematics is therefore that it is a conceptual hierarchy in which the student has to form concepts of a much higher order than is likely to be required of him in other subjects, or in everyday life. And a consequence of this is that the teacher must have a particularly clear awareness of the structure of this hierarchy if he is to help his pupils to construct it in their own minds.

(ii) Degree of abstraction

By the degree of abstraction of a concept, we mean something different from its order. A concept like, say, the derivative of a function may be built on many earlier concepts of successively lower order. But given proper presentation, these are not particularly difficult to form. 'Derivative' is a peak in a long hierarchy of concepts, but the height of the steps from one level to the next can all be made quite small, so the ascent need not be laborious.

What do we mean by this metaphor 'the height of each step'? This is the *degree of abstraction* involved in the formation of the new concept.

Consider these two examples. First, a child sees a number of mobile containers in which people ride about on the roads, each having four wheels and making a characteristic noise. To see that these have something in common, and class these objects together under the collective name 'motor-car', is not particularly difficult.

Second, consider the insight by which Newton perceived that the fall of an apple to the earth, and the orbits of the planets round the sun, have something in common.

What are the differences between these two processes of concept formation whereby the first is an everyday event of which any child is

---

[1] Unless, of course, he has chosen a textbook in which this choice has been correctly made for him.

capable, whereas the second is the kind of achievement which makes us regard Newton as a genius?

One difference is the remoteness of the conceptual property from what is perceptually available. There is considerable resemblance between the various kinds of motor-car which a child sees: there is very little resemblance between an apple falling to the earth, and the earth rotating around (and not falling to) the sun. The more remote the common property is from perceptual reality, the greater is the degree of abstraction, and the more does the achievement depend on that mental ability which we call intelligence. It takes more intelligence to see what three cows and three pennies have in common, than to see what three cows and five cows have in common.

Looking at this factor in another way, we could say the difference lies in the amount of irrelevant information which has to be ignored in order to form the concept. When identifying an object as a car, the irrelevant details (size, colour . . .) are much outweighed by the relevant ones (wheels, motion, general shape, doors, windows, people inside, characteristic noise . . .). In forming the concept of universal gravitation, *everything* is irrelevant but the masses of the two bodies and the distance between them.

When we say 'irrelevant', we mean of course only in relation to the concept which we have in mind. In this context, everything which does not contribute to the concept is called *noise* (a term taken from information theory). So we can say that one characteristic of a highly intelligent individual is in the amount of noise above which he can still form a concept.

This way of looking at it also suggests one method by which the abstraction of a particular concept can be made easier for those whose intelligence is nearer to the average: by reducing the amount of noise. The chief difficulty of a 'problem' is in abstracting the mathematical ideas from the total situation as presented. This is made easier if all the information given is relevant in some way or other: harder if the amount of noise is increased.

To the concept of any particular number[1], everything is noise except the separateness of the objects, and their being collected into a set. (When counting, we must have separate objects to count, and know which objects we are concerned with. Everything else we ignore.) So fairly plain objects, such as beads, cubes, matchsticks, contain less noise than trees, houses, and animals. Noise is reduced also

---

[1] Not the concept of *number*.

by having the objects in a set all alike: there is less noise (relative to the concept three) in a set of three cubes than in a set consisting of a bead, a cube, and a matchstick.

Care is needed, however, not to reduce noise so much that a child never learns to ignore it. Abilities are developed by the demands which are made on them, provided only that these demands are not so great as to be beyond the mental powers of the individual. A sound policy would seem to be to reduce noise in the early stages of learning, and for pupils of less ability; and to increase it when a concept is well formed, and for more intelligent pupils.

(The above paragraph contains the justification for this whole chapter to the reader who has no special interest in mathematics. The system of concepts which we call collectively 'schematic learning' is of great generality, and worth understanding by everyone concerned with education and human development. Mathematics offers examples of these concepts with minimal noise.)

The amount of irrelevant detail ignored by a particular concept is closely related to the amount subsumed by it – that is, to the generality and therefore the power of a concept. Clearly the more individual examples to which a concept is relevant, the more we can do with it. This is a function of the concept itself, but also of the extent to which we are able to use it. We can perceive easily the relevance of a concept in a situation where there is little noise; with more difficulty, as the irrelevancies become greater. So a concept can be powerful in itself (e.g. that of gravity), and an individual can also be powerful in his use of a concept – quick to see what is essential among a wealth of data. The concepts of mathematics are powerful partly because of their high degree of abstraction, which gives them a very wide range of application. Hence the importance of mathematics in our contemporary civilization. What is often lacking, unfortunately, is the ability to apply these powerfully – to see what are the mathematical concepts relevant to a particular problem. This may be partly due to a weakness of the concepts themselves, and partly to lack of practice in overcoming noise.

(iii) The search for structure

Mathematicians have always been interested in searching for general laws: or as I prefer to call them, general properties. These are simply statements which are true for a wide range of particular cases, so they are statements about relationships between concepts. Individual cases are then obtained by replacing each concept by one of its examples.

The best way to get an idea of the kind of general laws with which mathematicians concern themselves will be to follow through one particular line of thinking in some detail. But before beginning, there is a mathematical concept which is particularly useful in this context, namely that of a variable. A variable is simply an un-named member of some particular set. This means that it has every property which is common to all objects in the set, but that we must not assume for it any individual or accidental property.

One of the commonest variables in mathematics is an un-named number. We call this a numerical variable, and much of algebra is devoted to finding general properties which are true for numerical variables.

Most readers will already be familiar with statements such as:

$$(a + b)^2 = a^2 + 2\,ab + b^2$$

and these certainly have many uses. Recently, however, there has been a partial change of emphasis. This can be illustrated by looking more closely into the above statement.

Though we have not said so, the reader may well have taken it for granted that a and b stand for numerical variables: that is, that they both represent numbers, though we do not say which. We should, however, say what *kind* of numbers. Are they ordinary counting numbers (called natural numbers), or fractions, or perhaps negative numbers? To begin with, we will take the simplest, the natural numbers:

$$(a + b)^2 \text{ means the same as } (a + b) \times (a + b).$$

How can we multiply the sum of two numbers, simultaneously, by the sum of two other numbers? Let us take it a step at a time.

The result of adding two numbers is always another number. So $(a + b)$ must stand for a number, although we do not know which. Let us call this number N.
We can now say:

$$(a + b) \times (a + b) = N \times (a + b)$$
$$= N \times a + N \times b$$

Now replace N again by $(a + b)$

We get
$$(a + b) \times a + (a + b) \times b$$
$$= a^2 + b \times a + a \times b + b^2$$
$$= a^2 + 2\,ab + b^2,$$
writing *ab* for $a \times b$

Straightforward enough, it may appear: but actually, several important points have been skipped.

We said that the result of adding two numbers is always another number, as if this could be taken for granted. But as a famous professor said to his students, 'Why are you not surprised?' If we combine two gases, we do not always get another gas. (Hydrogen + oxygen = water.) If we combine two poisonous substances, we do not always get another poison. (Sodium + chlorine = common salt.) This property of the natural numbers, that adding two of them *always* gives another natural number, is therefore both surprising and fundamental to algebra. It is called *closure*, and holds good also for multiplication of natural numbers; but not for subtraction or division, as the reader can easily verify.

We also said that

$$N \times (a + b) = N \times a + N \times b.$$

This statement is itself an important general property of the natural numbers, and represents what is common to all statements like:

$$7 \times (2 + 5) = 7 \times 2 + 7 \times 5$$
$$9 \times (4 + 3) = 9 \times 4 + 9 \times 3, \text{ etc.}$$

It is called the *distributive property* of multiplication over addition. It does not hold good if the multiplication and addition are interchanged, as can also be easily verified.

We also took it for granted that:

$$a \times b = b \times a$$

when we added $a \times b + b \times a$ to get $2ab$.

But again, why are we not surprised?

Fire burns paper does not mean the same as *Paper burns fire*, and this property of being able to interchange the two objects involved in some operation or other (called the commutative property) is indeed the exception rather than the rule in everyday life. Try pressing the starter-button of your car before switching on the ignition, for example; or putting on your shoes before your socks or stockings.

Mathematicians have found certain properties of the natural numbers, in conjunction with the operations of addition and multiplication, to be so fundamental that they have chosen them as the defining properties of a number system. These are:

Closure under addition and multiplication.

If a and b are any two numbers,

$a + b$ and $a \times b$ are both numbers.

Commutativity for addition and multiplication.

$a + b = b + a$, and $a \times b = b \times a$.

Associativity. Given three numbers to be added, or multiplied, it does not matter which two we add or multiply first.

$(a + b) + c = a + (b + c)$, and $(a \times b) \times c = a \times (b \times c)$

Multiplication is distributive over addition.

$$a \times (b + c) = a \times b + a \times c$$

The whole of algebra (and therefore also of those branches of mathematics which depend on algebra such as calculus, co-ordinate geometry, statistics) depends on these basic properties. So does much else. For example, a calculating machine multiplying 21 936 by 4 287 works out:

21 936 $\times$ 7
21 936 $\times$ 80
21 936 $\times$ 200
21 936 $\times$ 4 000   and adds them.

The machine is far quicker and more accurate at doing this kind of calculation than any human: but this derives from the intelligence of the men who understand the structure of the number system, and incorporate this structure in a machine.

Mathematicians build on this particular structure of concepts in three ways. First they make sure that these properties are kept whenever we extend our idea of number to other kinds such as positive and negative integers, fractions, or irrational numbers (such as the square root of 2). Second, they go looking for other combinations of a set of objects, with two operations, which have the properties of a number system. And third, they take those properties as their starting point and invent, or define, number systems of an entirely abstract kind. Through these stages can be seen a gradual shift of emphasis, first using the structure, then looking for other examples where it can be found, and finally treating a structure as something in its own right. This interest in structure *as such* is one of the major emphases of modern mathematics.

The process can also be described as a gradual change of emphasis from the *content* of a conceptual system to its *form*, The combination, form + content, is what constitutes any schema, mathematical or otherwise. So it follows that many of the structures which mathematicians study, especially the most basic ones, are the forms we can look for in any examples of intelligent learning, mathematical or other. Contemporary mathematicians are closer to being psychologists than they know!

As an example of the second of these processes, here is a kind of addition which we all do every day; 'clock-face addition'. Seven hours later than 8 o'clock is 3 o'clock, so in this system:

$$8 + 7 = 3, \text{ and so on.}$$

Multiplication is defined as repeated addition, so:

$$3 \times 7 = 7 + 7 + 7 = 9$$
and $$3 \times 8 = 8 + 8 + 8 = 0$$

Is this a number system? The reader may prefer to find out for himself, so the answer to this question will be given at the end of the chapter.

The following is an example of an entirely abstract number system. It has just two elements, which we will call m and n. (Since we do not know what they stand for, any other letters would do just as well.) The results of adding and multiplying these are given by the following tables:

Addition	m	n		*Multiplication*	m	n
m	m	n		m	m	m
n	n	n		n	m	n

To find out the result of, say, adding $n + m$, we use the first table. Find the first term (n) in the left-hand column, and the second term (m) in the top row above the line. The row containing the first, and the column containing the second, intersect at n in the body of the table, so:

$$n + m = n$$

Similarly for multiplication. With these rules, it is a straightforward matter to check that all the properties of a number system are satisfied. Before reading on, the reader is recommended to do this.

P

III. REALIZATION OF A STRUCTURE

The recommendation of the last sentence in the previous section had a particular purpose, beyond inviting the reader to verify the truth of the author's statement (that the abstract system given above is, in fact, a number system). This was, by experiencing the difficulties of working with pure abstractions, to gain some awareness of what it must be like for a young child in the same situation. The latter's difficulties are far greater, for his mental powers are less developed, and the abstract system he has to learn is much larger. In the table for addition (up to $10 + 10$) there are 100 elements instead of 4, and in the table for multiplication (up to 12×12) there are 144 elements instead of 4.

Part of the difficulty lies in the abstract nature of the elements and operations, as the reader will discover if he replaces the entirely abstract system above with any of the three systems which follow.

First, suppose that an explorer meets a primitive people whose counting has not progressed beyond the ideas of 'some' and 'none'. If we replace m and n respectively by these words, and let 'and' correspond to addition, 'of' to multiplication, we obtain the following tables:

and	none	some
none	none	some
some	some	some

of	none	some
none	none	none
some	none	some

The above tables can be read quite simply. For example: none of some is the same as none, none and some is the same as some, and so on.

Now let us replace the elements m and n with two switches: m by a switch in the open position, and n by a switch in the closed position. 'Adding' now means 'connecting in series', and 'multiplying' means 'connecting in parallel'.

Here are two examples:

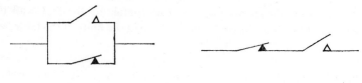

$n + m$	$m \times n$
(open in parallel with closed)	(closed in series with open)

The above system satisfies all the requirements for a number system. Closure, in this case, means that any parallel or series combination of two switches, open or closed, can be replaced by a single switch in one or other of these positions.

We can also replace m by 'false statement', n by 'true statement', addition by the disjunction 'or', multiplication by the conjunction 'and'. Then $m + n$ means a compound disjunctive statement (e.g. 'today is wet *or* today is Wednesday) which is true if either of the separate statements are true.

So $m + n = n$; and similarly for the other seven combinations.

Each of the three given examples satisfies the requirements for a number system, being what is called a *realization* of the abstract system given earlier. These three realizations have the same structure as the abstract algebraic system, and as each other. When this is so, we say that the systems are *isomorphic*. The reader may now care to construct the tables for 'adding' and 'multiplying' in the three later systems, using whatever notation commends itself to him: and, also, to check again that all three are all number systems.

Most people find the realizations much easier to comprehend initially than the abstract system; and also, that the abstract system then becomes clearer. Probably also the realizations were not equally easy for every one. Electrically minded people will probably prefer the second, philosophers the third, and those who enjoy puzzles will choose the first! But as each successive one is worked through, awareness of the structure increases: and understanding of each individual system is deepened by its relation to the common structure symbolized by the abstract system.

Realizations are particularly important to children, in such tasks as trying to comprehend the first number system they encounter (the natural numbers). For this purpose, the realizations are usually in concrete physical form, such as Unifix cubes, Multibase Arithmetic Blocks, Cuisenaire rods, and others. Their accessibility to the external senses satisfies the requirement that all concepts must originally be derived from primary concepts; and their simplicity minimizes 'noise', in the technical sense defined earlier. On these two criteria, there is little to choose between the various kinds available. Where they are very unequal is the accuracy with which they embody the required mathematical structure. Unfortunately a discussion of their respective merits would take us too far afield, particularly since it would have to begin with a detailed description of each.

Some general points may however be made. The first is that an abstract structure can best be formed from experience with several different realizations of it; which means that there is not one best 'number apparatus'. Moreover, unless a pupil encounters a sufficient number of different examples of a concept, he will not do the abstraction, and will remain at the level of concrete manipulation. Second: individuals will vary in the one which suits them best. Third: examples with more noise should be used as soon as the concepts are well formed. And finally, the function of realizations does not end with the learning of the natural number system. Concrete realizations should continue throughout the primary and junior years, with more sophisticated ones (such as pulleys and levers) entering in the secondary school. Mental realizations can make their first appearance quite early, and never become dispensable.

IV. ASSIMILATION AND ACCOMMODATION

There is a further function of the schema which is at least as important as those already discussed. As well as integrating what is known already, it is a valuable and often essential means for future learning. This is true in both everyday life and in school and college learning, from the most practical sensori-motor schemata to the most abstract theoretical systems. A child cannot walk till he can stand, nor play football till he can run and kick. The understanding of much of physiology depends on a knowledge of biochemistry, which depends in turn on ordinary chemistry. To learn aerodynamics, or the theory of oscillatory circuits, one must know calculus, for which a knowledge of algebra is first required; and this in turn derives from arithmetic. These are all large-scale examples, but the same dependency can also be seen in detail at every stage within them.

By schematic learning is meant learning which makes use of this ability of the schema to facilitate, often to make possible, further learning. In the process, the schema itself is always amplified, and sometimes further extended. To these complementary events are given the names *assimilation* and *accommodation*. Assimilation refers to the incorporation of new knowledge into an existing schema, and accommodation to the corresponding changes of the schema itself.

These sometimes appear simply as two aspects of the same process. For example, when a child obeys a teacher in the same way as he has previously obeyed his parents, he is assimilating this new experience to an existing schema. Since the teacher's requirements will not be identical with those of either of his parents, the schema itself will develop (accommodate) in the process of incorporating the new relationship. In so doing it will be preparing itself for further assimilations (needing further accommodations) as the individual encounters an increasing assortment of authorities in the course of finding his place in the adult social structure of his country and the world.

For a mathematical example, let us look again at the simple binomial expansion quoted at the beginning:

$$(a + b)^2 = a^2 + 2\,ab + b^2$$

We can multiply both sides of this by $(a + b)$, obtaining (after simplification):

$$(a + b)^3 = a^3 + 3\,a^2b + 3ab^2 + b^3$$

To do this requires no drastically new thinking: simply the further application of what is already known. The process can be repeated, giving:

$$(a^4 + b)^4 = a^4 + 4\,a^3b + 6\,a^2b^2 + 4\,ab^3 + b^4$$

It is clear that we could continue to get expansions of $(a + b^5), (a + b)^6$, ... as long as our motivation lasted.

But suppose now that we want to know the expansion of $(a + b)^{100}$. Few mathematicians would tolerate the tedious repetitions necessary to obtain the result by repeated multiplication. A search is made to find a pattern common to all the right hand sides, so that this can be used to determine any particular case which may be desired. This is not particularly easy: which is another way of saying that a considerable accommodation of the schema is required. When this has been achieved, the enlarged schema includes all the earlier examples as special cases – the new schema is continuous with the old. It is, moreover, now capable of assimilating new examples, such as $(1 + t)^{30}$, with great ease.

Assimilation thus depends on accommodation. Where the differences between new examples and those already incorporated into the schema are small, assimilation is effortless and intuitive. How wide a gap can be bridged in this way depends partly on the abstracting ability of the individual – that is, on his intelligence. A child who has only seen black and white cats, and tabbies, will readily accept marmalade cats, Siamese, and Persians into his feline schema. To realize that lions, tigers and leopards are also members of the cat family makes greater demands on powers of abstraction, but is still possible at the intuitive level.

V. REFLECTIVE INTELLIGENCE

There comes a stage, however, when the accommodation required is greater than can be done entirely in this way (though throughout mathematics, the importance of the intuitive leap must never be underestimated). In the binomial example just given, an impasse would be reached but for the ability not only to *use* the schema but to *examine* it, to make it conscious, to look for and eventually discover the pattern: in brief, the ability to use one's intelligence to reflect on one's own thoughts.

This is an ability which most of us use so habitually that we take it for granted. But I repeat, 'Why are you not surprised?' We can see the external world because we have eyes, hear it because we have ears. But no dissection has yet revealed any anatomical basis for our ability to see mental images, hear verbal thinking. And if we can do more – we can manipulate both of these. We can, for example, mentally experiment with images of possible actions, from which we select or construct the one which seems to us the most desirable; after which we put this pre-constructed behaviour into effect.

This remarkable ability underlies many of mankind's greatest achievements; yet it has, so far, aroused little surprise and given rise to few psychological experiments. So we know far less than we ought either about its functioning, or about how it develops.

We do, however, know a little – not enough – about when. One thing is sure: we must form concepts before we can reflect on them, so the intuitive level of functioning precedes the reflective level. The work of Inhelder and Piaget (1958) gives some guide to the ages when the latter develops, and suggests that formal reasoning – the ability to consider form apart from content – does not develop fully until adolescence.

If this is so, the implications for teaching are clear. We must not use methods which require the reflective use of intelligence in children who have not yet developed it. Piaget has shown (1928) that children can give the correct answer to a simple arithmetical problem without being able to say how they did it. I came across a good example myself recently, in a lesson on measurement for 11-year-olds. The teacher said that he wanted some rope, for a swing. The shopkeeper told him that 'This much' (from hand to hand, stretching his arms out horizontally) 'costs two shillings.' There were two men in the shop: a little, clever looking man, and a big, stupid looking man. 'Which,' asked the teacher, 'would you have asked to measure the rope?'

On a show of hands, about twenty-five out of thirty children chose the bigger man. But of the six children who were asked why they would choose him, not one gave the correct answer. (The bell then rang for the end of the lesson, so there was not time to ask any others.) Some were misled by the 'noise', i.e. the information that the bigger man also looked stupid, while others gave quite other and even more irrelevant reasons. Yet all the children questioned had intuitively given the correct answer.

Teaching for the lower ages must therefore be adjusted to the intuitive level of assimilation. This means a careful conceptual analysis by the teacher, the resulting concepts being communicated to the children in a suitable order for easy synthesis by them.

But we have not finished our job, as teachers, until we have made ourselves unnecessary. Until pupils can themselves begin to reflect on and analyse their own schemata, they are only half-way to being mathematicians (see Skemp, 1961). So at the ages when we are not yet assuming reflective ability in our pupils, we must nevertheless be trying to stimulate its growth. And although, as already said, too little research has yet been done into how or why it develops, it is a reasonable working hypothesis that asking children to give reasons for their answers will help. Any other situation, which forces one to think about one's ideas, such as trying to explain them to someone else, will also have this effect. In an experiment of my own with 12-year-old boys, those who had to teach something to a partner did better in a final test than their class mates who had spent the time in further practice on the same topic. Class discussions, in which an individual may have his ideas challenged and be called on to justify them, also provide conditions which stimulate reflection.

VI. THE POWER OF A SCHEMA

Material which can be assimilated to an existing schema is more easily learned, and better retained, than material which can only be rote-memorized.

In an experiment (Skemp, 1962a) with two grammar school first forms, it was found that schematic learning resulted in twice as much material being recalled immediately after learning, and seven times as much after four weeks, compared with rote-memorizing. The material to be learnt by the two methods was in this case identical, the only difference between the two groups of subjects being in the existence or absence of an appropriate schema to which the material could be assimilated. It was also noticeable that the boys seemed to enjoy the schematic learning task, while they reacted negatively to the rote learning one.

The superiority of schematic learning on these grounds alone is thus overwhelming – and we must also recall the other two related advantages: the integrating of what is known already, and the development of a mental tool for learning yet to come.

This also means that anything which does not fit into an existing schema has a very poor chance of being remembered. The facilitating effect of the schema for ideas which are easily assimilated to it acts also as a limiting effect against ideas which are not. In his account of Fleming's early work on lysozyme, Maurois (1959) relates that when he read a paper on his discovery to the Medical Research Club, 'The reception accorded to the paper was cold beyond belief. . . . Only utterly worthless papers were treated in this manner.' Yet this paper was anything but worthless, the audience anything but stupid. The occurrence can, however, easily be explained by one simple assumption, that the new ideas contained in Fleming's paper struck out in such a new direction that they were not assimilable to the schemata of his hearers. Similar receptions have been the fate of all too many other innovators – the reader can make his own list.

In any subject, the early schemata are therefore of crucial and far-reaching importance. And since, in children, they are being formed at an age when the learners' critical powers are undeveloped, in a situation where they have little freedom of choice, it is the responsibility of parents and teachers to see that so far as possible the right schemata are formed. And by 'right', we mean 'having the greatest possible powers of assimilation and accommodation'.

Inevitably, a major role will be played by the concepts and relations which form the schema. To guide its development aright, a teacher must know his subject with the utmost thoroughness, in two dimensions. He must know its content, and also have arrived by a conceptual analysis (which may be his own, or that of someone else) of its structure.

There is another factor still to mention. This is, the conditions in which pupils learn. Piaget has pointed out (1950), that in what appears to be trial-and-error learning, the trials are not random, but determined by the existing schema. We must therefore picture a schema not so much as an inanimate structure on to which further bits are gradually fitted (like a construction toy), but as something living and organic, actively reaching out for and seeking food for its own growth. The 'food' in this case is new ideas, some of which can be assimilated and some not.

Up to now we have been emphasizing the role of the teacher as dietician. But he has another function, too, which can be likened to that of the physical education teacher. Powers of accommodation, increasingly important as the rate of growth of human knowledge increases, are best developed in a situation which calls for active search by the schema, not just passive absorption.

This is the psychological basis of what is commonly called 'Discovery methods'. Implicit in this is the partial restriction of *guided* discovery, for without some guidance, children cannot be expected to make, in a few years, discoveries which have taken mankind many centuries. Our problem is to provide children with a challenging enough situation to evoke their interest, in free enough conditions for their own schemata to determine the kind of exploration and experiment which they do, while at the same time making a careful enough selection of the experiences offered to them to ensure that the new concept will be formed.

Who chooses these concepts? We do: it is a responsibility which we are not entitled to abdicate. If the next generation is to see further than we can, we must help them to climb on our shoulders, not leave them to repeat exactly the same ascent as we had to make. But we must not only 'give them a hand up'; we must also provide them with enough difficulty on the way, to develop their own strength and agility for the climb ahead.

The teacher's task is thus seen to be more complex, and more far-reaching in its consequences, than it ever appeared to be in the past. We are determining not only what a pupil learns while he is with us, but also his powers to learn (not to mention his appetite) in the future. And we have to try to bring about the right kind of development, only partly by direct activity on our own side: largely, by providing the right conditions for the children's own activity, and then standing back. The second of these approaches is by far the harder, and it is to the better understanding of it that I hope that this chapter may have contributed.

REFERENCES

INHELDER, B., and PIAGET, J. (1958). *The Growth of Logical Thinking*. London: Routledge and Kegan Paul.

LORENZ, K. Z. (1952). *King Solomon's Ring*. London: Methuen.

MAUROIS, A. (1959). *The Life of Sir Alexander Fleming*. London: Jonathan Cape.

PIAGET, J. (1928). *Judgement and Reasoning in the Child*. London: Routledge and Kegan Paul.

PIAGET, J. (1950). *The Psychology of Intelligence*. London: Routledge and Kegan Paul.

SKEMP, R. R. (1961). Reflective intelligence and mathematics. *Brit. J. Educ. Psychol.* **31**, 45–55.

SKEMP, R. R. (1962a). The need for a schematic theory of learning. *Brit. J. Educ. Psychol.* **32**, 133–142.

SKEMP, R. R. (1962b). The teaching of mathematical concepts. *Mathematics Teaching*. No. 20, 13–15.

SKEMP, R. R. (1965). Concept formation and its significance in mathematics teaching and syllabus reform. *Aspects of Education*. Hull University, Department of Education.

Yes: clockface addition and multiplication is a number system.

14

Psychology and the Teacher

E. A. LUNZER

I. EDUCATION AND THE PSYCHOLOGY OF LEARNING

EDUCATION is the process whereby a society passes on its knowledge, its skills and its attitudes. The recipients are of course members of the society, usually younger and less experienced than the educators. The latter, in primitive societies, may be simply the adult members, or those who interact most closely with the child. In most contemporary societies, a great deal of education is institutionalized. There are nurseries, schools and colleges, usually purpose-built and equipped. There are also teachers and professors to whom society delegates some of its educational functions, and sometimes, but not always some or all of these may be accorded quite a high status. And there are rules for the observance of the various parties: teachers are required to attend the schools and to teach; pupils must attend and are expected to learn; parents and guardians must 'send' their children to school, and so on. On all of these there are negative sanctions and positive incentives. Teachers and professors may be dismissed for conspicuous failure to perform their duties, or they may be promoted for apparent devotion and success. Parents may be punishable by law for failure to send their children to school, and the children may be punished by their parents, or by the school, or even sent to a corrective institution for failure to attend. Both may be expected to share in some measure the attitude that education is necessary for success, and that knowledge and skill are somehow worthy ends in themselves. This last is, of course, not something that can be taken for granted, for attitudes vary. Finally, there is a great administrative paraphernalia, ranging from ministers of education to educational welfare officers, and including various kinds of inspecting and examining bodies, all of whom are concerned either with decision-making as to the how and what of education, or with the enforcement and implementation of decision, or with both.

Underlying all this machinery is the assumption that knowledge,

439

skills and attitudes can be transmitted from one individual to another. There is also an assumption that the delegation of education to special- ists is an effective way of achieving this end. The teacher in the classroom is the front line of education. Without him the activity of the officials would be meaningless, whereas without them one presumes that he might still carry on, albeit less effectively for want of resources and various kinds of support.

Suppose we call knowledge, skills and attitudes, behaviours. There is still a great deal of doubt as to whether there can be genetic trans- mission of acquired behaviours in human beings. What positive evidence we have relates to worms. There is no doubt about the pos- sibility of the transmission of acquired behaviour through education. The culture of societies depends on it. But how? The teacher–pupil relation involves the interaction of two parties, both human beings. As such it is of interest to psychologists, since psychology is the scientific study of the regulation of human behaviour. Even if their analysis were of no practical value, psychologists could not easily neglect so arresting a phenomenon as the transmission of acquired regulations (if the behaviour is transmitted, then so are the regulations). But, of course, there is every reason for believing that the scientific analysis of this transmission process can lead to greater efficiency in educational prac- tice. In some ways it has done already.

The aim of educational psychology is to construct an adequate scientific theory to account for the process of education, i.e. the trans- mission of behaviour. 'To account for' means to describe the inter- relations of all its underlying inferred processes. This is the difference between description and explanation, which somehow still continues to puzzle many. I am not sure why. Everyone knows the difference between describing the performance of a motor-car and explaining it. Of course engines and pistons are 'there' in the same sense as motor- cars. If one chooses to deny that inferred regulating processes are 'there' simply because they are not directly observed, one is liable to land up in confusion. I will say they are 'there', there in the brain, quite often physiologically observable (see Volume I, *passim*, and especially Chapters 2 and 4, Sections I, III), even though their functions are always inferred.

The aim of educational psychology is not simply, or even mainly, to devise techniques for measuring whether behaviour has been trans- mitted or not, i.e. whether learning has occurred and how much. But it cannot get very far without such techniques. Nor is its aim confined to the evaluation of individual differences in the learner which facilitate or obstruct the process of transmission. Clearly, this too is one of the problems that it must face. But it is not the central problem. To the extent that we understand the process of behaviour transmission, the characteristics of the learner take on the character of parameters to the process: not a part of the process itself, but a part of the larger system within which the process occurs, the values of which are modifiers to the process: e.g. the learner is a slow learner or a fast learner, specifically slow in bringing representational strategies to bear on a problem, or in the verbalization of relations, or in the visualization of spatial transformations, and so on. But first we must know how these sub-processes themselves interrelate in the process of transmission. This is the central problem of educational psychology considered in the present volume. And this is why we have considered the problems of individual differences in the learner along with the effect of various social determinants on the learner's attitudes, bracketing both under the single heading of the *Contexts of Education* (Volume III).

It is important to say this because too often – since Thorndike – educational psychology has been concerned precisely with these important but secondary problems. The central problem tends to be neglected. Instead, the discussion of individual differences and of environmental pressures will be prefaced by a perfunctory account of some features of behaviour in the laboratory rat, by way of lip-service to the fact that educational psychology is concerned with learning. Undoubtedly the fault lay mainly in the limitations of psychological theory and inquiry as a whole. Psychology took a wrong turning when it came to assume that, because theory stands or falls by experimental verification, and because experimental verification requires the specification both of controls and of observations, therefore the statements of the theory must be limited to statements of correlations between the two sorts of specified elements: stimuli and responses. What was left out of account was the consideration of the regulatory processes within the organism by virtue of which it becomes differentially selective in its response to combinations in the environment. Inevitably, this kind of psychology led to a serious under-estimation of the complexity of behavioural regulation even in the rat – especially in the 'free-field' situation, while the infinite complexity of human learning was neatly brushed under the carpet and all but dismissed as an artefact of 'symbolic response', or 'verbal mediation'. By way of innocent camouflage, we were invited to inspect the results of quite trivial 'learning' experiments involving human subjects (usually students, who are handy and tractable, just like rats), consisting in the memorization of words or nonsense syllables. The artificiality of such experiments is, of course, bound up with the fact that words do not exist in isolation but in the context of the very complex system of communication which we call language.

Because of the great importance of language in human learning, two chapters in this book have been devoted to a consideration of some of the relevant problems. A point I would like to emphasize here is that it is precisely in the area of language that psychologists are most keenly aware of the inadequacy of stimulus – response theory. Thus Lashley (1951) first called attention to the fact that the production of sentences required the imposition of a syntactic order on words, an order which is by no means implicit in the strength of associative bonds between groups of words related in meaning. Semantics, syntactics and phonology are three different levels of behavioural organization which interact in the determination of utterance. There can be no question of the determination of each element (phoneme or word) being simply a function of the feedback input from its predecessor. This is a part of the story (as shown in the disturbances that result from delayed feedback), but it is not the whole: for instance, there is evidence of backward determination of words by their successors (see Chapter 6). More than this, language provides some of the clearest evidence that the subject imposes a patterning on things, on which is not a product of experience but a product of his own brain. This is strongly suggested by the structure of elementary two-word sentences which splits all words into two broad classes: words that can take another word as prefixes or suffixes (pivot) and words that cannot (see Chapter 6 and Braine, 1963). This may well be a 'grammar' not modelled on adult grammar but based solely on a differentiation between subject and predicate. But there are other interpretations. Even more telling, however, is the evidence from negation and interrogation (Klima and Bellugi, 1966).

The proper way to negate '*Teddy is naughty*' is '*Teddy isn't naughty*': what one finds is that children begin with such forms as '*No Teddy* [*is*] *naughty*' and go on to invent a number of intermediate rules before fully adopting adult grammar. Quite generally, one may ask, what is the experience corresponding to negation? The very fact that the earliest understanding relates to '*No*', in the sense of '*Refrain*' (Chapter 5), illustrates that negation is something that relates to the activity of the subject and not to the object: one cannot be a passive receiver of stimulation from something that is not there, but one can look for it and find it absent. A similar grammatical history, and similar epistemological considerations, apply to the interrogative form.

The inadequacy of much psychological theory in explaining language has led Chomsky to postulate the existence in the human brain of a specific *Language analysing device* (LAD) to account for the understanding and production of new grammatical sentences. It is argued that certain structural properties of sentences, notably the subject-predicate relation and the negative, interrogative and passive transformations, are imposed on the language from within, both in production and in reception (Chomsky, 1965; McNeill, 1966). But it seems to me that Lashley was nearer the mark, in recognizing the generality of mechanisms which are not accounted for in linear chain models of behaviour, and especially of serial mechanisms. Although the fact is most obvious in language behaviour, it is apparent in all integrated behaviour, down to such instances as the succession of leg movements in insects. By the same token, the subject-predicate relation corresponds to the differentiation between subject and object which is elaborated in the first few months of life and which culminates in the conservation of the object (Volume I, Chapter 5); it is not peculiar to language. Similarly, the negative and interrogative transformations reflect the fact that a line of behaviour or 'strategy' can be evoked in the absence of the input which would be required for its completion. To an important extent, the running off of the behaviour consists precisely in varying performance so as to achieve a match between input and anticipation, which means that failure of anticipated input (negation) is implicit in the mechanisms of behavioural regulation in general, and not something which is first manifest when the child acquires spoken language (Miller, Galanter and Pribram, 1960, and cf. the extended discussion in Volume I, Chapter 4).

All this may seem rather a long way from where we began, so let us recapitulate the argument thus far. Education is concerned with the transmission of behaviour, or, more properly, with the transmission of mechanisms or rules governing behaviour, i.e. generalizable behaviour, and it is this that we call teaching. Modification of the mechanisms governing the behaviour of the subject, whether or not it occurs as a result of teaching, is what we call learning. Therefore the psychology of learning is quite central to educational psychology, and in so far as one attempts to arrive at a correct analysis of the fundamental mechanisms involved in the learning process, one is trying to lay the foundations of a science of education, or what Bruner terms a scientific 'theory of instruction' (Bruner, 1966). Stimulus-response theories yield a model of learning which is far too simple to be of much value to those interested in human education. This is probably the main reason why educational psychology has tended to concentrate on what should properly be regarded as secondary aspects, especially the evaluation of individual differences in the human learner. Although it has always been recognized that man's possession of language is bound up with an altered quality of learning, it is only recently that the activity of language has come to be seen as implying a totally different kind of relation between subject and object from that which is assumed in conventional or stimulus-response learning theory. Having looked at some of the reasons why this is so, we went on to conclude that these features of behavioural regulation are not peculiar to language after all, but are evident in many of the co-ordinations that are achieved during the sensori-motor period of development, i.e. before speech has come to play a dominant role in behavioural regulation.

What we must do now is to look at the problem of learning from this new vantage point, to see how far the interests of contemporary psychologists as outlined in *The Regulation of Behaviour* and in the present volume coincide with those of teachers who are concerned with the practical problems of improving the efficiency of learning. To begin with, therefore, let us recall what were the principal features of this new approach, as outlined in Volume I.

II. BASIC MECHANISMS IN THE REGULATION OF BEHAVIOUR

For detailed criticisms of earlier theories and for a summary of the evidence which supports the present theory, at least in its broad mode of attack, the reader will need to refer to Volume I. All we can do here is to list the principal features of this 'New Look' psychology, using the language of Volume I, which is really one version of ideas which are coming to be increasingly accepted in one form or another. Its chief features were these:

(1) The stimulus or stimulus complex does not act directly on the subject. The input to the behaviour control mechanisms depends on the transmission of signals representing cues from primary receptor structures to pre-sensitized detectors. The latter in turn form part of a systematic network – termed the comparator system. The comparator system acts

as a filter. At any given moment the greater part of stimulation is ineffectual.

(2) The behaviour of the subject is not a linear sequence of responses. It reflects the activity of a network of strategies. By virtue of their interrelations, including their relations with the comparator system (for it is their activity which leads to the differential sensitization of specific detectors), strategies in their combination are taken to represent schemata. These may be likened to circuit-diagrams for the regulation of behaviour. They are therefore held to function as the internalized reflexion or 'image' of the world elaborated by the subject. Our knowledge of the world and the differentiation of our behaviour are one and the same thing.

(3) The operation of one strategy does not necessarily exclude those of others. Their organization is partly hierarchical. In so far as it is, the activity of a higher-order strategy (say hunger) facilitates that of a lower-order strategy (say turning into a road with a café). Also the final form of overt behaviour often represents the simultaneous activity of several hierarchies. These may be independent, as when we do two or more things at once, say blinking, scratching and listening to a conversation. Or they may be co-determinative, as in speaking. For in speaking the choice of words, the structure of sentences, and the imposition of a tonal and rhythmic form on the utterance must all enter into the final form of the expression.

(4) The systematic interfacilitatory and inter-inhibitory structures of schemata and strategies are in great part learnt. So also, inevitably, are the detector mechanisms in the comparator system, as well as the behavioural patterns mediated by effector mechanisms. There is no doubt that the formation and consolidation of connexions involves the intervention of specific reinforcement centres. But this does not imply at all that learning depends on the reduction of physiological needs. A general functional mechanism which would fit nearly all the facts of reinforcement learning may be stated as follows: when the activation of a strategy is blocked by failure of input, other strategies to which the input lends itself are activated in turn, and if the activity of these brings about the necessary input for the running off of the original strategy, then they, together with the detector facilitations which they imply, are incorporated as sub-strategies within the original strategy.

(5) The question of the origin of higher-order strategies such as those entering into the formation of learning sets is more problematical (see Chapter 3 of the present volume and Volume I, Chapter 5). The

difficulty is that such strategies do not exist until they have been formed and their principal mode of action cannot be a direct relation to input but must be assumed to be one of selective inhibition of other, lower-order strategies. One can be fairly certain that whether they arise or not depends on the availability of suitable structures within the brain, so accounting for inter-species differences in learning. Their formation is likely to involve a mechanism of conditioning and progressive specification of connexions, perhaps under the influence of reinforcement. However, once they have arisen, they are subject to the same laws of reinforcement and they enter into trial-and-error behaviour.

(6) What this means is that reinforcement learning is not confined to the acquisition of specific behaviours ('habits'), but extends to the acquisition of regulatory strategies common to different behaviours. It is the latter which give rise to 'transfer'. For instance, a subject who has learnt to select a red square from two blue squares will not necessarily select a triangle from among two circles. We know that such 'abstraction' is acquired progressively when a suitable intelligent subject, viz. a primate (monkey, ape or child) is presented with a number of problems having the same form.

III. THE CHILD'S CONSTRUCTION OF THE EVERYDAY WORLD

While the summary I have just given is brief and over-simplified, I have tried to make it fairly precise and explicit. In order to do so, I have had to use the language of systems, and this means that the account tends to sound rather abstruse. Let us see what it all amounts to in the language of common sense.

To begin with, let us recognize that the treatment of developmental and educational psychology given in these volumes is very much influenced by the work of Piaget. This does not mean that the contributors to this volume, or even the writer in Volume I, have adhered slavishly to a faithful presentation of Piaget's work, to the neglect of the many significant contributions made by many others. An attempt has been made to present the gist of Piaget's ideas in sections of both volumes (cf. Chapters 1, 8 and 9). At the same time, some at any rate of the contributors to this volume are certainly very sceptical about many of Piaget's ideas, as well as justifiably critical of much of his methodology. Nevertheless, all are aware of the significance of his work for a clearer appreciation of the growth of the child's understanding (see especially the very clear statement by Blank in Section V of Chapter 3).

Now Piaget has sometimes been described as at least as much a philosopher as he is a psychologist. It is true. One of Piaget's principal theses is that the study of development in children's thinking can shed light on what is one of the oldest philosophical problems, the question of the origin of knowledge. Granted that all our awareness is mediated by the activity of our own nervous apparatus, what leads it to take the forms that it does? In particular, is it entirely a reflexion of the patterning of stimulation impinging on our end organs, or is it in any important way of reflexion of a patterning originating from within, i.e. from the constitution of our own nervous system? The importance of such questions, long neglected, is recognized more readily in this second half of the century, e.g. by Kessen (1966). As to the answer, Piaget is strongly attached to the second view, that the structure of our knowledge is largely determined by that of our own cognitive apparatus as it develops.

There are really two worlds that we know, or at least that we know of; the world of particle physics and mass-energy transformations and the world of solid objects with sensible properties. Now we know that however objective and real the world of the scientist, there is nothing at all obvious about it: it is very much a construct, the product of some very hard thinking and experimentation, which it has taken many centuries to build up. But the world of common sense seems real in a very different kind of way, not simply in that it corresponds with the properties of the world, but also in that its categories are ready-given, and do not require any painful process of construction on our part: unlike the waves and particles of the physicist, the objects of the everyday world are there for all to see, large or small, stationary or moving, quick or slow, hard or soft, red, white or magenta, odourless, perfumed or stinking.

Nevertheless, rationalist philosophers have long recognized that knowledge of the everyday world is not direct, immediate and uninfluenced by the the operations of our own brains. But it is Piaget who first set out to look at the behaviour of very young children in order to see how this knowledge comes to be built up. What he showed is that every baby builds up this image that we have of the everyday world through a process of construction which is in some ways parallel to that in which scientists have constructed the other. We set out from the very reasonable standpoint that it makes very little sense to imagine that the child 'knows' things in some special, direct, intuitive way, without in any way betraying this 'knowledge' through his behaviour. What we know is potentially plain for all to see, by our behaviour and by our words, which are themselves a form of behaviour. If, then, one takes the child's behaviour as one's criterion, one sees that what he knows is precious little. True, the ultimate limiting factor on the knowledge that a young infant might realize is set by his powers of perceptual discrimination. But the mere fact that he possesses the nervous equipment necessary for making a discrimination is not enough. He cannot be said to know a difference (a differential property of things) unless he in fact makes the discrimination. For, in the final resort, the child's knowledge of the world is fully expressed in the patterning of his actions with respect to it. This is of course equally true of our knowledge, but our actions include internalized actions in the form of images and words, where the infant's repertoire lacks these possibilities of expression.

Piaget's detailed studies of development in the first eighteen months of life (Piaget, 1953, 1955) are designed to show how, starting from the basis of a few reflexes (especially grasping, sucking, following movement with the eyes) together with a considerable capacity for perceptual discrimination which is at first unrealized, the child elaborates what amounts to an internal image of a stable world occupied by objects with more or less clearly differentiated properties, disposed in a space which may be explored by several means (visual, kinaesthetic, etc.) with congruent results, and subject to causal laws, especially those that relate to the permanence of objects, to the relative stability of their sensible properties, to the experience of gravitational phenomena (things fall as they are dropped) and to certain very general aspects of the mechanics of movement and rest (moving objects tend to continue in their line of motion, objects sealed in a container may be rediscovered in the container after this has been moved – and not in the place where they were first sealed, etc.). Among the achievements of this period, Piaget attaches particular importance to the successive appearance of anticipation of the effects of rotation of a visually perceived object (turning a milk-bottle to get hold of the business end), the ability to search for an object which has been screened or covered, the use of a support to pull a desired object towards one, the use of a stick as a rake to achieve the same end, and finally, the mental rehearsal of the effects of intended actions (e.g. moving an object the child has been carrying out of the way of an opening door while opening it so as to be able to retrieve the object when the door has been opened – once a task as difficult to execute as it still is to describe!).

This, then, is a long way towards the world of common sense as we know it. But the important point is that the child who ignores the milk-bottle when proffered to him back to front or who tries to suck at the wrong end is not operating in the common-sense world. Nor is the child who loses all interest in a fascinating object as soon as it is hidden from view. One of the first steps taken by the child in his construction of the everyday world is the integration of information from his several senses, and in particular the co-ordination of vision and prehension. This is a matter of learning the relation between the relevant visual cues and the motor and visuo-motor actions which they permit. But since the behaviour is guided by the visual input, we were surely right in arguing that the comparator system is filtering out irrelevant information and enabling the relevant cues to communicate with the relevant strategies. Later, when the child learns to move an object out of the way to obtain another, there is little doubt that the first action is subordinated to the second, and also that while the first is being executed two strategies are operating simultaneously (for the child may complete the movement even while keeping his eye on the target cues). Nor can one doubt that it is in the course of active exploration that these developments are achieved: the child tends to apply a strategy which he possesses to new perceptual inputs, resembling those to which the strategy was applied in the past.

The limits of similarity of the inputs (the things to which the child acts in similar ways) may be very wide. I tried to show in Volume I, Chapter 5, that there are important analogies between the systematic application of familiar schemata (strategies) to new objects and the laboratory phenomenon of learning set. Both imply an elasticity in behaviour sufficient to allow the putting into operation of a higher-order strategy which consists essentially in putting one *kind* of strategy into operation rather than another. In other words, the transfer occurs not to objects which are perceptually similar, but to objects which allow the same class of alternative behaviours (see the description of error factor theory in Chapter 3).

It is the application of familiar strategies to new objects which, according to Piaget, permits the conservation of the object. The object, as defined in Volume I, is simply the intersection of all the strategies that can be applied to it. We know by what we do. And so does the child. The child's world comes to resemble our (everyday) world in the measure that the patterning of his actions comes to resemble that of ours.

Summing up, the details of this early construction may be of less interest to the non-specialist than the proper characterization of the process by which it is achieved. What is central both to the argument of Volume I, summarized in the last section, and to Piaget's analysis, summarized in this, is that learning does not consist merely in the attachment of responses to stimuli and in the chaining of responses in a linear sequence. Behaviour represents a co-ordination of many different activities occurring simultaneously, and hence a study of the way in which these co-ordinations are achieved is central to the learning process. In so far as new learning involves trial-and-error, the trial-and-error is not an alternation of responses, or even of chains of responses, but of co-ordinated strategies, ways of processing input (experience) that have already been built up. Similarly, in so far as it involves the activity of reinforcing centres in the nervous system, the reinforcement does not operate simply on responses but on the strategies which give rise to these responses, and the integration of these trial strategies within the original schema that was aroused leads to new co-ordinations, and hence to new strategies and schemata which may now be applied to other situations, situations which do not resemble the learning situation in any ordinary perceptual sense.

Of course, if that were all, if the development of behavioural co-ordination in the first eighteen months or so did result in an 'image' of at least the everyday world which is in all essentials similar to our own adult world picture, then matters for the teacher, concerned with learning in middle and late childhood, would be far simpler. School learning would consist in the acquisition of new information only, coupled with the perfection and routinization of skills such as calculation and reading. Indeed these do form a major part of learning in the older child.

One again, Piaget's work in particular, but a great deal of other work besides, goes to show that co-ordinations built up in early childhood are not sufficient. The disciplines that we require children to master in the course of their schooling require new co-ordinations, implying both the intervention of a new capacity, the capacity to represent or reconstruct the features of experience (or the sequence of perceptual input) in its absence, by means of symbols of one form or another, especially language, and new levels of integration.

IV. THE LOGICAL STRUCTURING OF EXPERIENCE

Both the observational approach and the experimental approach to language indicate that the child achieves a remarkable facility in representing the significant features of his experience at a very young age. Differentiation of present, past and future tense, of singular and plural, of objects and stuff (count nouns and mass nouns), all these are achieved by the end of the fourth year of life if not before (see Chapters 5 and 6).

Yet research has shown that in spite of this facility with language and representation, the structurization of the child's experience remains at a relatively primitive level until at least the age of 5. It is only from that age on, and especially during the period from 6 to 8 years on average that children learn to compare one experience with another, and sort out the critical features that link them to one another. In introducing Chapter 8, Lovell recalls how the average child of 6 is apt to reproduce the elements of a story or of an explanation in higgledy-piggledy fashion, omitting some which are crucial, and introducing others too early or too late. Equally characteristic in the way in which he describes a route from one place to another, featuring fixed turnings and landmarks, in an entirely subjective way, although the content should be objective, so much so that he fails to realize that the landmarks he encounters when travelling in one direction are bound to be met with on the return journey and that the two distances are equal. In other words, all experience is assimilated directly to the action sequence in which it occurs.

If we recall the way in which the child's construction of the world is built up, it is easy to see why this should be so. It is true that the regulation of his behaviour involves a recognition of the permanence of objects and of spatio-temporal relations. But this is a recognition which is expressed only in action. To say that the child of 12 months has an interiorized model of the world is correct in the sense that the programming of his own behaviour with respect to the input which derives from the world accurately reflects the relations between events that produce this input. At 12 months there is little representation in the sense that the child has no access to this model except when the perceptual input is there to activate the relevant schemata and strategies. Representation develops gradually from anticipation in action, through deferred imitation and imagery, to increasingly symbolic recall, using language. But the representation is initially just that, a representation of action sequences using a substitute input (play, imagery or language), an input which is still largely self-produced. The fact of representation hardly alters the character of what is represented. It is still an amalgam of action and expected input, much more than a reconstruction of an objective reality.

As shown in Chapter 8, the most general weaknesses in young children's reasoning are these: Although a child of 5 or 6 may be able to arrange objects in groups in terms of an obvious criterion, he cannot classify systematically, with the result that he is very apt to change the criteria of his classifications without realizing it, that he cannot cross-classify, and that he cannot handle nesting classifications. Similarly, although he can arrange objects in series when differences are obvious, he cannot do so systematically when the number of elements is greater than four or five and when the differences between adjacent elements are not immediately apparent: just as he cannot compose the relations between two classificatory criteria, so he fails to compose two relations in seriation. Likewise again, as shown in the many conservation experiments, he fails to grasp the systematic invariances in terms of which we are able to reason precisely about the properties of things.

What all these behaviours have in common is a lack of precision in conceptualization – which is why both Vygotsky (1962) and Piaget agree in selecting the term 'preconceptual' to describe the reasoning of young children. To take an example at random, one may consider an experiment relating to movement and speed (Piaget, 1946; Lovell and Slater, 1960). Two dolls are seen to travel along parallel rails; they are set to start and stop at the same time, but one outdistances the other. Young children now reason that the doll that went faster and farther must have travelled over a longer time interval. The concepts are global and undifferentiated: farther implies faster implies more time implies better all round!

The failure of the child to use unambiguous criteria in solving problems of conservation and of classification contrasts strangely with his handling of language. The semantic and syntactic structures of language imply both classifications and strict causal implication, yet children of 4 show a remarkable facility with the linguistic structures themselves combined with an equally remarkable imperviousness to the relations which they imply. Considering this contrast, Bruner quotes an instructive simile from Sapir: 'It is somewhat as though a dynamo capable of generating enough power to run an elevator were run almost exclusively to feed an electric doorbell' (Bruner, Olver and Greenfield, 1966).

Yet one may go further and ask whether in fact the generator is of the type that could run an elevator. It is true that the language of young children implies a classification. But so do their actions. The very fact that the child discriminates between objects that can be moved and those that cannot be shifted, within the former, between those that can be pulled towards him and those that cannot, and within the former of these, those that can be pulled by means of an extension (string) and those that can be pulled by means of the support on which they rest, all this is surely a very clear example of classification in action (Piaget, 1959).

A summary overview at the end of a book is no place for an adequate discussion of the very thoughtful and thought-provoking volume of studies by Bruner and his associates, a work which appeared after many chapters in the present volume had already been completed. Like Piaget, Bruner recognizes that in such situations as the conservation problems, the reasoning of the younger child tends to be dominated by perception. Co-ordination is therefore in part a freeing from perception. Unlike Piaget, however, Bruner attributes a far greater part in this freeing from perception to the structuring imposed by the patterning of language. In particular, the structure of language is seen as abstracting and bound up with a functional mode of classification, while the structure of perception is seen as 'complexive', or to use Piaget's term, 'global'. The development of cognition is seen as a progression in representation from 'enactive' representation, through 'eikonic' (perceptual and imaginal) to symbolic, the last especially representing a higher level.

What we then find is that language tends to be used by the young child in the service of a pre-conceptual mode of representation: in Bruner's terms, in disregard of the structuring implied by the 'symbolic level' itself, the symbol is used to convey or represent an 'eikonic' or 'enactive' content. Now it is true that language can be used to good effect to help wean the child away from 'egocentric' or 'global' thinking, as is apparent both in a number of studies reviewed by Lovell and in some more recent work (Kohnstamm, 1967). Our own view, which is much nearer to that of Piaget, is that the achievement characterized as operational reasoning is due not so much to the use of a different 'level' of representation as to the emergence of a new kind of co-ordination (cf. Inhelder, Bovet, Sinclair and Smock, 1966). In other words, what is represented is always in the final analysis a relation between action and perception or a relation between one action and another. To the extent that a phenomenon like conservation depends in part on reversibility, i.e. on the child's recognition that alterations in the appearances of things have been created by his own action and can be negated by the inverse action, the superior co-ordination is actually more 'enactive' rather than less so. Similarly, although all researchers from Goldstein and Scheerer (1941), through Annett (1959) to Olver and Hornsby in Bruner's team find a progression from perceptual sortings of objects to sortings in terms of abstract and often functional categories (e.g. from red things, etc., to things to eat, things that sustain life, etc.), this is not necessarily a reflexion of the power of language (which in any case permits both kinds of categories). For what it also argues very clearly is an ability to bring together for comparison situations or events which, although perceptually different, permit the same action strategies.

There is, of course, something paradoxical in this: the more objective our reasoning becomes, the more heavily it relies on co-ordinations in the actions of the subject. But leaving aside philosophical consideration, it can be argued that the achievement of precision in conceptualization depends on the subject's ability to focus on the criteria of his own actions. To take an example, we showed in Volume I, Chapter 5, that younger children could be quite successful in the solution of the oddity problem, including the formation of an oddity learning set (picking out the one that is different out of three, where the actual objects are changed from one trial to the next, and what is constant is only the similarity of two of them and their difference from the third). But younger children were unable to explain how they solved the problem and were also unable to make up similar problems of their own. Although the action strategy was available to them, they had no higher strategy for recapturing the first out of its context and comparing it with others. It is surely a similar restriction on young children's thinking that prevents them from anticipating the form of cross-classificatory arrangement although they are only too liable to switch from one criterion of classification to another. Again, in the conservation experiments, the achievement of conservation closely parallels the child's increased ability to make systematic judgements and calculations involving number, weight, volume, etc. In effect, the child must recognize a criterial property of things, defined by enumeration, weighing, etc., not only in the original situation (the initial identity preceding the transformation in conservation experiments) but also in other transformed situations, where its applicability is not perceptually obvious.

If the above argument is correct, then the distinction between the structuring of experience at the sensori-motor level and the operational co-ordinations achieved at the age of 5-plus is the distinction between doing a thing and knowing what it is that one is doing. The cognitive formulation is illuminating, recalling as it does M. Jourdain's feeling of pride at the realization that he had never spoken anything but prose. It is difficult of course to speak with any certainty as to the mechanism which enables the subject to achieve this awareness of his own activity. What would it mean if we tried to think of the subject objectively, simply as an information-processing system?

A possible and tempting suggestion, in line with the argument presented in Volume I, is that this higher co-ordination which implies awareness of the criteria of one's own actions stands in much the same relation to learning set behaviour as the latter to direct perceptuo-motor learning. Broadly following Harlow, we suggested that learning set represents a higher order strategy, which acts in such a way as to suppress irrelevant (lower order) strategies by assimilating the present input to a class of inputs which would permit a class of such alternative strategies (Volume I, Chapter 5). The corollary would be that operational behaviour acts on the representational input by assimilating it to a class of *generalized* strategies all of which are of the order of learning set itself. Let us take concrete examples to clarify our meaning. The oddity learning set is one of several possible strategies of the same order, notably the non-oddity or matching learning set (of two different objects select the one which resembles the standard matching object). Recognizing that one has been using an oddity procedure implies a review of that strategy by a higher-order strategy which simultaneously scans other strategies such as the non-oddity procedure. So, in classification, sorting into groups implies the use of a criterion. But being able to single out this criterion and relate it to other possible criteria implies a more general strategy which is capable of reviewing the various possible sorts. And so on.

One may add that such a co-ordination is necessarily representational since it either acts backwards on the behaviour already executed or forwards, anticipating it, and since it does so by establishing a relation between that behaviour and others which are not executed at all. Because it is representational it is necessarily symbolic (i.e. it uses a substitute input instead of or in addition to direct perception). And this is one reason why generally operational co-ordination does not appear until language is fairly well developed. Achieving such a level may well imply first and foremost the realization of an immediate memory span capable of handling three or four 'chunks' of information (one is after all establishing a relation between two possible judgements) – see Mc-Laughlin (1963).

But although the use of symbols is a necessary condition for operational co-ordination, it is not a sufficient condition, as we have seen, and the essence of this co-ordination is not the use of symbols as such, but how they are used, and what relations are established between the actions themselves. It is understandable that, since language offers a tremendous facility for pinpointing criteria of all sorts unambiguously, the deliberate use of verbalizing strategies helps the child to achieve co-ordinations, once he has reached a sufficient level of maturity (Chapter 8). At the same time, the distinctions enshrined in natural language may well be unimportant in the achievement of at least some kinds of co-ordination as is apparent from the relative success of deaf children compared with hearing children of similar ages (Furth, 1966).

At this point we can go back over an earlier formulation and amplify it. We said that operational co-ordination implies knowing what one is doing. We now see that this may be spelt out further. Knowing what one is doing entails knowing the relation between the effect produced by the given course of action and the effect of other alternative actions. For instance, in measuring a length with a standard rule, it is often convenient to measure the difference between the object and the standard. Here the relation is one of equivalence. Other examples of systematically related sequences are given in Chapter 8. Considering only the possible relations between related sets of actions, and ignoring the specific characteristics of the actions and of the objects on which they bear, the kinds of possible relations turn out to be quite limited in number, and they can be formulated in terms of a logic.

But here a word of caution is necessary. For the evidence reviewed in previous chapters makes it abundantly clear that what the child is learning is not a logic as such, but certain ways of thinking (i.e. of symbolic action) which conform to a logic. The thinking, and the overt behaviour to which it gives rise (e.g. in problem solution) always occur in a specific context, and it is the co-ordination of the specific behaviours relative to these contexts which the child learns rather than the general form of their relations. Whether the deliberate teaching of logic can help to facilitate the acquisition of such specific co-ordinations is still an open question, and recently a number of research workers have begun to turn their attention to this question (Mays, 1965; Allen, 1965; Suppes, 1965; Davydov, 1965; Furth, 1966). So far all that can be said with confidence is that the elements of logic can be taught at far younger ages than was once thought; certainly at 10, and probably at 7 or perhaps even younger. How much carry-over there would be from such teaching to the actual use of logical thinking in reference to concrete problems we still do not know.

Throughout this discussion, we have insisted again and again that in the final analysis all knowledge is matter of actions. This idea, that knowledge itself can only be understood as a determiner of behaviour, is one that is common to nearly all psychological formulations, including the earlier-stimulus response psychologies and the kind of conceptions analysed here. At the same time, we have gone further in our insistence that the behaviour involved may be a direct action upon objects, or it may be an indirect action using a representational or symbolic input. Even if the behaviour takes the form of direct activity, this does not at all imply that the mechanism which governs it is a simple chaining of responses. A hierarchical organization is essential both to the execution of skilled activities like walking, talking (even in respect of its motor aspect only) and singing, as well as in the co-ordinations implicit in sensori-motor intelligence (object permanence, etc.). As to symbolic behaviour, we have just seen that this may take one of two forms. It may be no more than a re-enactment of overt behaviour, with only this difference that the strategies act on a self-produced symbolic input which represents the objects of sensori-motor experience, and where this is so one finds an inability to separate out the part of the subject and that of the object, and a consequent inability to recognize the criteria of one's own actions. Or the symbolic behaviour may go beyond the mere re-enactment of direct behaviour and extend to the realization of its criteria by a co-ordination of related actions. In the measure that the child achieves such a co-ordination, the mental actions which he performs are related to one another in accordance with a logical structure.

V. KNOWLEDGE AND SKILL

1. *Similarities*

Starting from the recognition that knowledge is co-ordinated behaviour, many psychologists find it useful to make a comparison between the acquisition of knowledge and the acquisition of physical skills.

Perhaps the most general conclusion that emerges from Reed's excellent review (Chapter 4) is that skilled behaviour involves the efficient processing of information. Such efficiency depends on the automatization of component sub-skills and their integration within the overall plan that governs performance as a whole. By automatization we understand that there is the greatest possible degree of anticipation of relevant variations in input (the cues which guide the behaviour of the skilled performer). Irrelevant information is filtered out (presumably by the pre-setting of the comparator system) with the result that there is less information to cope with. At the same time decision-making becomes automatic in the sense that the selection of the appropriate strategy within the schema occurs once and once only, and there is no need for a conscious verbal review of the situation and of the various action possibilities. This enables the eventual performance to appear effortless and unhurried. At any given moment the skilled performer has fewer decisions to make (owing to the correct matching between his action strategy and those changes in input that are predictable in the light of earlier perceptions and decisions), and the decisions which he must make are easier (again because the transition probabilities of events have been correctly anticipated).

On the effector side, Reed notes, following Bartlett, an economy of effort marked by such things as the suppression of flourishes. The interpretation may well be similar, that there is efficient processing of information, save that the information involved here is the feedback of the effects and effectiveness of the subject's own actions. Unnecessary flourishes argue a mistaken exaggeration of irrelevant features of performance and a deliberate matching of strategies mediating such performance so as to produce these features.

If on the one hand performance in physical skills is interpretable largely in terms of efficiency in information-processing while on the other the acquisition of knowledge depends ultimately on the co-ordination of actions, the boundary between the two begins to appear very thin. The reason is that the most useful analysis of behaviour is the systems approach: the regulation of all behaviour depends on the evolution and acquisition of effective ways of matching output to input, of sifting relevant information and programming action so that behaviour is maximally effective. Such an approach is quite general, and applies equally to all co-ordinated aspects of performance.

Nevertheless, as we will presently see, there are important differences between physical and cognitive skills, and these relate principally to the critical role of timing in the former and to the greater range of the latter. For the present, let us recall a number of ways in which the analogy with physical skills is useful in thinking about the most effective ways of promoting learning in general.

To begin with it was noted that often, though perhaps not always, the acquisition of skills proceeds unevenly, with periods of rapid improvement alternating with learning plateaux. Where this occurs, the interpretation seems to be that the subject requires a certain amount of practice with partial skills before these can be integrated within larger units. One may go even further, supposing that during the phase of no improvement the subject is learning to economize in the amount of redundant information being processed. Although there is no improvement in overt measures of performance, there is probably a reduction in the number of decision processes being made: hence a greater automatization of the part-skill which will allow of its integration within a larger whole (cf. Chapter 7). Because of the very complex structural dependencies in the conceptual disciplines forming part of the scholastic curriculum, well brought out in the case of mathematics by Skemp in Chapter 12, one would not be surprised to find a similar phenomenon even more prevalent. At the same time, one is not absolved from the need to study in each instance what seem to be the causes of such breaks in the continuity of learning, and whether a different structuring and sequencing of the material might produce greater efficiency.

A second group of findings relates to the effectiveness of distributed practice. Here, again, the results of experiments on physical skills and rote learning are not always easy to interpret. Nevertheless, the balance of evidence strongly supports the thesis that learning is most effective when units of activity with the material are interspersed with short but frequent rest periods. The idea that the rest pauses allow the subject to forget or inhibit erroneous responses has been criticized (e.g. by Osgood, 1953) on the ground that this does not account for the selective character of this inhibition: why are right responses not inhibited? Another suggestion is that the rest pauses allow time for the consolidation of the behaviour (Eysenck, 1957, 1967). The objection to this formulation is its vagueness: what is consolidation? However, it is possible that, in some as yet undefined manner, the rapid rate of decision-making entailed during the periods of active learning interferes with the integration of these strategies within the higher-order strategy governing the behaviour as a whole. The most significant empirical finding, it will be recalled, was the asymptotic effectiveness of the pauses:

quite brief pauses are as effective as pauses of a day or more. Once again there is every reason to believe that similar processes will be found to operate in the acquisition of knowledge. Incidentally, it cannot be assumed that the subject himself will automatically discover the most effective ways of distributing his effort. This is probably one reason that experiments on group administration of programmes, usually 'paced', are not found any less effective than self-paced individual work (see Chapter 13).

Third, Chapter 4 contained a discussion of the controversy centred on the issue of part-learning versus whole-learning. Here, again, one cannot but agree with the conclusion that the question is wrongly formulated, the problem being rather: what are the most effective units for the breakdown of this or that specific acquisition and what is the most effective sequencing? Stated in these terms, the questions do not permit of any general solution, for every body of acquisitions needs to be examined in its own right. One point which did emerge with some force was that wherever possible, difficult sub-skills should be practised separately before integration within the performance as a whole. As we will see in the next section, there is fertile ground for co-operation between psychologists and subject-specialists in discovering just what are these difficult junctures, and what are the most effective ways of overcoming them.

Finally, considering the common ground between the acquisition of skills and the acquisition of knowledge, we turn to the problems of transfer. The evidence reviewed in previous chapters (especially Chapters 4 and 8) suggests two major conclusions. First, that the degree of generalization or transfer to be expected from one task to another depends not only on criterial achievements but also on the strategies invoked by the subject in reaching these. In particular, where teaching has been of a character to induce the activation of higher-order heuristic procedures, more positive transfer can be expected than when the learning of the first task relied on more limited understanding, or less generalizable action strategies (cf. the discussion of 'action feedback' and 'learning feedback' in Chapter 4). The second point of agreement is that transfer can be positive or negative: the interference of past learning with new learning depends on processes which are in principle identical with those that operate, under other circumstances, to produce facilitation. Broadly speaking, in so far as the transfer task involves cues which are common to the original task and these have already been assimilated to strategies which are well accommodated to the transfer task, positive transfer may be expected; if the strategies aroused by these cues compete with strategies needed to solve the transfer task, the transfer tends to be negative. Negative transfer may also be expected to the extent that automatization of the original task has led to an excessive economy in attention to cues: information which is redundant in a limited context ceases to be redundant when the context is widened (cf. the negative features associated with look-and-say controlled vocabulary methods of teaching reading considered in Chapter 7).

2. *Differences*

All learning, we have said, involves the acquisition of regulating mechanisms. The integration of these mechanisms, the advantages of consolidation pauses, the usefulness of breakdown of the task and concentration on difficult areas, all these point to problems that are common to all forms of learning. We have also seen that the considerations governing the expectation of positive or negative transfers are similar for physical skills and scholastic learning. Nevertheless, it would be a mistake to ignore the differences, for their importance is critical to the psychological analysis of the kinds of learning that have concerned us most in these volumes.

While the importance of automatization and timing is critical both in physical skills and in advanced cognitive behaviour, their analysis is different. It seems probable that the progressive integration and automatization in skills are entirely subordinated to the end of achieving the very high levels of accuracy in timing of movements and decisions that are necessary to skilled performance. There are two corollaries. One is that, even if representation of the performance as a whole and its associated variables may be useful or even indispensable at various stages in the acquisition of the skill, or even in the evaluation of past performance, it remains that the actual execution of skilled behaviour involves a minimum of representation. It is a direct operation on the environment in which there is literally no time to think in the sense of thinking back over one's moves and correcting them, or going over the structure of one's actions in one's head prior to execution (of course, if 'thinking' is used in the sense of anticipation, then thinking is the critical factor in the whole process, but such a usage is too wide to be helpful). The second is that physical skills are irreversible. Lack of reversibility, as Piaget insists, is the prime differentiator between sensori-motor behaviour, however skilled, and the systematic co-ordinations of representational behaviour. Often it is the irreversibility in

Q

the environment itself which imposes the restriction on the correction of errors: a climber who misses a hold may not get a second chance, and an amateur carpenter is apt to find that the use of a hammer, simple though it seems, is complicated by the irreversibility of its effects. In competitive games, where the operative environment consists largely of the other participants, the irreversibility is built into the rules. In artistic performance, it is the irreversibility of perception (by the viewer or listener who tolerates a minimum of 'noise' in the communication).

Nevertheless, the fact that the higher cognitive schemata are reversible does not mean that timing is irrelevant. For although it is true that errors in thinking can be corrected, we must remember that the reversibility itself is a product of the co-ordination of related strategies and the differentiation of the part of the subject in their execution (Section IV). The symbolic representation of action is initially as irreversible as the action itself. Consequently, it is not unlikely that the co-ordination of judgements which eventuates in the representation of reality as governed by systematic relations which may be read in any direction (reversibility) depends on speed of transition from one judgement to another, just as skilled movement relies on such anticipation. Such, essentially is the argument advanced by Piaget in his model of equilibration discussed in Chapter 8.

In other words, although the final product of the co-ordination is a reversible structurization, with all the implications of a complex system, any part of which may be perused at leisure, the achievement of this structurization depends on speed and selectivity in the passage of representation. One may think of the way in which an experienced map-reader uses a map to solve any one of a large number of problems as he chooses, once the systematic relations between the map and the relevant features of the ground have been thoroughly mastered. But the mastery of these depends on the ability to shift very rapidly from thinking about the ground to thinking about the map, preserving the uniformity of all changes in scale and the isomorphism of relations of direction (which are identical on map and ground), while accepting that features which are observable on the ground but not represented in the conventions of the map are to be rejected as noise.

At several points in the discussion, both in this chapter and in Chapter 8, we have had occasion to draw attention to the important role played by immediate memory in the structurization of representation. It certainly looks as if, in order to achieve the co-ordination of relations involved in conservation, in the recognition of criteria of classification, and in reversible seriation, the subject needs to retain in immediate memory some representation of both the strategies to be reconciled and of their relation to one another. The co-presence of these elements in immediate memory does not necessarily imply that they are simultaneously active in the determination of behaviour (although they may be). What it does imply above all, however, is that they are all available for immediate scanning – by the determining strategy. It is interesting to note in this connexion that backward repetition of digits or words is very little more difficult than forward repetition, and the span for the latter, which increases from two at age $2-2\frac{1}{2}$ to eight or nine in the adult, seldom exceeds that for the former by more than a single unit. If McLaughlin's argument, referred to earlier, is correct, then the growth of immediate memory capacity poses a maturational limit on the child's potential for imposing a systematization on his representation of the environment.

But it is no more than a limiting factor, for the achievement of the necessary maturational level does not by itself assure the co-ordination with respect to this or that content area. Thus it must be recalled that the 'elements' of the immediate memory span can only be defined functionally: as units which can be comprehended or redintegrated by means of a single symbol. The span for disconnected words, each composed of many letters, is as great as that for disconnected letters, and so on (see the article by Miller, 1956 on which much of this argument is based). Therefore the facility of systematization, in so far as it depends on immediate memory, will be greatly aided by the availability of strategies for 'chunking' the critical features of the environment, and identifying them by means of a single word, image, etc.

In so far as considerations of timing and speed enter into the performance of cognitive tasks, they do not act on the same mechanisms as those that are relevant to skilled physical performance. Instead of directly affecting action control by pre-sensitization of the effector and comparator systems, they are relevant mainly to the regulation of immediate memory as a factor in the recognition of logical relations.

Automatization and the building up of complex structures, too, seem to be characteristic of learning both in physical skills and in the acquisition of knowledge. But, here again, the reversibility of the latter makes for a difference in character. Skilled performance is one-directional and irreversible. What this means is that although considerable automatization and integration is possible, the resulting structures remain less powerful than those which are available to conceptualization. In effect, the subject has to learn a relatively larger number of controlling strategies, and these retain a relatively greater independence from one another. Also, the automatization and integration remain largely subordinated to the more delicate timing which they permit.

Turning now to the acquisition of cognitive structures, we find that any area of knowledge extends over an enormous content area, and that the interrelations and inter-implications that it entails are far more numerous than is the case for skills. Both the extension of content and the greater comprehensiveness of structure pose problems of their own.

As to the first, we recall that all knowledge ultimately derives from action, overt or symbolic. The teacher cannot expect to add significantly to the range of content area available to the learner except in the measure that he also supplies him with a large number of the action strategies relative to it which he himself possesses. The fact that language can by-pass this construction by means of ready-made categorizations can easily be a trap. As an instance we may take the (partial) definition of the functions of Parliament as the responsibility for the government of the country through the ratification of laws. Such a definition has meaning only in the measure that the learner also has a clear idea of the sort of thing a law is, how it is administered, how it affects others, how the ratification is carried out, and so on. Or one may consider the statement that a place A is 100 miles south of another, B. This is significant to the learner only in the measure that he can also bring to bear other information and experience concerning both, that he understands their relation to other places C, D, etc., that he can envisage the significance of the named distance, and so on. Just as the acquisition of knowledge of the child's immediate surroundings in the first two years of life is achieved only by means of actions and their integration, so the extensions of this knowledge which one seeks to promote depend in the final analysis on the availability of a rich variety of symbolic actions which can be related to real actions. In this respect, educational psychology reinforces the experience of the gifted teacher who realizes the value of richness of information and concreteness of presentation.

But it is probably the interrelations of the different units of knowledge which poses the greatest problems for education and at the same time provides the most fruitful field for research and advance.

VI. PROGRAMMING FOR EFFECTIVE LEARNING

The main argument of this chapter is that educational psychology has an important part to play in improving the efficiency of education, conceived as an institution for the transmission of knowledge and skills. But it would be absurd to suggest that the skills of the psychologist are by themselves sufficient to discover what improvements can be made. Any of the recognized 'disciplines', and many more, as yet unrecognized, represent an extremely complex, ill-defined, and at the same time ever-growing set of facts and relations. Each is a specialization, and inevitably, only those who are themselves familiar with the given area of knowledge are in a position to map out the kinds of competence that they consider to be most necessary in the pupil, and the specific principles and data which they need to command. Likewise, only they are in a position to chart the structure of their subject bringing out the relations between concepts and especially the specification of what concepts and what types of skill are essential preliminaries to the acquisition of others. Chapter 13 includes a discussion of ways of constructing such plans in general terms, and we have tried to construct such an analysis for reading in Chapter 7. But reading is a symbolic skill more than an area of knowledge.

Nevertheless, sufficient has been said both in this and in preceding chapters to substantiate the claim that educational psychology has a legitimate interest in studies concerned with improvements in curriculum and in method, and involves specialized knowledge and skills which are not usually available to the subject-specialist. In other words, educational research is or should be a multi-disciplinary endeavour, involving the participation of psychologists alongside subject specialists.

One of the most significant concrete contributions of educational psychology to educational practice has been the development of the techniques of programmed learning. Such techniques, whether linear, branching or adaptive, draw on the most general principles of learning established in the laboratory. They have as their aim the maximization of learning efficiency by substituting deliberately planned sequences of learning for *ad hoc* and unsystematic presentations which are apt to overlook the structural dependencies of the to-be-learnt behaviour, and to place excessive reliance on incidental learning – often without knowing it. At the same time programmed learning provides constant and usually immediate feedback, carefully directed to ensure that the strategies which are to be learnt are also those that are reinforced rather than any other behaviours which might have occurred between the original behaviour and the knowledge of its results. Finally, feedback operates in the opposite direction, in the construction of the programme itself. For, as Kay insists, programmed learning is geared to the learner in that his responses play a controlling part both in the construction of programmes and in their use. Thus the programme deliberately ensures that what needs to be 'received' is 'transmitted' in such a way that it will be received.

The last consideration brings to mind an important application of programmes which is their use in research. Any methods experiment tends to be confounded by lack of controls. For what is called the teacher variable includes not only differences in the relations between teacher and pupils but also large differences in the actual content that is transmitted and received, ostensibly within the same method. Learning programmes have the advantage that the content is permanently stored, available for inspection and the same for all learners. Some studies of this kind have in fact been carried out and were discussed in Chapter 10 (I refer to the work of Gagné on guidance and discovery, which uses learning programmes as a research method).

However, the relevance of educational psychology is not confined to the development of programmed learning, especially programmed learning in the narrow sense (see below). For, as Bruner (1966) has emphasized, the structure of systematic interdependencies in an area of knowledge referred to earlier rarely admits of only one learning sequence. Usually there will be great deal of choice both in the sequences which are equally possible, and in the specific content to be included by way of example within each unit in the sequence. It is here that the developmental analysis of the acquisition of knowledge outlined in the foregoing pages assumes most relevance. Educationists have always recognized the need to reconcile the conflicting claims of subject-teaching and teaching designed to promote the happiness and personal adequacy of the pupil. In similar vein, one recognizes the importance of teaching which will bring about an enhanced willingness to exploit the pupil's curiosity and initiative (see the discussion of creativity in Volume III, Chapter 2). But the chief lesson to be learnt from Piaget's developmental approach to knowledge concerns the importance of establishing exactly the nature of the understanding which the child brings to bear initially to the learning of any topic at any given stage, and hence the nature of the reorientations (new strategies and schemata) that he needs to acquire.

To take an example, a comparatively recent review of studies of children's understanding of history by Jahoda (1963a) brings out the lack of understanding of temporal relations which persists until a very late age. A study by Coltham (1960) illustrates the very confused understanding that children often have of concepts which, at a verbal level, enter quite readily into their repetitions of lessons in history ('king', 'subject', 'ruler', 'early man', etc.). Both studies suggest that it may be useful to approach the teaching of history by beginning with the comparatively recent past, rather than with the most distant periods, as is often the practice. A second study by Jahoda (1963b) shows how the structural relations implied in geographical concepts demand a mental construction and a breadth of experience which cannot easily be taken for granted. The relations between Glasgow, Scotland and Britain were very imperfectly understood by many Glasgow children up to the age of 10 or over, and the lack of understanding was directly related to a failure to apply an adequate schema of spatial inclusion to a sufficiently rich representation of places and countries.

All this does not imply that there are insuperable barriers which prohibit the introduction of any specific content area until the child has reached a sufficient level of intellectual development. The problem is rather one of deciding, in the individual case, what is the importance of introducing the topic early rather than late, and if it is to be introduced at one stage rather than another, what is the best way to treat it, having regard to the initial understanding which may be assumed in the child and the relevance of the new learning for transfer at future stages in the learning. By way of example, both mathematicians and psychologists have increasingly come round to a recognition of the value of an early introduction of what were once taken to be highly sophisticated concepts (Chapter 12).

Much of the content of this volume has been concerned with development in learning in general, and the research which we have considered was usually undertaken with specifically psychological questions in mind, and as such the selection of content was dictated largely by considerations of feasibility in the laboratory, unambiguity in measurement, and so on. Taken as a whole, it is legitimate to look on this kind of work as an introduction to educational psychology. But what we are suggesting here is that there exists a largely unexplored field for development which would consist in the practice of educational psychology as an applied science. Undoubtedly one of the main ways in which this can be pursued lies in the collaboration between psychologists and other specialists in detailed curricular work.

Such curricular planning is certainly programming in a broad sense. But it is not programming in the specialized sense discussed in Chapter

13. In point of fact, as Kay recognizes, psychologists working in the field of programmed learning and educationists studying curriculum development are converging on a much wider conception of programming, one which is not based exclusively on the use of programmed machines or texts, but which extends to a consideration of the educational environment as a whole (cf. Leedham and Unwin, 1965). This includes capitalization on factors of social incentives in learning (group learning, etc.), variation in input (use of visual and audial aids, etc., and relation of in-school to out-of-school activity), and establishing the most effective distribution of the pupil's time. In regard to the last, it is easy to see that the considerations of distributed practice and of part-learning as treated in Chapter 4 and in Section V of the present chapter is limited to the elaboration of general principles. It remains to work out in detail how these are to be applied in educational practice.

Looking ahead, it is unrealistic to assume that the pattern of education which has continued for so long, centred on the blackboard, the textbook and the exercise book, is one that will continue to predominate in the not very distant future. Constant developments in material techniques as well as advances in educational thinking make it far more likely that learning will in time be a largely self-directed activity, within the limits of carefully devised and elastic 'programmes' (in the wider sense), such activity including work on programmes (in the narrow sense), reference to textbooks and audio-visual aids, and references to the teacher, functioning as guide, consultant and specialist. Having regard to the concrete problems which inevitably arise in the field of personal difficulties, individual differences and inter-individual relations, it is not too fanciful to foresee, working alongside such teachers, a sprinkling of trained educational psychologists, participating in such consultant work, within the educational establishments themselves.

REFERENCES

ALLEN, L. E. (1965). Toward autotelic learning of mathematical logic by the WFF'N PROOF games. In Morrisett, L. N., and Vinsonhaler, J. (eds.), Mathematical learning. *Monogr. Soc. Res. Child Developm.* **30,** No. 1 (Serial No. 99), 29–41.

ANNETT, M. (1959). The classification of instances of four common class concepts by children and adults. *Brit. J. Educ. Psychol.* **29,** 223–236.

BRAINE, M. S. (1963). The ontogeny of English phrase structure. *Language*. **39**, 1–13.

BRUNER, J. S. (1966). *Towards a Theory of Instruction*. Cambridge, Mass: Belknap.

BRUNER, J. S., OLIVER, R. R., and GREENFIELD, P. M. (1966). *Studies in Cognitive Growth*. New York: Wiley.

CHOMSKY, N. (1965). *Aspects of the Theory of Syntax*. Cambridge, Mass: M.I.T. Press.

COLTHAM, J. B. (1960). Junior school children's understanding of some terms commonly used in the teaching of history. Ph.D. Thesis, University of Manchester.

DAVYDOV, V. (1965). Learning barriers. *New Education*. January, 12–15.

EYSENCK, H. J. (1957). *The Dynamics of Anxiety and Hysteria*. London: Routledge.

EYSENCK, H. J. (1967). Intelligence assessment; a theoretical and experimental approach. *Brit. J. Educ. Psychol.* **37**, 81–98.

FURTH, H. G. (1966). *Thinking without Language*. New York: Free Press.

GOLDSTEIN, K., and SCHEERER, M. (1941). Abstract and concrete behaviour: and experimental study with special tests. *Psychol. Monogr.* No. 239.

INHELDER, B., BOVET, M., SINCLAIR, H., and SMOCK, C. D. (1966). On cognitive development. *Amer. Psychologist.* **21**, 160–164.

JAHODA, G. (1963a). Children's concepts of time and history. *Educ. Rev.* 15, 87–104.

JAHODA, G. (1963b). The development of children's ideas about country and nationality. *Brit. J. Educ. Psychol.* **33**, 47–60, 143–153.

KESSEN, W. (1966). Questions for a theory of cognitive development. In Stevenson. H. W. (ed.), Concept of development. *Monogr. Soc. Res. Child Developm.* **31**, No. 5 (Serial No. 107), 55–107.

KLIMA, E. S., and BELLUGI, U. (1966). Syntactic regularities in the speech of children. In Lyons, J., and Wales, R. J. (eds.) *Psycholinguistic Papers*. Edinburgh: Edinburgh Univ. Press, 181–219.

KOHNSTAMM, G. A. (1967). *Piaget's Analysis of Class-Inclusion: Right or Wrong?* The Hague: Mouton.

LASHLEY, K. S. (1951). The problem of serial order in behaviour. In Jeffress, L. A. (ed.), *Cerebral Mechanisms in Behaviour*. New York: John Wiley, 112–136. (Reprinted in Saporta, S. (ed.) *Psycholinguistics: A Book of Readings*. New York: Holt, Rinehart and Winston (1961). 180–198.)

LEEDHAM, J., and UNWIN, D. (1965). *Programmed Learning in the Schools*. London: Longmans.

LOVELL, K., and SLATER, A. (1960). The growth of the concept of time: a comparative study. *J. Child Psychol. Psychiat.* **1,** 179–190.

MCLAUGHLIN, G. H. (1963). Pyscho-logic: a possible alternative to Piaget's formulation. *Brit. J. Educ. Psychol.* **33,** 61–67.

MCNEILL, D. (1966). Developmental psycholinguistics. In Smith, F., and Miller, G. A. (eds.), *The Genesis of Language*. Cambridge, Mass: M.I.T. Press, 15–184.

MAYS, W. (1965). Logic for juniors. *Teaching Arithmetic.* **3,** No. 3, 3–10.

MILLER, G. A. (1956). The magical number seven, plus or minus two: Some limits on our capacity for processing information. *Psychol. Rev.* **63,** 81–97.

MILLER, G. A., GALANTER, A., and PRIBRAM K. M. (1960). *Plans and the Structure of Behaviour*. New York: Henry Holt.

OLVER, R. R., and HORNSBY, J. R. (1966). On equivalence. In Bruner, J. S., Olver, R. R., and Greenfield, P. M. *Studies in Cognitive Growth*. New York: Wiley, 68–85.

OSGOOD, C. E. (1953). *Method and Theory in Experimental Psychology*. New York and London: Oxford University Press.

PIAGET, J. (1946). Le développement de la notion de temps chez l'enfant. Paris: Presses Univ. de France.

PIAGET, J. (1953). *The Origin of Intelligence in the Child*. London: Routledge.

PIAGET, J. (1955). *The Child's Construction of Reality*. London: Routledge.

PIAGET, J. (1959). Apprentissage et connaissance. In Piaget, J. (ed.), *Etudes d'épistémologie génétique*. **7,** 21–67 and **10,** 159–188. Paris: Presses Univ. de France.

SUPPES, P. (1965). On the behavioural foundations of mathematical concepts. In Morrisett, L. N., and Vinsonhaler, J. (eds.), *Mathematical learning. Monogr. Soc. Res. Child Developm.* **30,** No. 1 (Serial No. 99), 60–94.

VYGOTSKY, L. S. (1962). *Thought and Language*. New York: Wiley.

INDEX